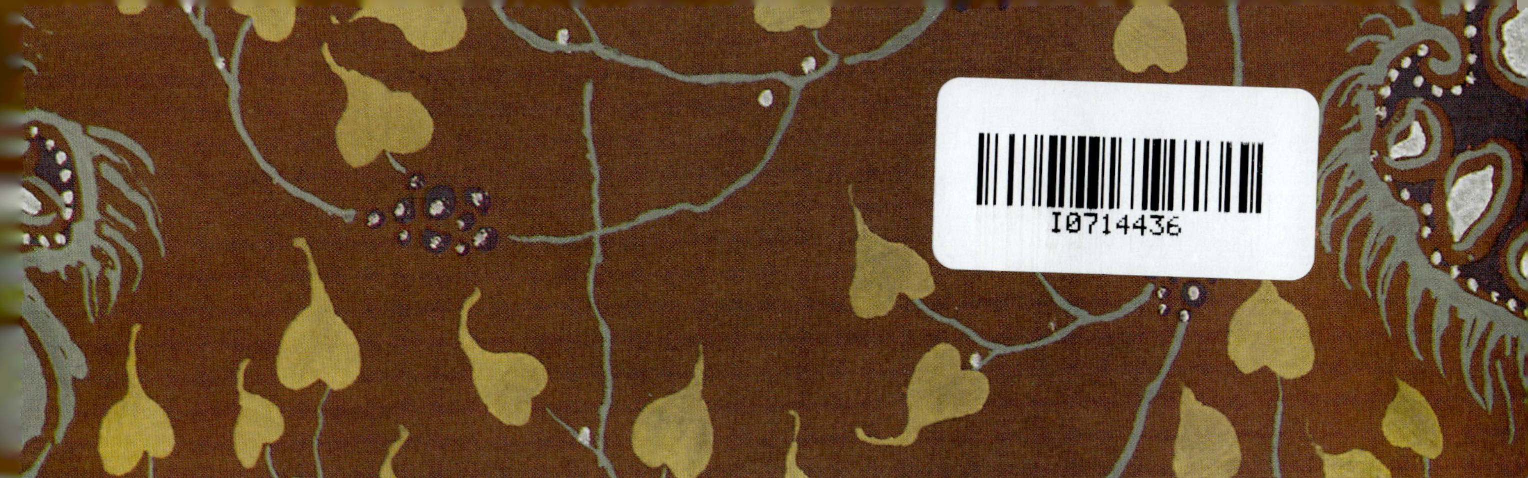

ART NOUVEAU
THE ESSENTIAL REFERENCE

CAROL BELANGER GRAFTON

DOVER PUBLICATIONS
GARDEN CITY, NEW YORK

Source of chapter opener images:
The Spectacular Color Floral Designs of E. A. Seguy

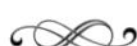

Art Nouveau: The Essential Reference is a new compilation of images reprinted
from authoritative sources. For detailed source information see page 137.

ISBN-13: 978-0-486-79983-4
ISBN-10: 0-486-79983-2

Printed in China
79983205   2025
www.doverpublications.com

INTRODUCTION

On December 26, 1895, Siegfried Bing, a successful German art dealer based in Paris opened a new gallery at 22 rue de Provence which he called the Maison de l'Art Nouveau ("House of New Art"). The new gallery was devoted to what was then considered modern art, including works by Henri de Toulouse-Lautrec, and artifacts in glass by Louis Comfort Tiffany. A few years later at a Parisian World's Fair, the 1900 *Exposition Universelle*, Bing expanded his reach by displaying complete installations featuring furniture, textiles, and other objects of all kinds created in this new and modern style by his substantial roster of artists and designers. Because of its central role in popularizing this new movement, the name of Bing's gallery became the name of the style it featured, and what we now simply call Art Nouveau left its home on the rue de Provence and entered its peak years all over Europe and in parts of the world beyond. The artists and designers represented in this book were from France, Germany, Austria, Czechoslovakia, England, and the United States.

The intent of this book is to give the reader a sense of what Art Nouveau was about, what it looked like, who some of the people were who created and developed it, and especially—because news of Art Nouveau spread around the world in those early decades of the twentieth century mostly by means of the printed page—what their books and portfolios were about. Art Nouveau is a vast subject. The Art Nouveau style spread quickly throughout Europe, to Germany where it was named Jugendstil ("Youth Style") because of the central role played there by the Munich periodical *Die Jugend*, to Austria where it was named Sezessionstil ("Secession Style"), because many of the artists interested in this new style were members of the Vienna Secession, a group formed in 1897 by artists who were looking for something new and modern, different from the historical conservatism in which they had been brought up. In some other areas it became known, in different variations, simply as the "Modern" style. A single volume such as this one can only hit some of the high spots, but our hope is that provided here is some visual inspiration and information for the reader and researcher who would like to go further into this world, and details of some of the essential sources which could be, and should be, consulted in that quest.

Art Nouveau might be difficult to define concisely, but it isn't hard to describe. Sinuous, long and flowing lines and curves; a fascination with adapting natural forms, plants and animals of all kinds, exotic as well as everyday, for stylized and decorative purposes; obsession with the female form and a new freedom in working with interpretations of that form. Above all, Art Nouveau meant elegance and energy and precision in the way anything and everything was presented, from bookplates and business cards, to huge opera posters and advertising placards. This collection features examples of Art Nouveau decorative art, geometric and other patterns, textile and wallpaper designs, designs for decorative stencils, jewelry, tiles, and other ceramics, furniture, bookplates, alphabets and monograms, typographical ornaments, advertising signs, book covers, and periodical illustrations, stained glass windows, posters, labels, and other advertising materials.

A quick glance through these pages will convince even the casual reader that one thing which can surely be said about Art Nouveau artists and designers is that they went outside, into the sunlight and the world of nature for their material. Plants and flowers are steady and perennial themes, butterflies and peacocks were obvious, given the style and the period's bias toward charm and elegance, but even a humble rooster or everyday common bird could make a stylized appearance. The designer E. A. Seguy took some of the world's most exotic insects and turned them into unforgettable design motifs. Seguy and the others understood most of all that they were living in a new world of color, colors that were both vivid and subtle, often combined in new and adventurous ways that only magnified their elegance. Anything could be done in the Art Nouveau style, from an opera poster to the label on a jar of pickles, and in a sense the message was often somewhat the same—this is what's new, modern, well designed, happy, smart, and elegant.

It isn't possible to study these books and portfolios from the turn of the nineteenth century without feeling that the designers who created them were fully aware that they were on to something new, different, and in its way, profoundly meaningful, even if it was in the form of advertising—advertising for everything from the theatre and the opera, the great new hotels and restaurants, champagne and brandy, newspapers and the new magazines which were both the agents and the products of this vast new artistic movement, to the most ordinary of everyday objects, bicycles and tires, household products, appliances and umbrellas. When before had an artistic avant-garde played such a role in the commercial life of such a prosperous era? It is pleasant to think of those early days on the rue de Provence in the 1890s, with the brand new Eiffel Tower looming in the sky not far away, and Mr. Bing's many artists coming and going with their new and marvelous designs and creations. The building at number 22 is now a post office and, it being Paris after all, it is equally pleasant to report that the exterior hasn't changed.

This book is organized by the sources used to create it, with typically a few pages devoted to material from each of the many books on Art Nouveau design which Dover has published in the past several decades. What became a very sizeable collection started with a few books based on material from some of the best-known Art Nouveau portfolios and periodicals, and when it was found that there was a substantial market among designers for this material, Dover's collection grew with new additions almost every year. Many of the books and periodicals from which selections are reproduced here were acquired at book auctions held by Swann Galleries, Inc., in New York and from other auction houses, and many others came from antiquarian bookdealers in the U.S. and England. Several were loaned to Dover by the late Charles Rahn Fry, one of the first collectors to approach this subject in a systematic way, whose collection is now at the Princeton University Library. Our thanks, of course, to all.

John Grafton
Princeton, NJ
June, 2015

CONTENTS

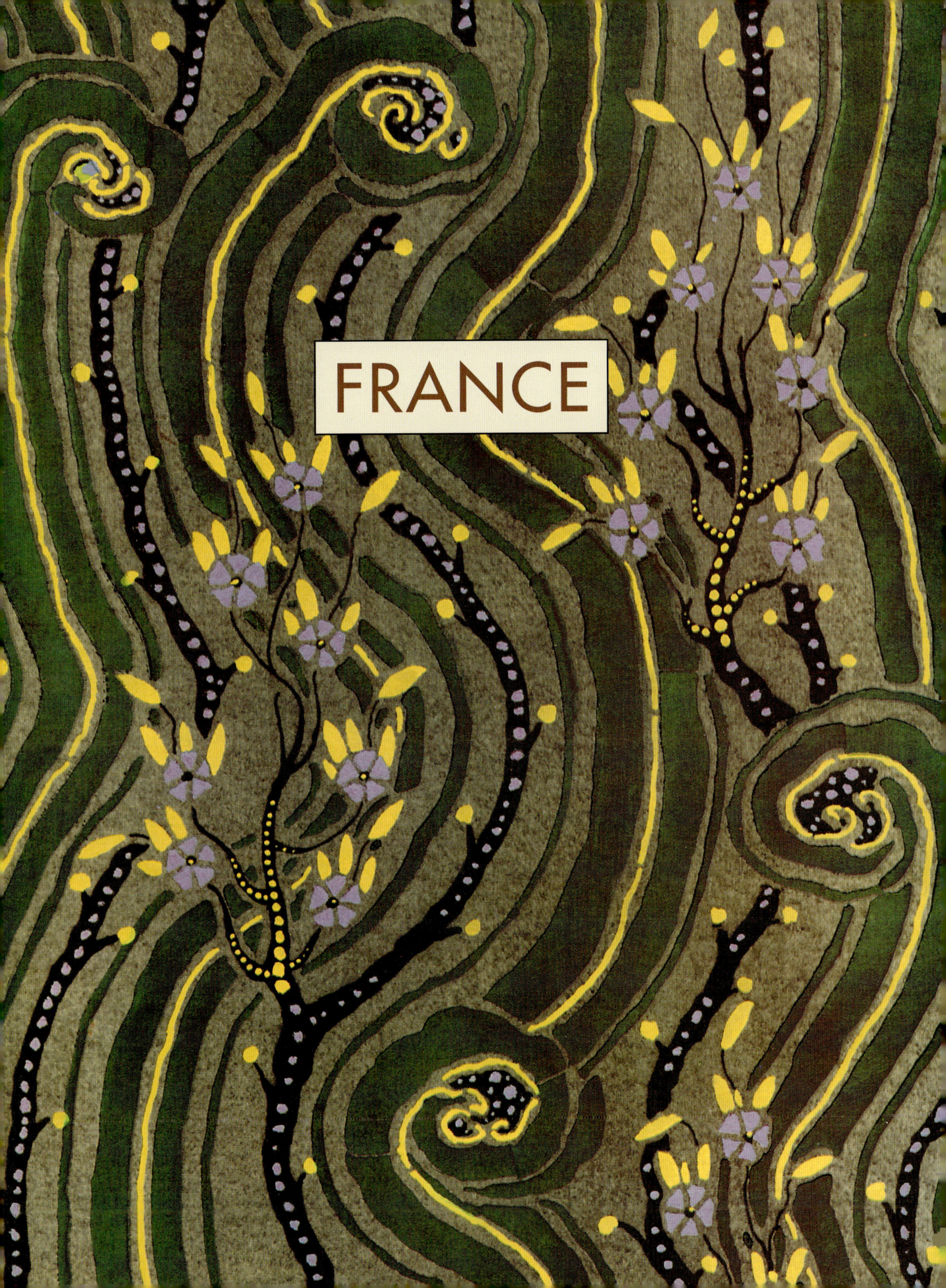

FRANCE

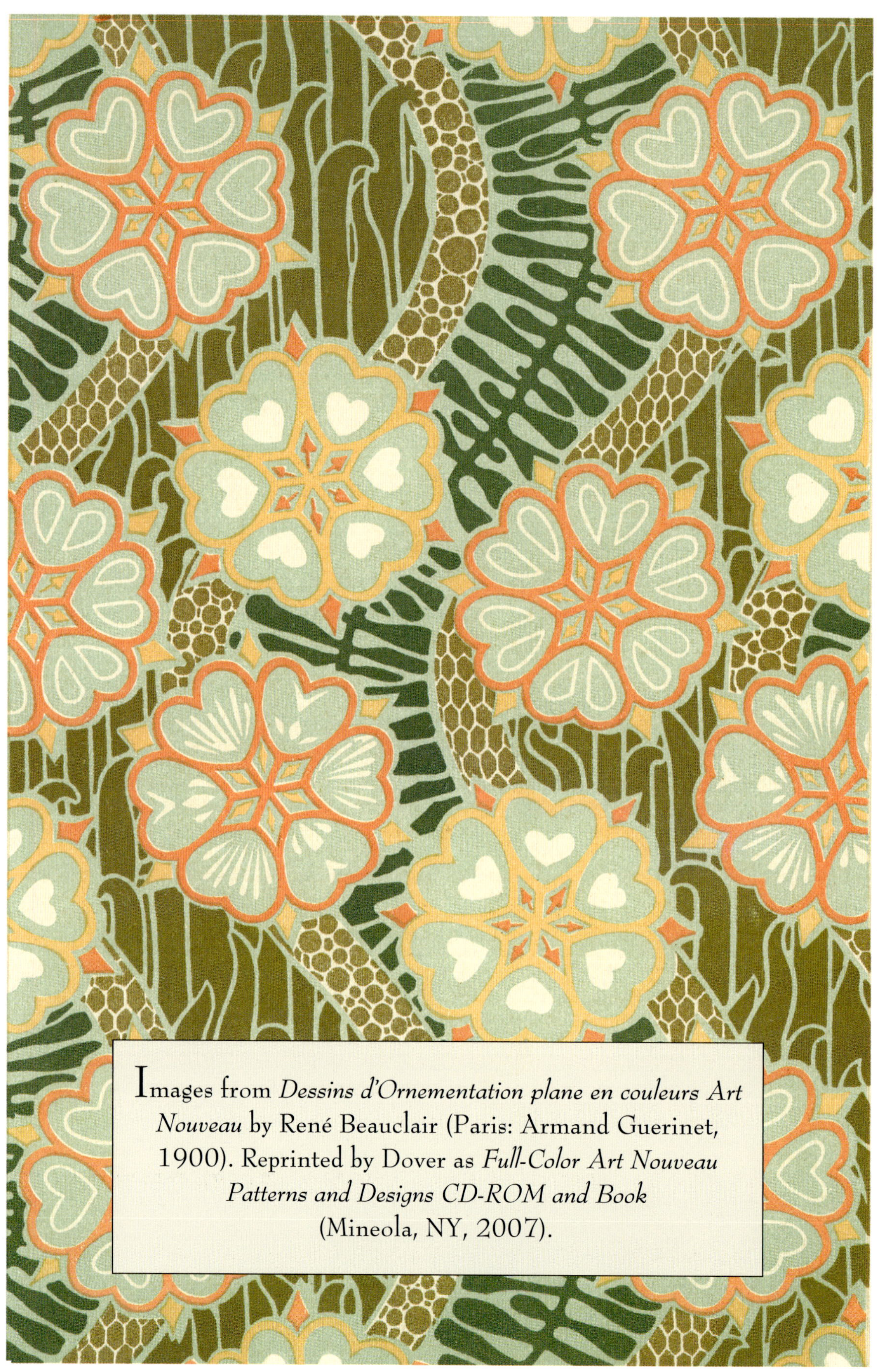

Images from *Dessins d'Ornementation plane en couleurs Art Nouveau* by René Beauclair (Paris: Armand Guerinet, 1900). Reprinted by Dover as *Full-Color Art Nouveau Patterns and Designs CD-ROM and Book* (Mineola, NY, 2007).

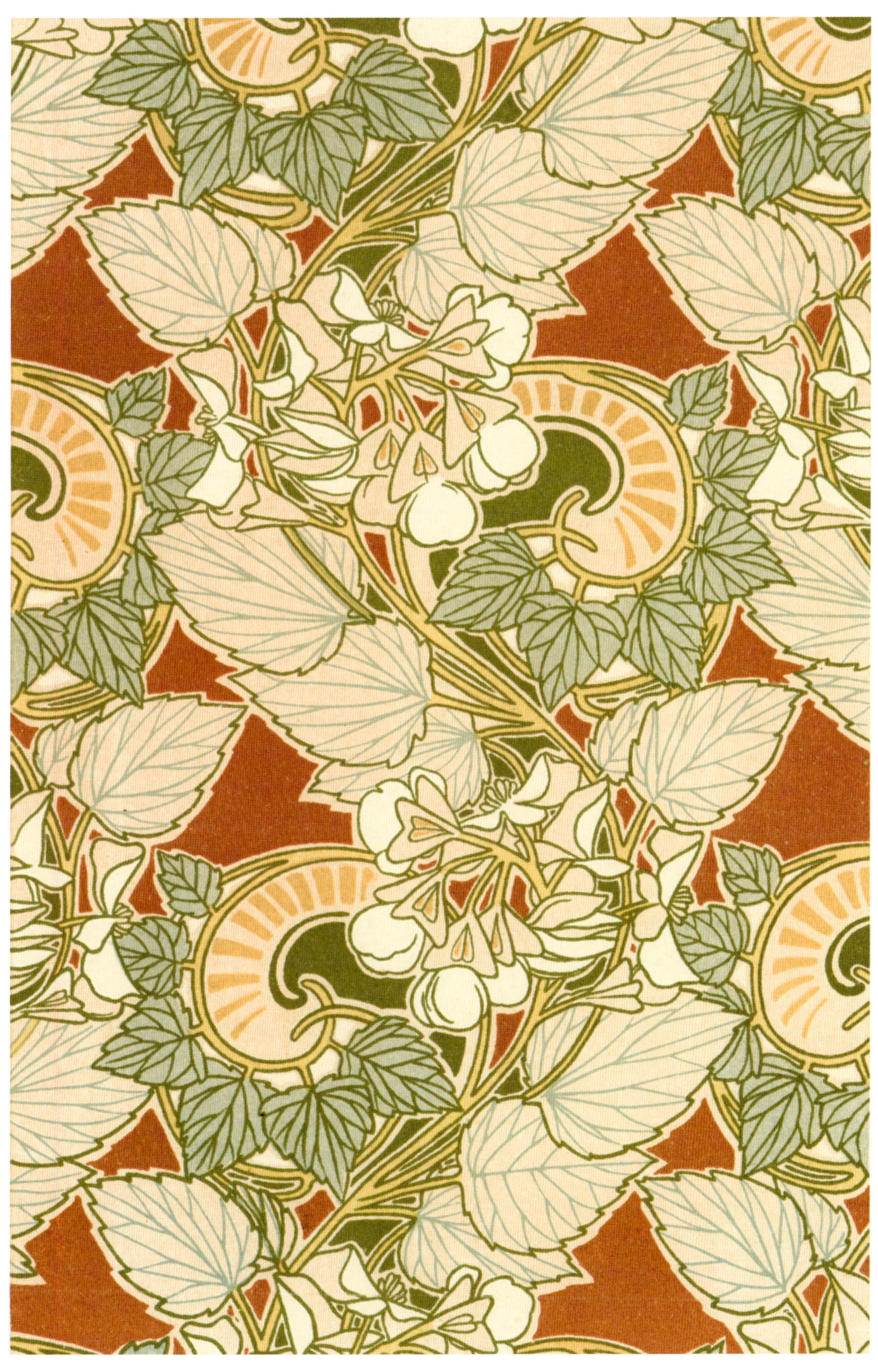

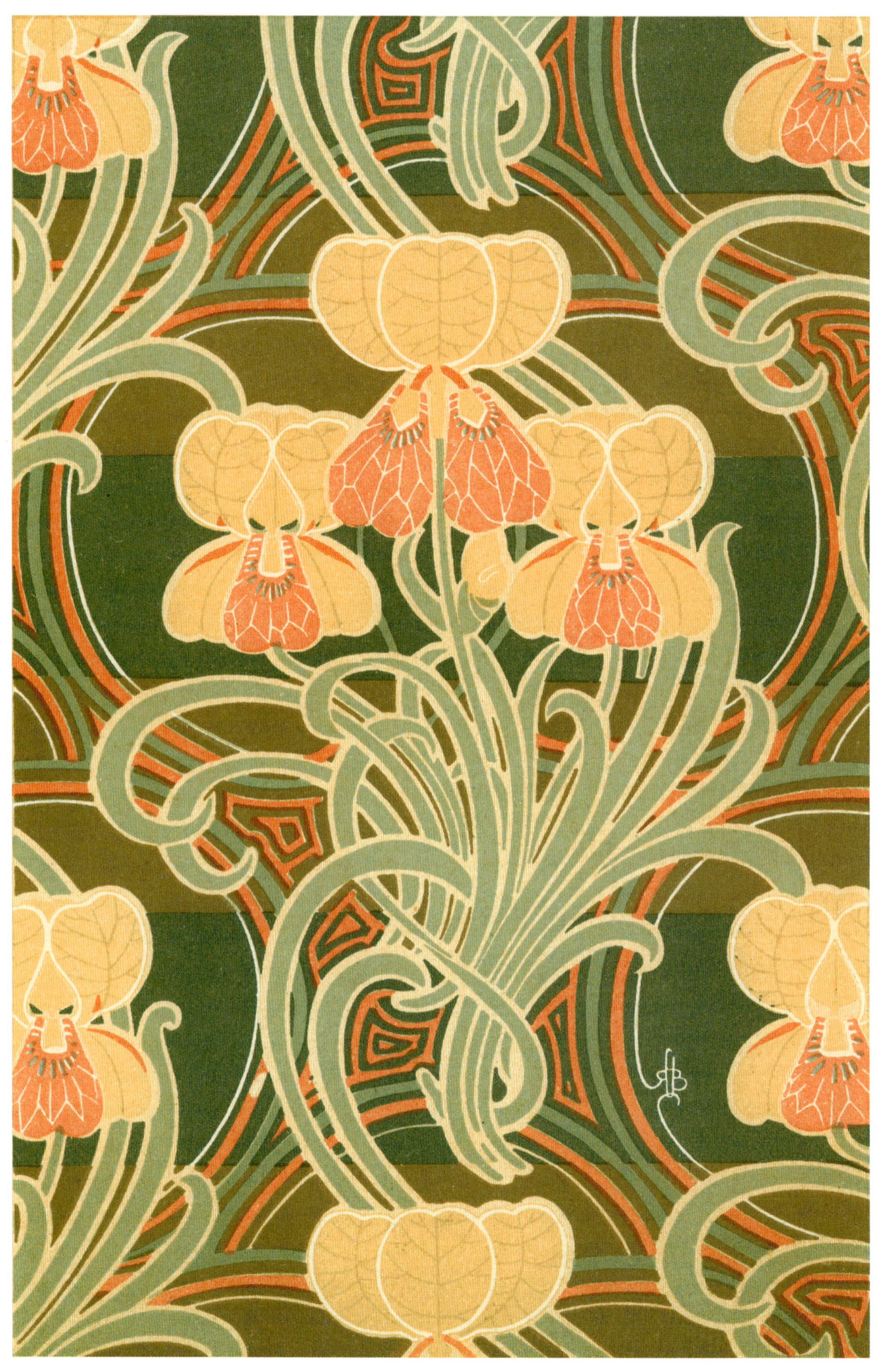

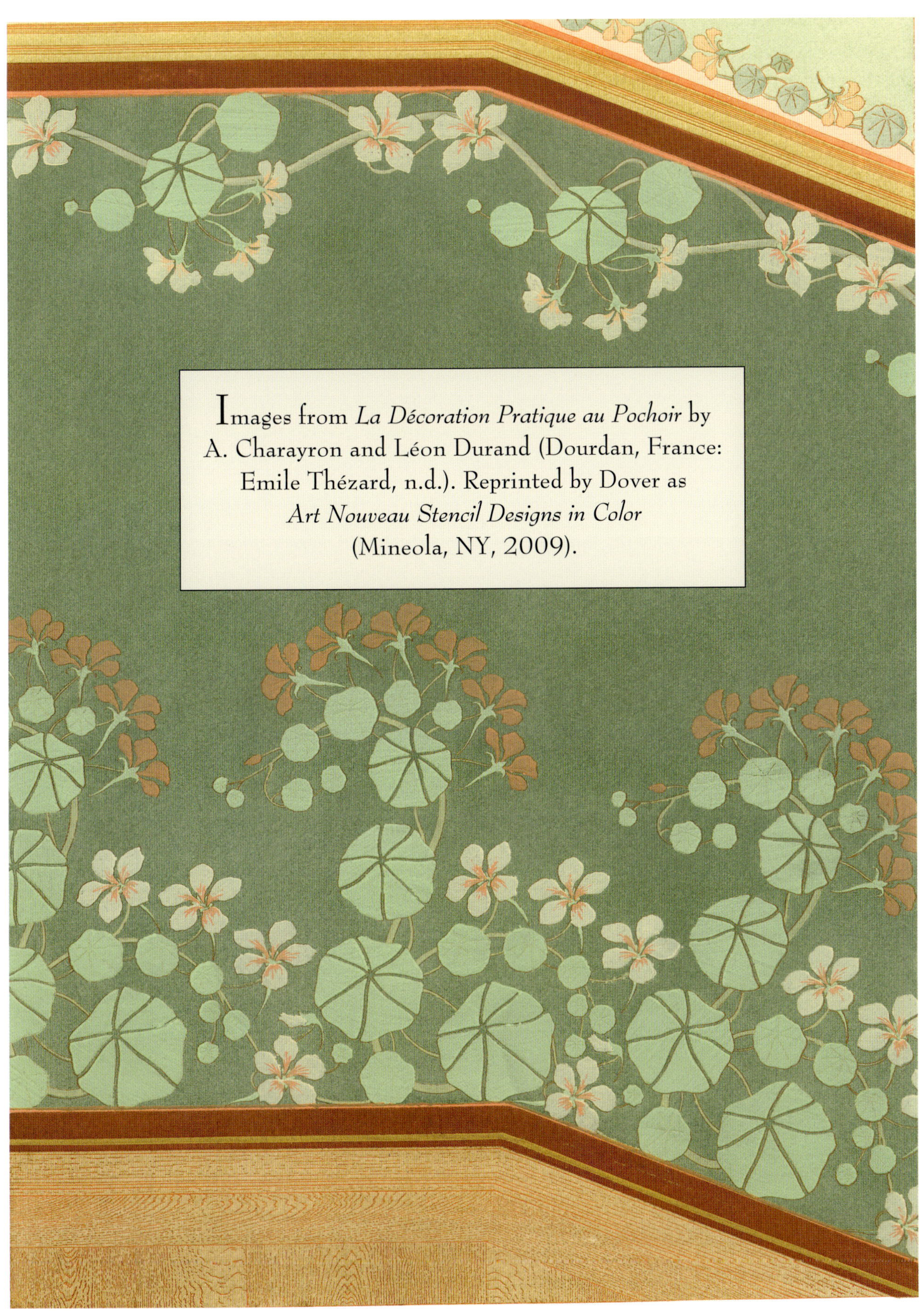

Images from *La Décoration Pratique au Pochoir* by
A. Charayron and Léon Durand (Dourdan, France:
Emile Thézard, n.d.). Reprinted by Dover as
Art Nouveau Stencil Designs in Color
(Mineola, NY, 2009).

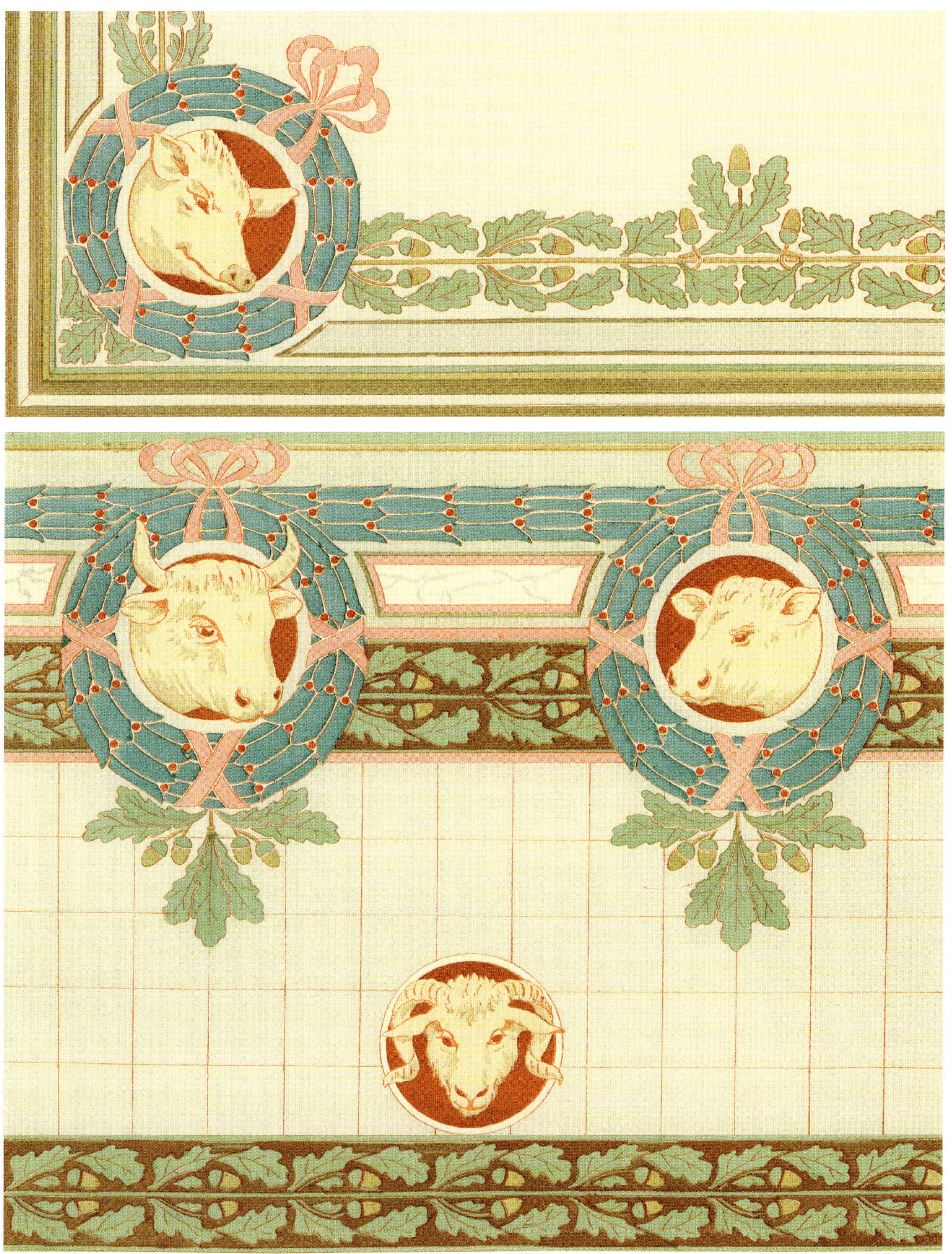

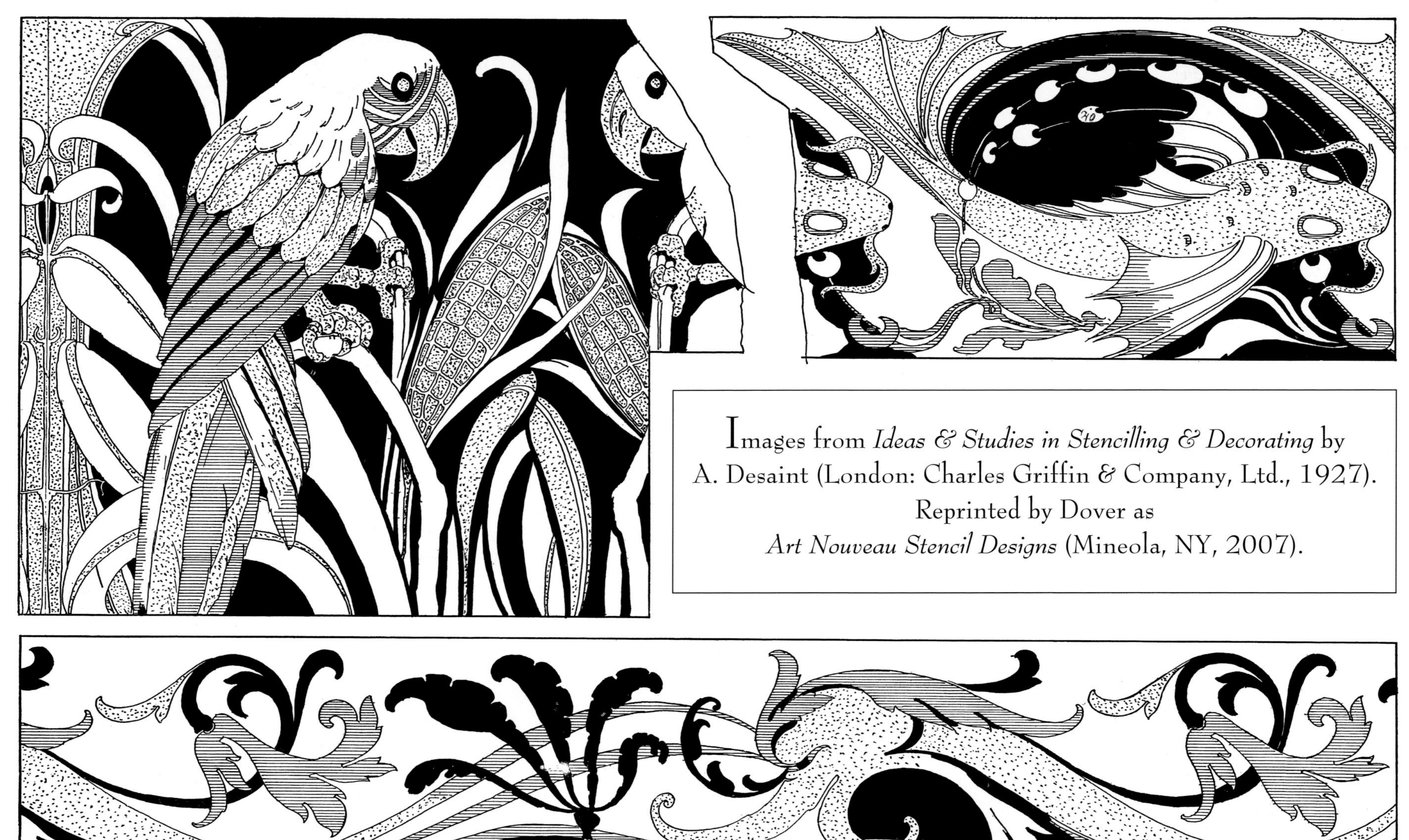

Images from *Ideas & Studies in Stencilling & Decorating* by A. Desaint (London: Charles Griffin & Company, Ltd., 1927). Reprinted by Dover as *Art Nouveau Stencil Designs* (Mineola, NY, 2007).

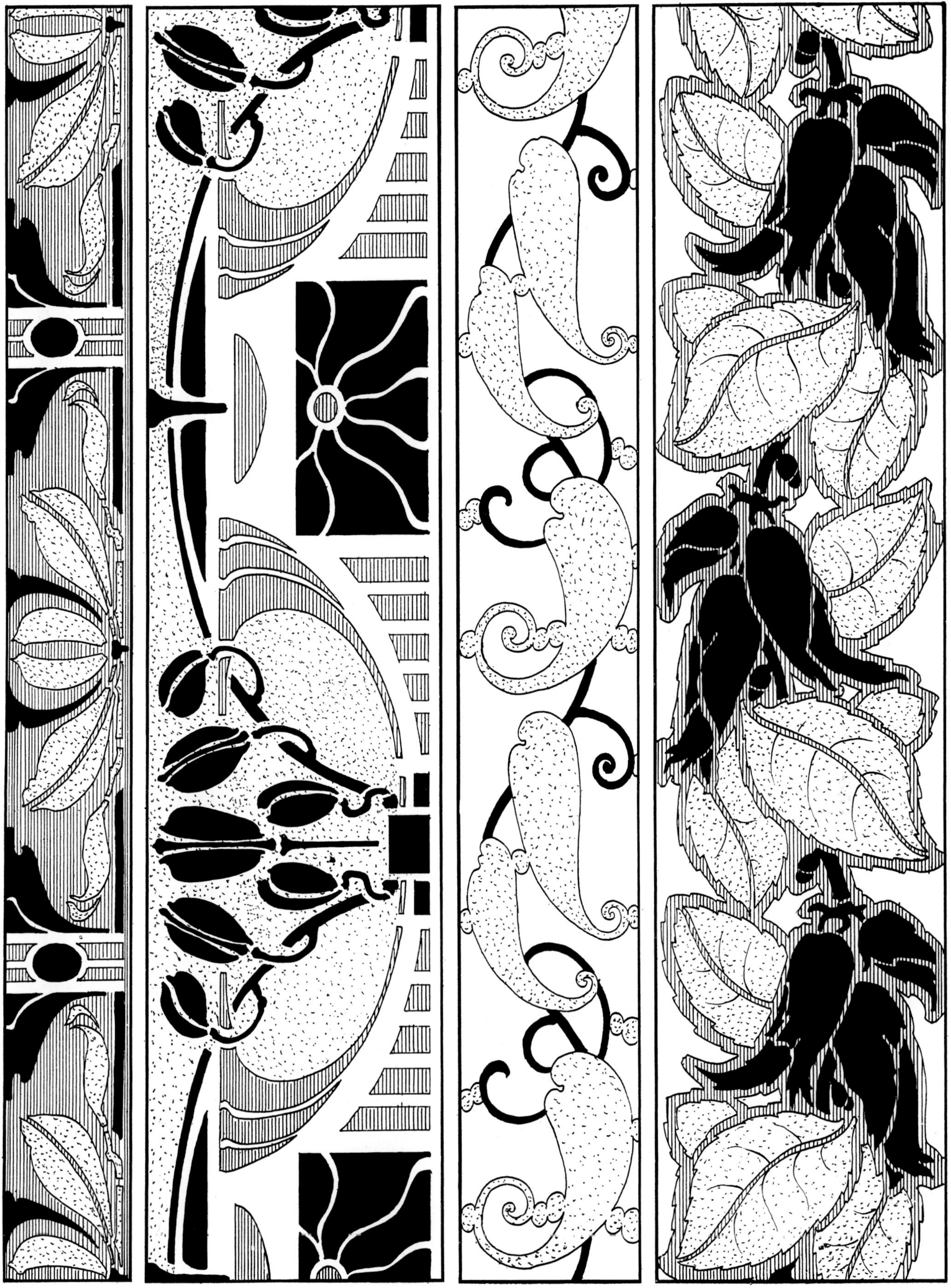

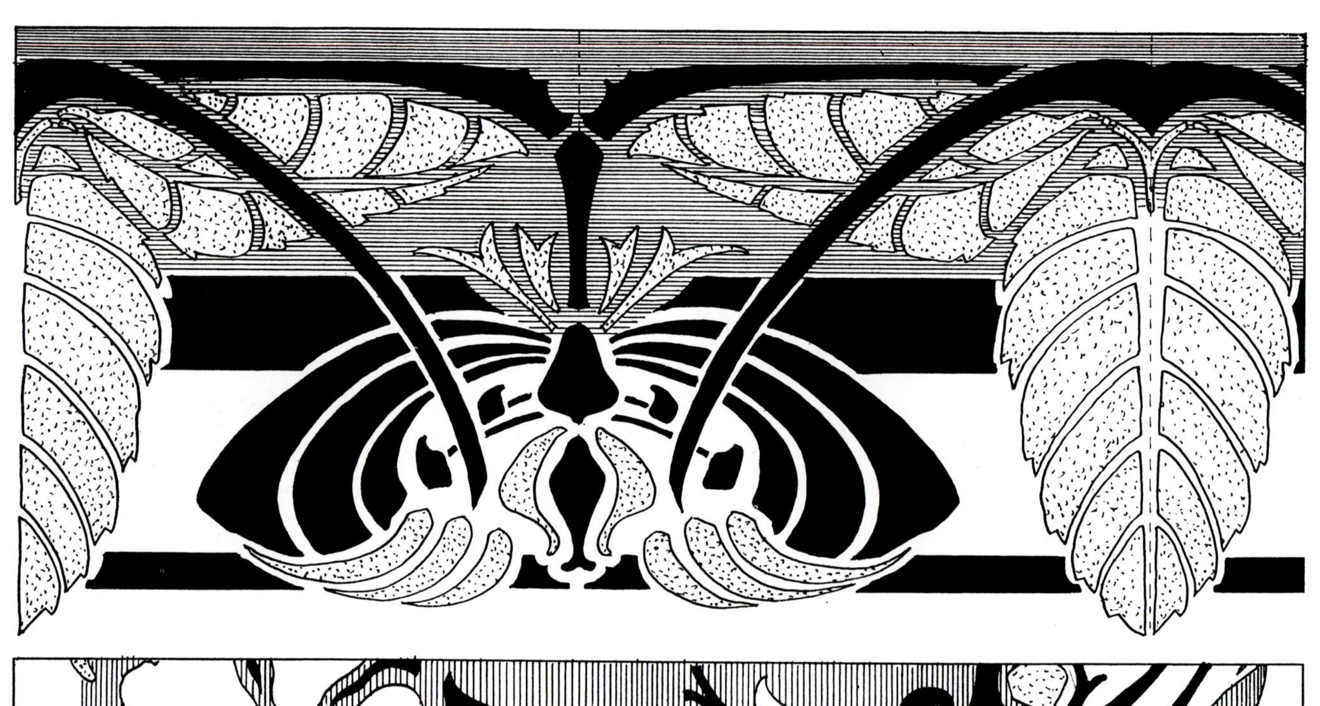

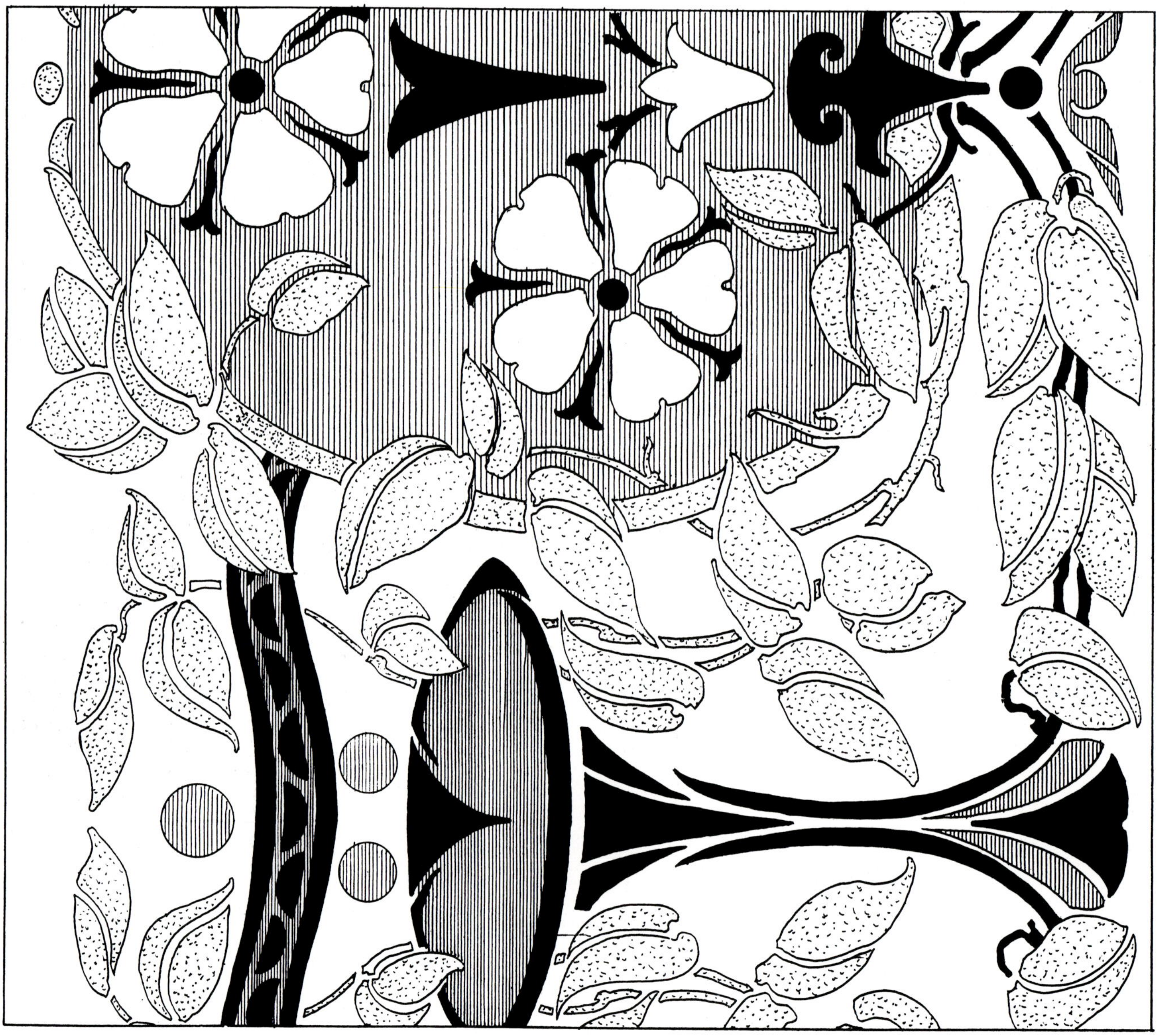

Images from *Les Bijoux* by Maurice Dufrène (Paris: Librairie des Arts Décoratifs, A. Calavas, c. 1900). Reprinted by Dover as *305 Authentic Art Nouveau Jewelry Designs* (New York, 1985).

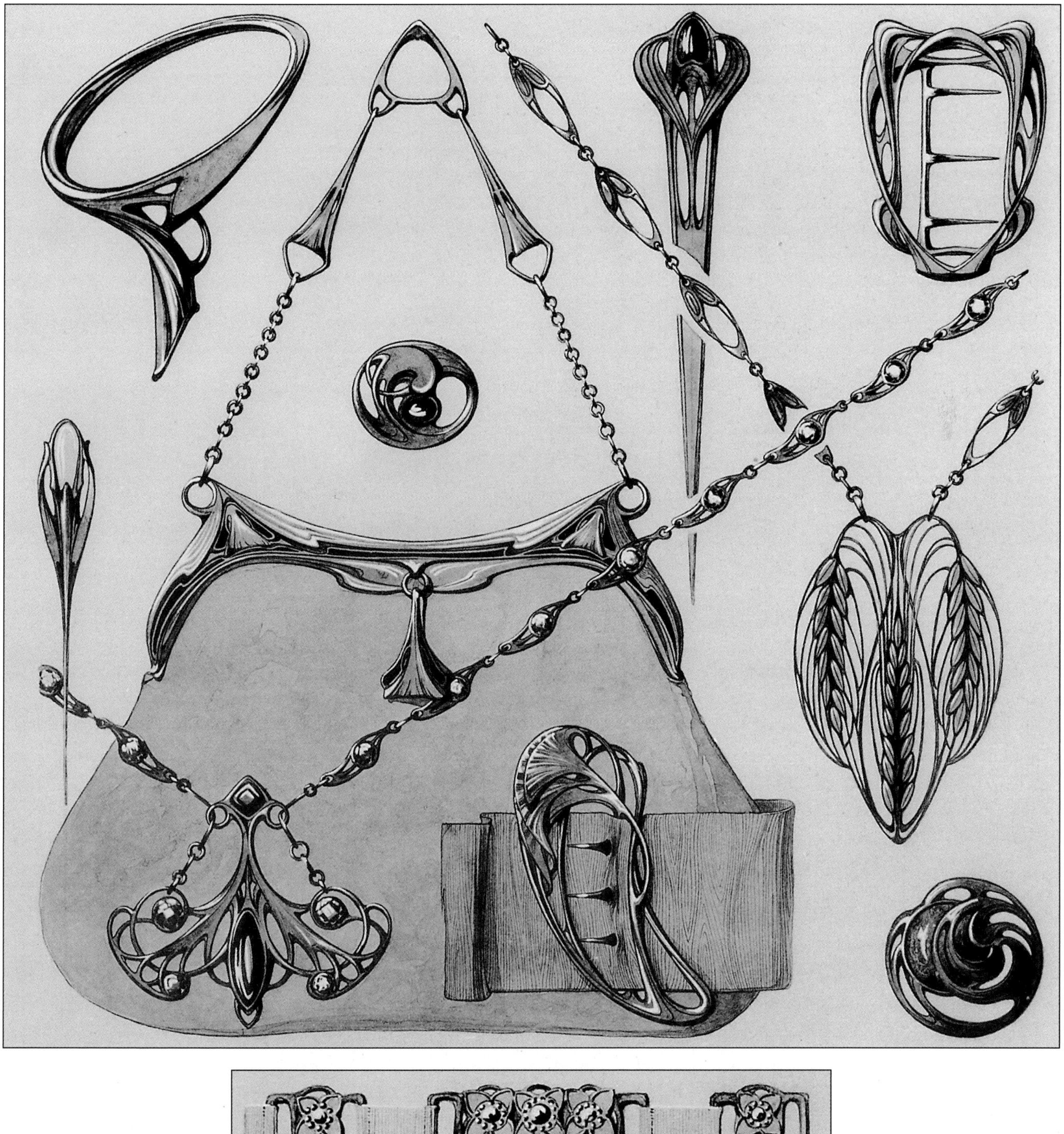

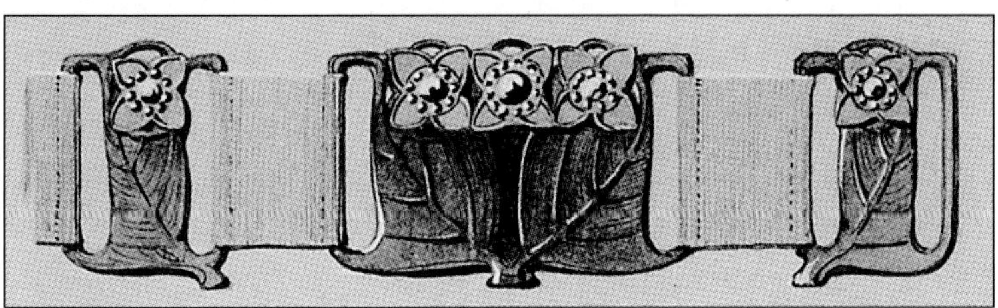

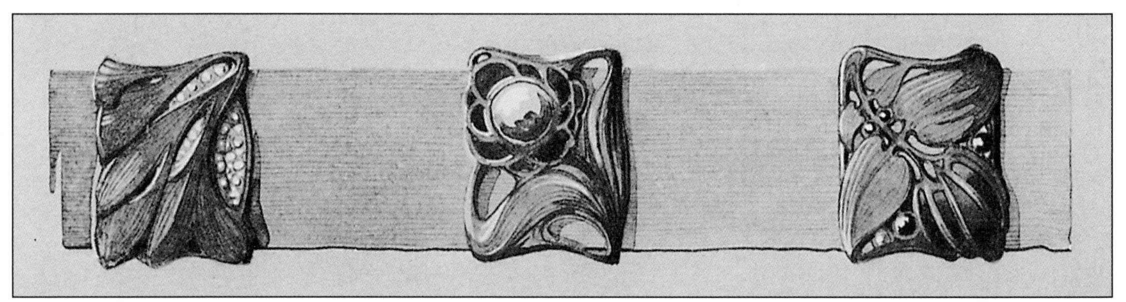

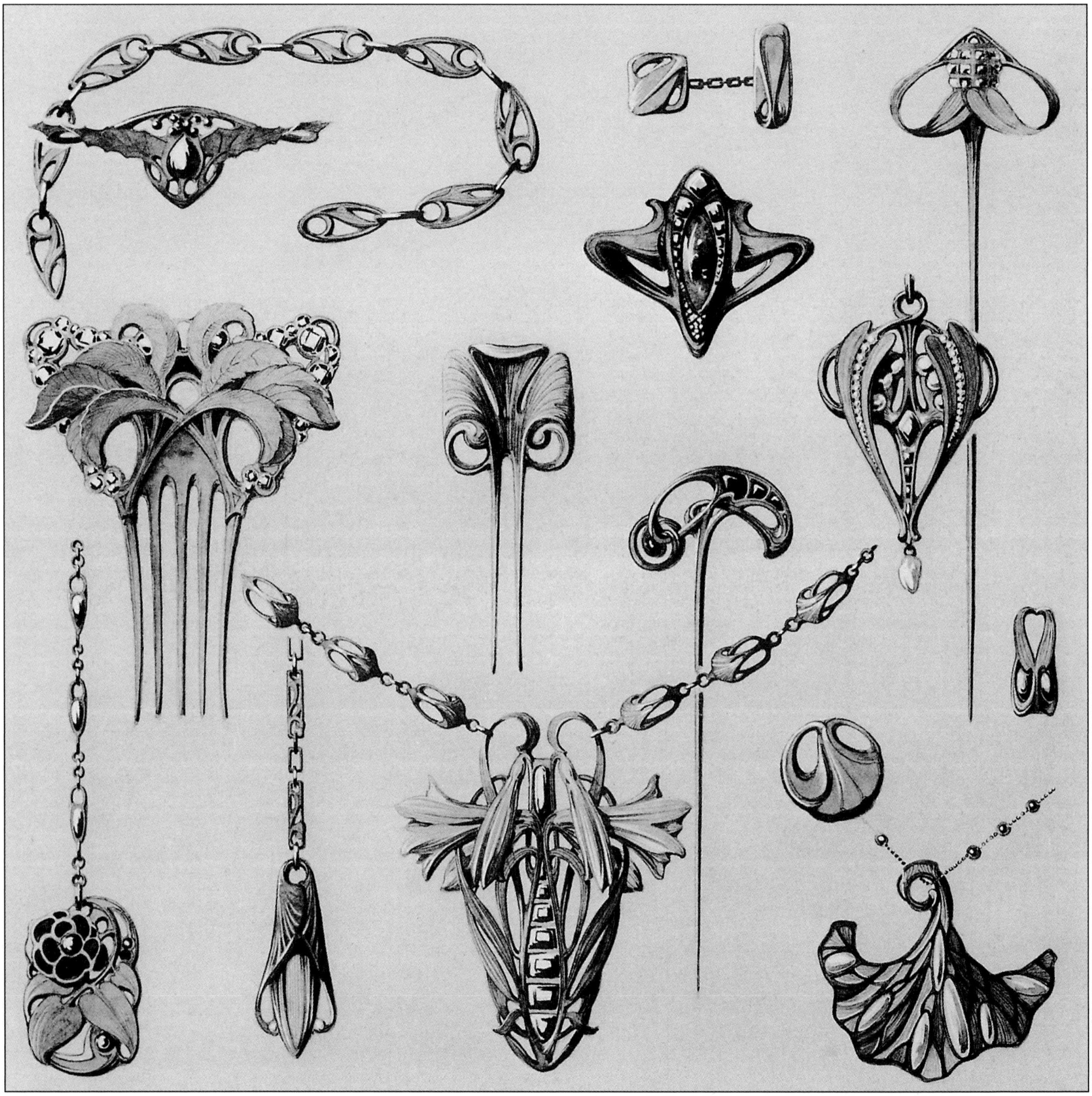

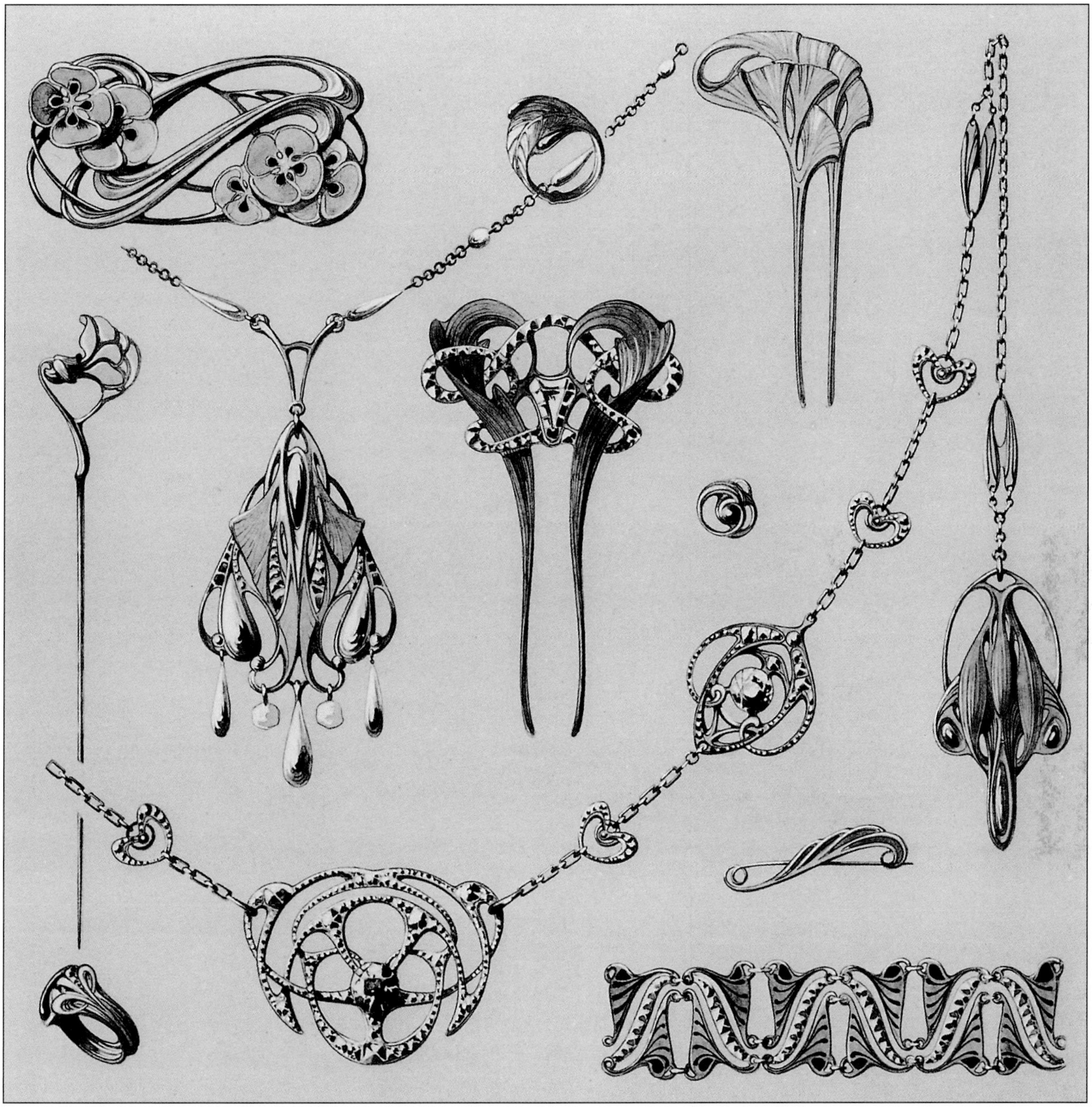

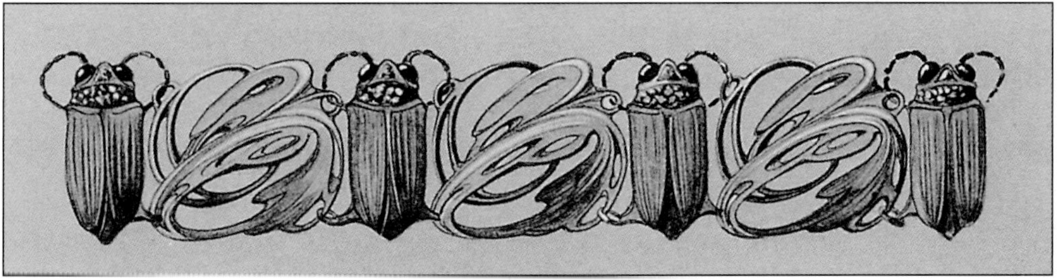

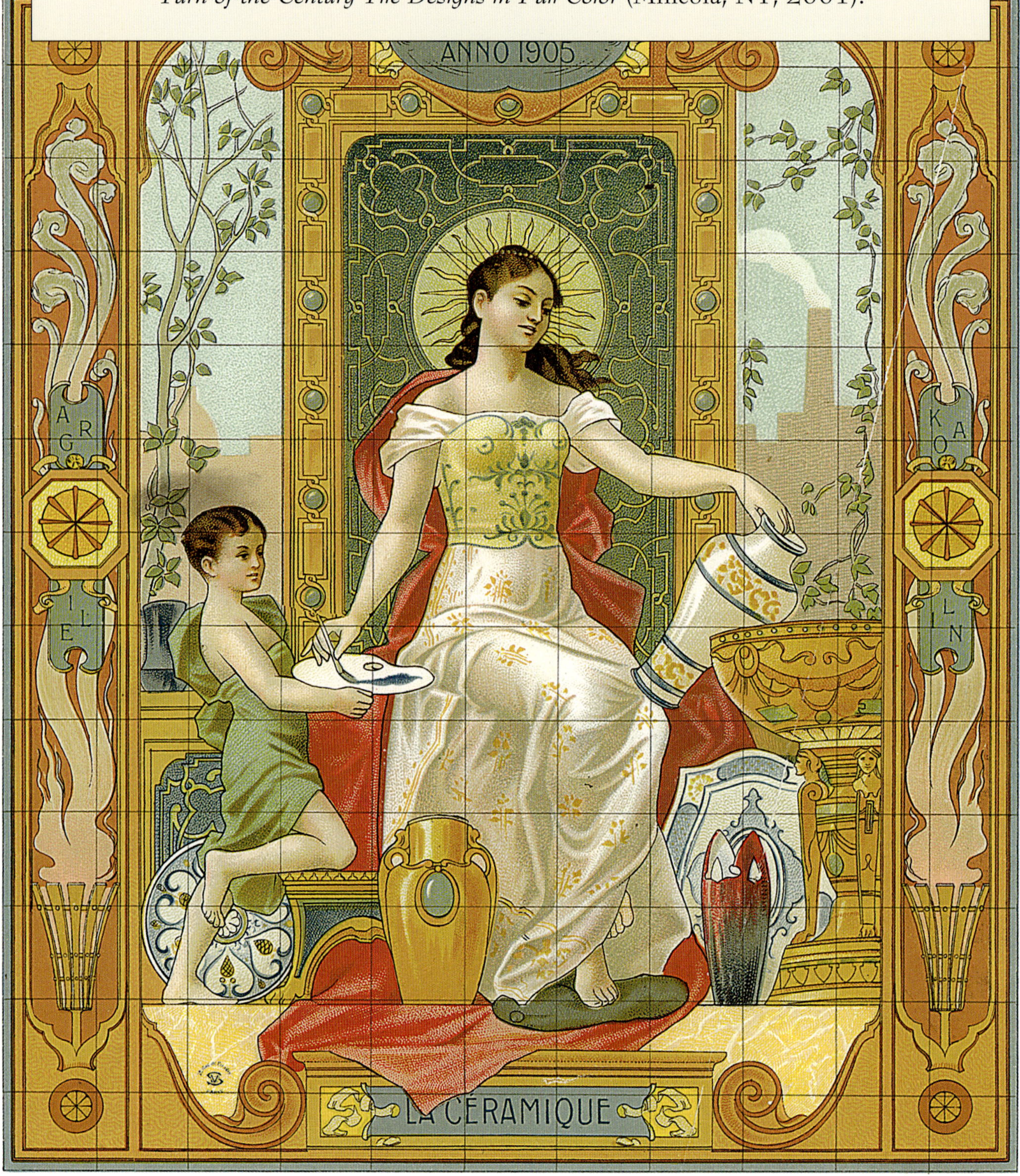

Images from *La Céramique Architecturale/Revetements Decoration: Album de Carreaux pour Revetements,* edited by L. François. (Paris: Faienceries de Sarreguemines, Digoin et Vitry-le-François/Utzschneider & C[ie.], 1905). Reprinted by Dover as *Turn-of-the-Century Tile Designs in Full Color* (Mineola, NY, 2001).

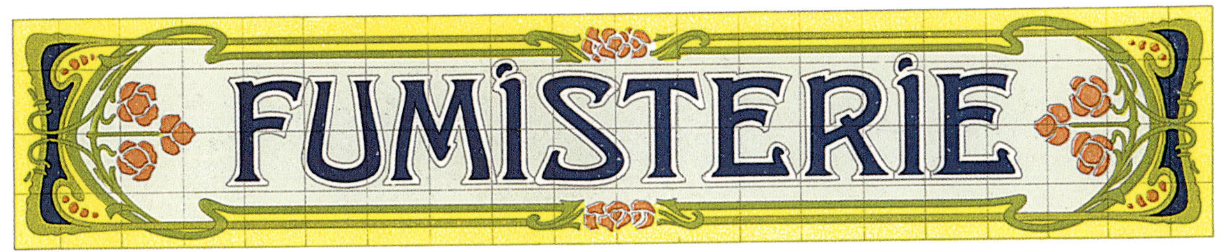
FUMISTERIE

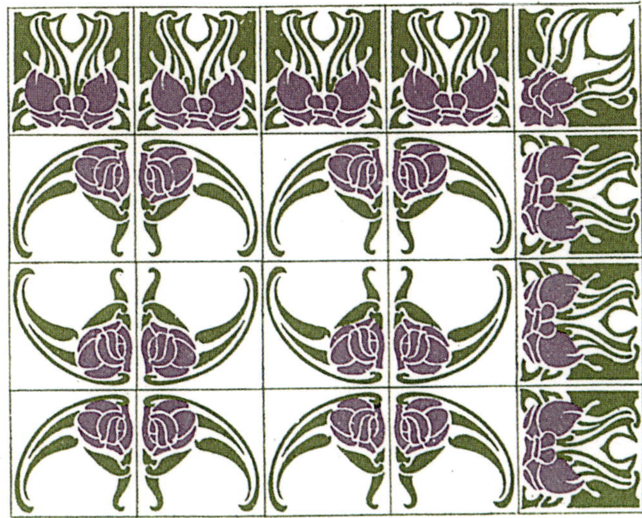

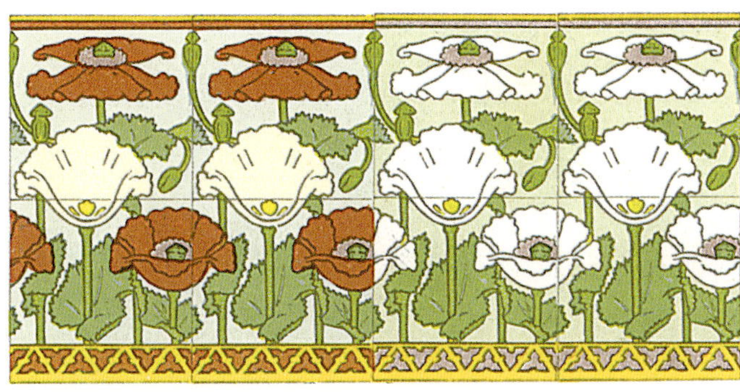

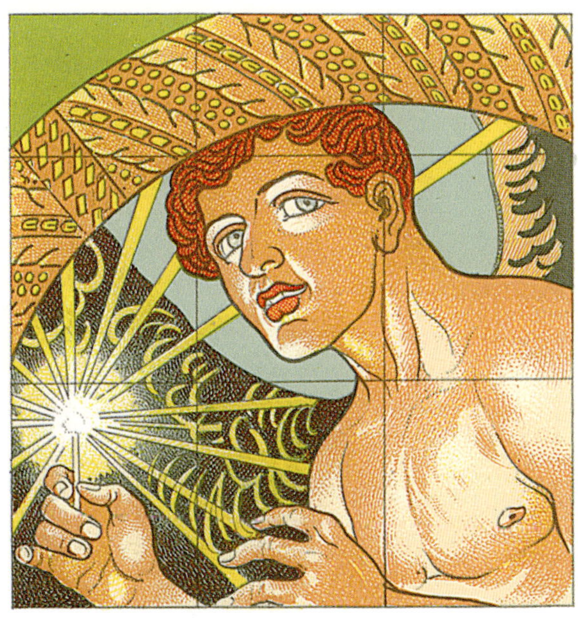

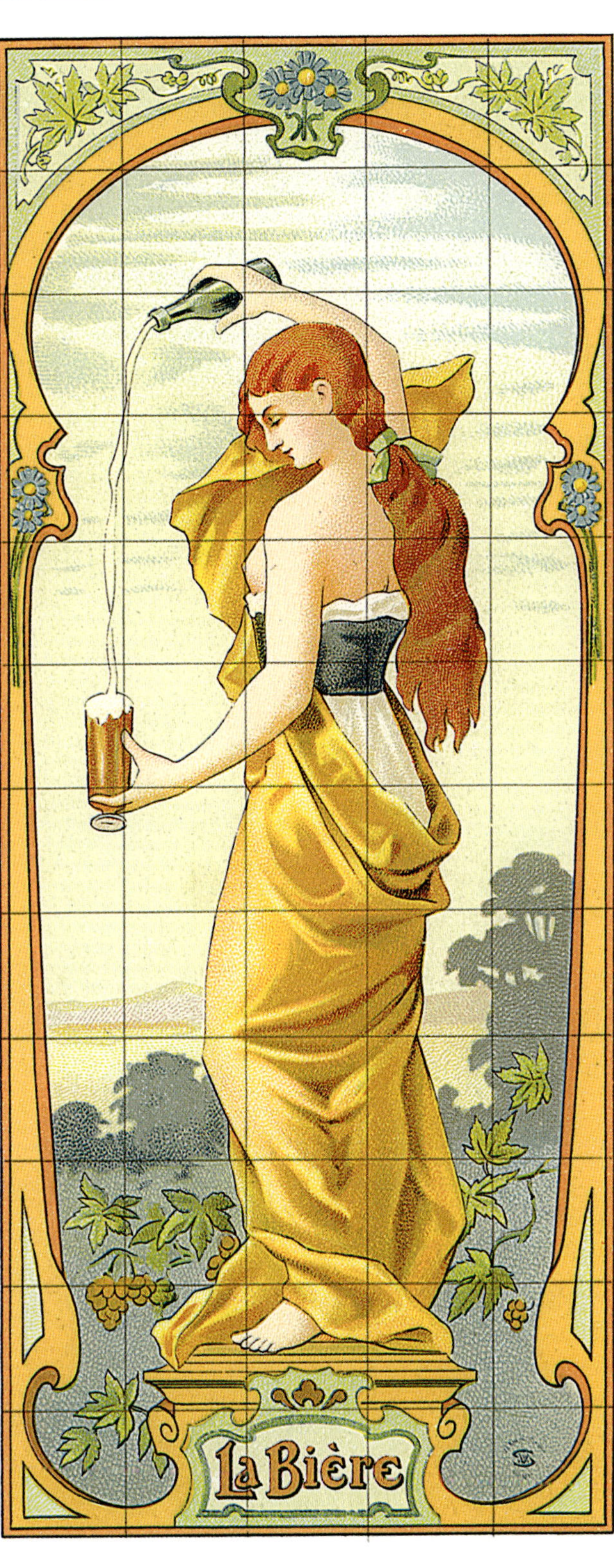
La Bière

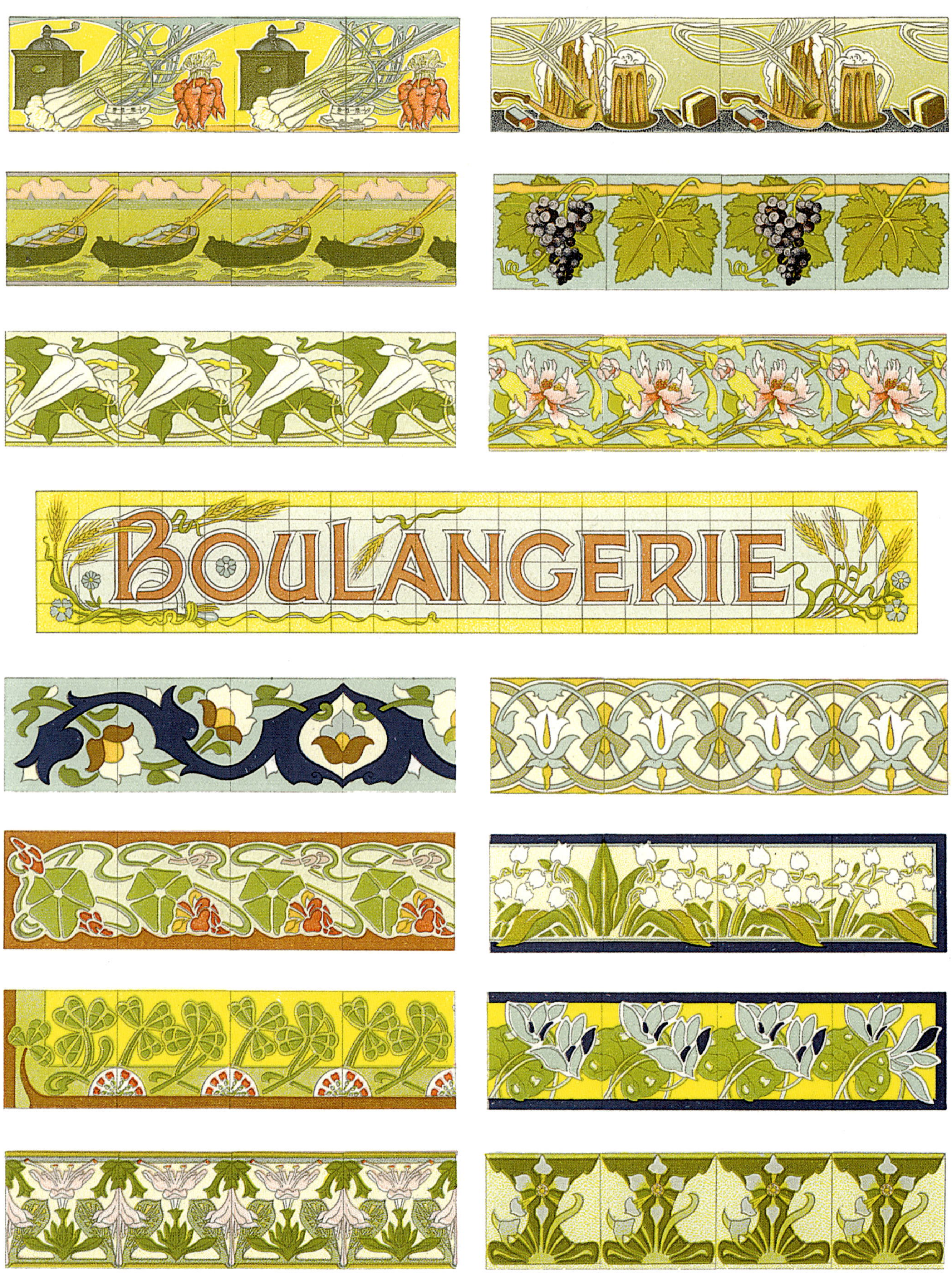

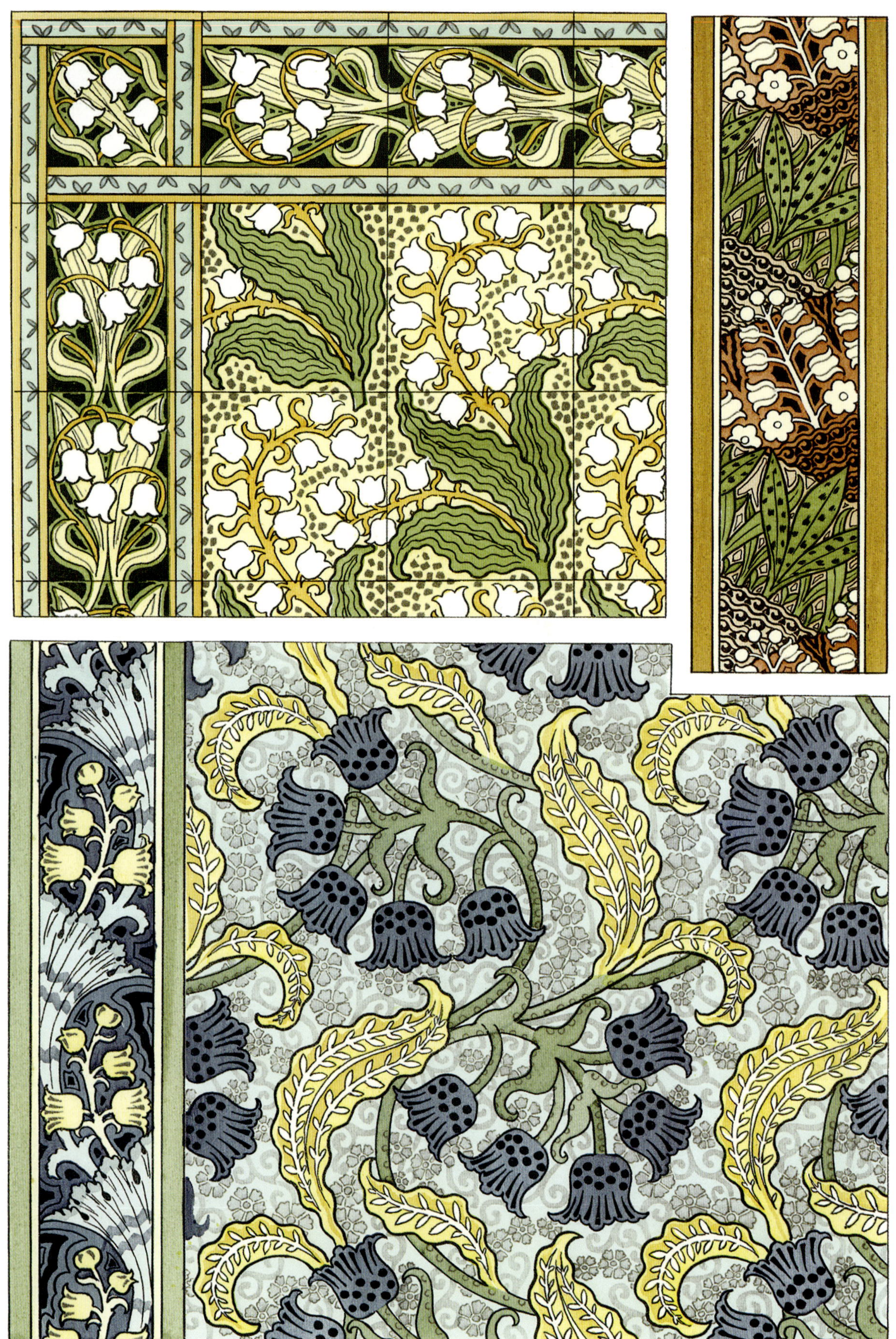

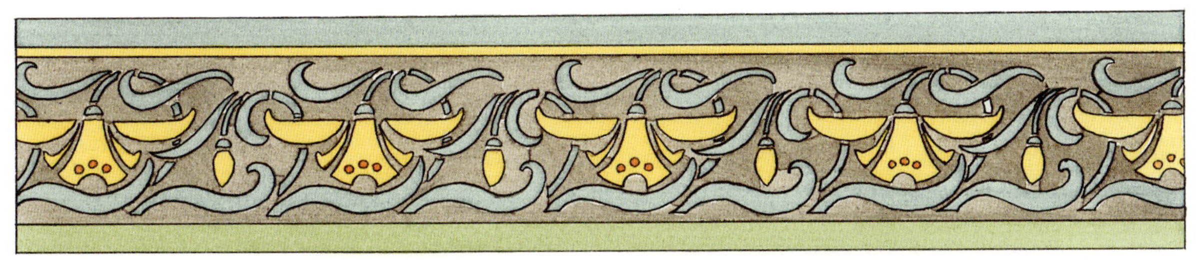

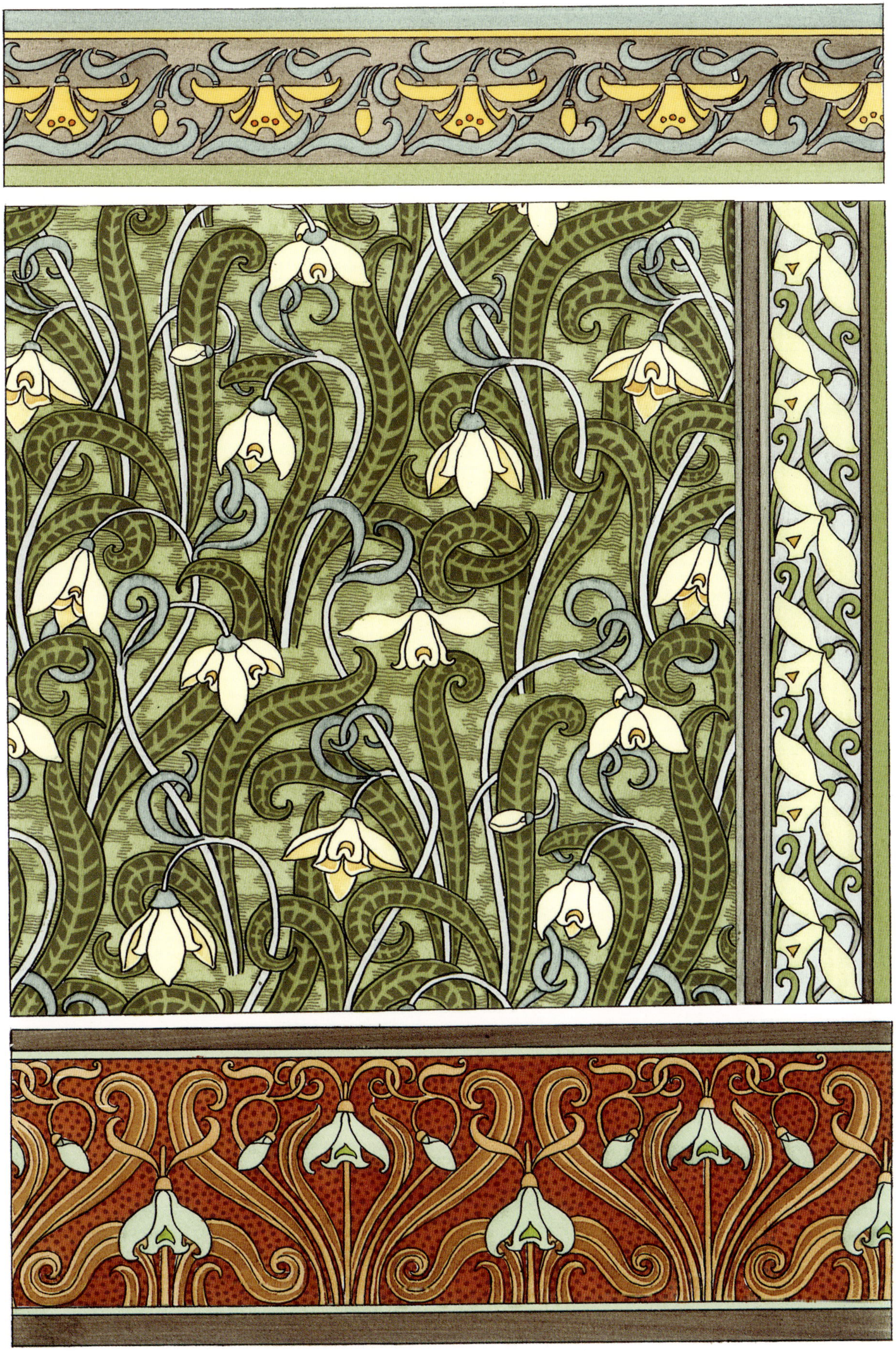

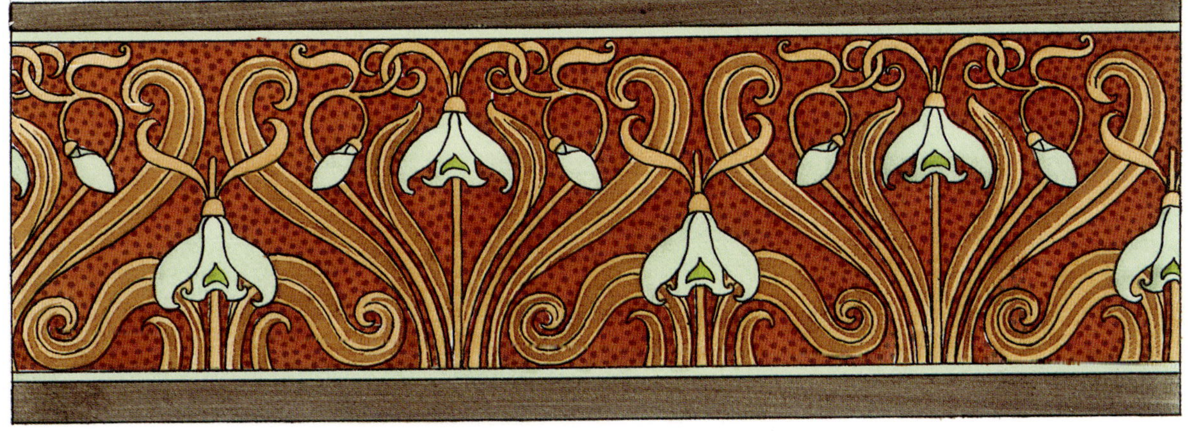

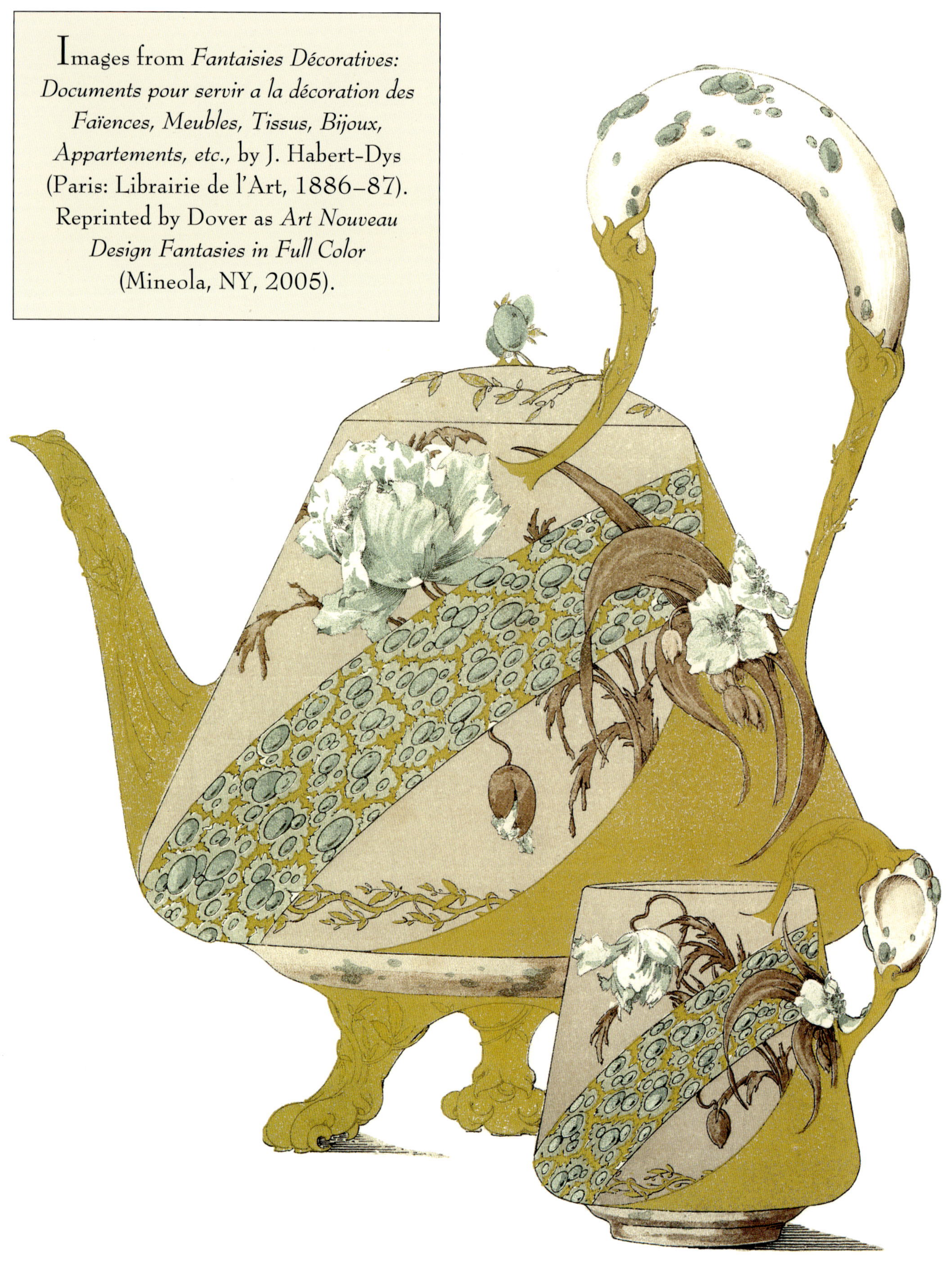

Images from *Fantaisies Décoratives: Documents pour servir a la décoration des Faïences, Meubles, Tissus, Bijoux, Appartements, etc.*, by J. Habert-Dys (Paris: Librairie de l'Art, 1886–87). Reprinted by Dover as *Art Nouveau Design Fantasies in Full Color* (Mineola, NY, 2005).

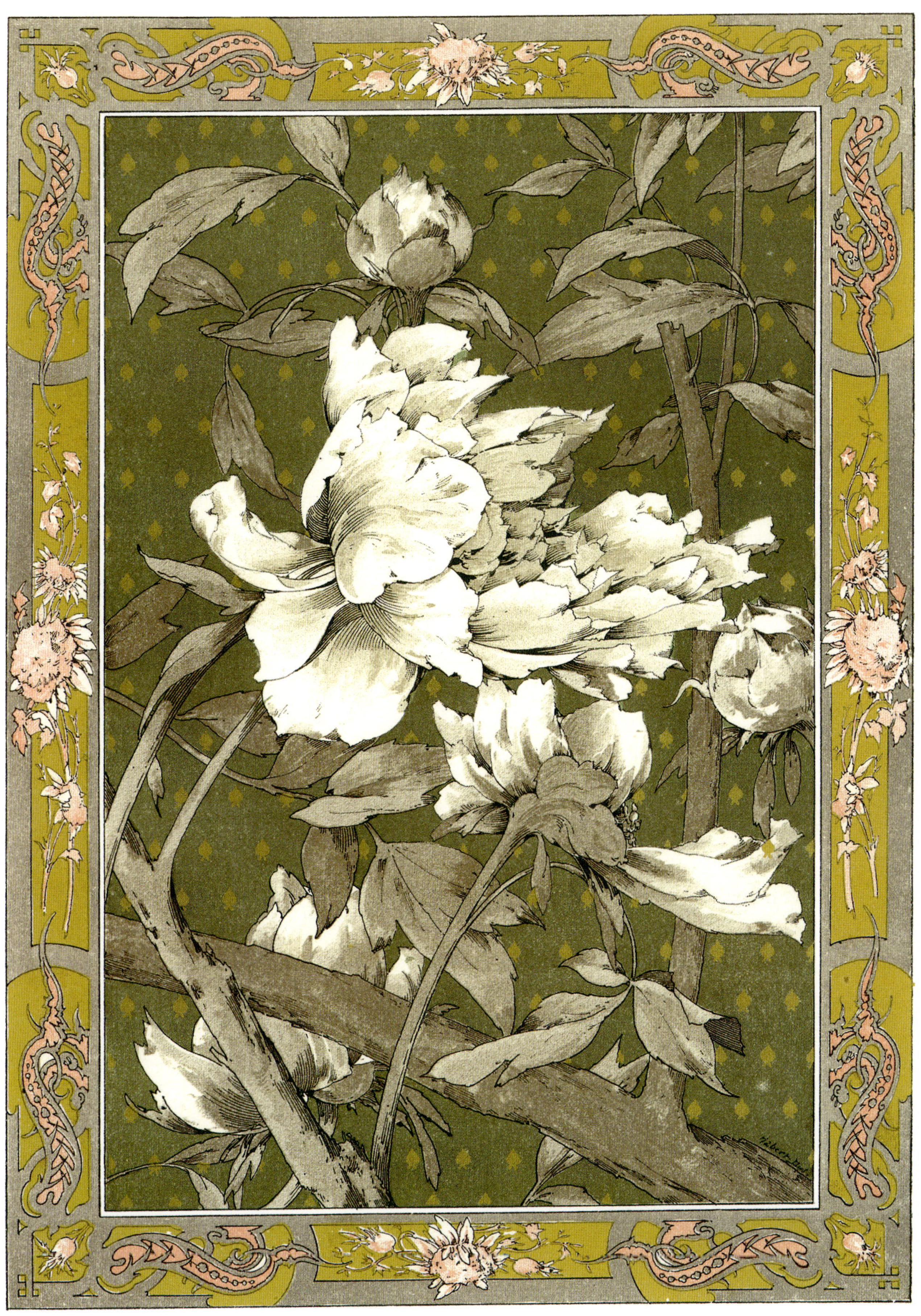

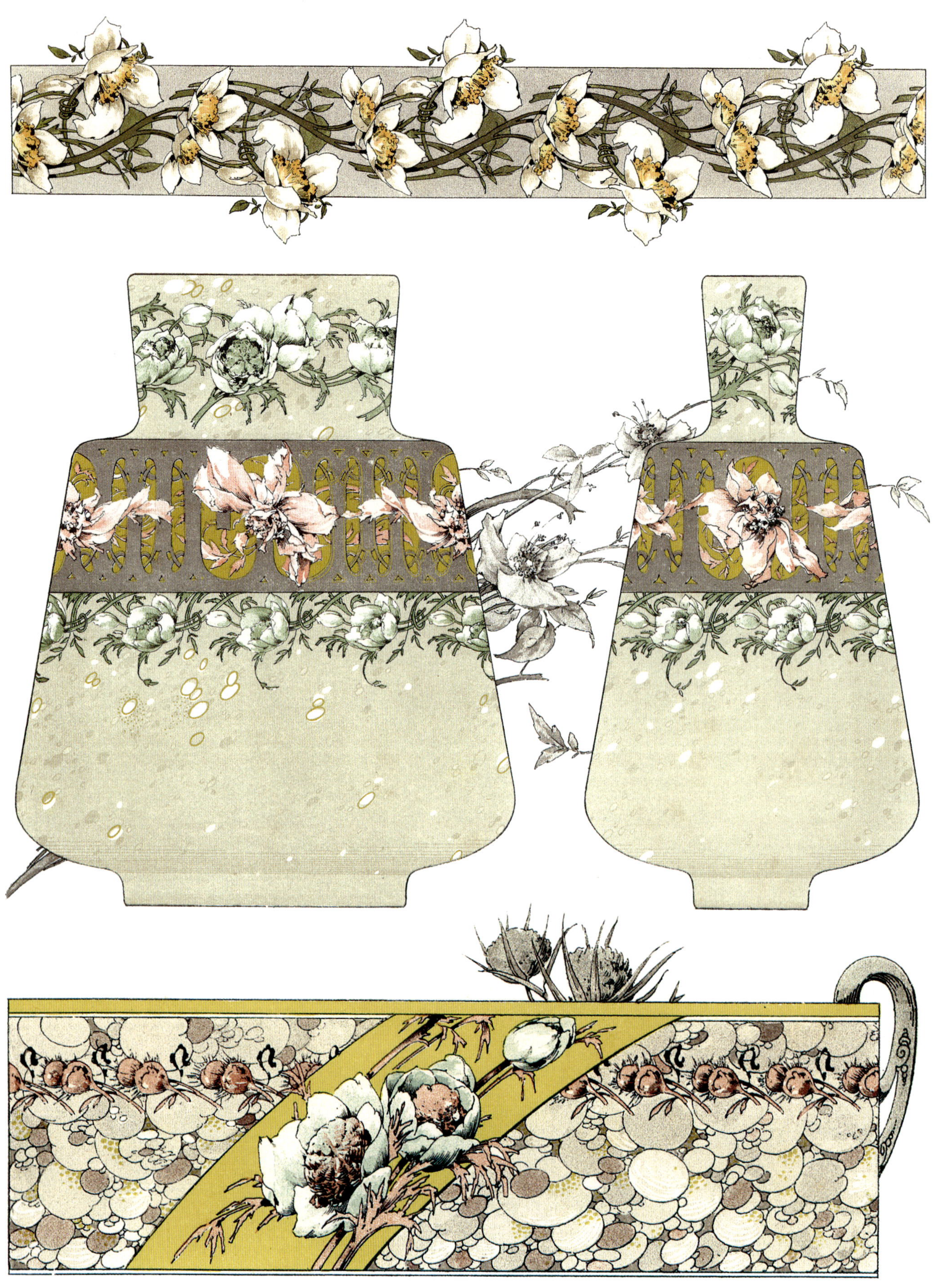

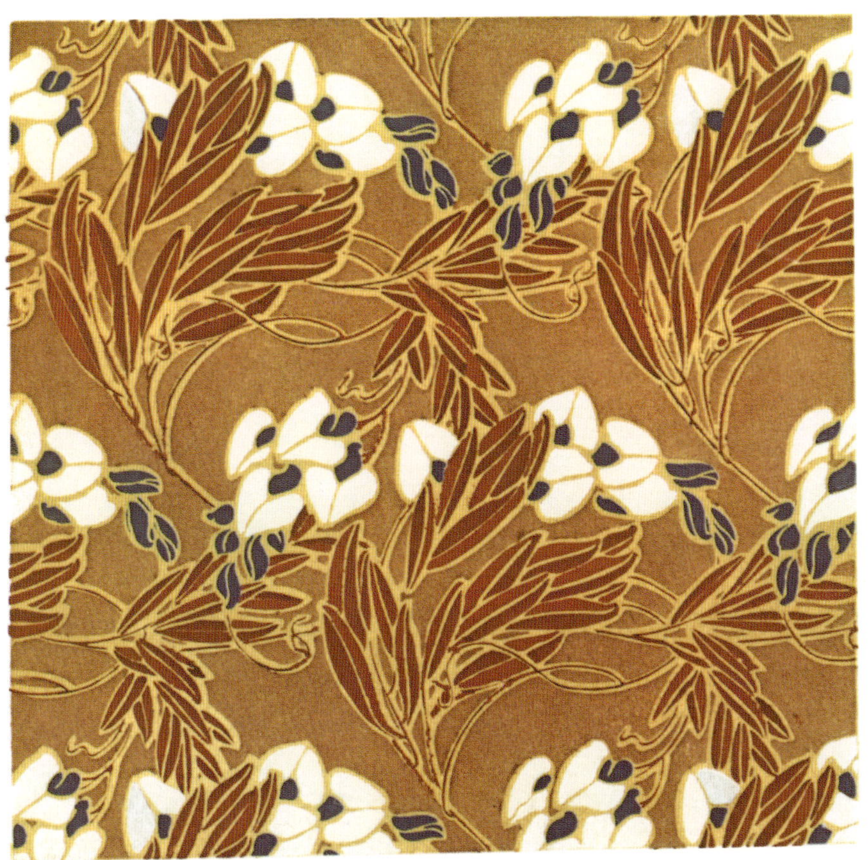

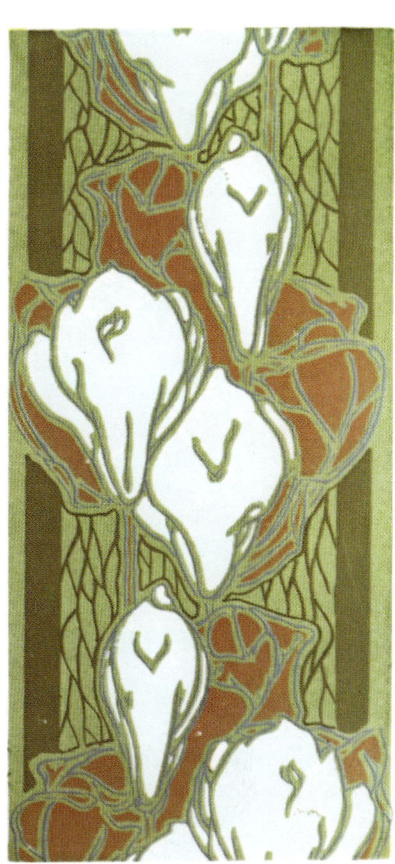

Images from *Les fleurs et leurs applications décoratives* by E. A. Seguy. (Paris: Librairie des Arts Décoratifs (A. Calavas), c. 1902. Reprinted by Dover as *Full-Color Floral Designs in the Art Nouveau Style*, edited by Charles Rahn Fry (New York, 1977).

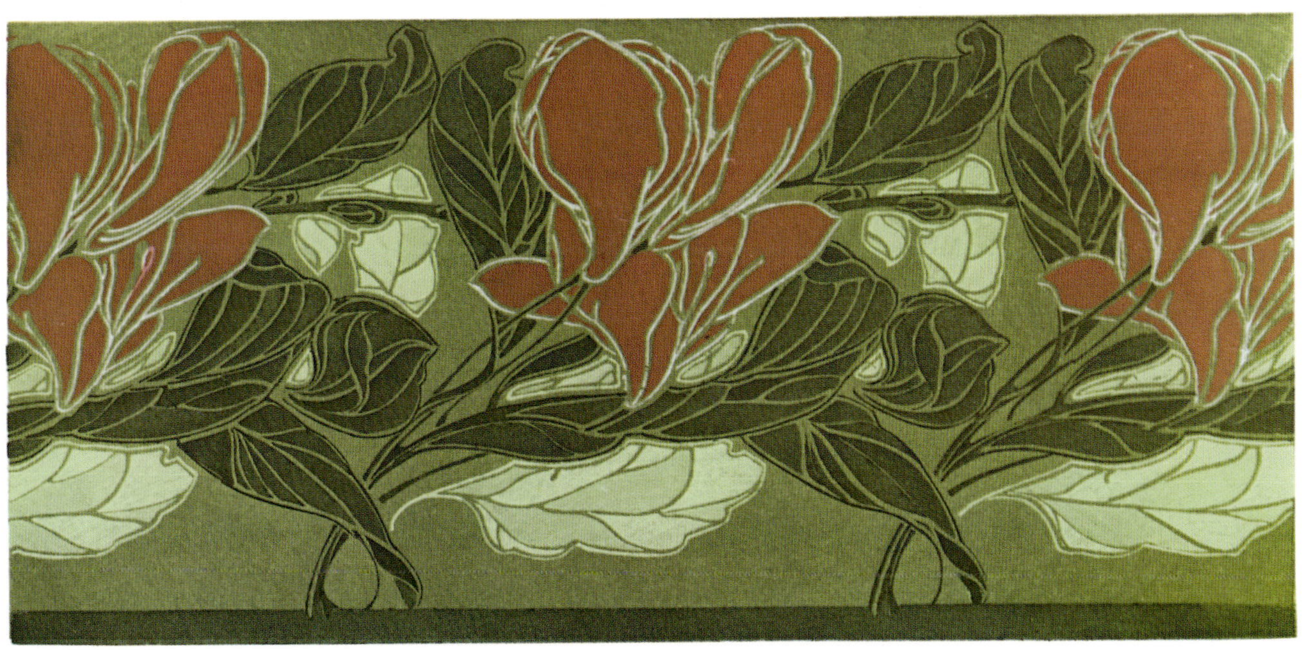

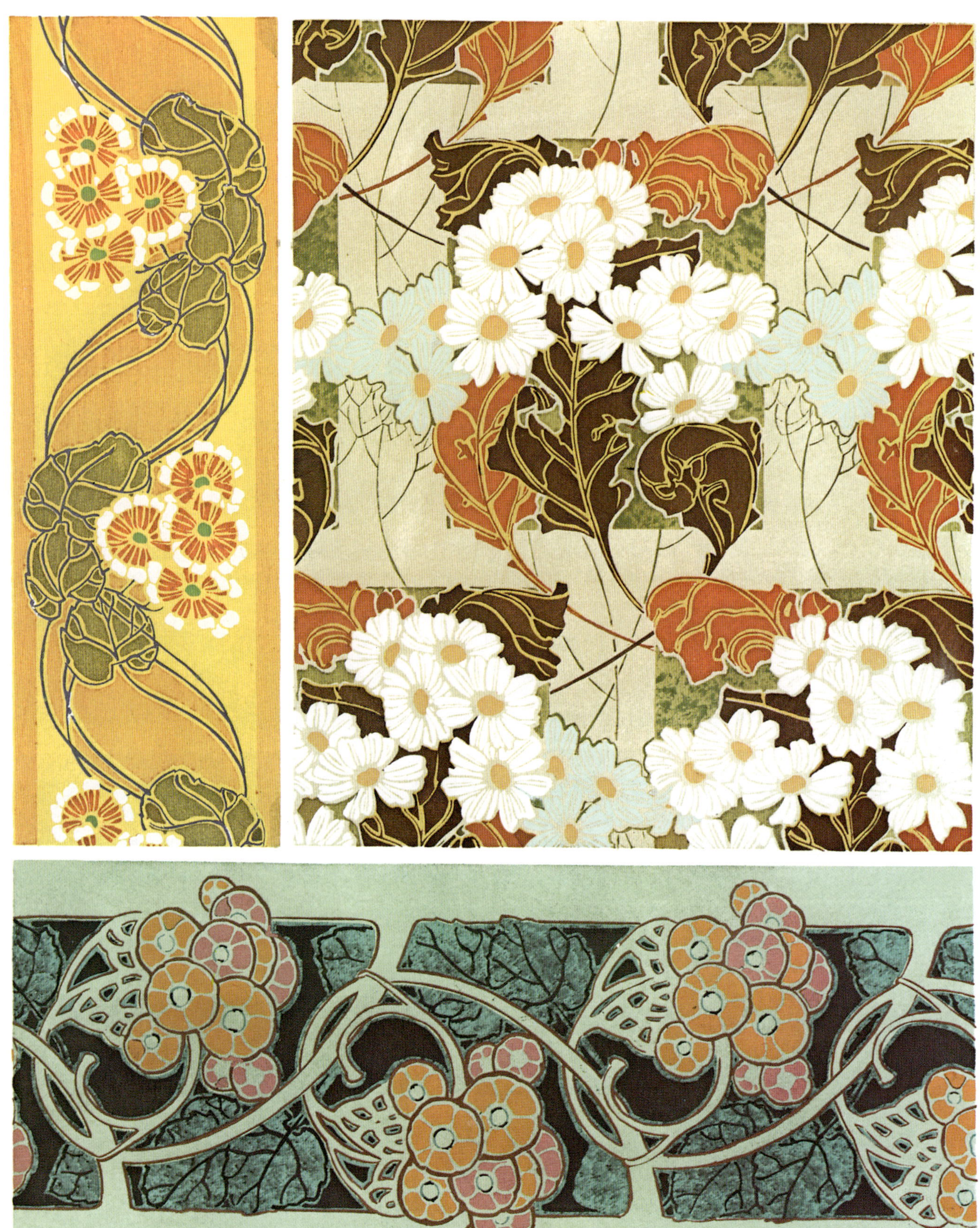

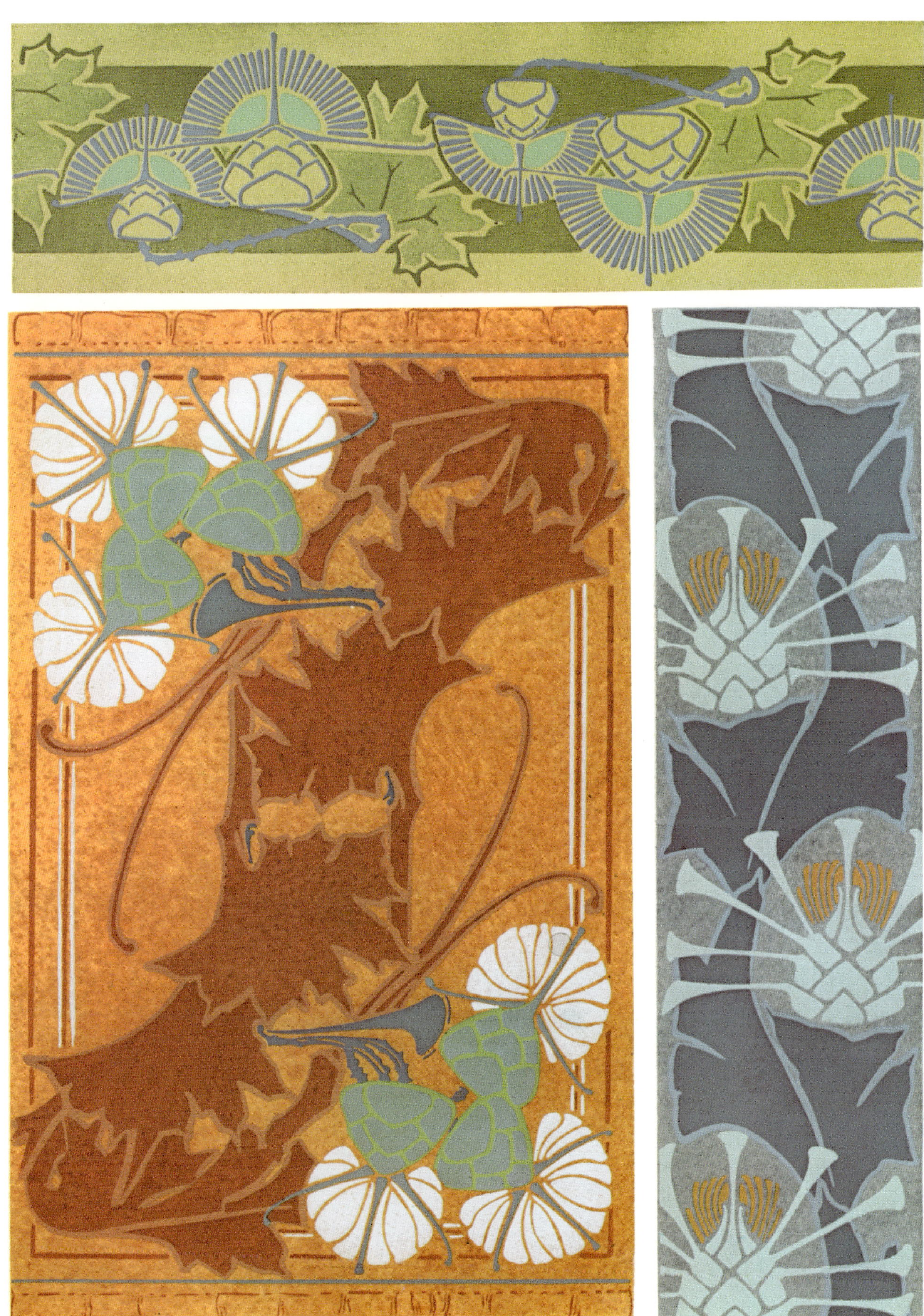

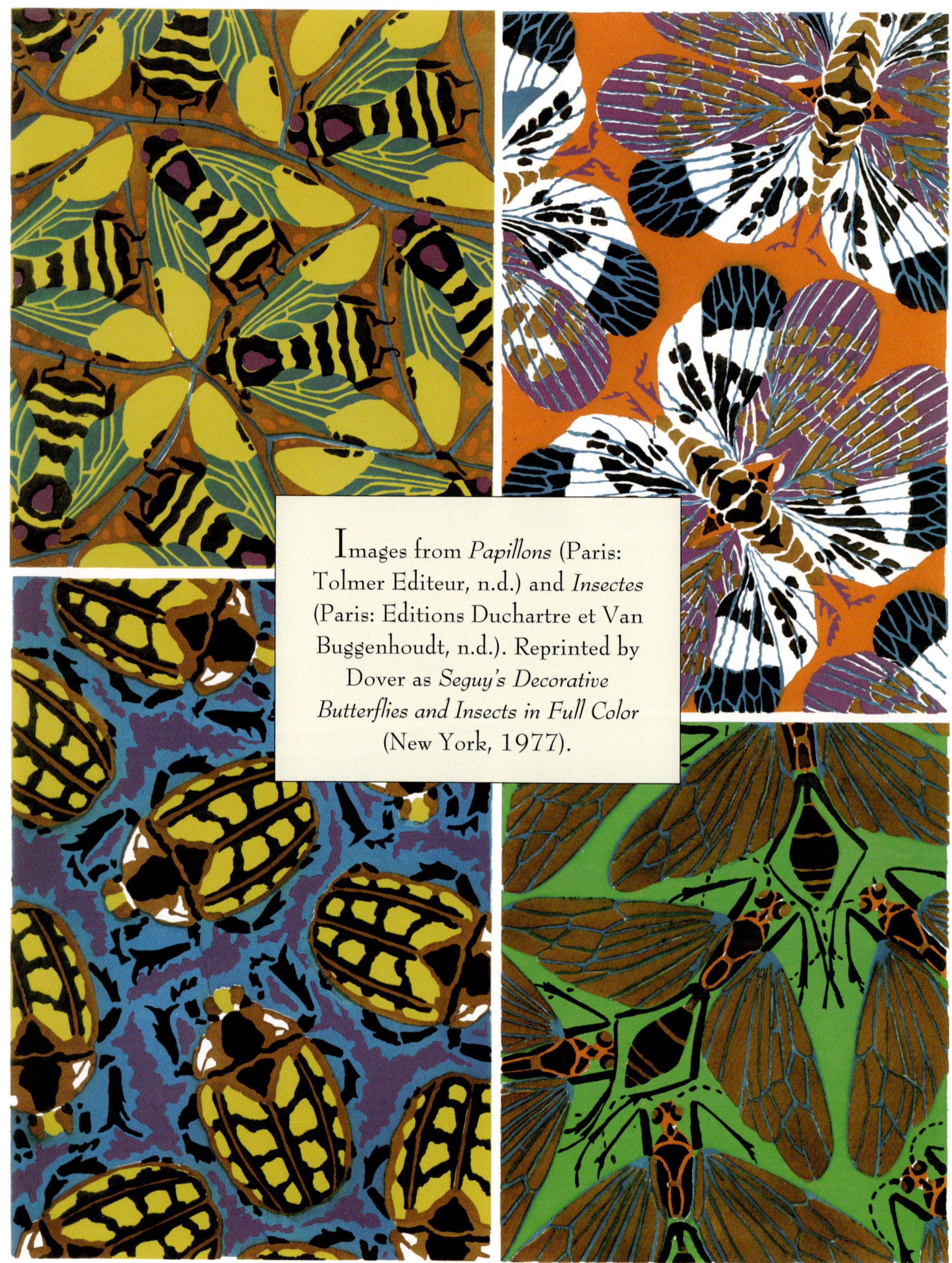

Images from *Papillons* (Paris: Tolmer Editeur, n.d.) and *Insectes* (Paris: Editions Duchartre et Van Buggenhoudt, n.d.). Reprinted by Dover as *Seguy's Decorative Butterflies and Insects in Full Color* (New York, 1977).

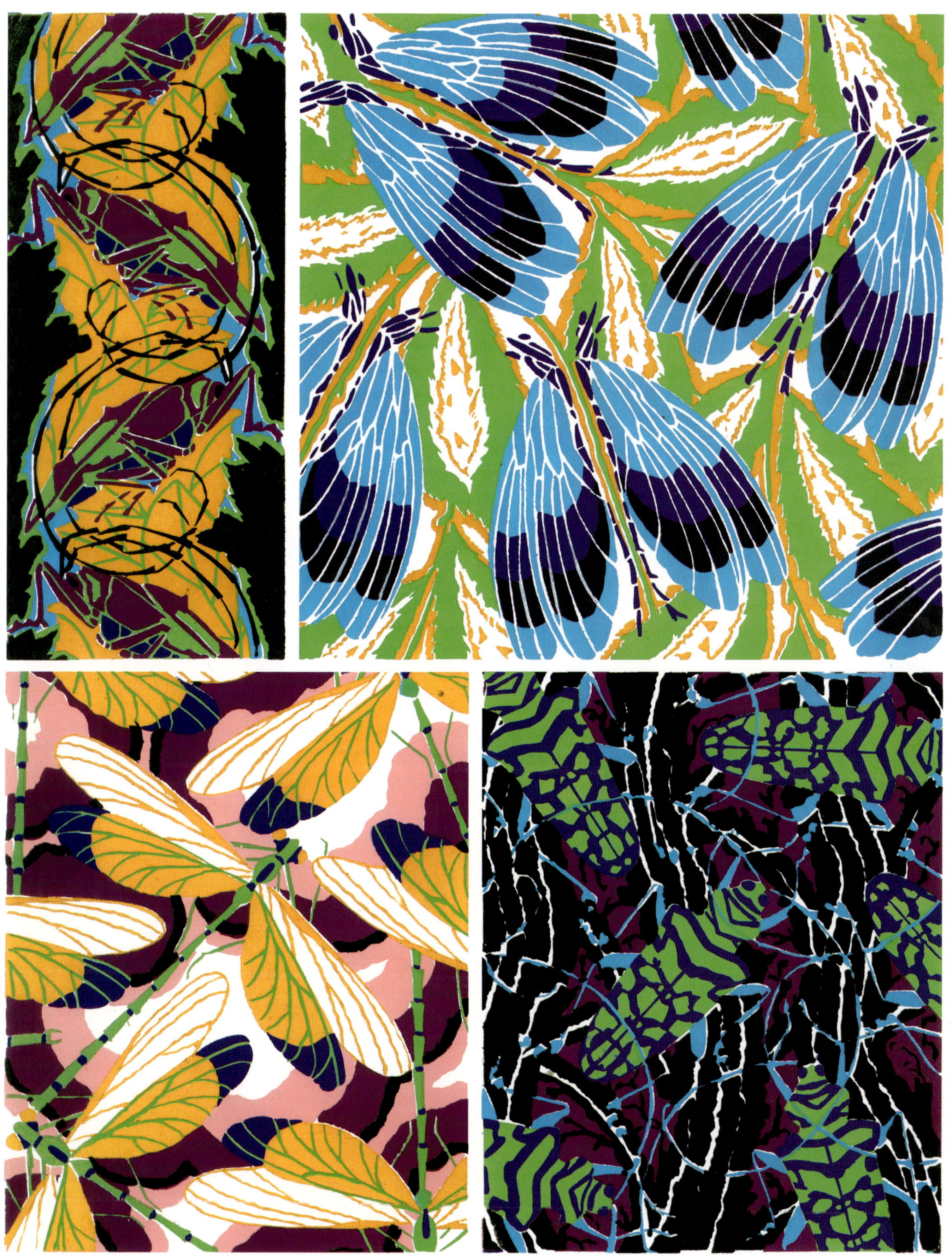

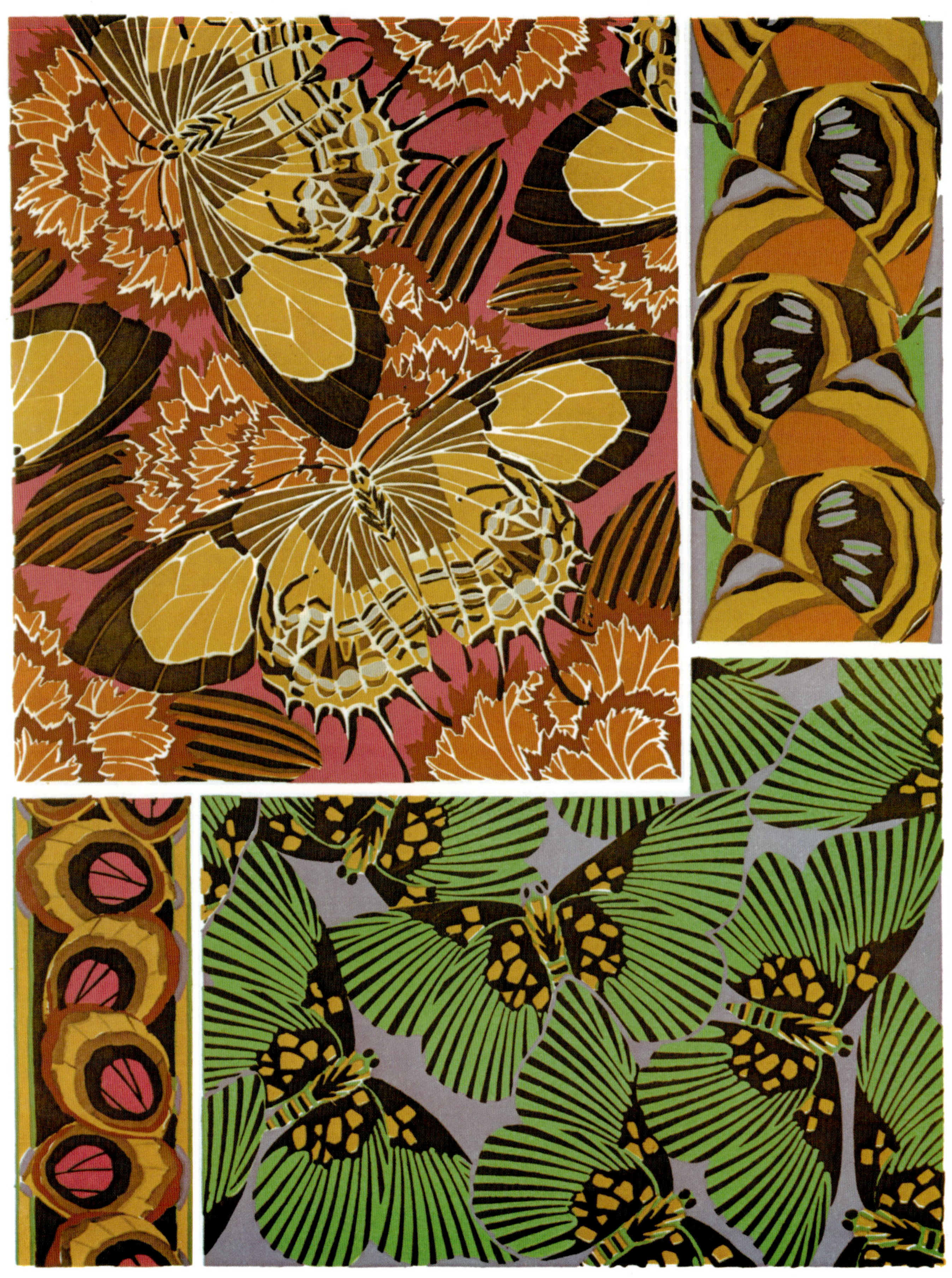

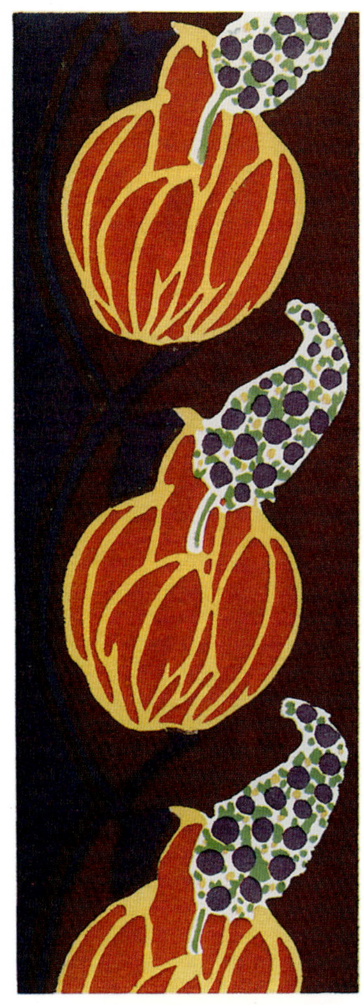

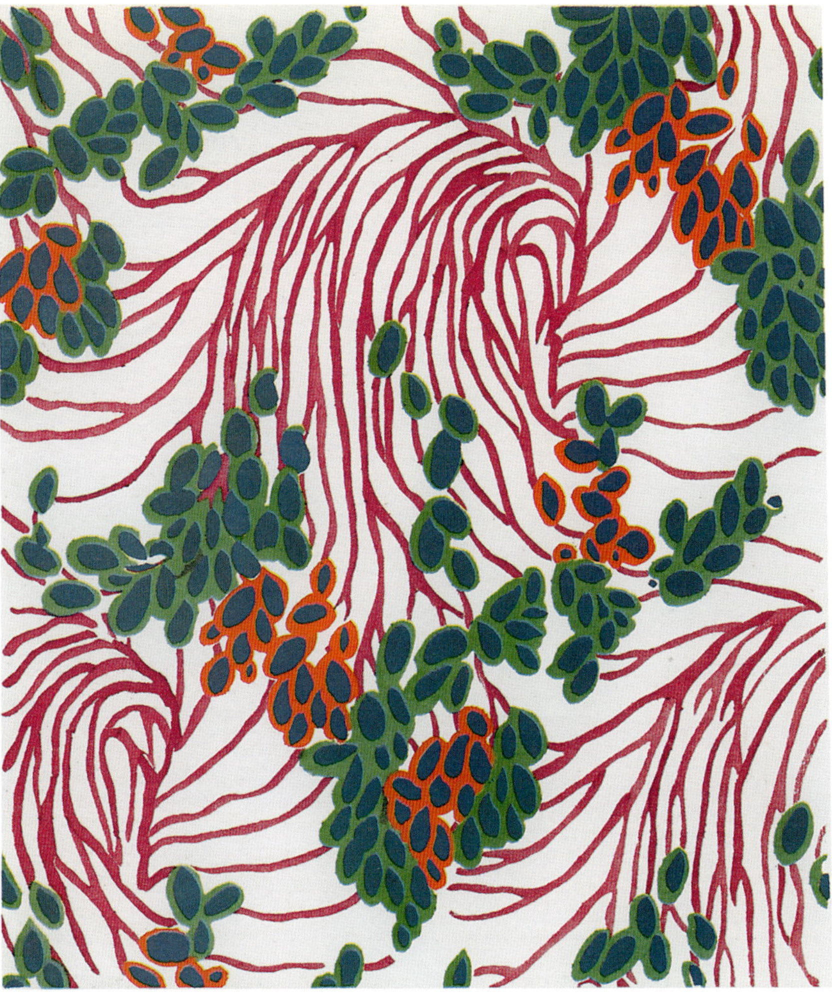

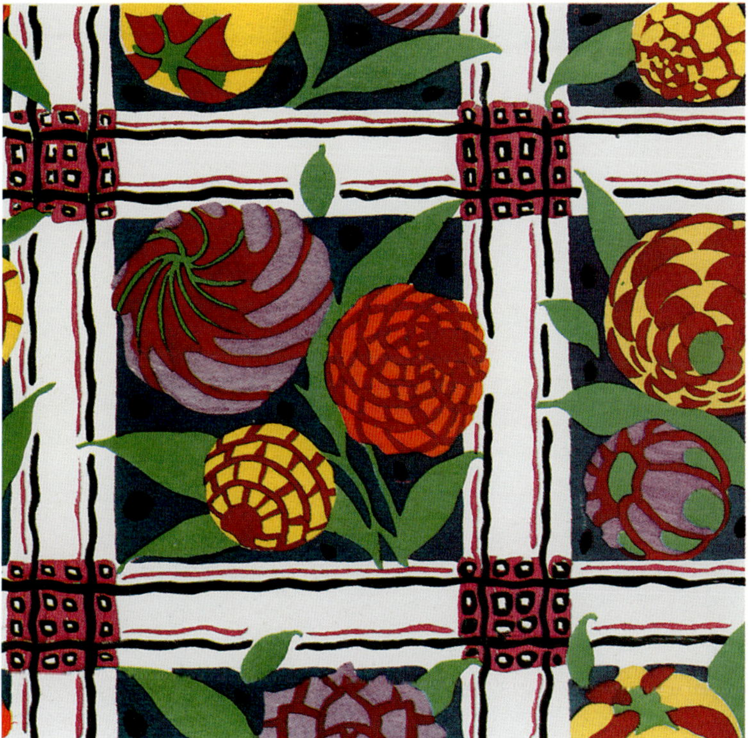

Images from the following three books by E. A. Seguy: *Primavera: Dessins & coloris nouveaux* (Plauen, Germany: Christian Stoll, n.d.), *Floréal: Dessins & coloris nouveaux* (Paris: A. Calavas, c. 1914), and *Samarkande: 20 compositions en couleurs dans le Style oriental* (Paris: Ch. Massin, c. 1920). Reprinted by Dover as *The Spectacular Color Floral Designs of E. A. Seguy* (New York, 1983).

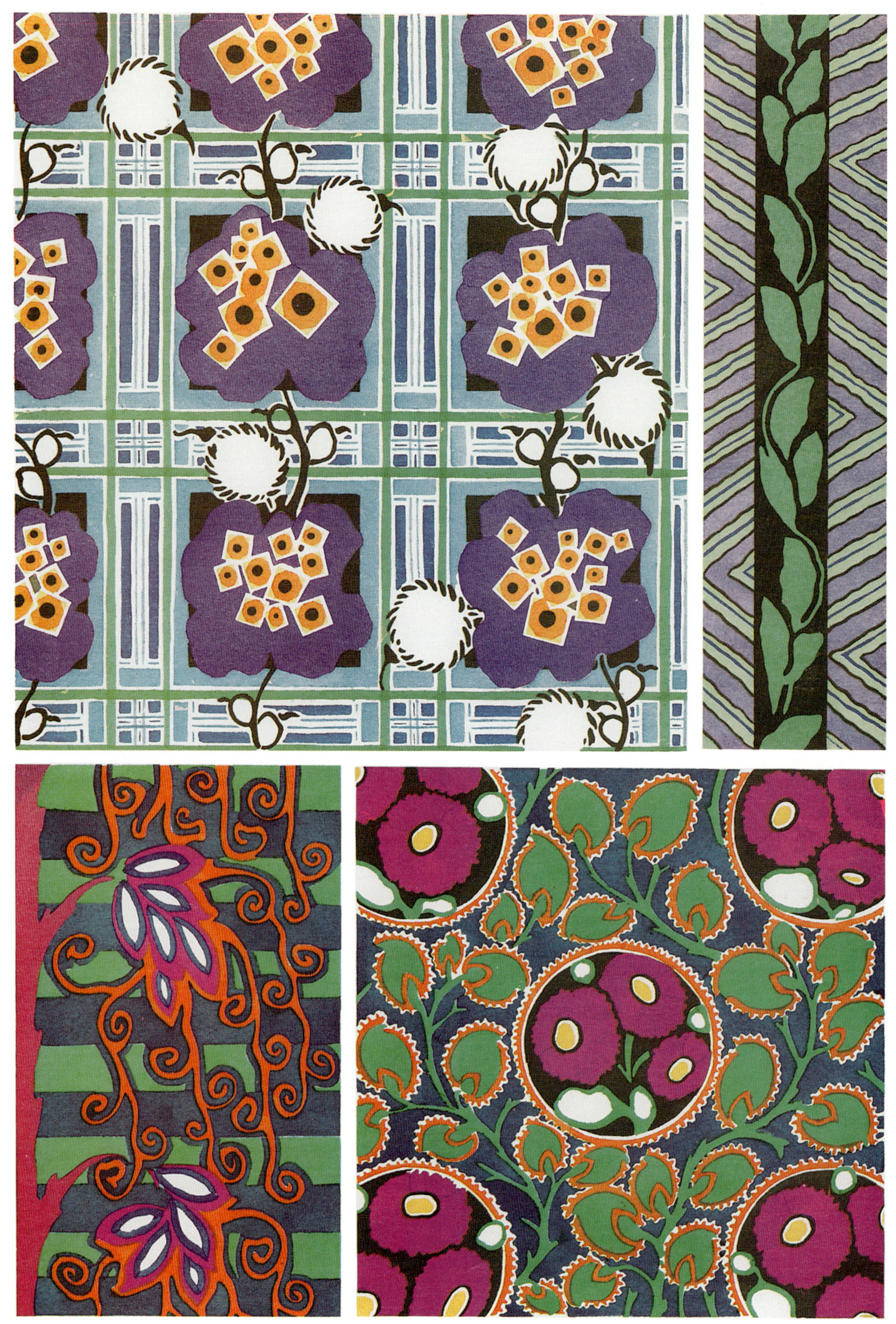

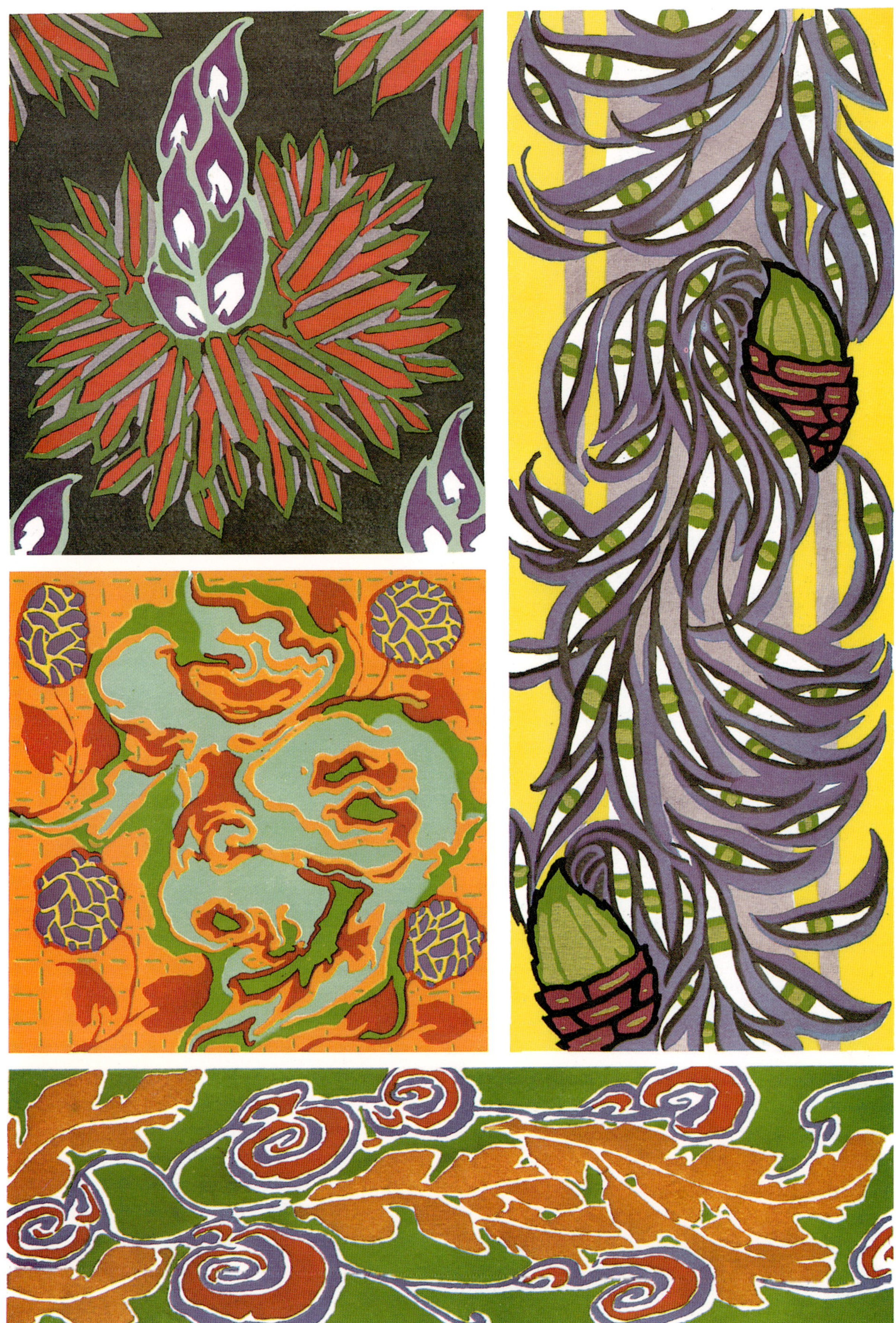

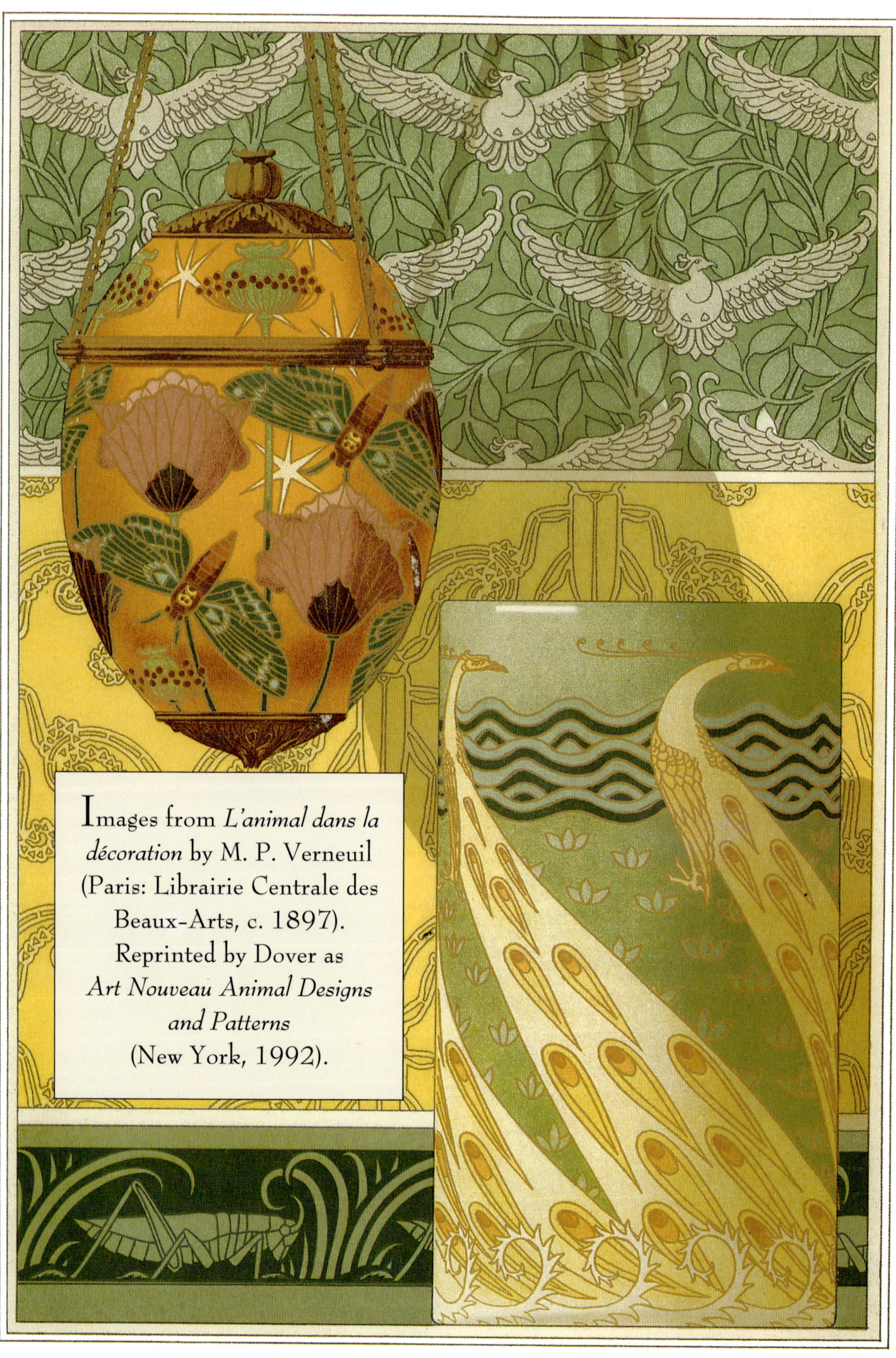

Images from *L'animal dans la décoration* by M. P. Verneuil (Paris: Librairie Centrale des Beaux-Arts, c. 1897). Reprinted by Dover as *Art Nouveau Animal Designs and Patterns* (New York, 1992).

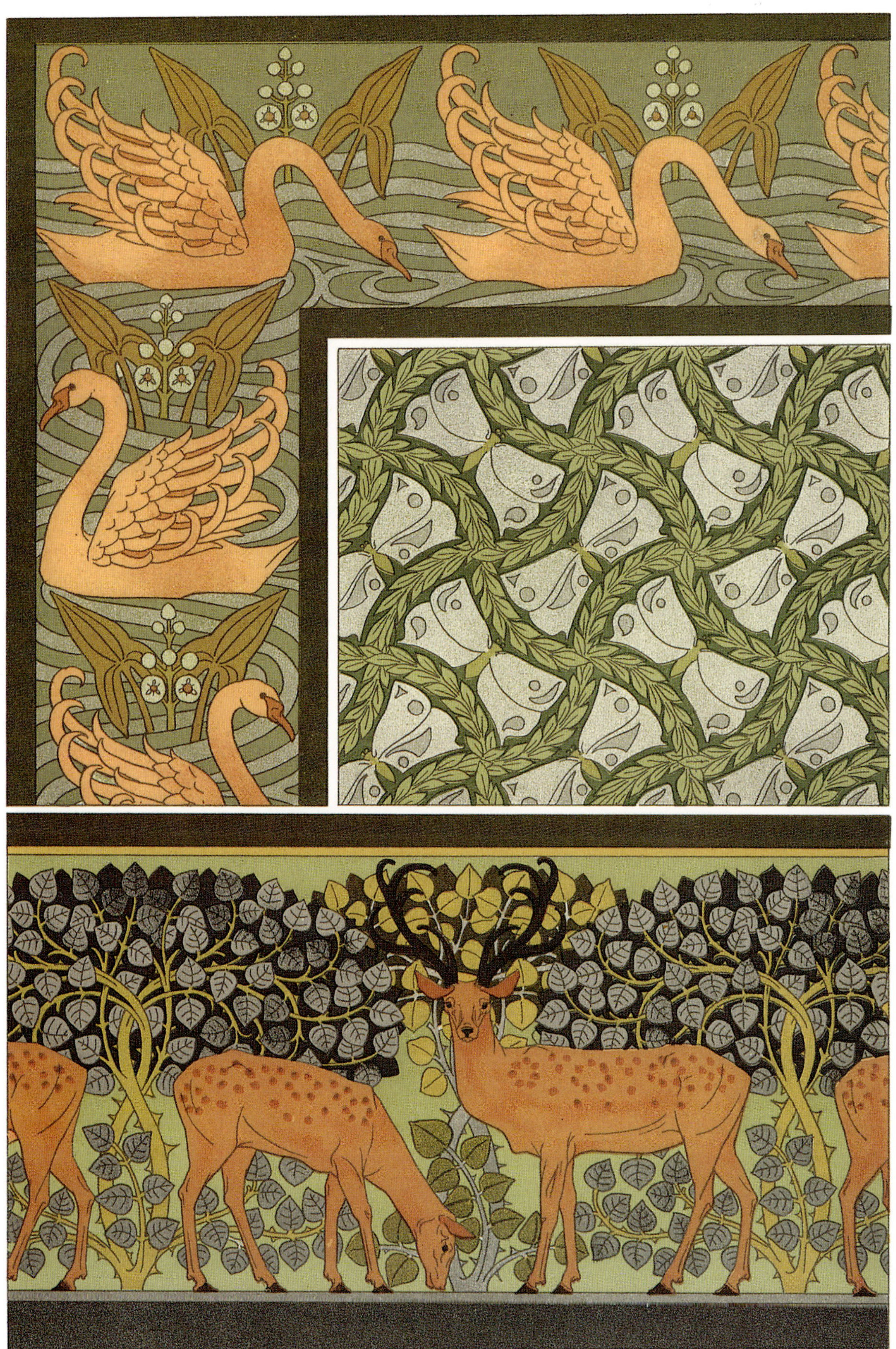

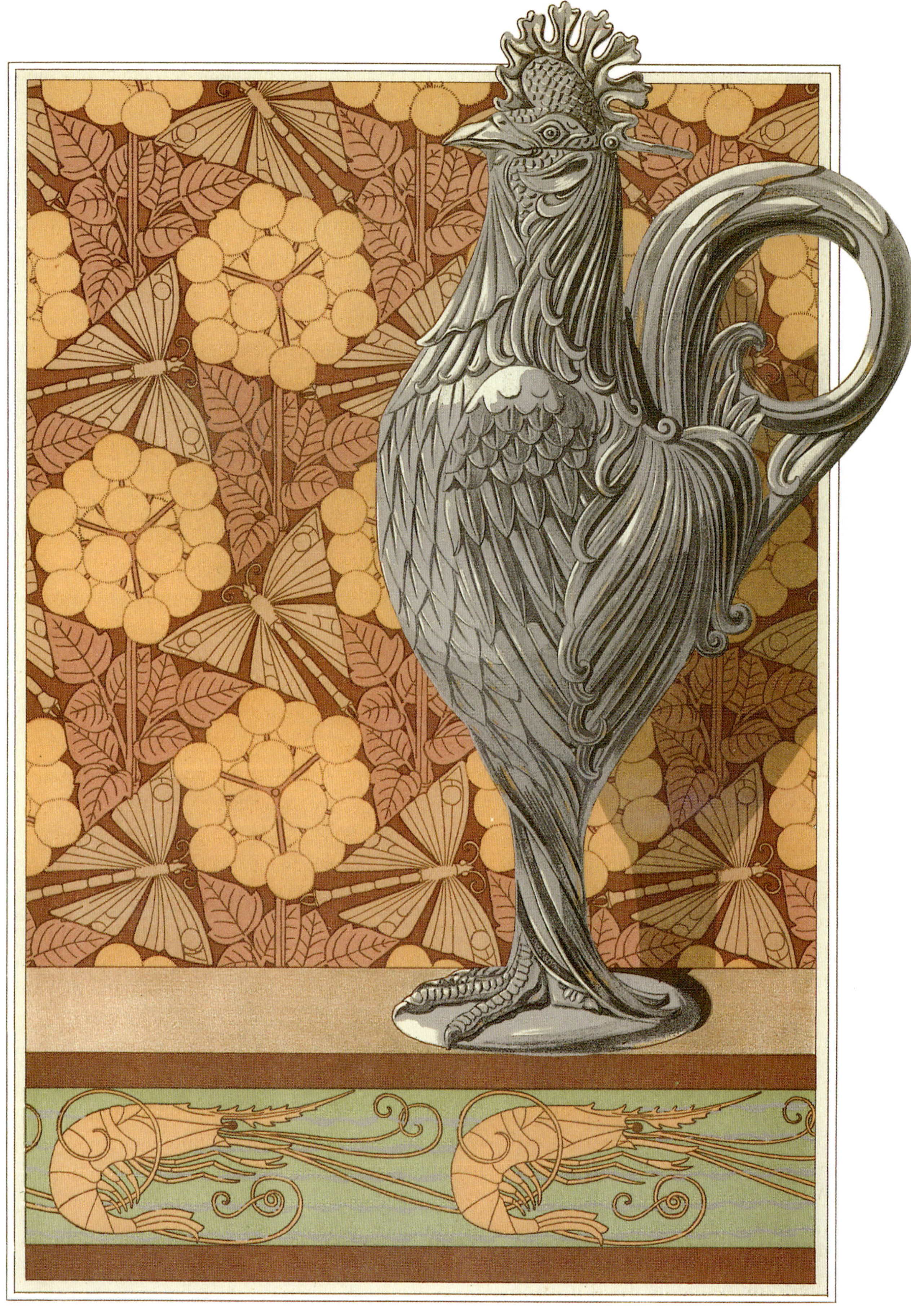

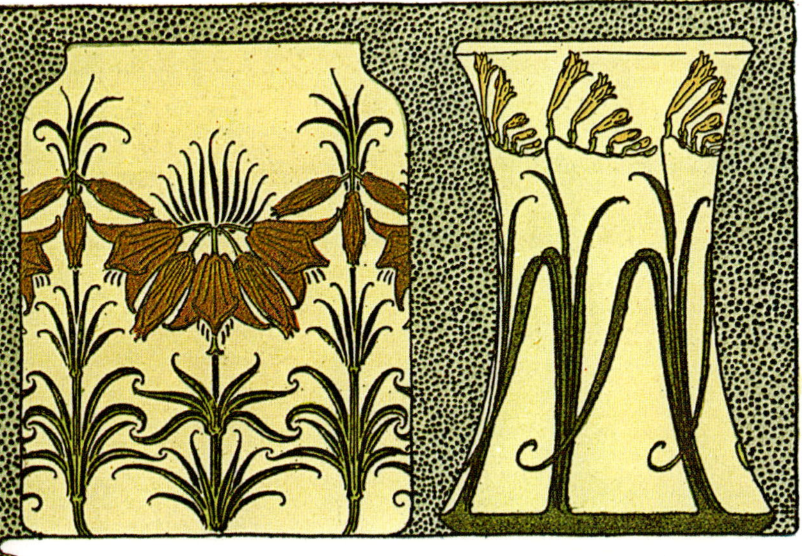

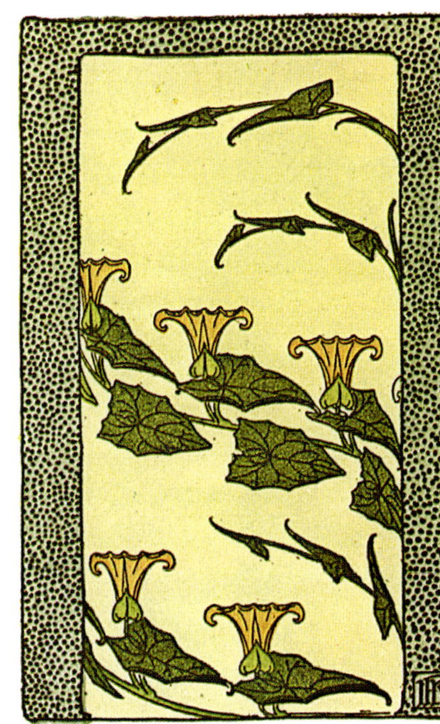

Images from *Étude de la Plante: son application aux industries d'art* by M. P. Verneuil (Paris: Librairie Centrale des Beaux-Arts, c. 1900), and from *L'ornementation par le Pochoir* by M. P. Verneuil (Paris: Schmid and Laurens, n.d.). Reprinted by Dover as *Art Nouveau Floral Patterns & Stencil Designs in Full Color* (Mineola, NY, 1998).

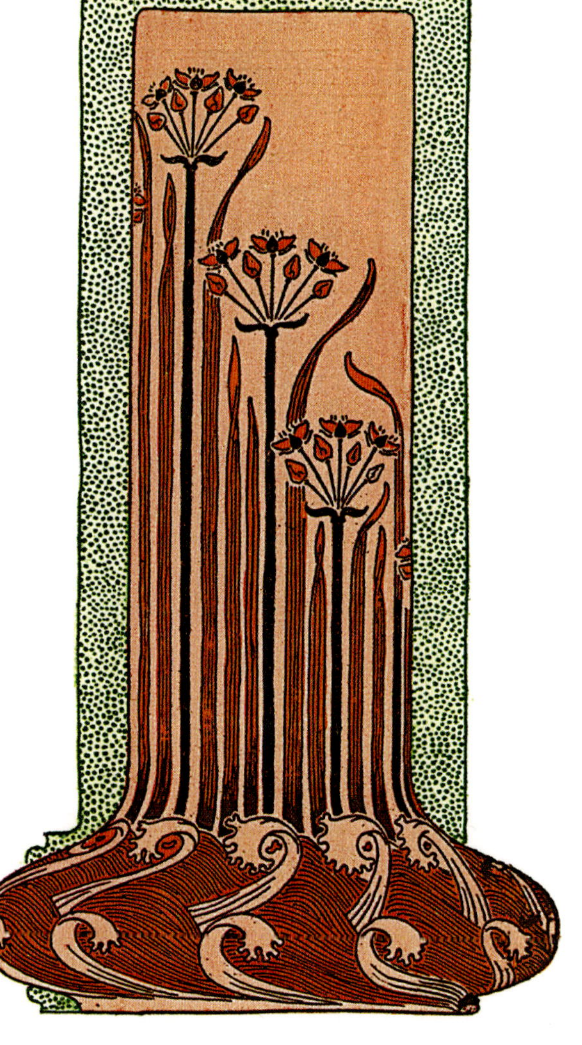

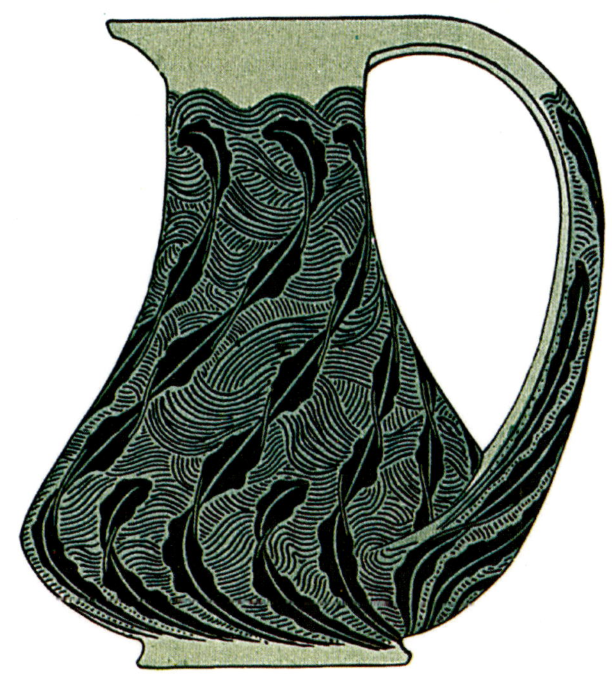

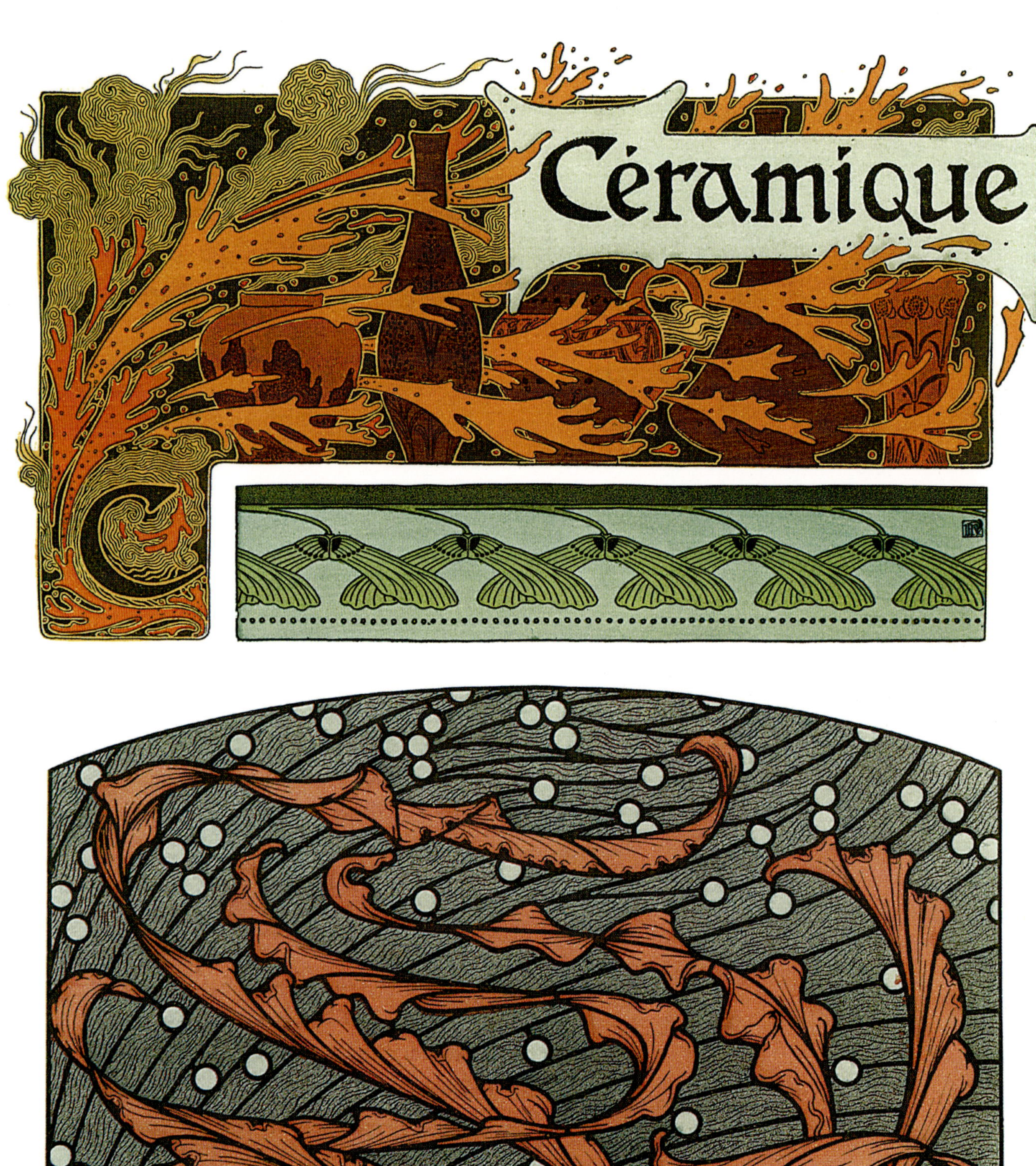
Céramique

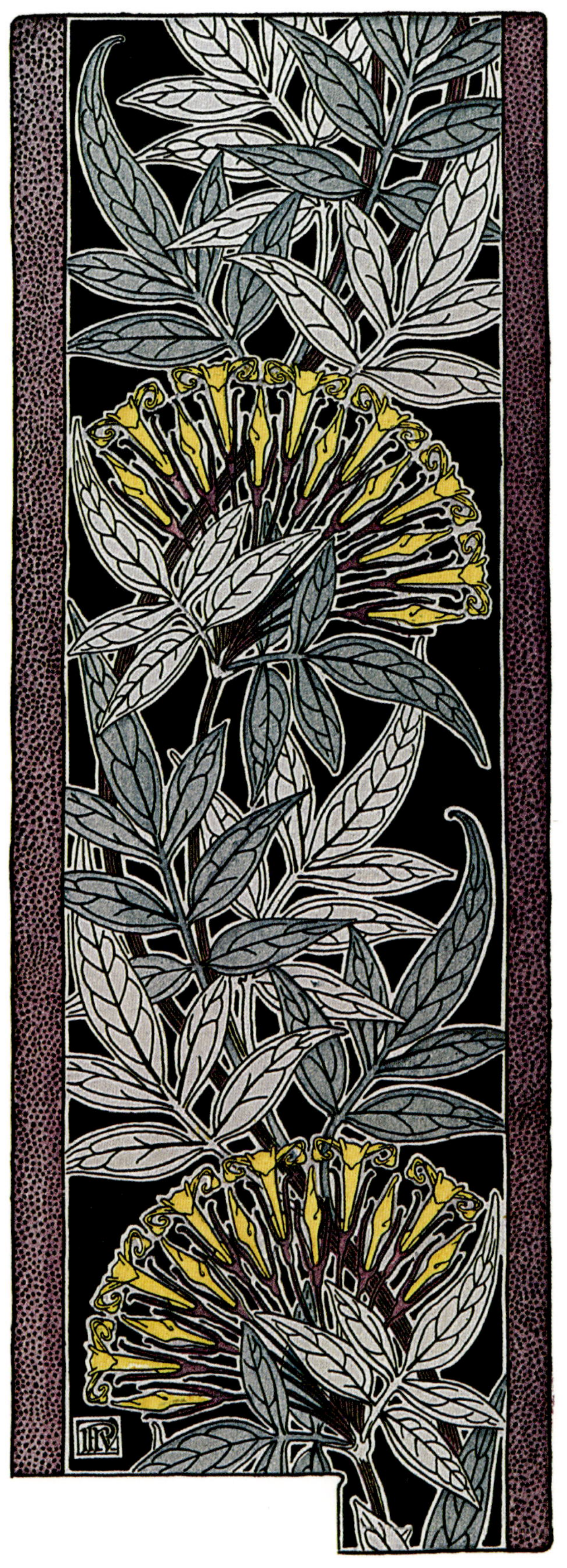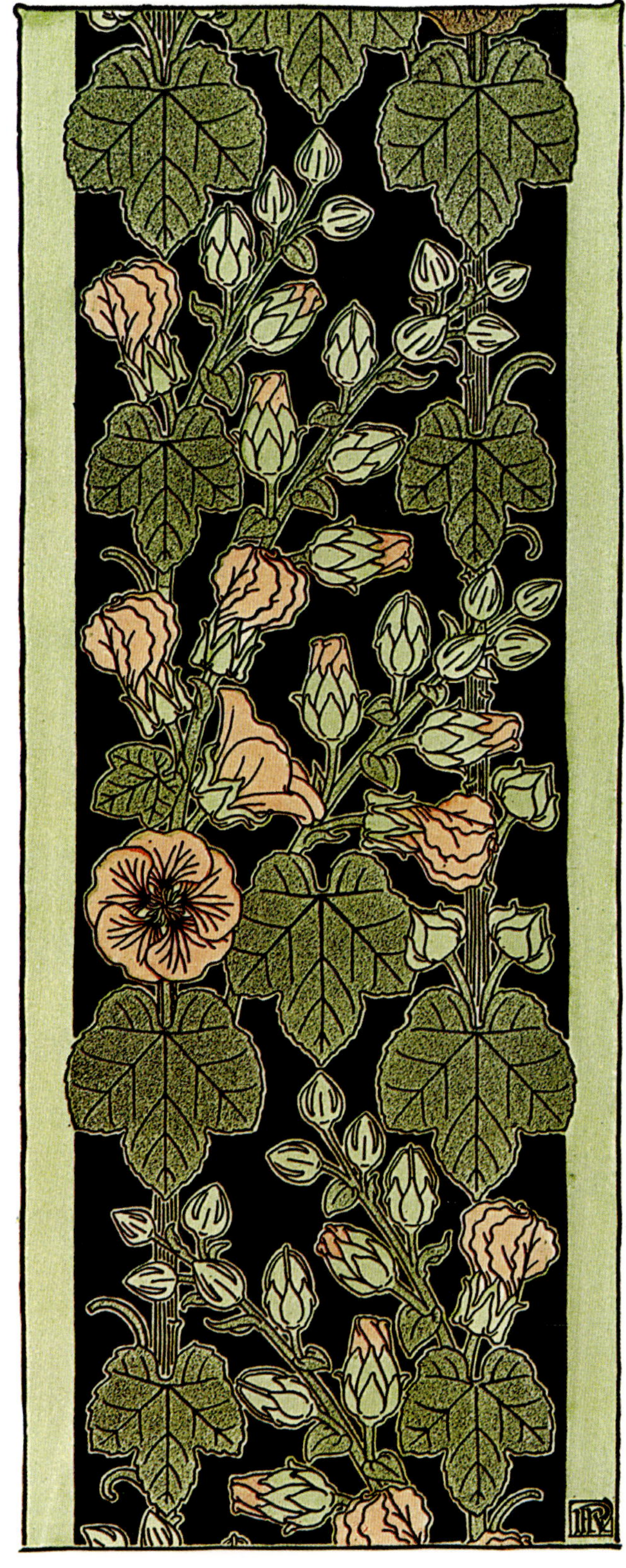

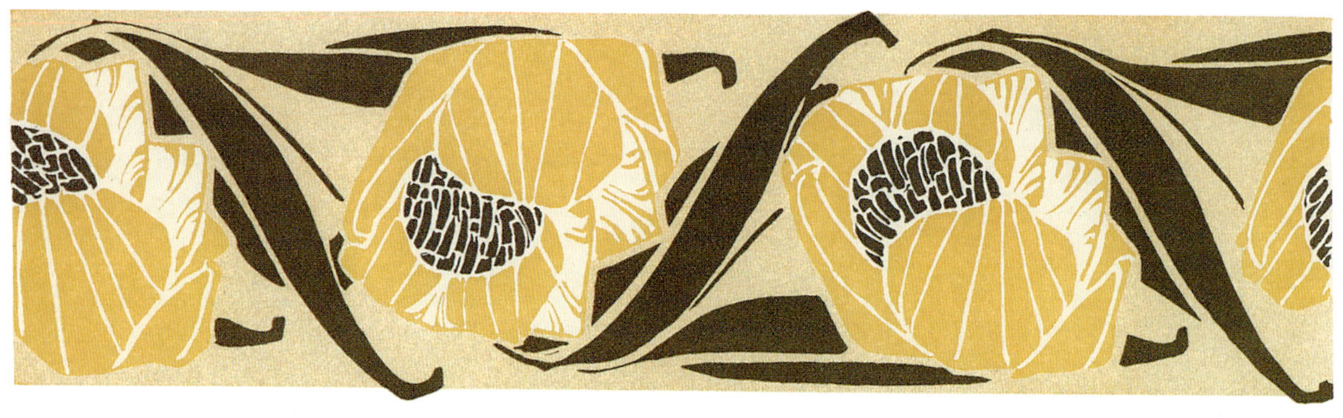

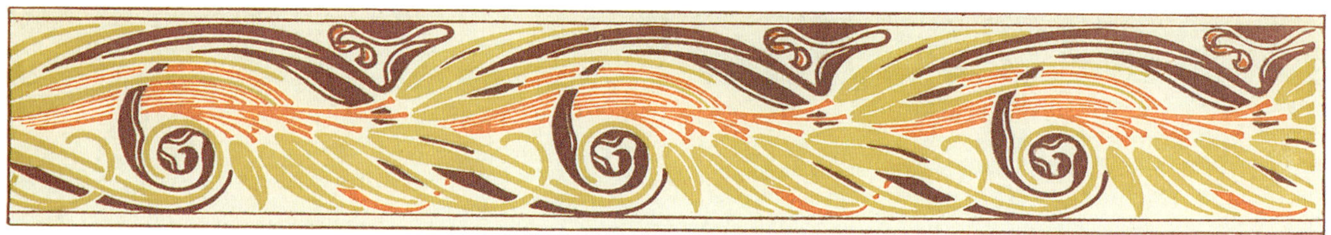

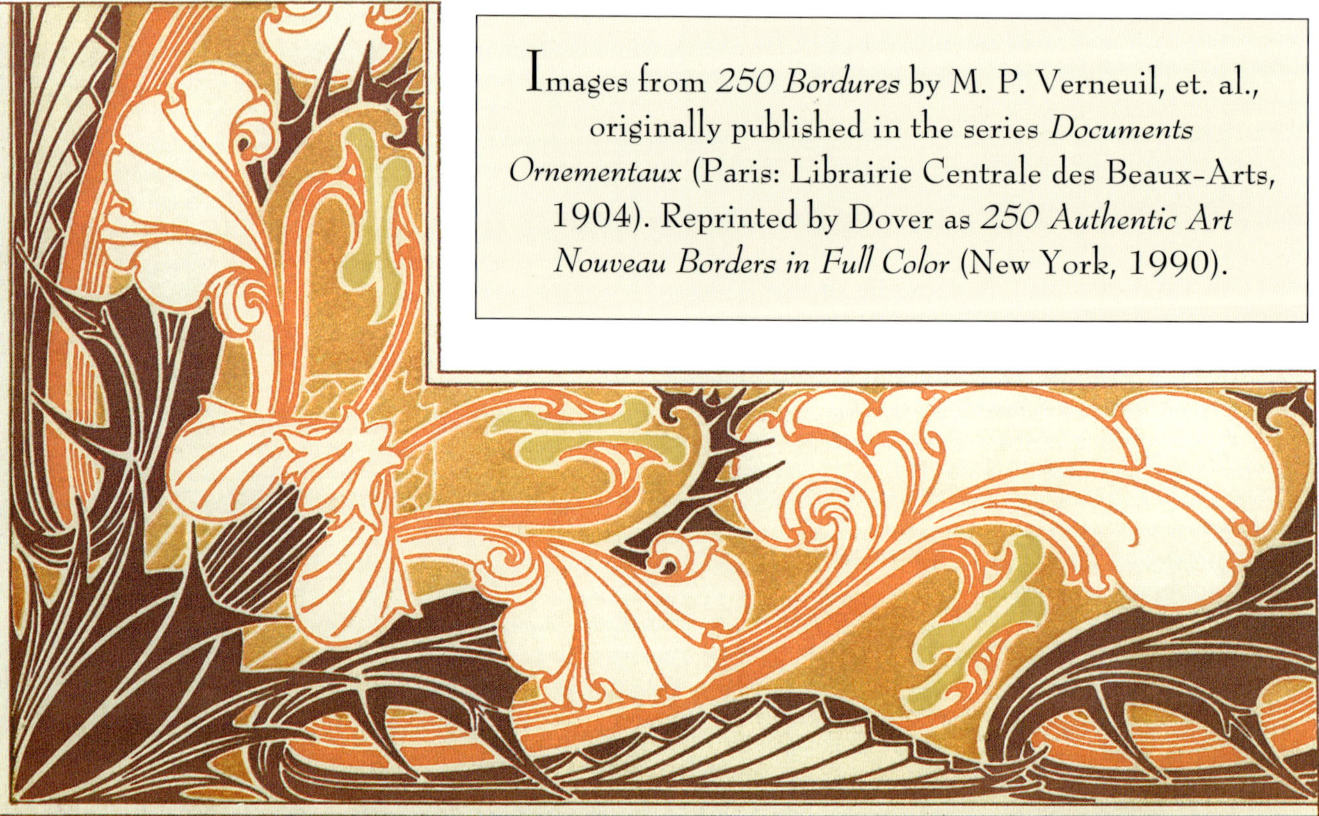

Images from *250 Bordures* by M. P. Verneuil, et. al., originally published in the series *Documents Ornementaux* (Paris: Librairie Centrale des Beaux-Arts, 1904). Reprinted by Dover as *250 Authentic Art Nouveau Borders in Full Color* (New York, 1990).

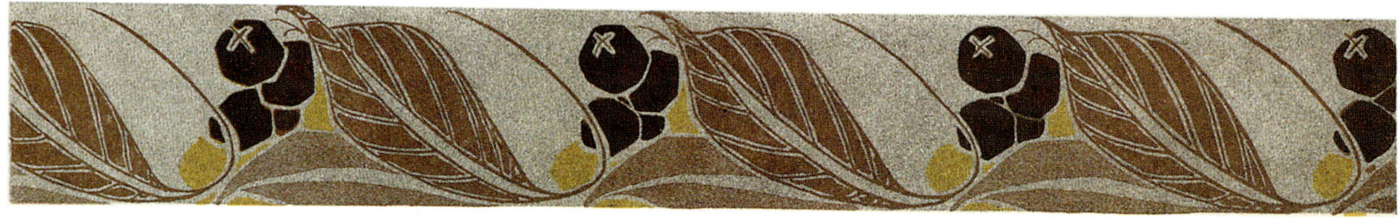

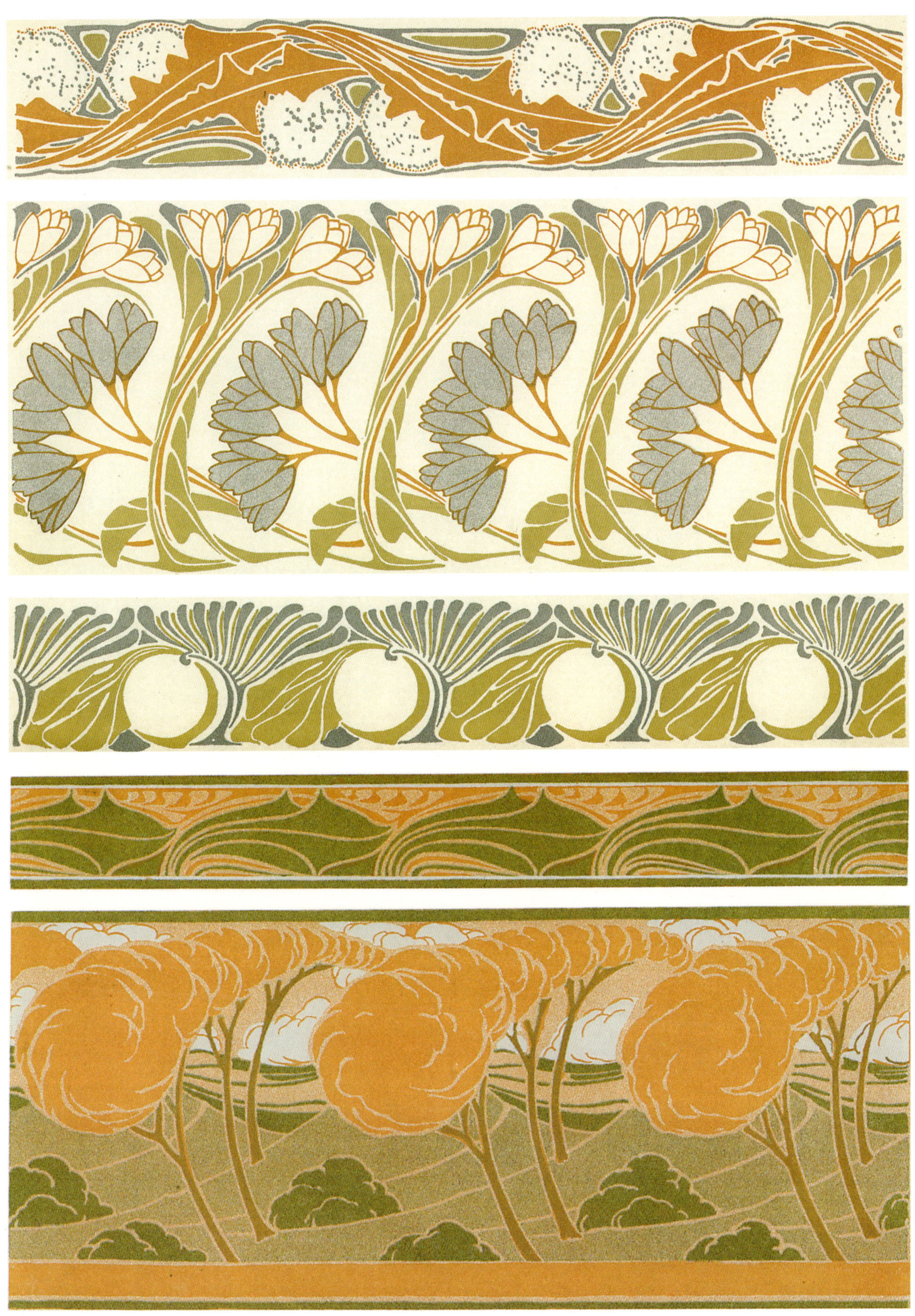

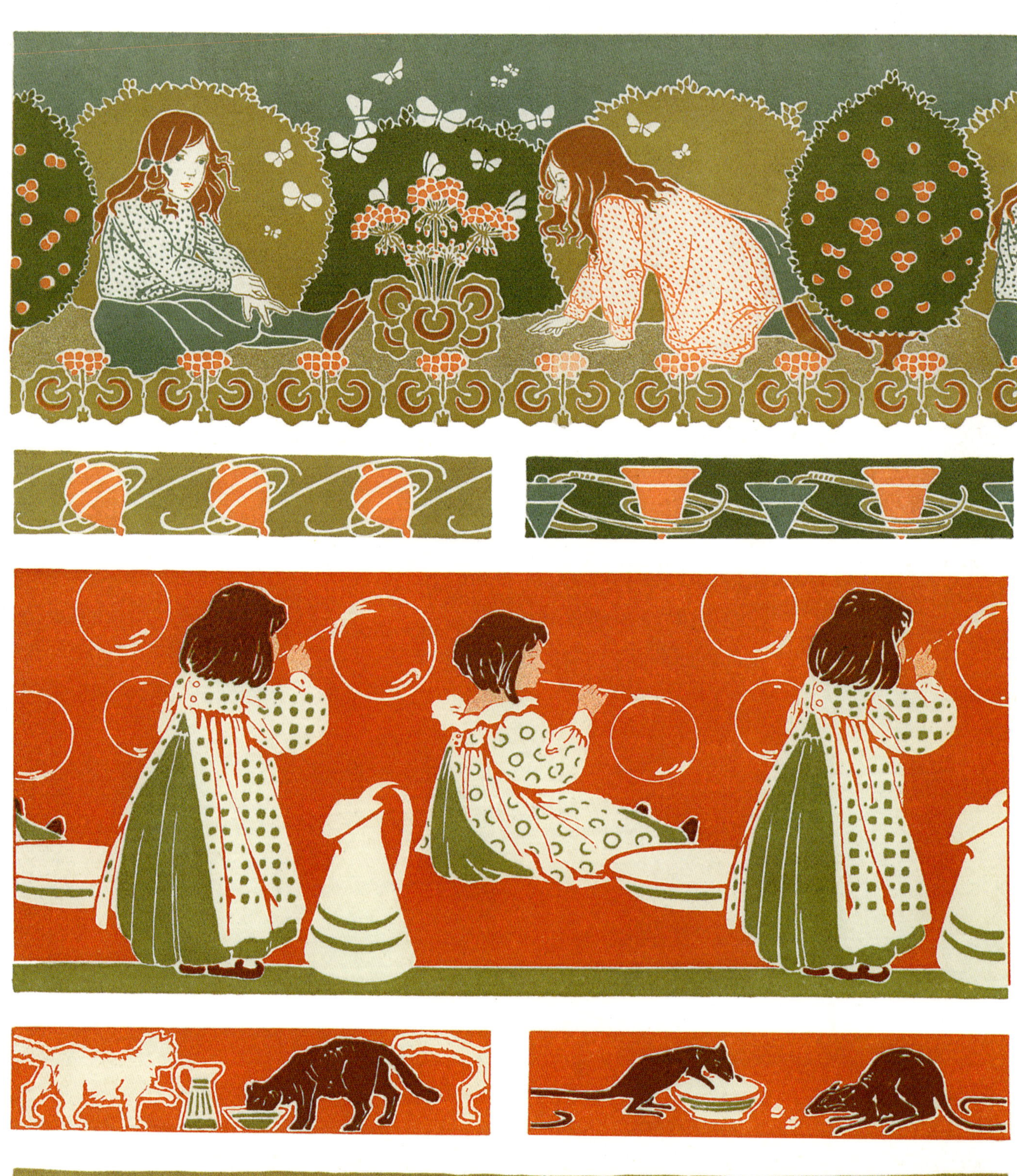

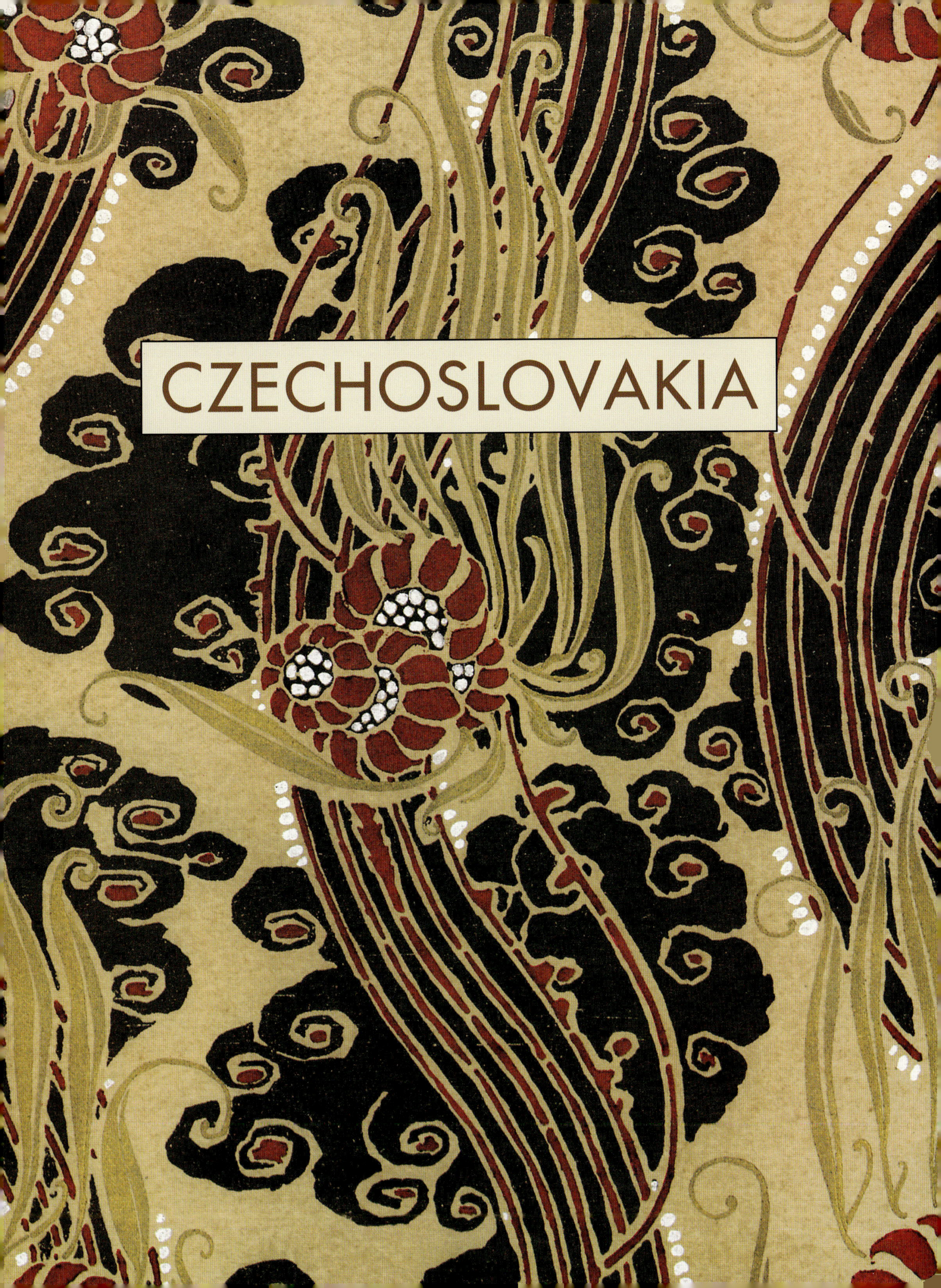

CZECHOSLOVAKIA

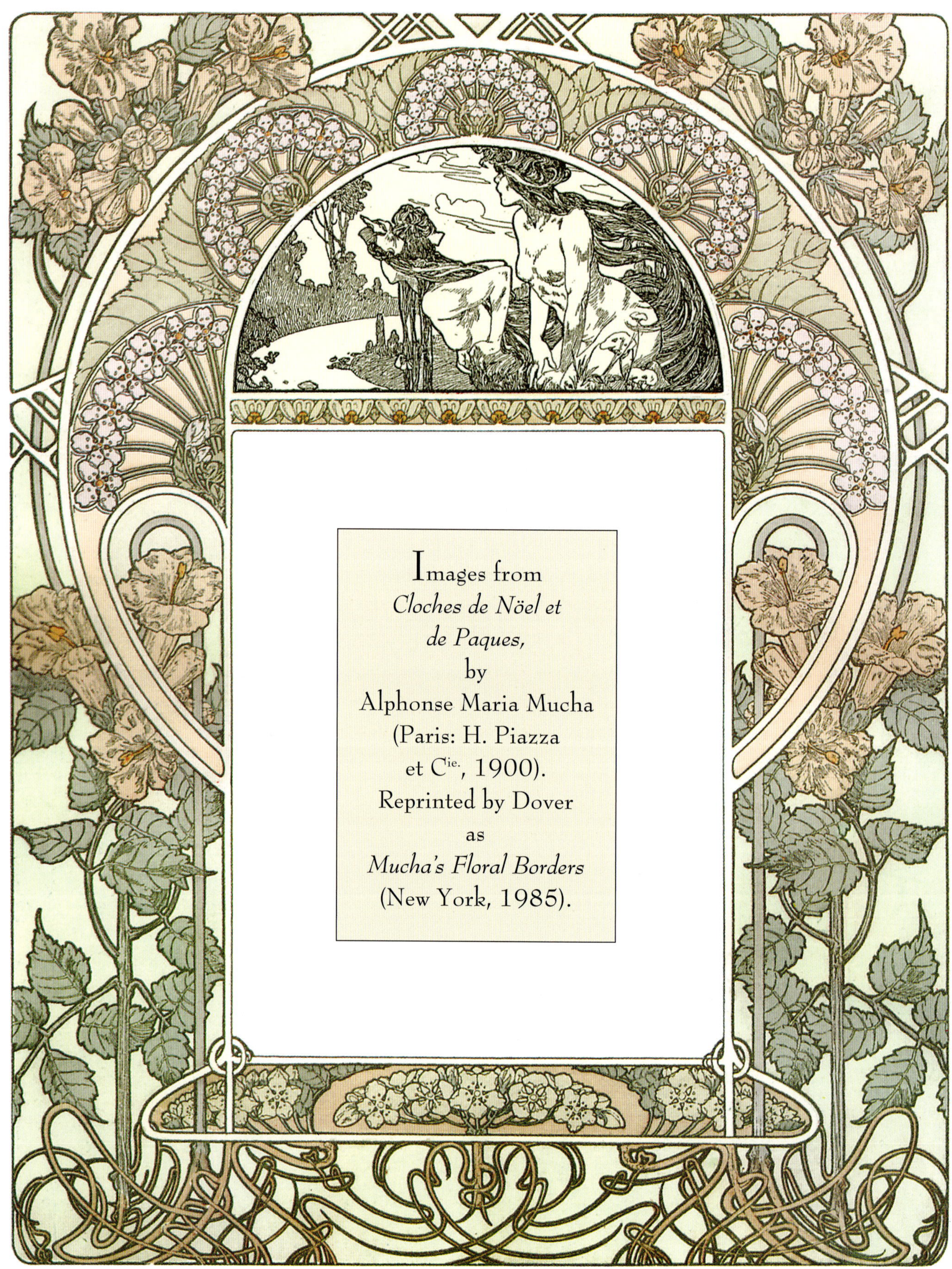

Images from
Cloches de Nöel et de Paques,
by
Alphonse Maria Mucha
(Paris: H. Piazza
et Cie., 1900).
Reprinted by Dover
as
Mucha's Floral Borders
(New York, 1985).

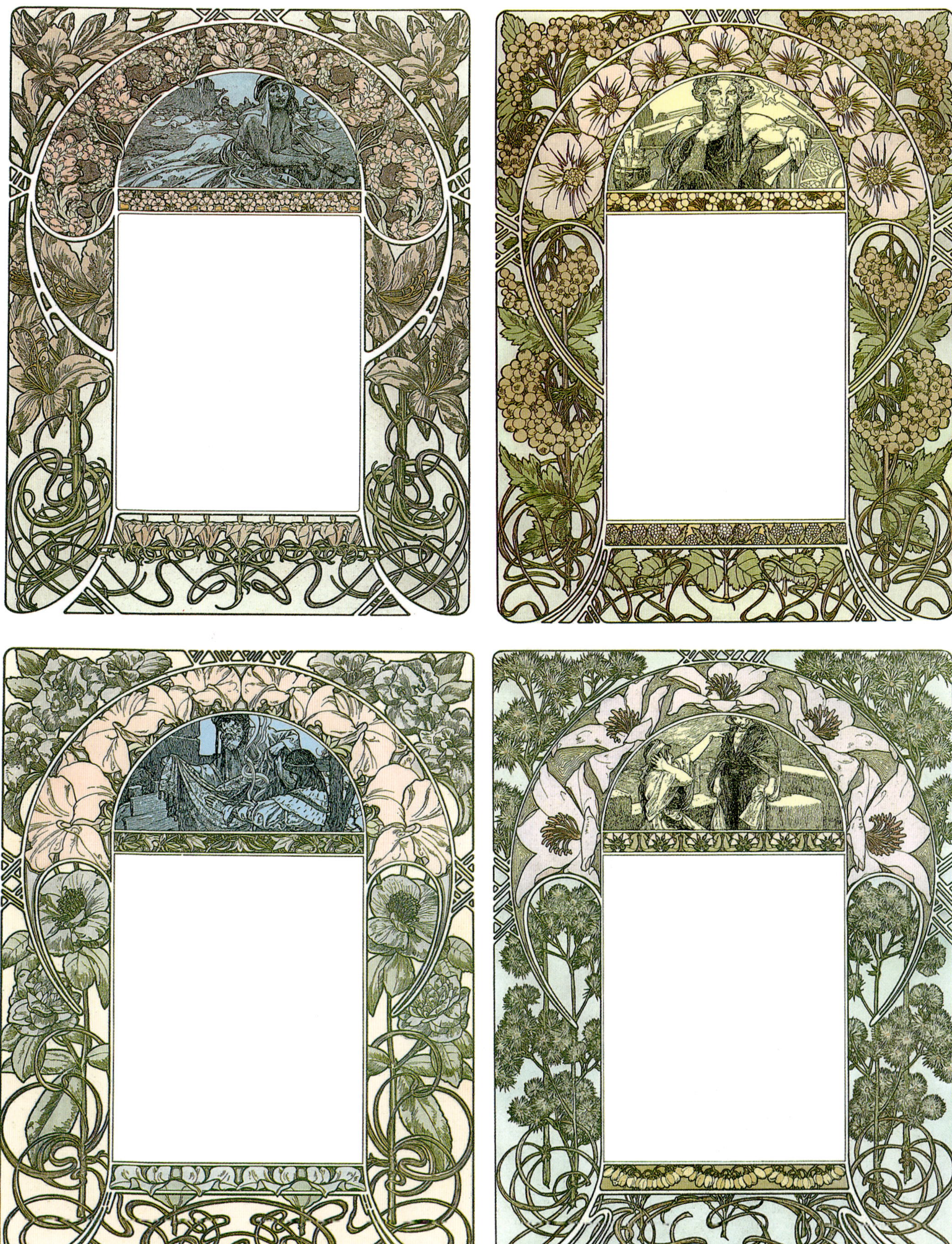

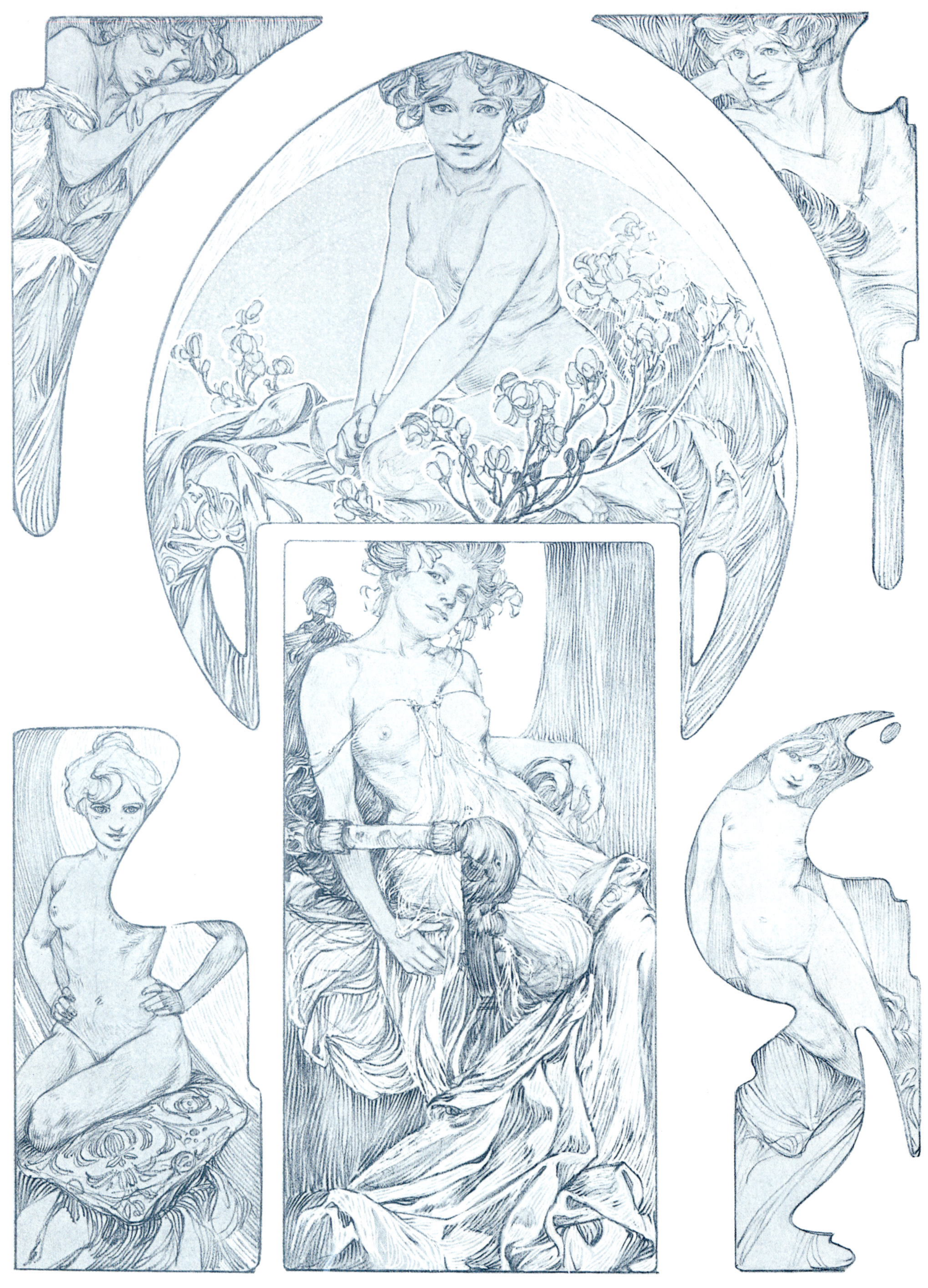

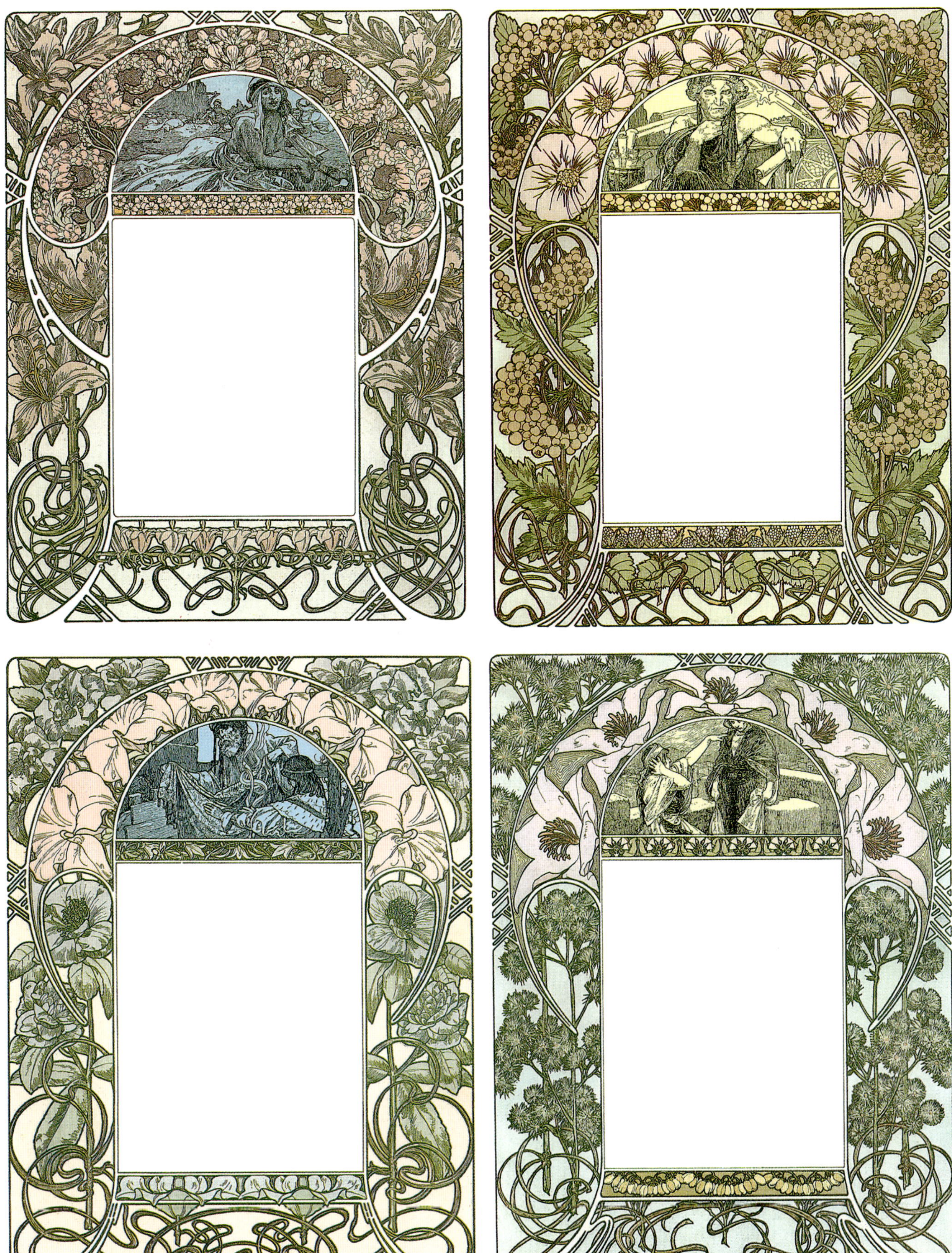

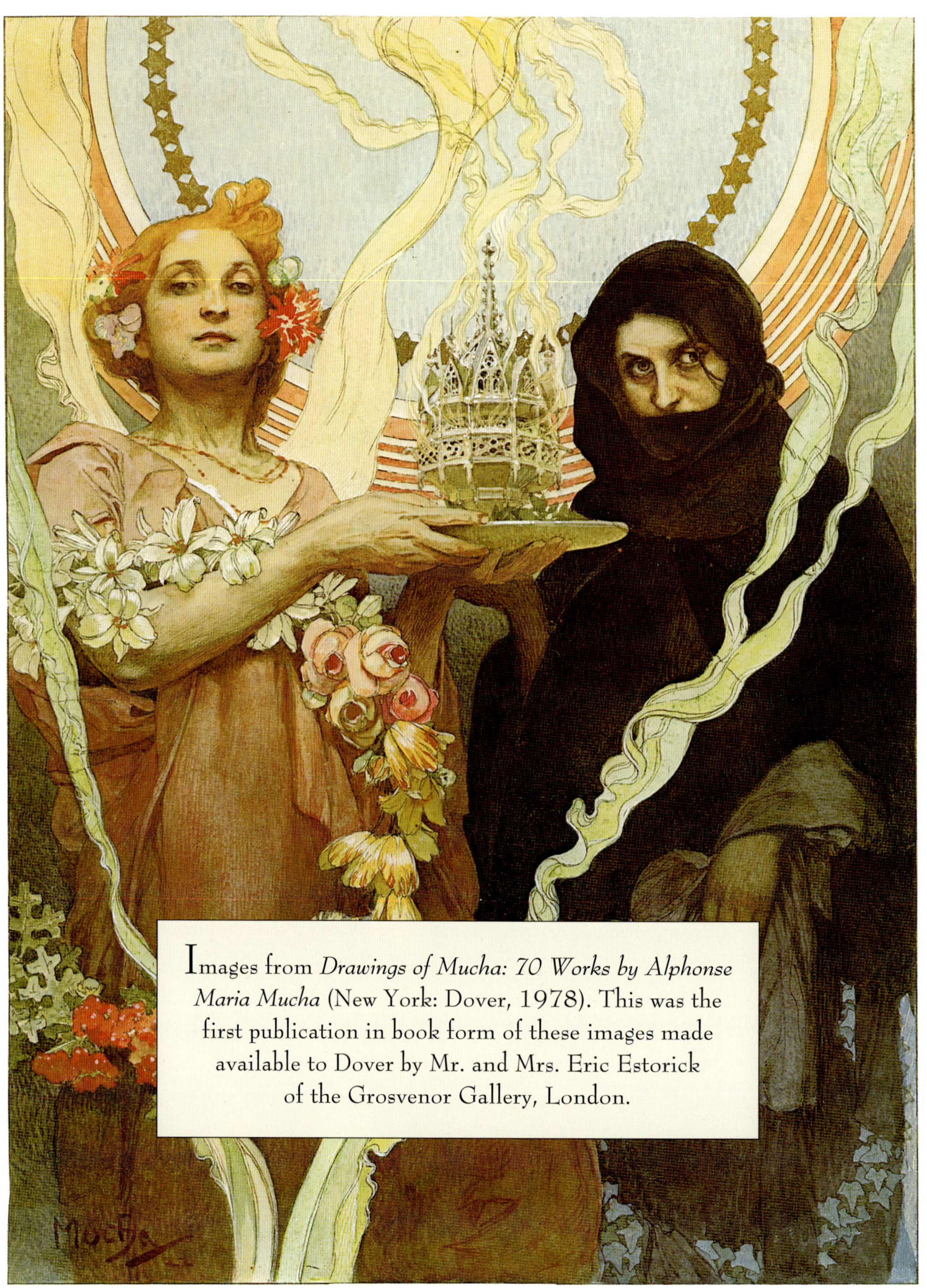

Images from *Drawings of Mucha: 70 Works by Alphonse Maria Mucha* (New York: Dover, 1978). This was the first publication in book form of these images made available to Dover by Mr. and Mrs. Eric Estorick of the Grosvenor Gallery, London.

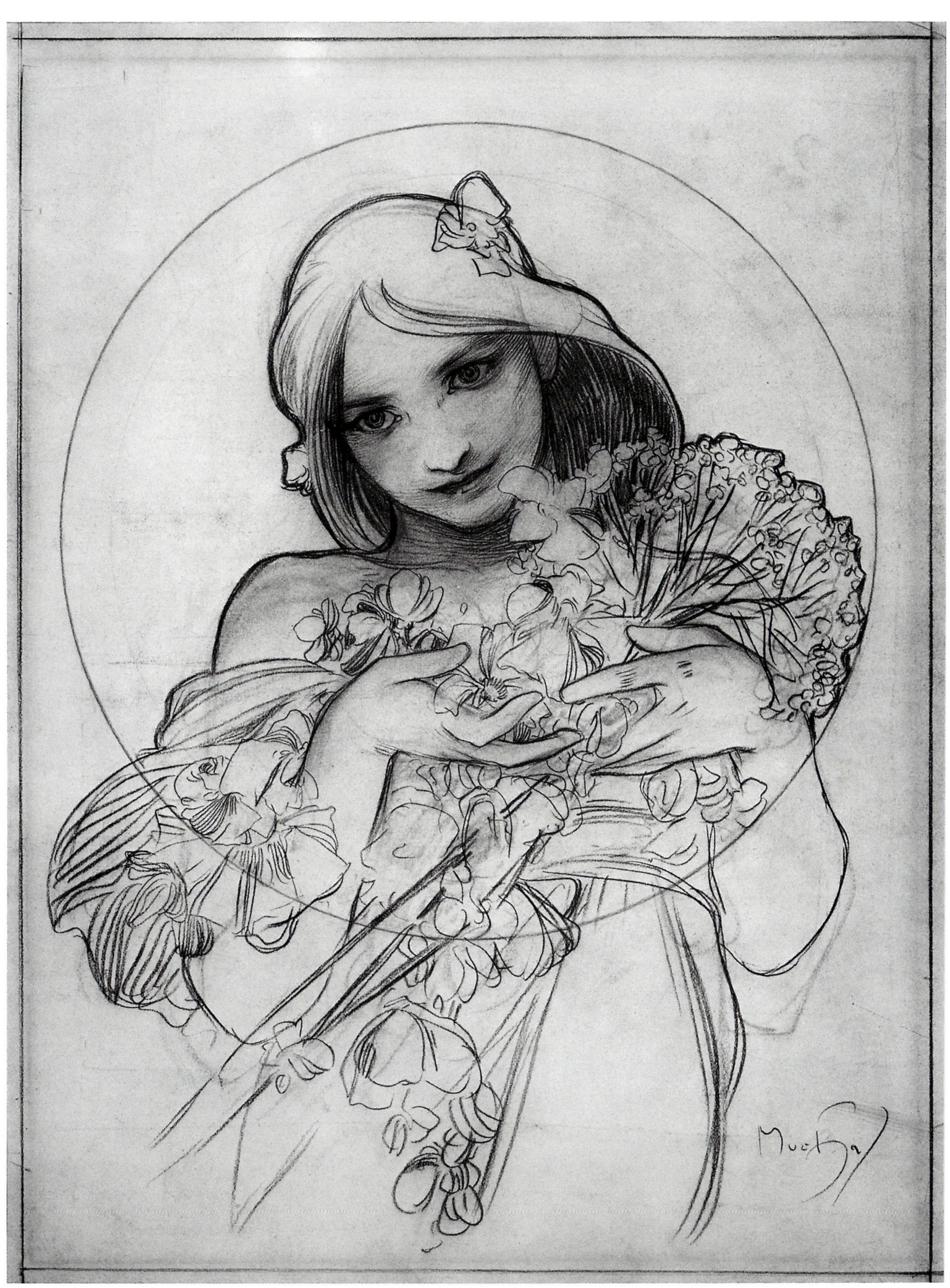

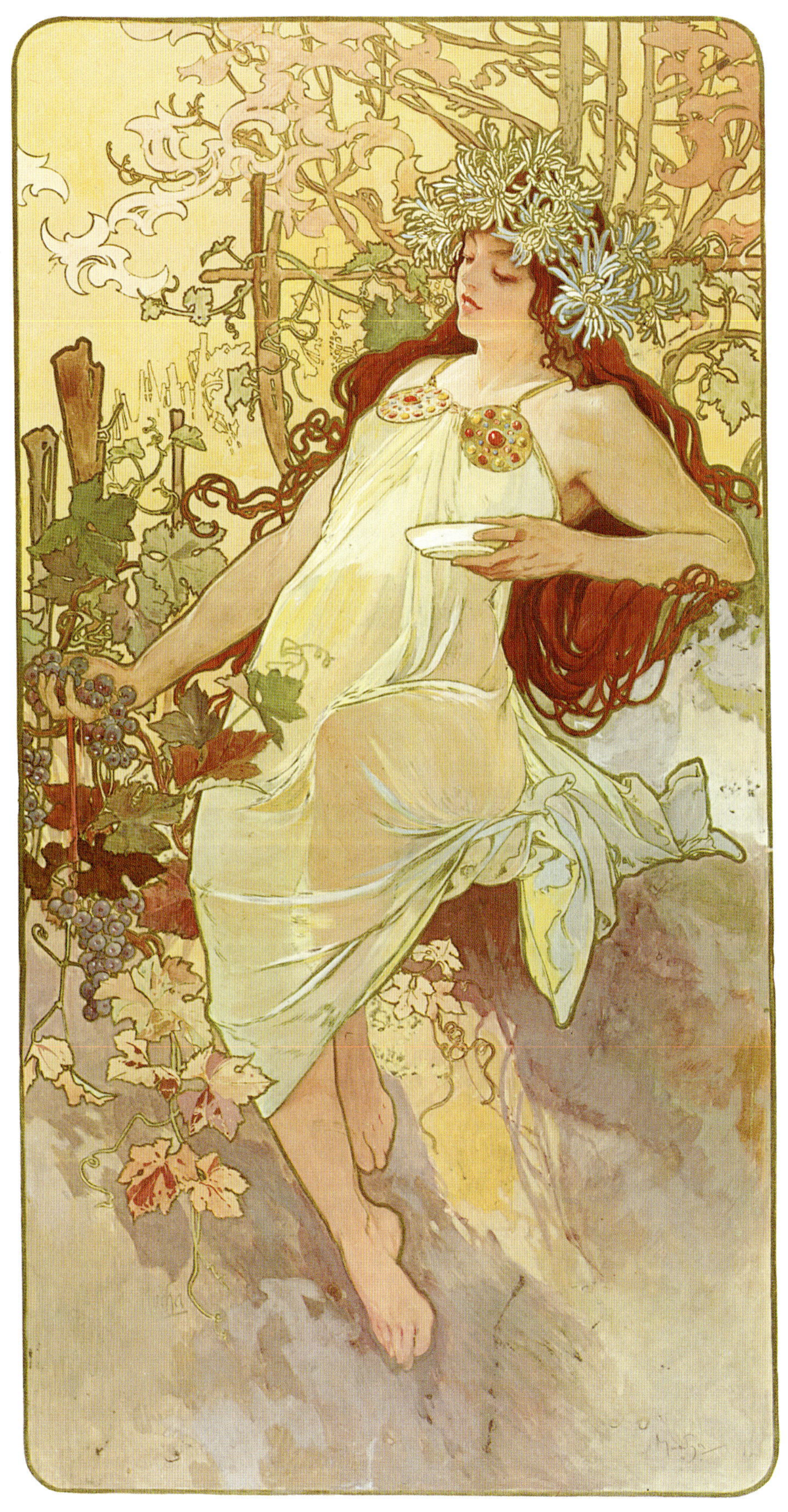

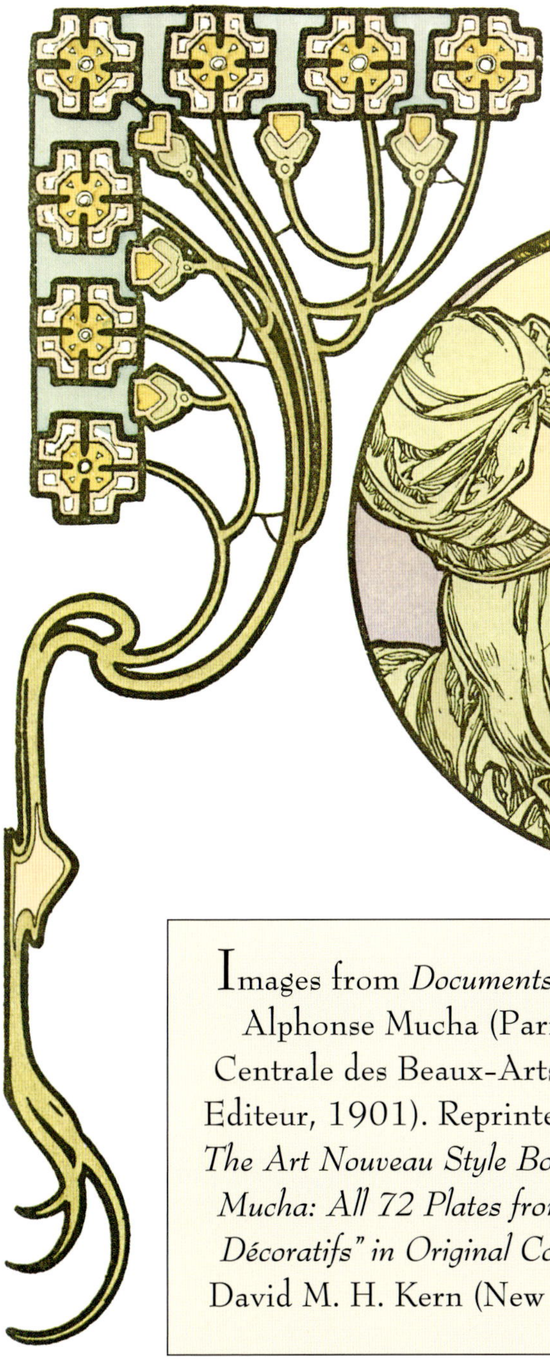

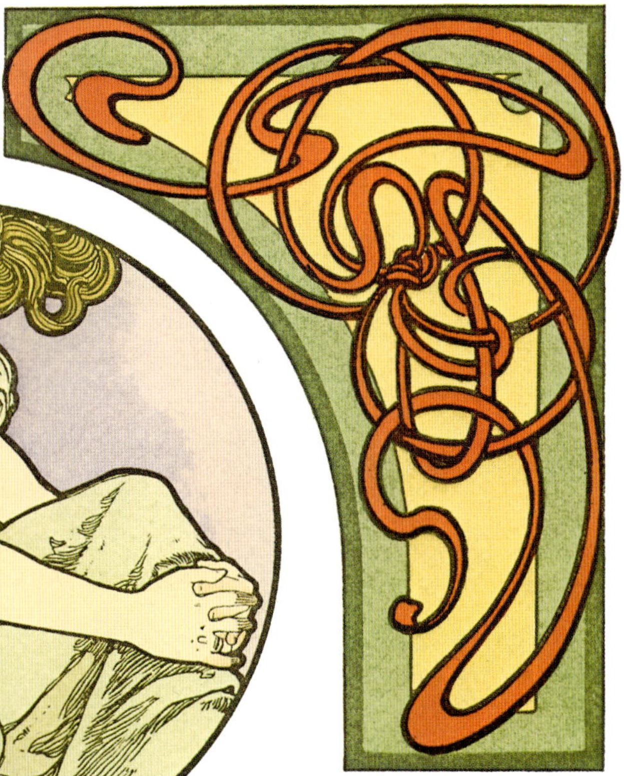

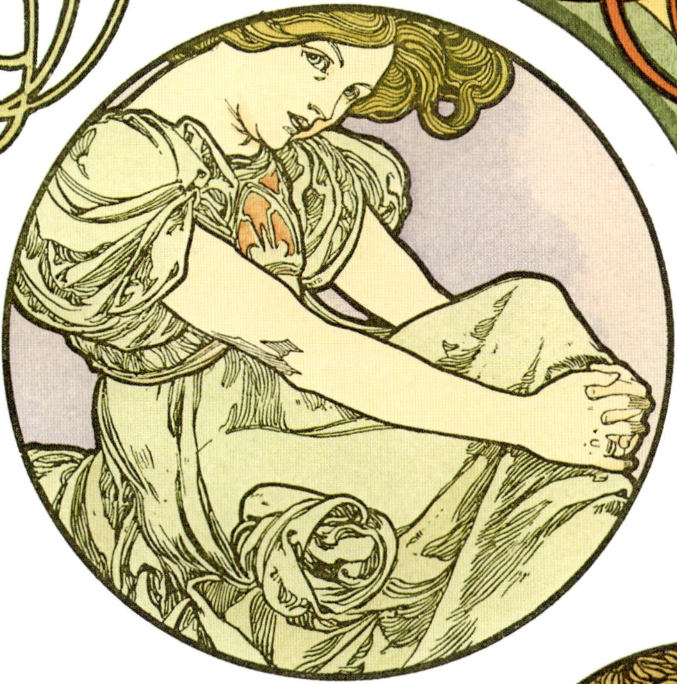

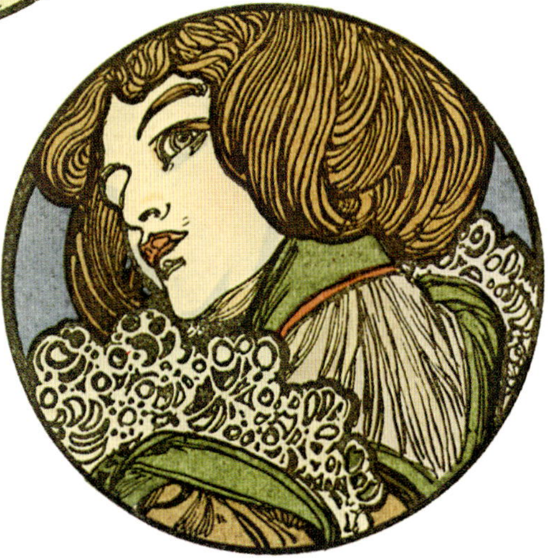

Images from *Documents Décoratifs* by Alphonse Mucha (Paris: Librairie Centrale des Beaux-Arts/Émile Lévy, Editeur, 1901). Reprinted by Dover as *The Art Nouveau Style Book of Alphonse Mucha: All 72 Plates from "Documents Décoratifs" in Original Color*, edited by David M. H. Kern (New York, 1980).

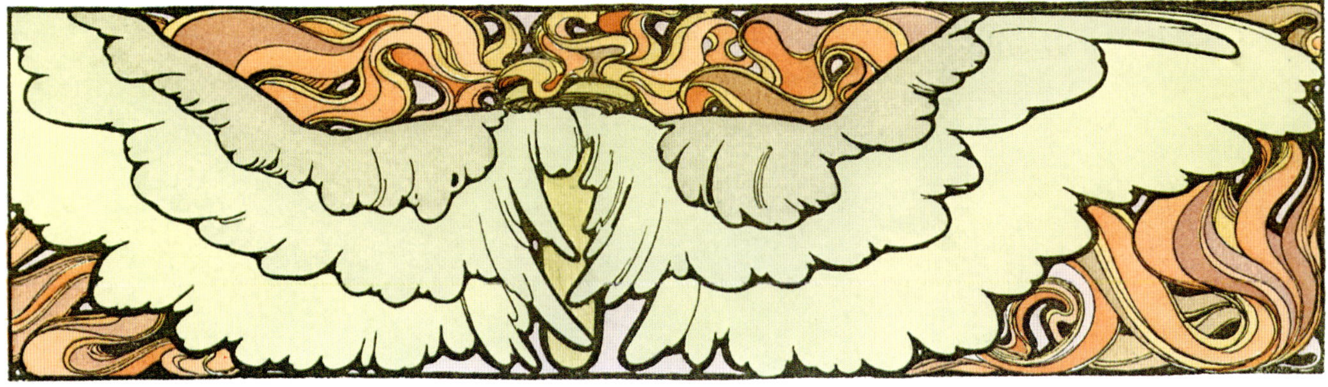

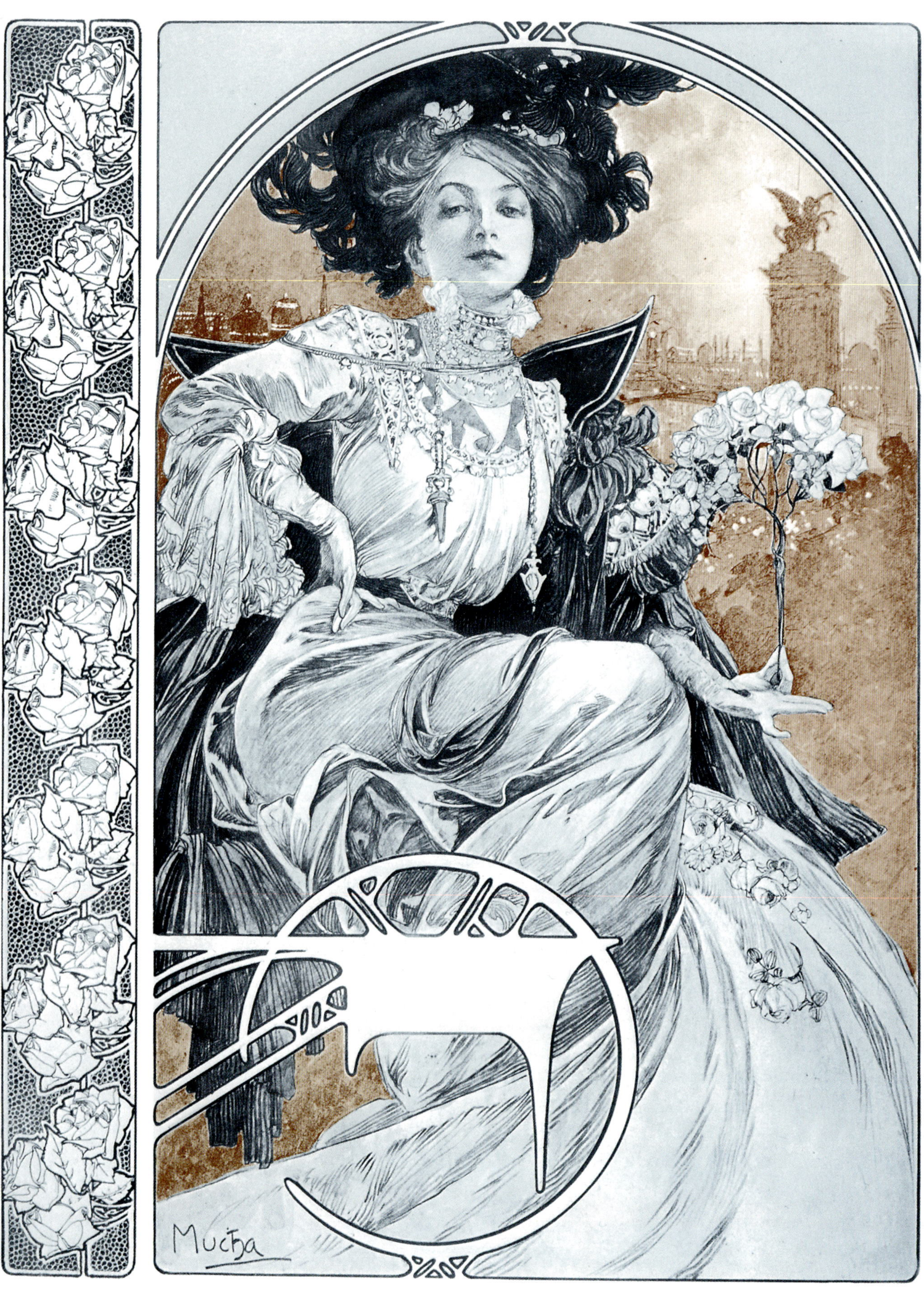

Mucha

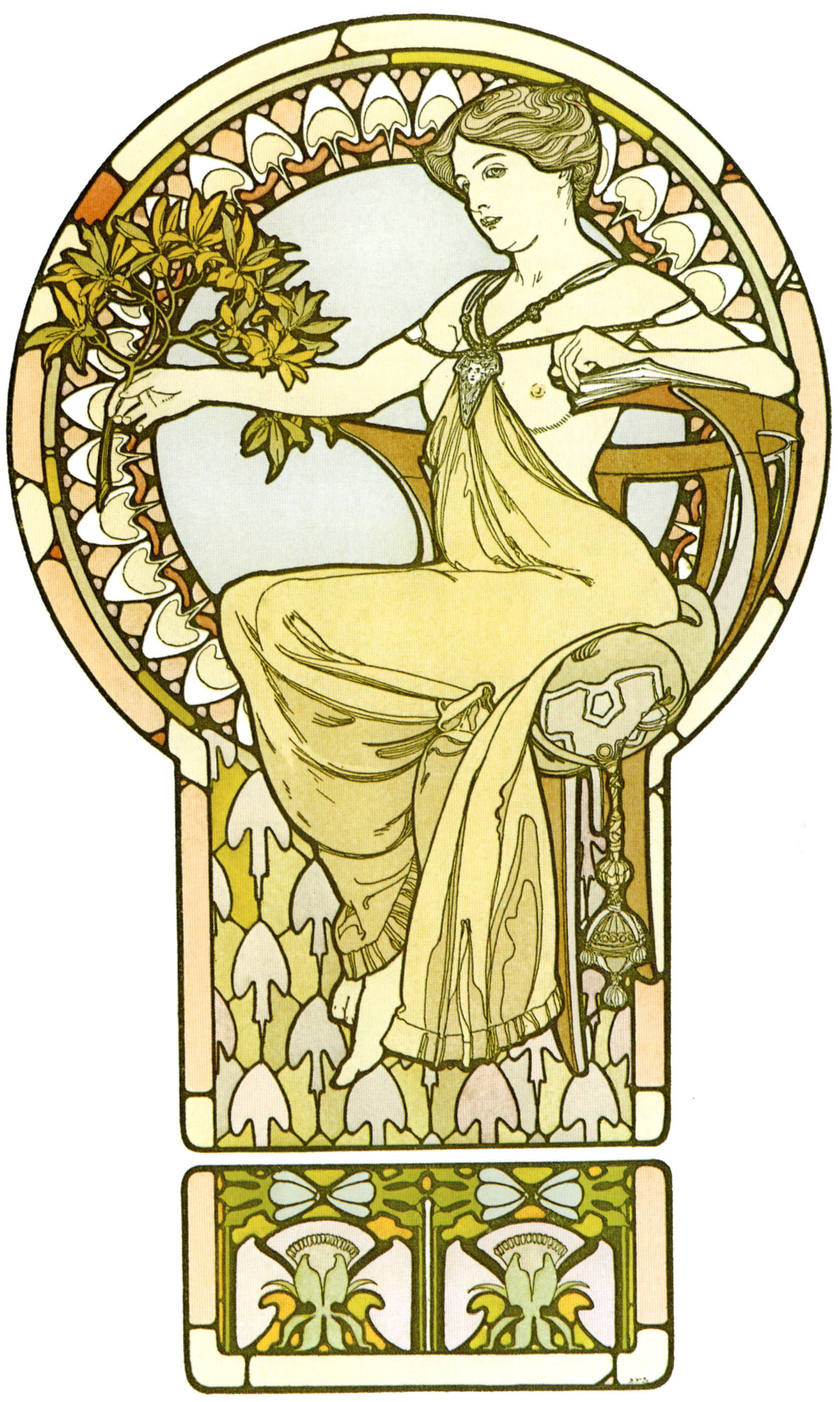

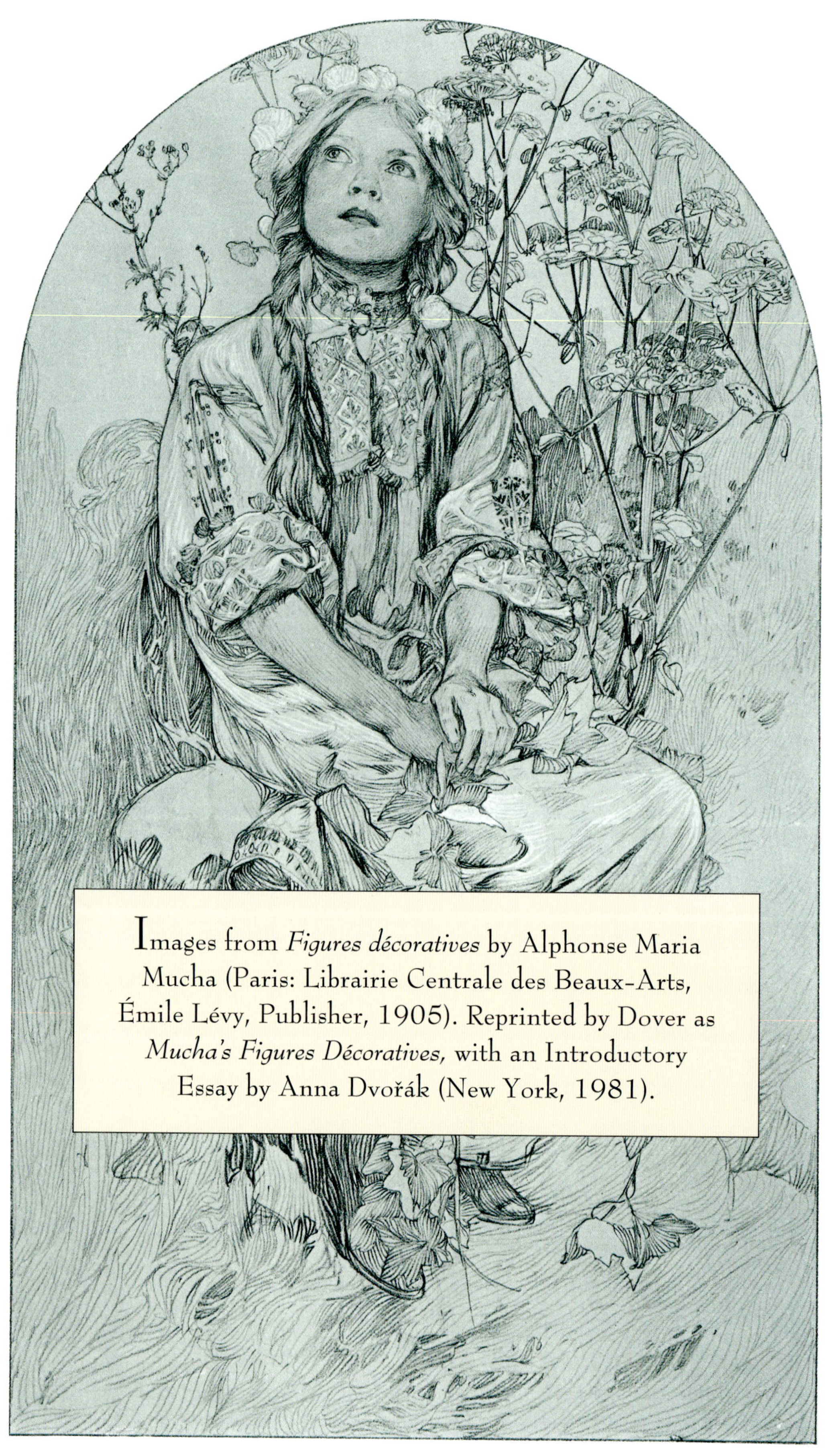

Images from *Figures décoratives* by Alphonse Maria Mucha (Paris: Librairie Centrale des Beaux-Arts, Émile Lévy, Publisher, 1905). Reprinted by Dover as *Mucha's Figures Décoratives*, with an Introductory Essay by Anna Dvořák (New York, 1981).

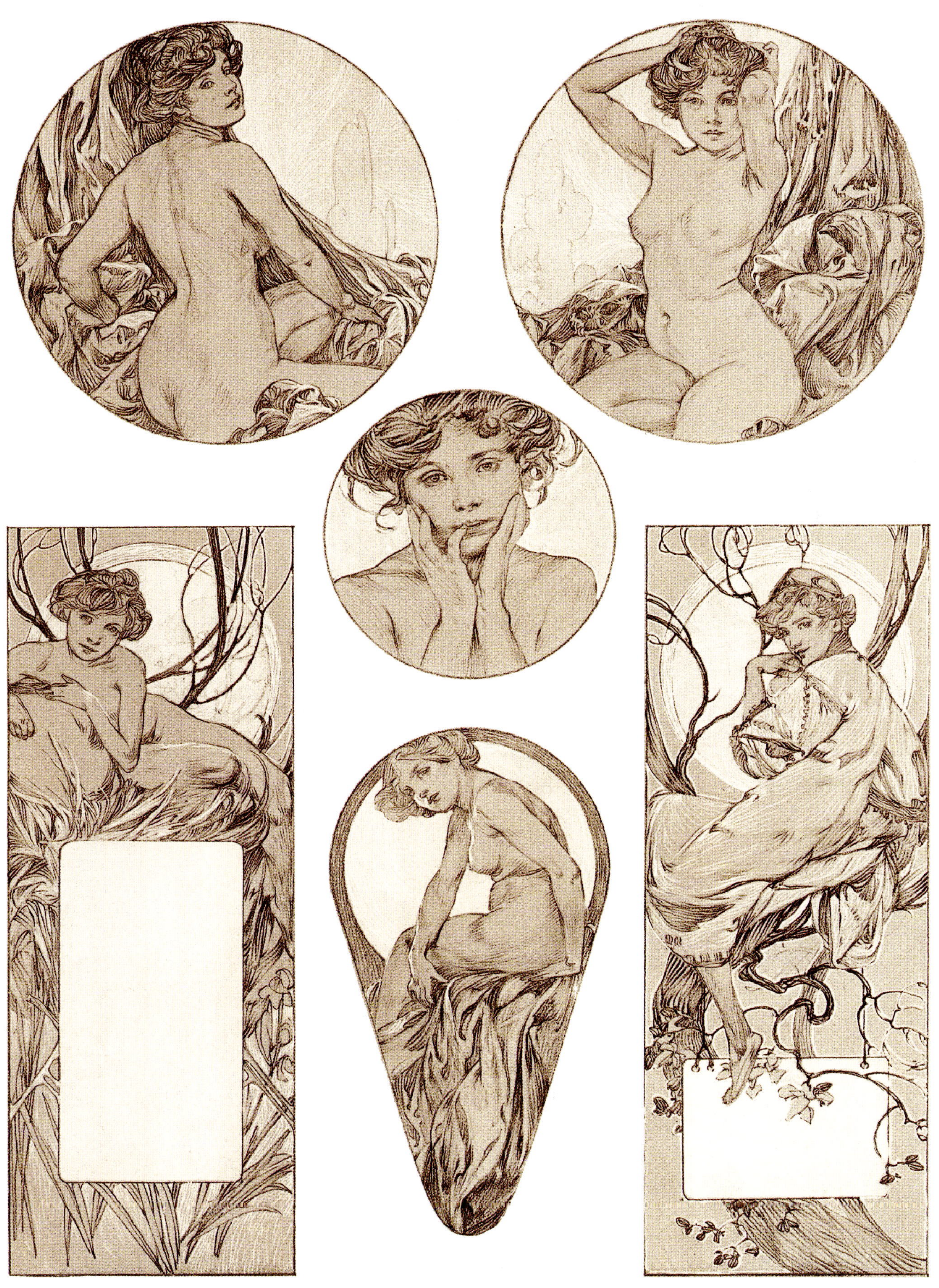

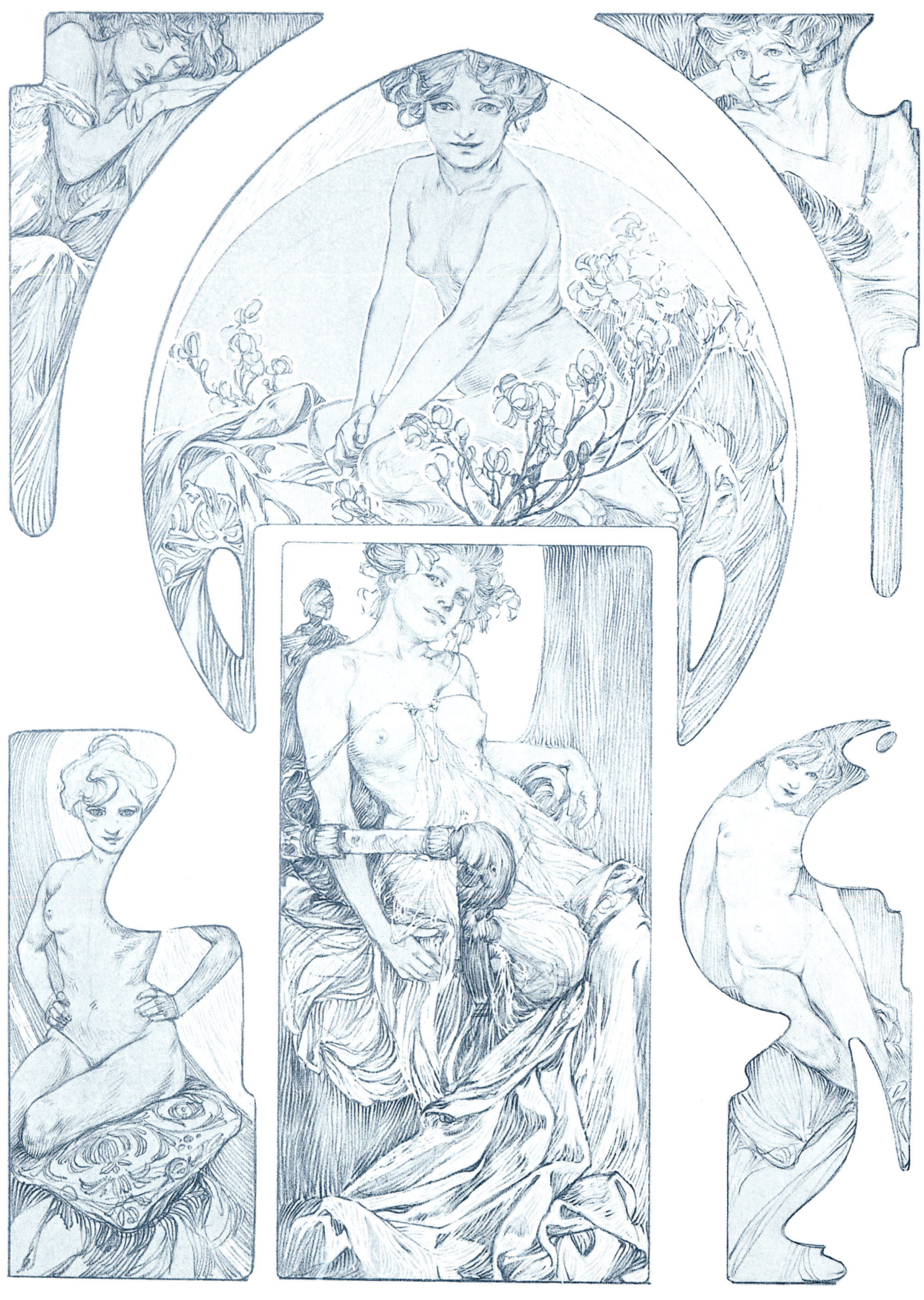

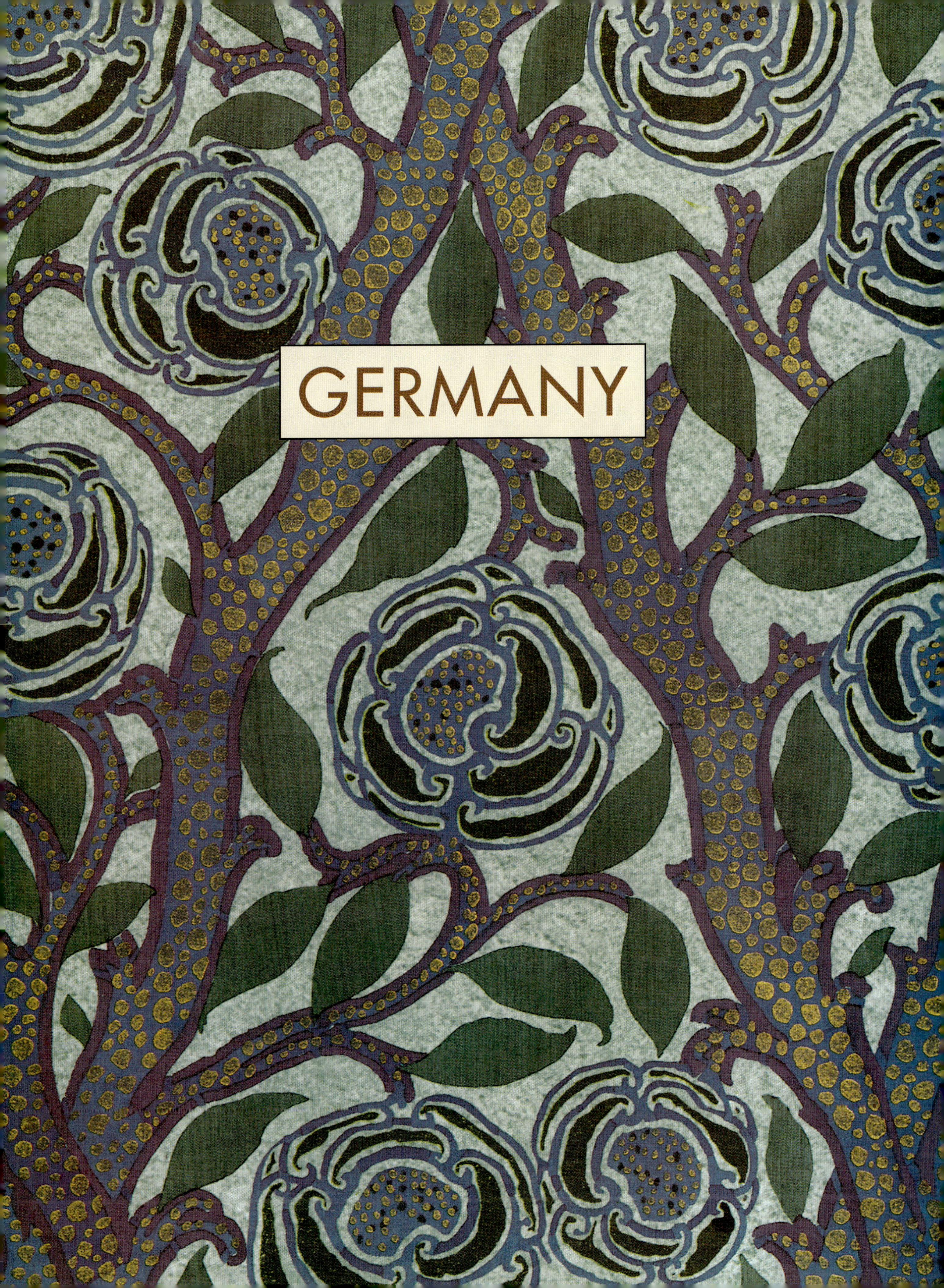

GERMANY

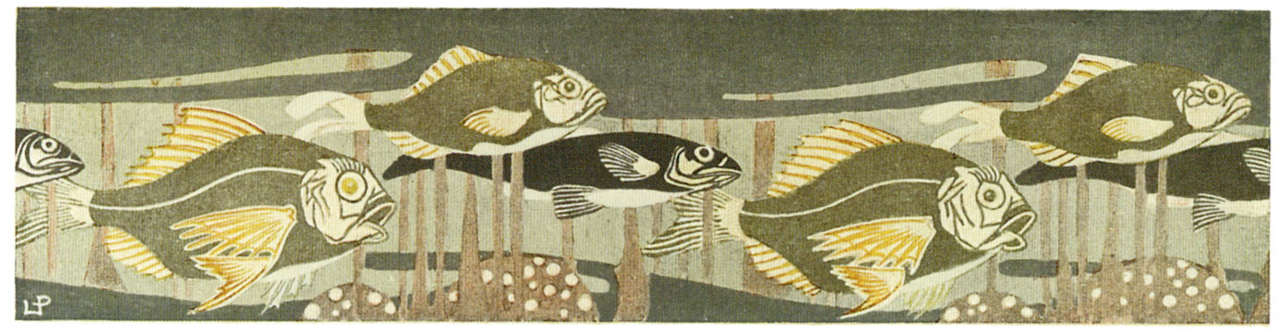

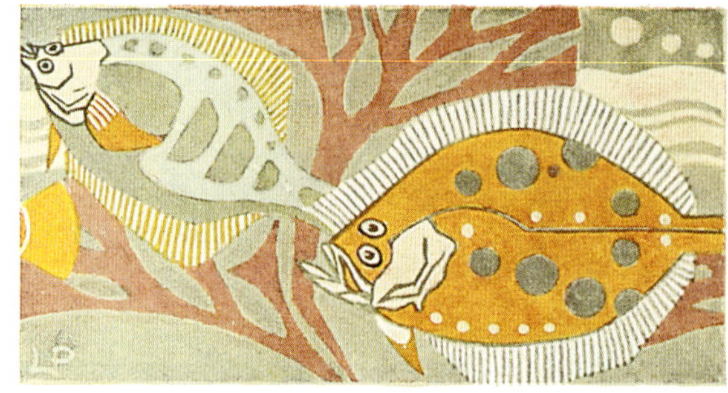

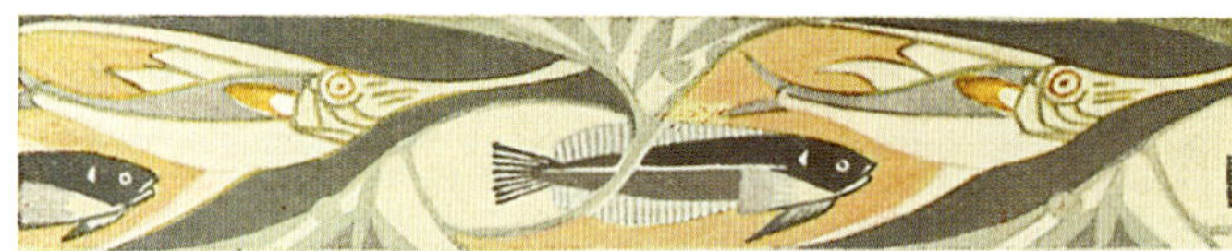

Images from *Dekorative Vorbilder* (Stuttgart: Verlag von Jul. Hoffmann, Volumes 8, 10–11, 13, 15–21, 23, 1897–1912). Reprinted by Dover as *300 Art Nouveau Designs and Motifs in Full Color*, edited by Carol Belanger Grafton (New York, 1983).

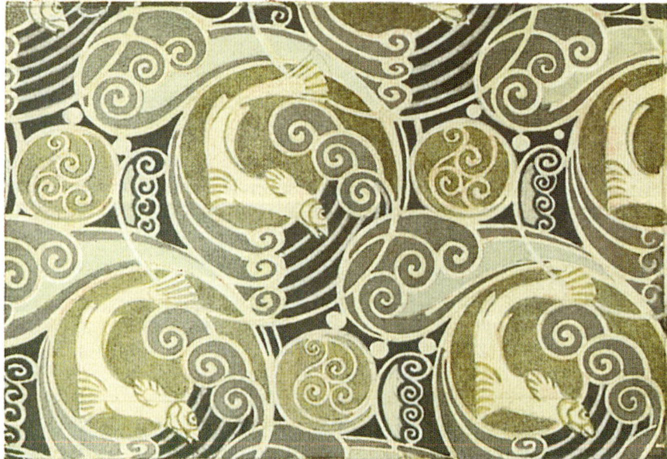

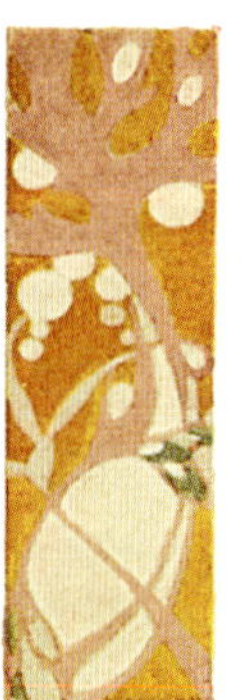

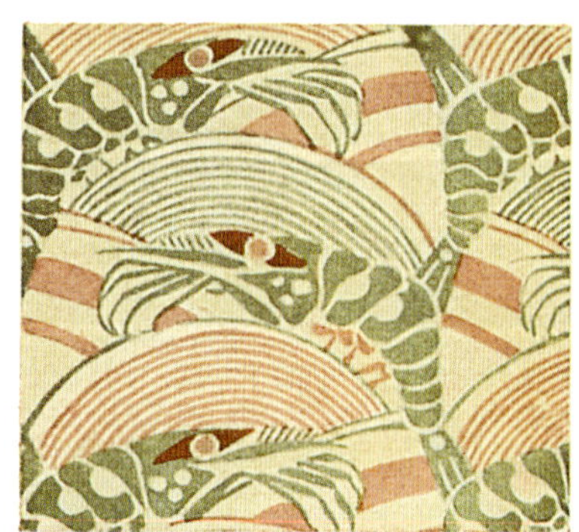

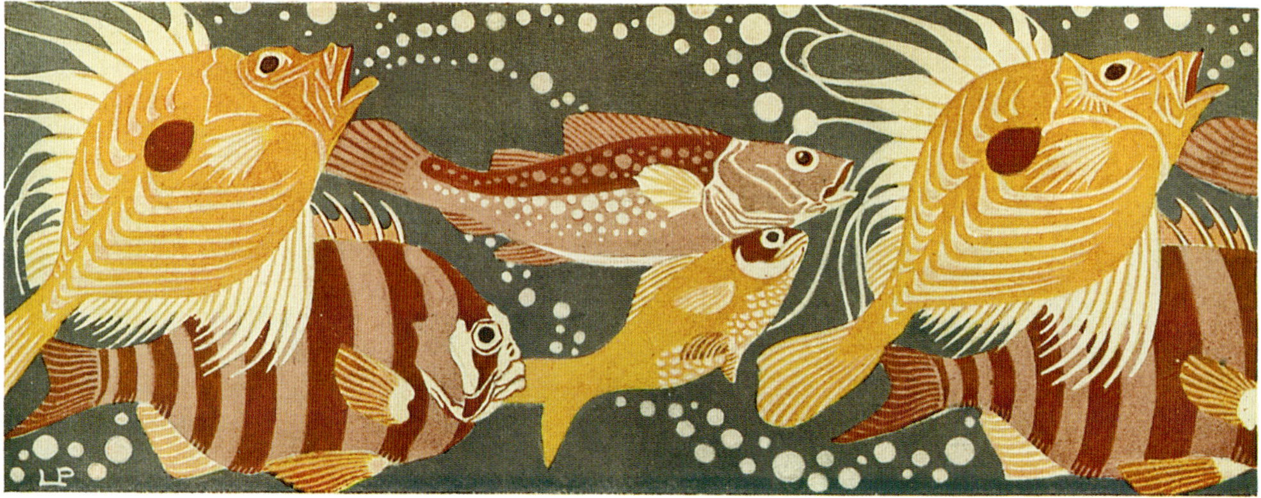

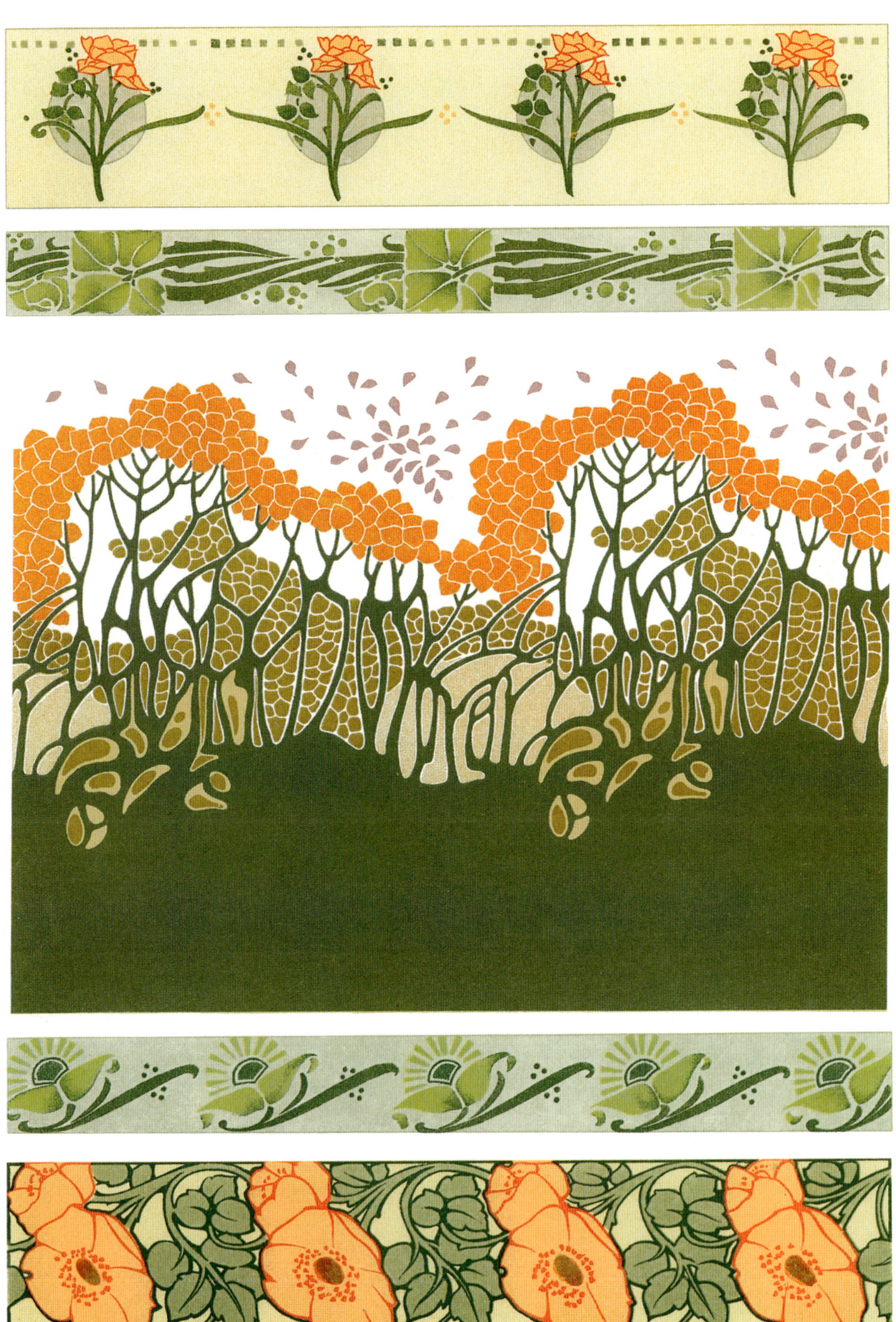

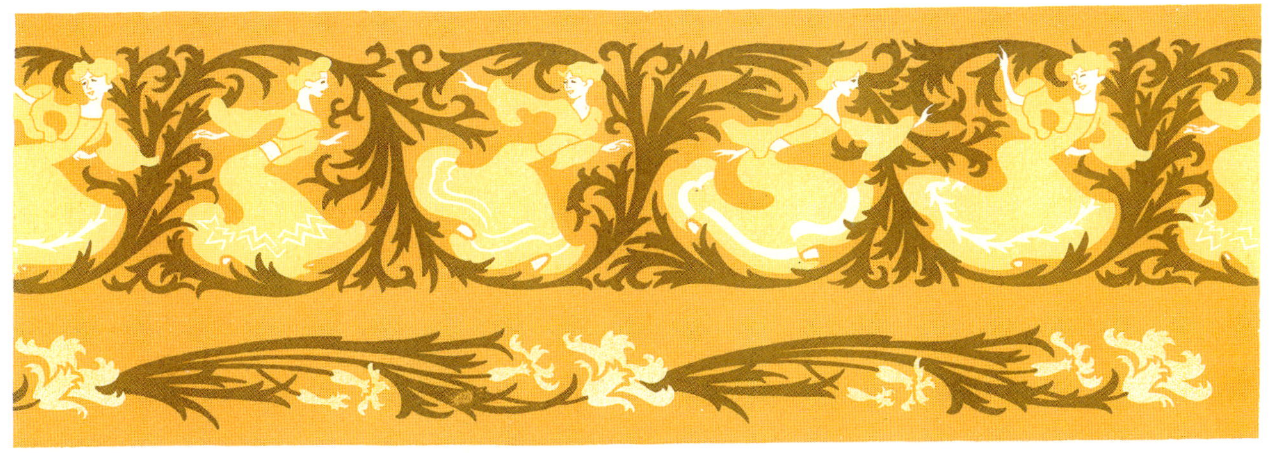

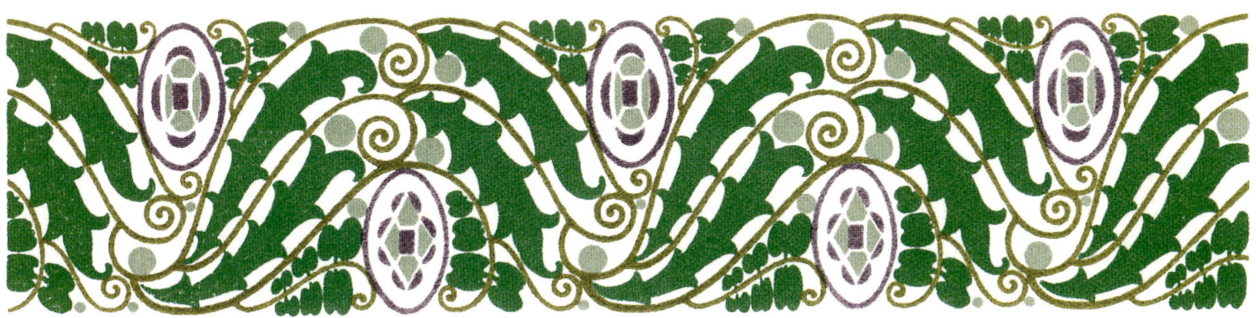

Images from *Dekorative Vorbilder: eine Sammlung von figürlichen Darstellungen, kunstgewerblichen Verzierungen, plastischen Ornamenten, dekorativen Tier- und Pflanzen-typen, Allegorieen, heraldischen, Motiven, Traphäen, etc.* (Stuttgart: Verlag von Jul. Hoffmann, 1889–1928). Reprinted by Dover as *356 Art Nouveau Floral Designs CD-ROM and Book* (Mineola, NY, 2007).

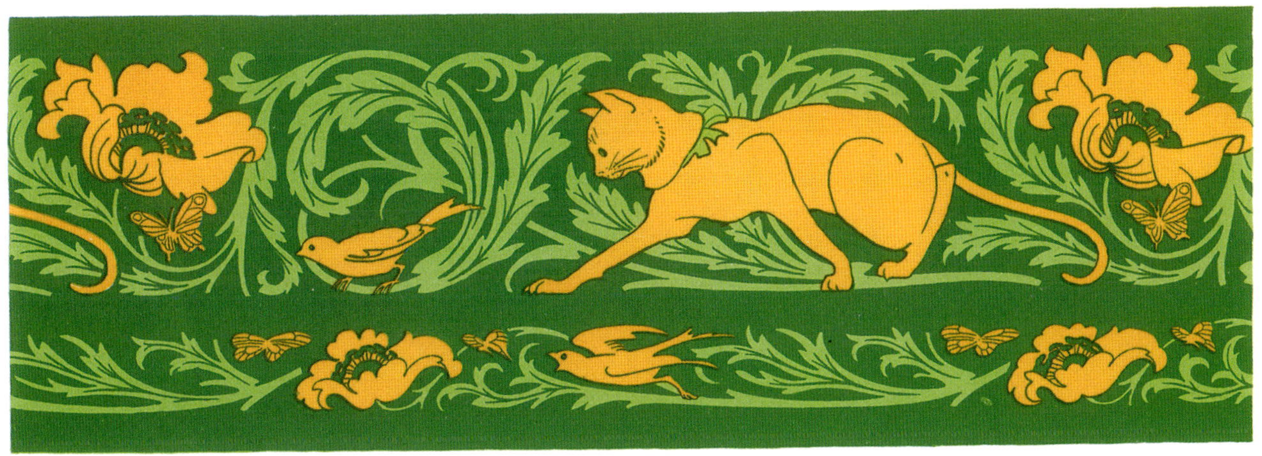

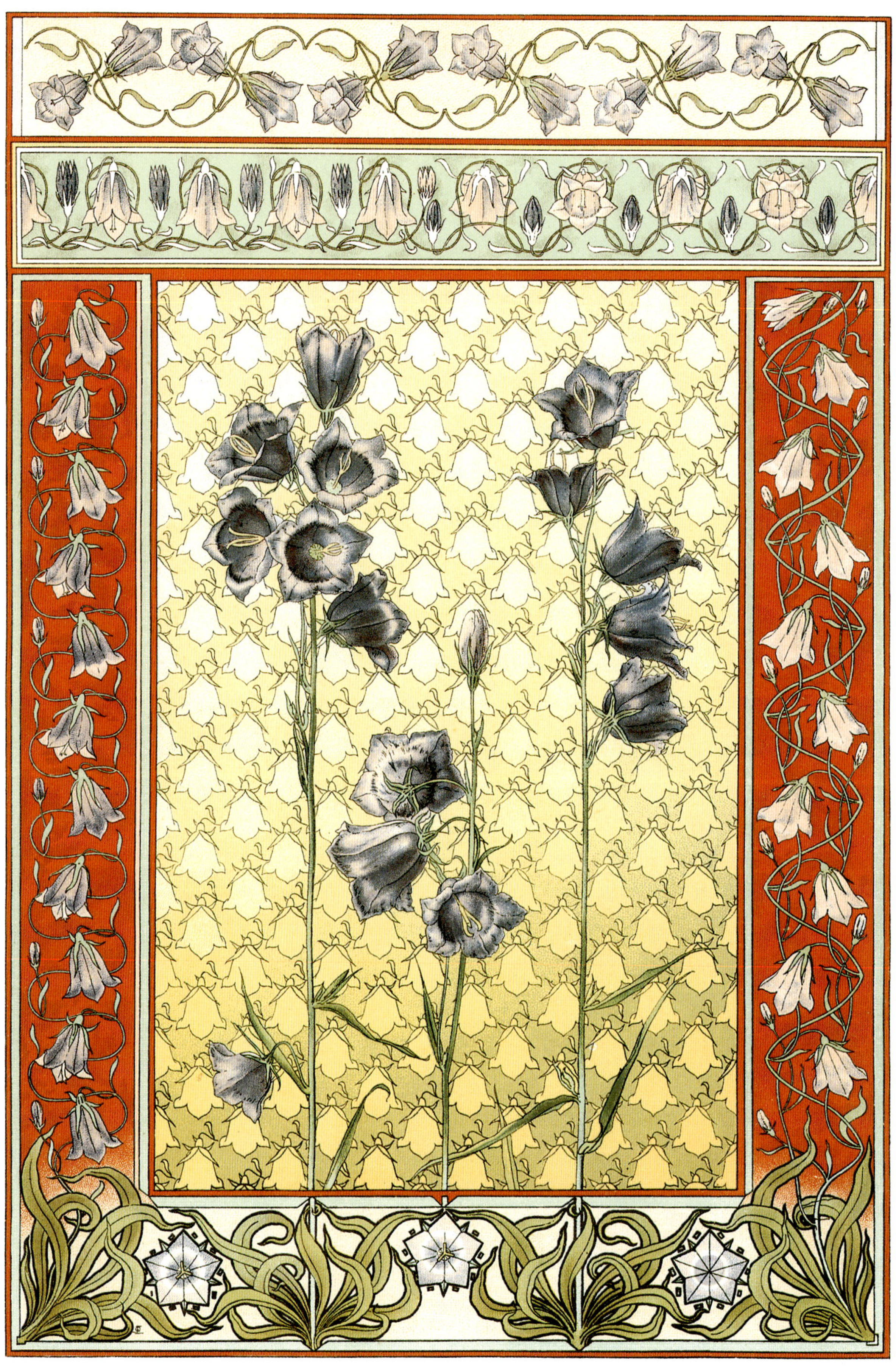

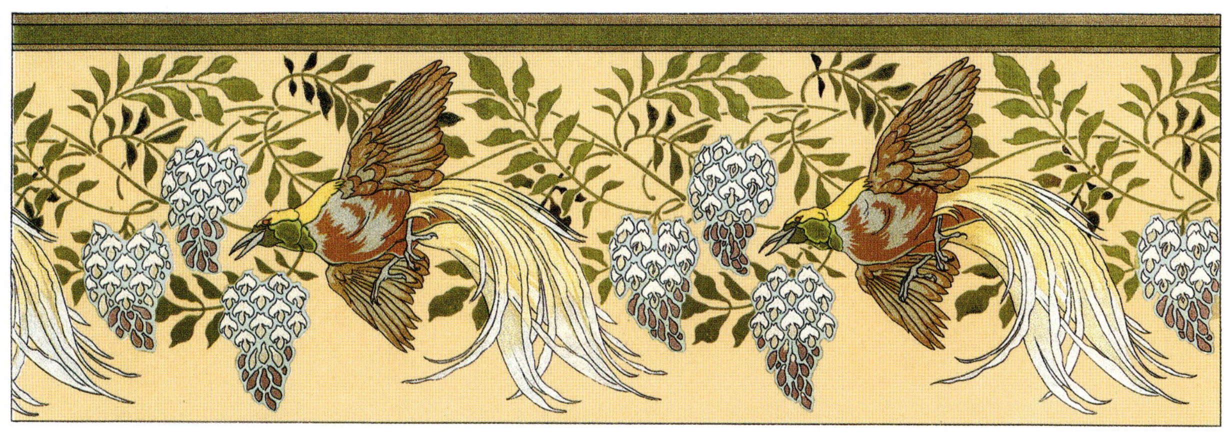

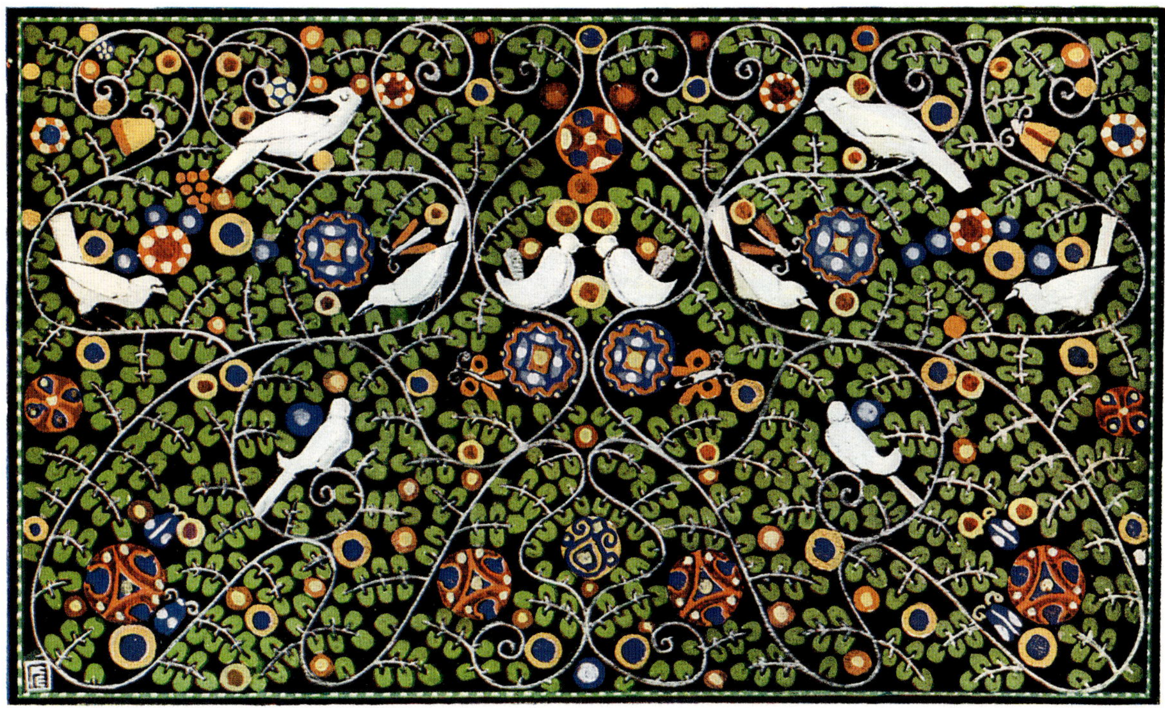

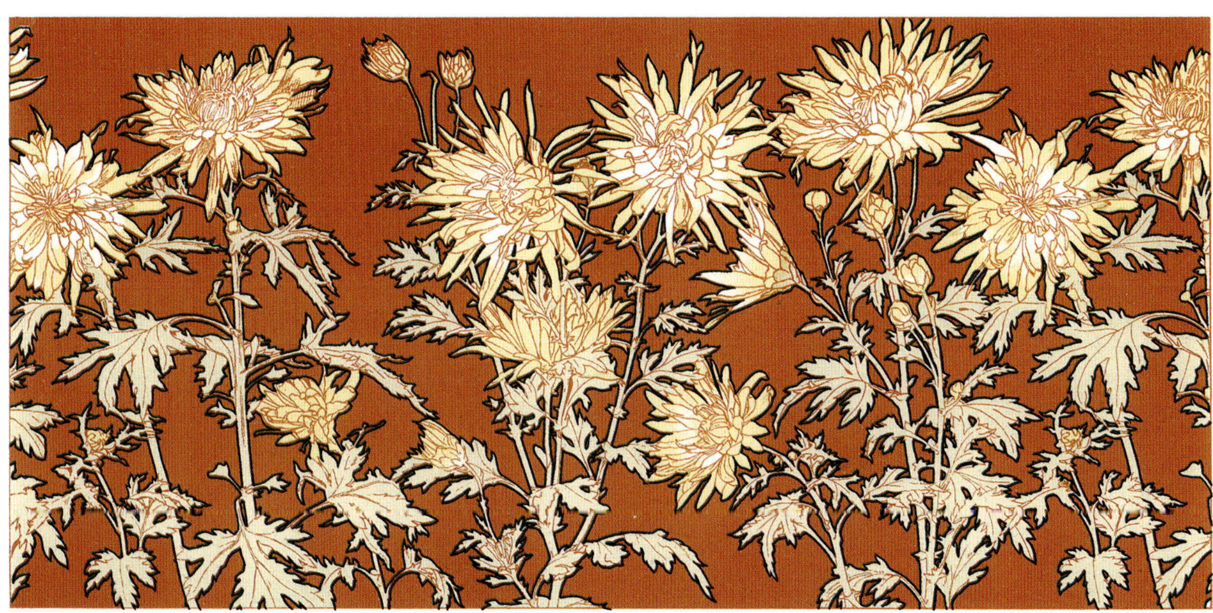

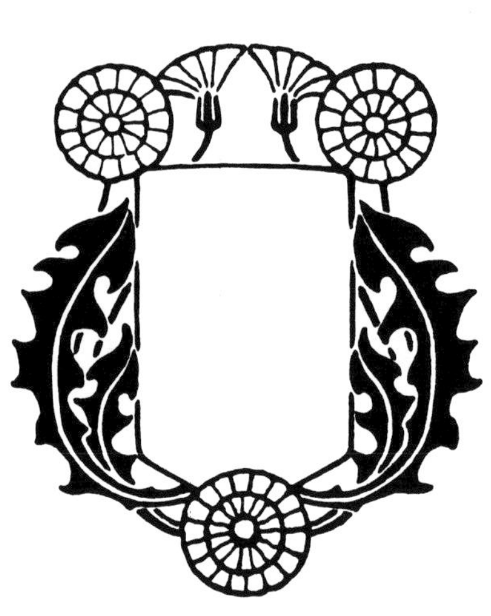
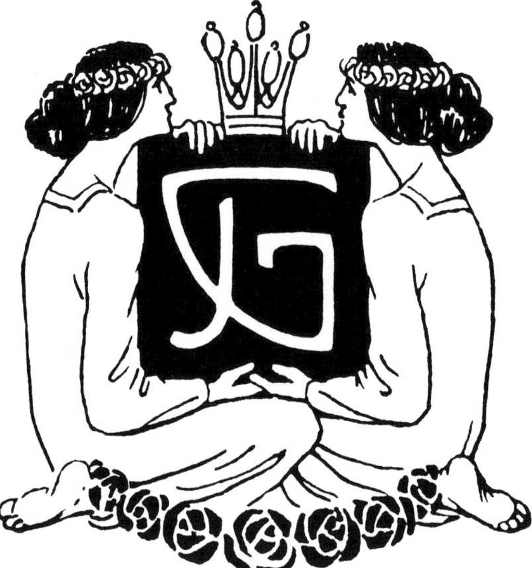
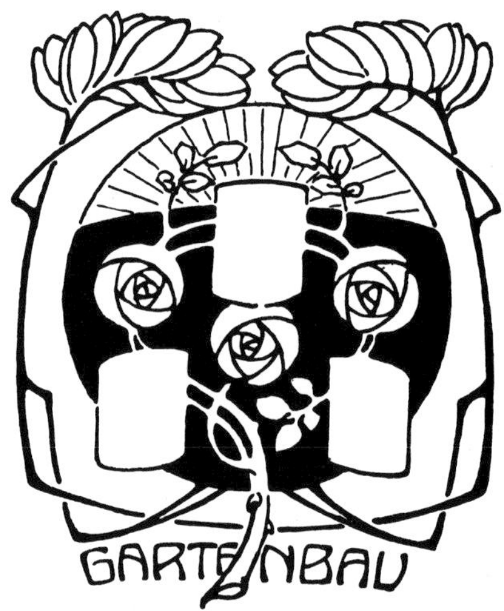

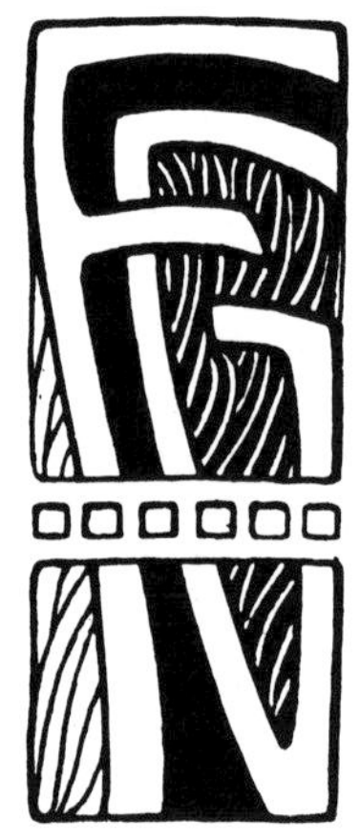
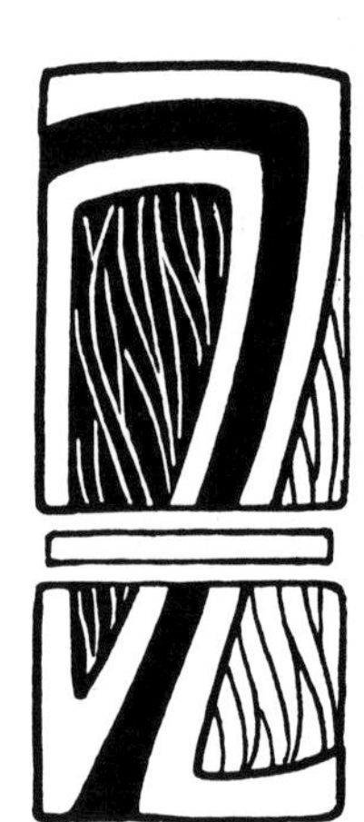

Images from *Monogramme und Dekorationen* (Leipzig: Verlag von Wilhelm Diebener, 1911). Reprinted by Dover as *Monograms and Decorations from the Art Nouveau Period,* edited by Wilhelm Diebener. (New York, 1982).

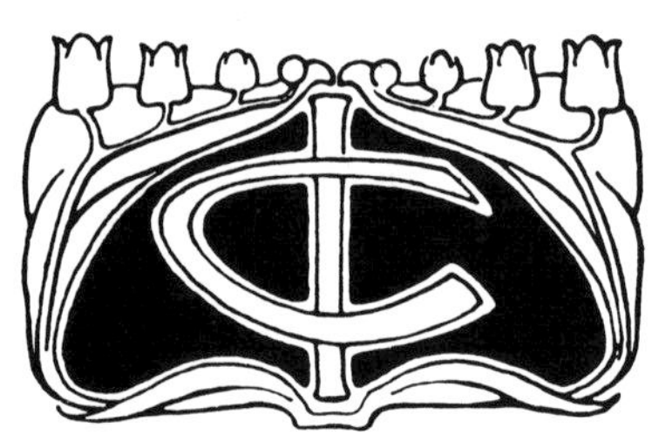
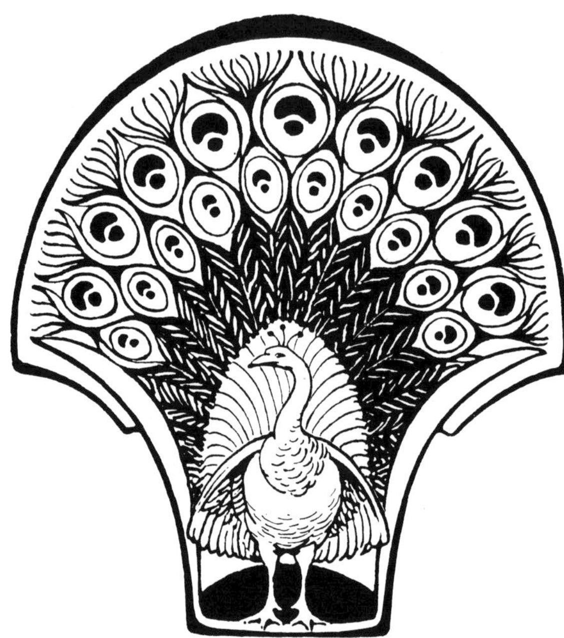
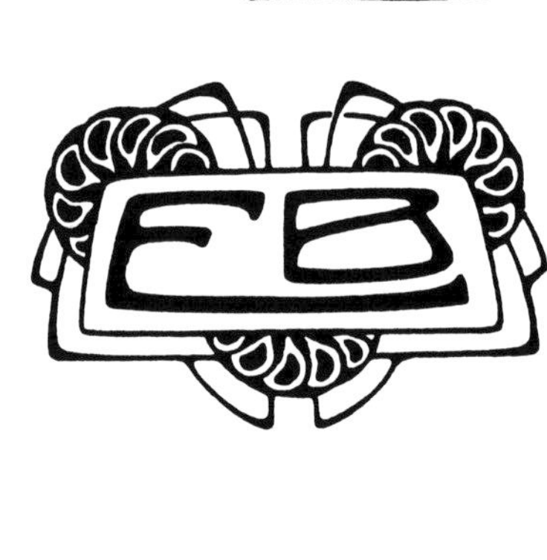
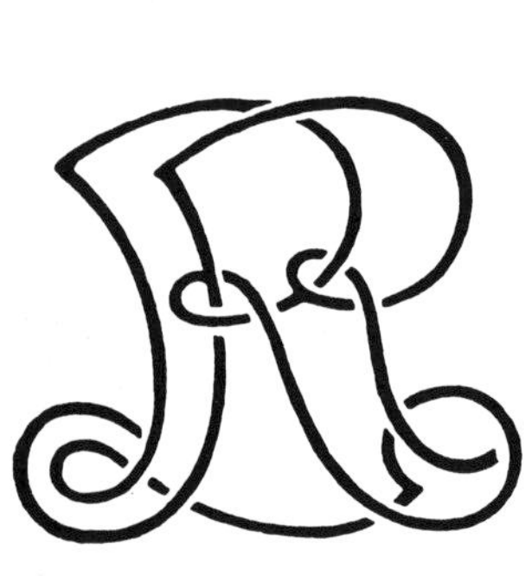
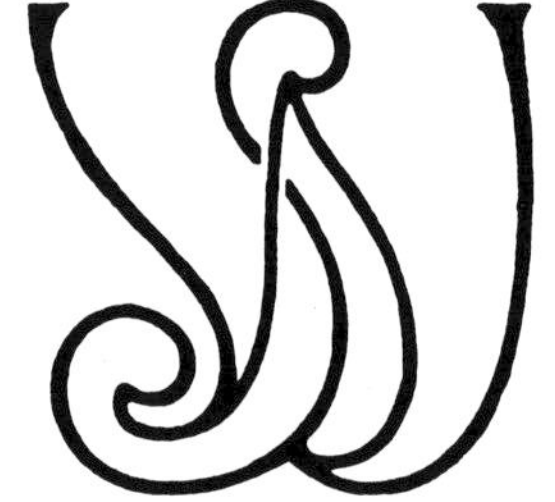

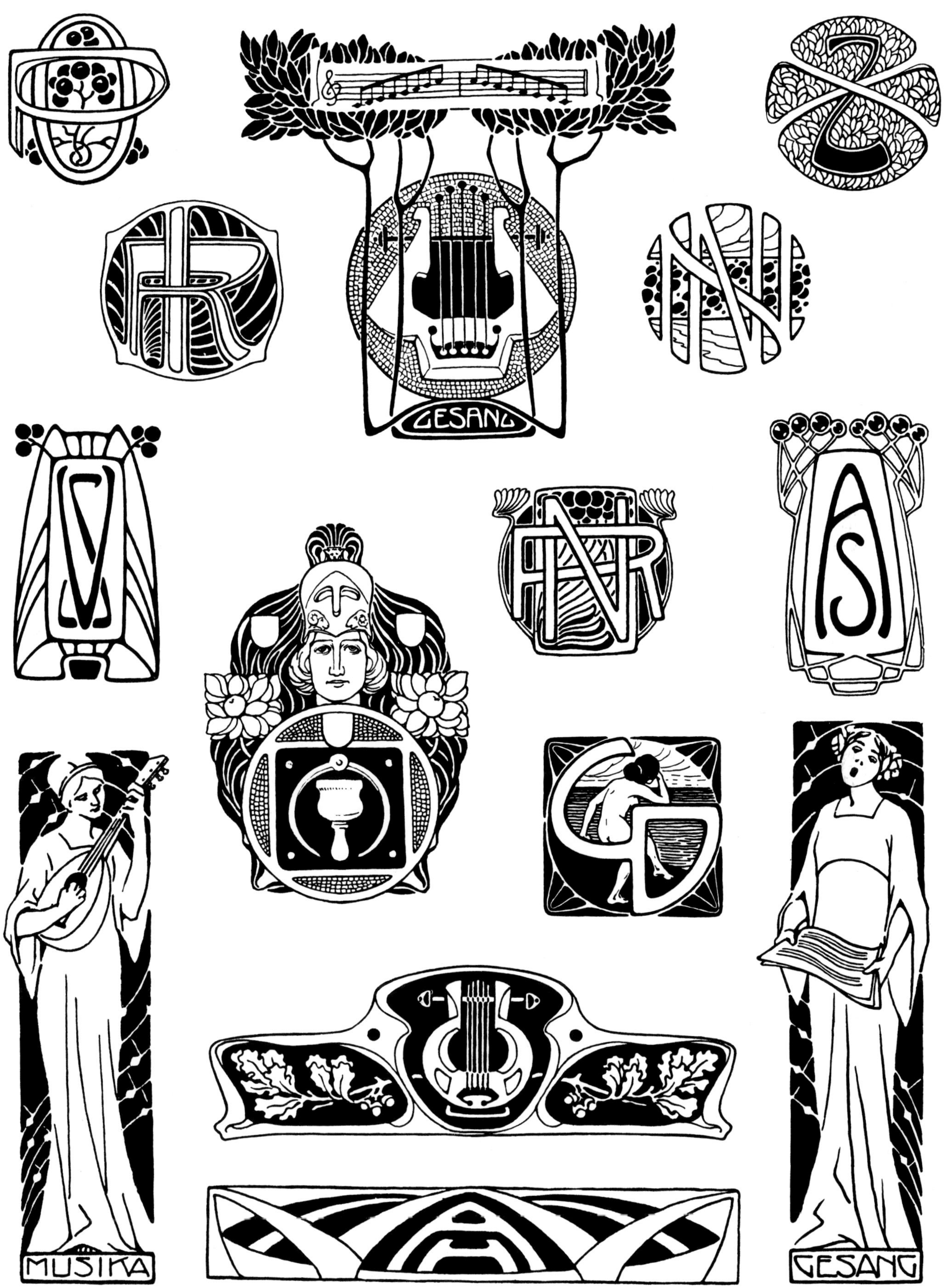

MUSIKA
GESANG
GESANG

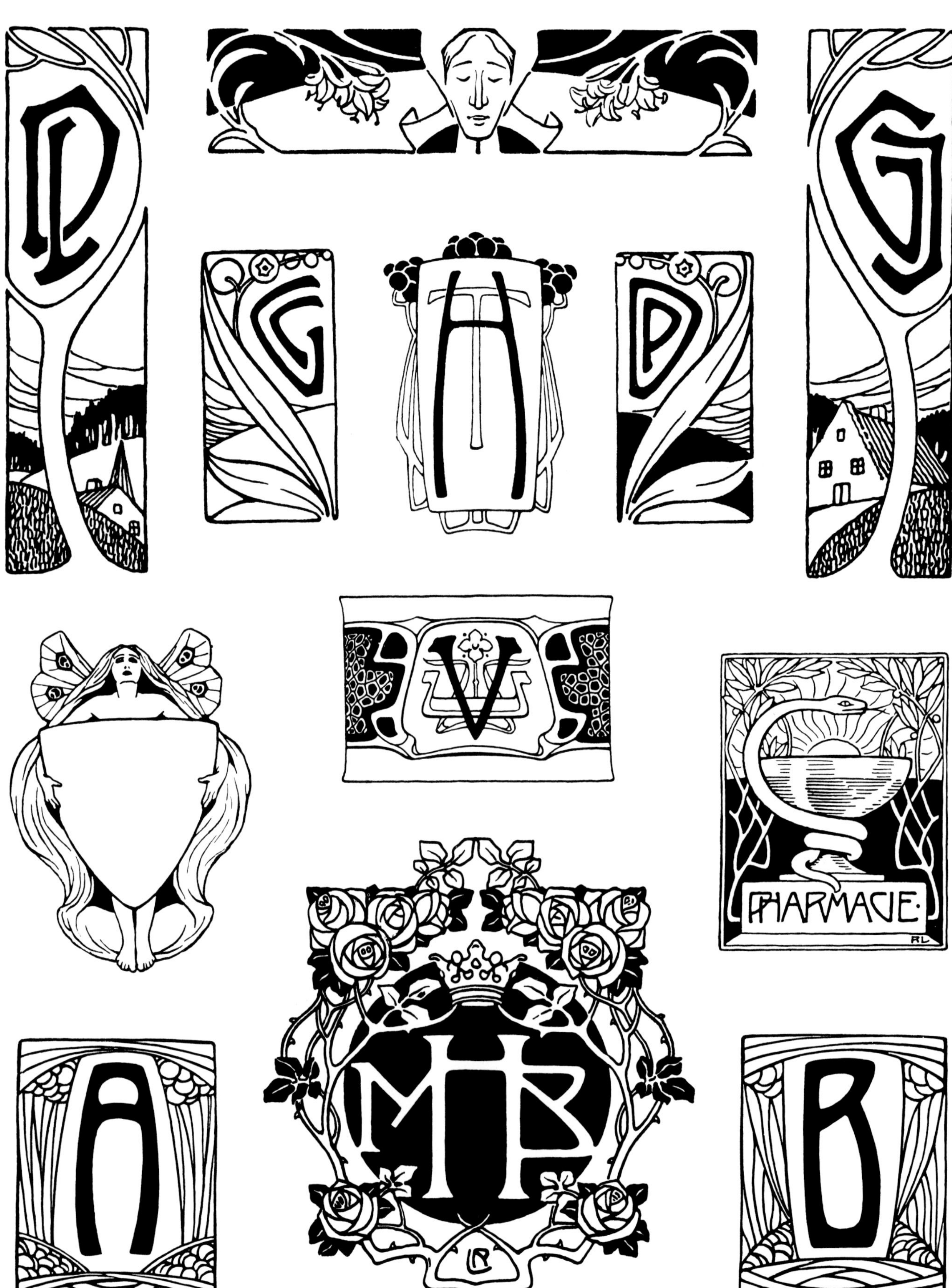

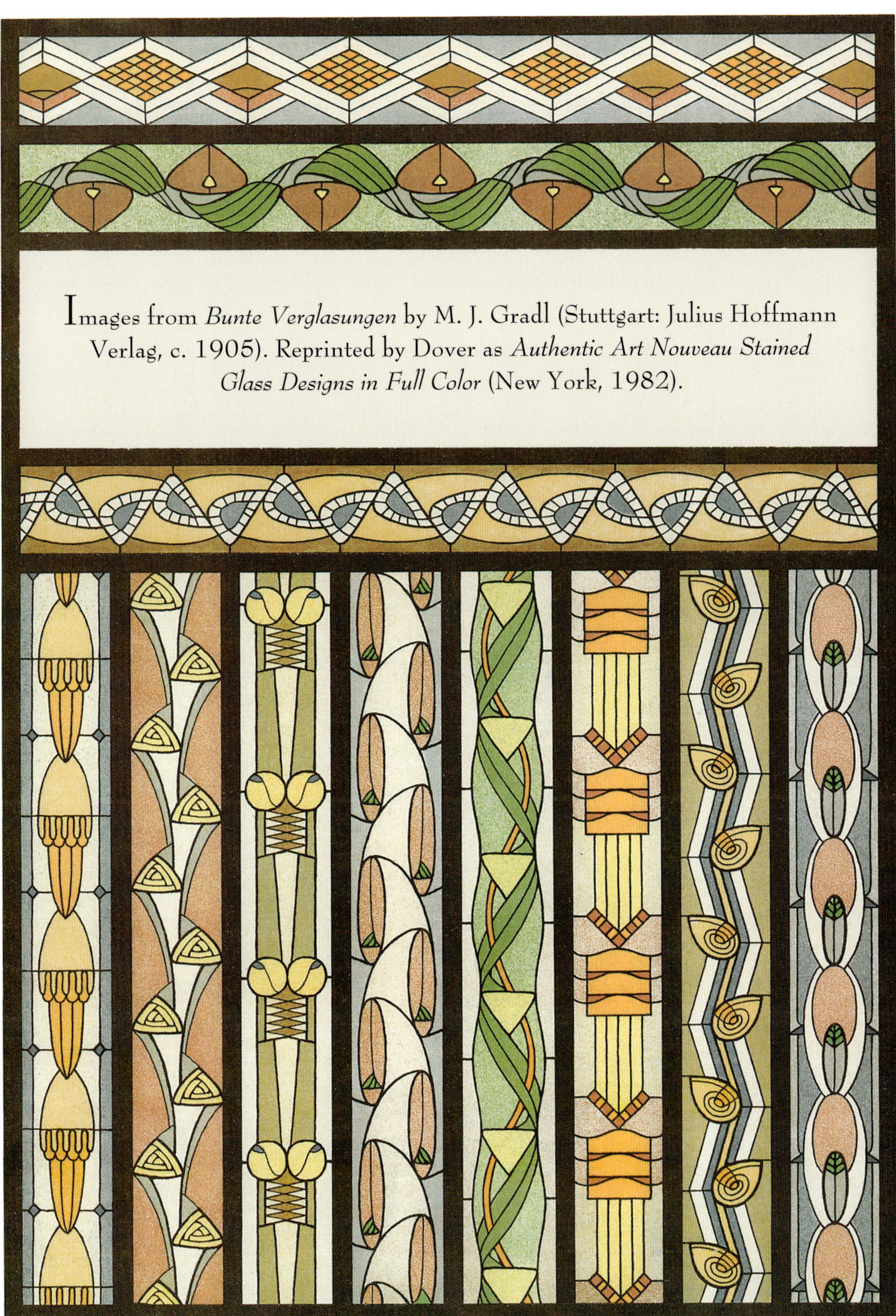
Images from *Bunte Verglasungen* by M. J. Gradl (Stuttgart: Julius Hoffmann Verlag, c. 1905). Reprinted by Dover as *Authentic Art Nouveau Stained Glass Designs in Full Color* (New York, 1982).

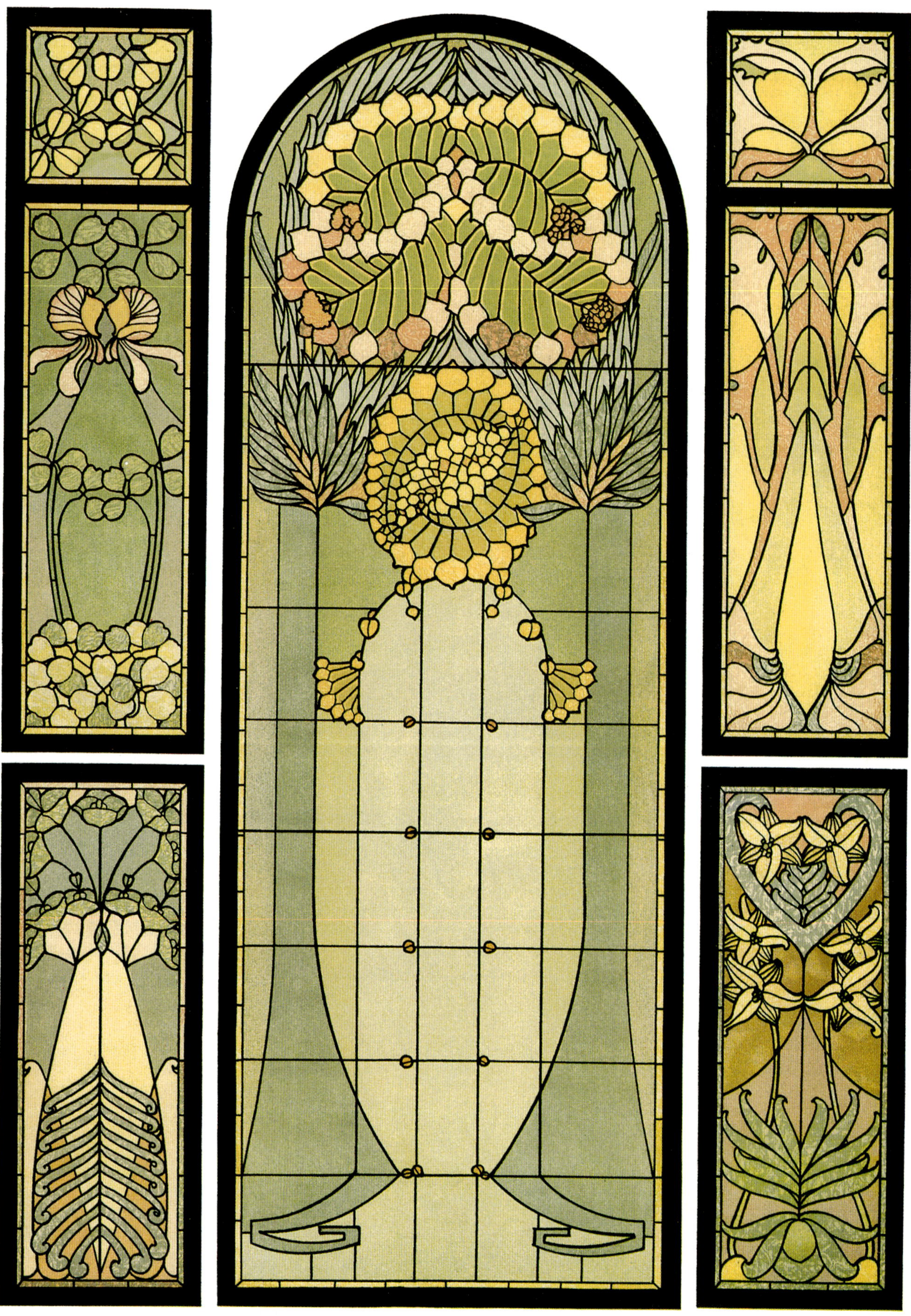

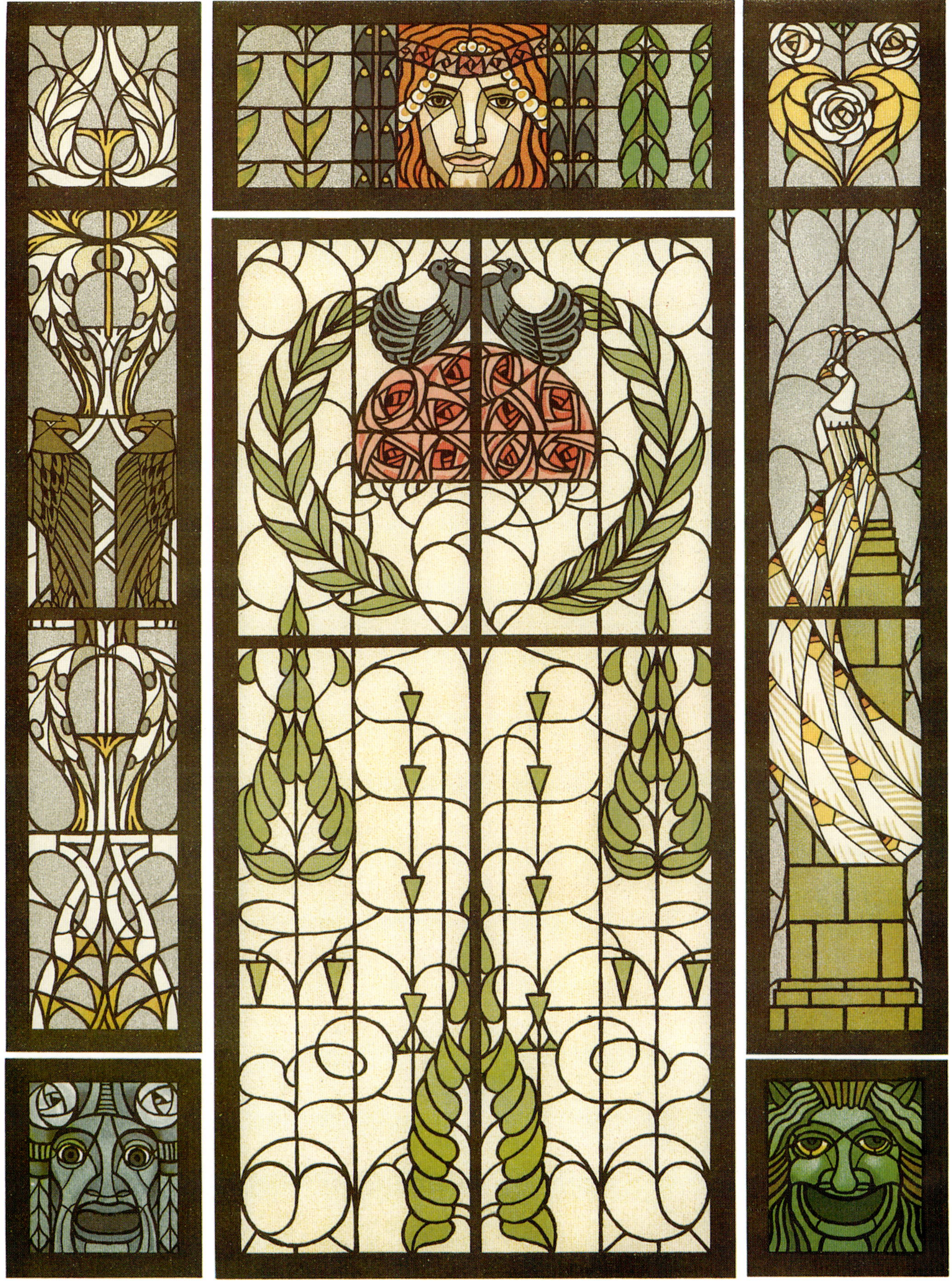

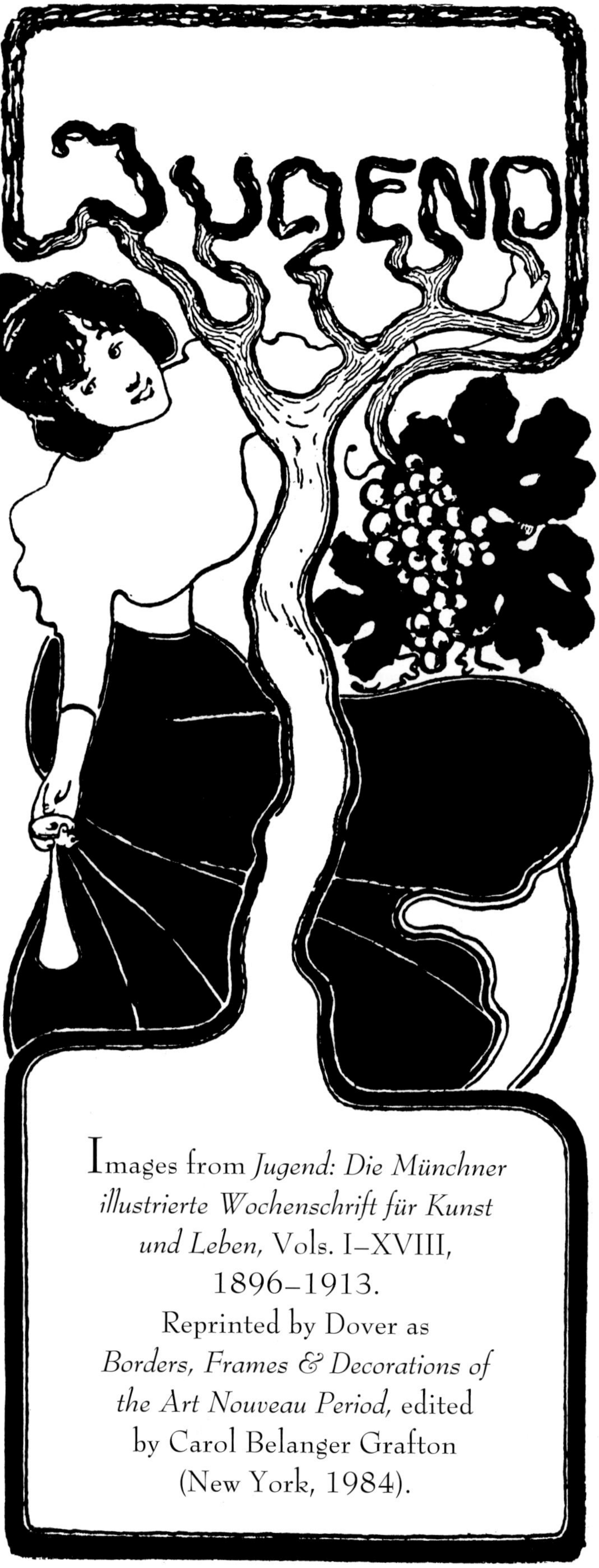

Images from *Jugend: Die Münchner illustrierte Wochenschrift für Kunst und Leben*, Vols. I–XVIII, 1896–1913.
Reprinted by Dover as *Borders, Frames & Decorations of the Art Nouveau Period*, edited by Carol Belanger Grafton (New York, 1984).

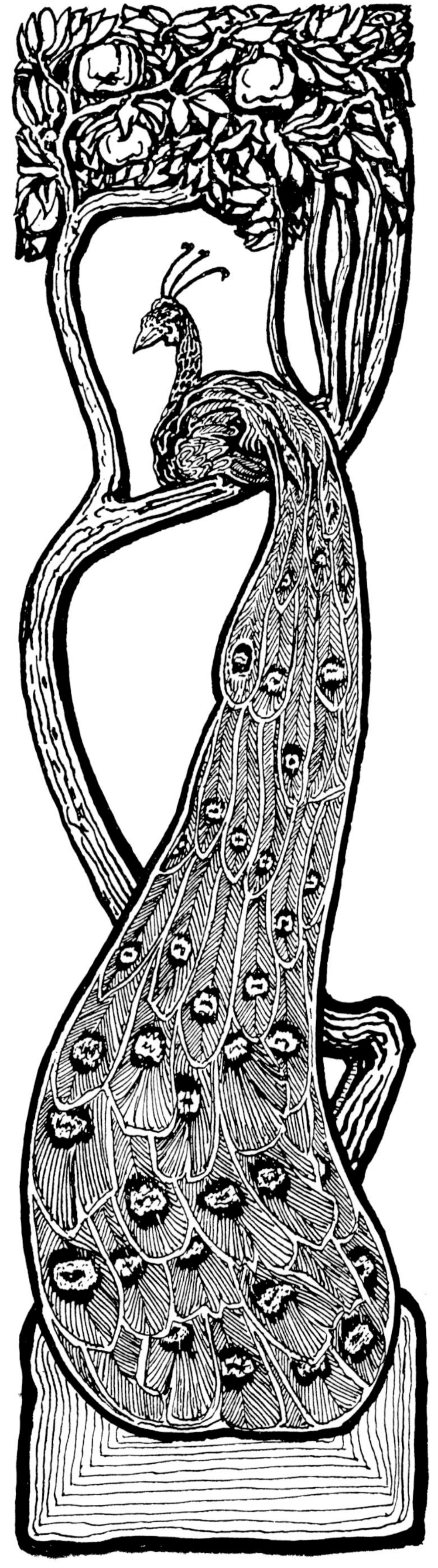

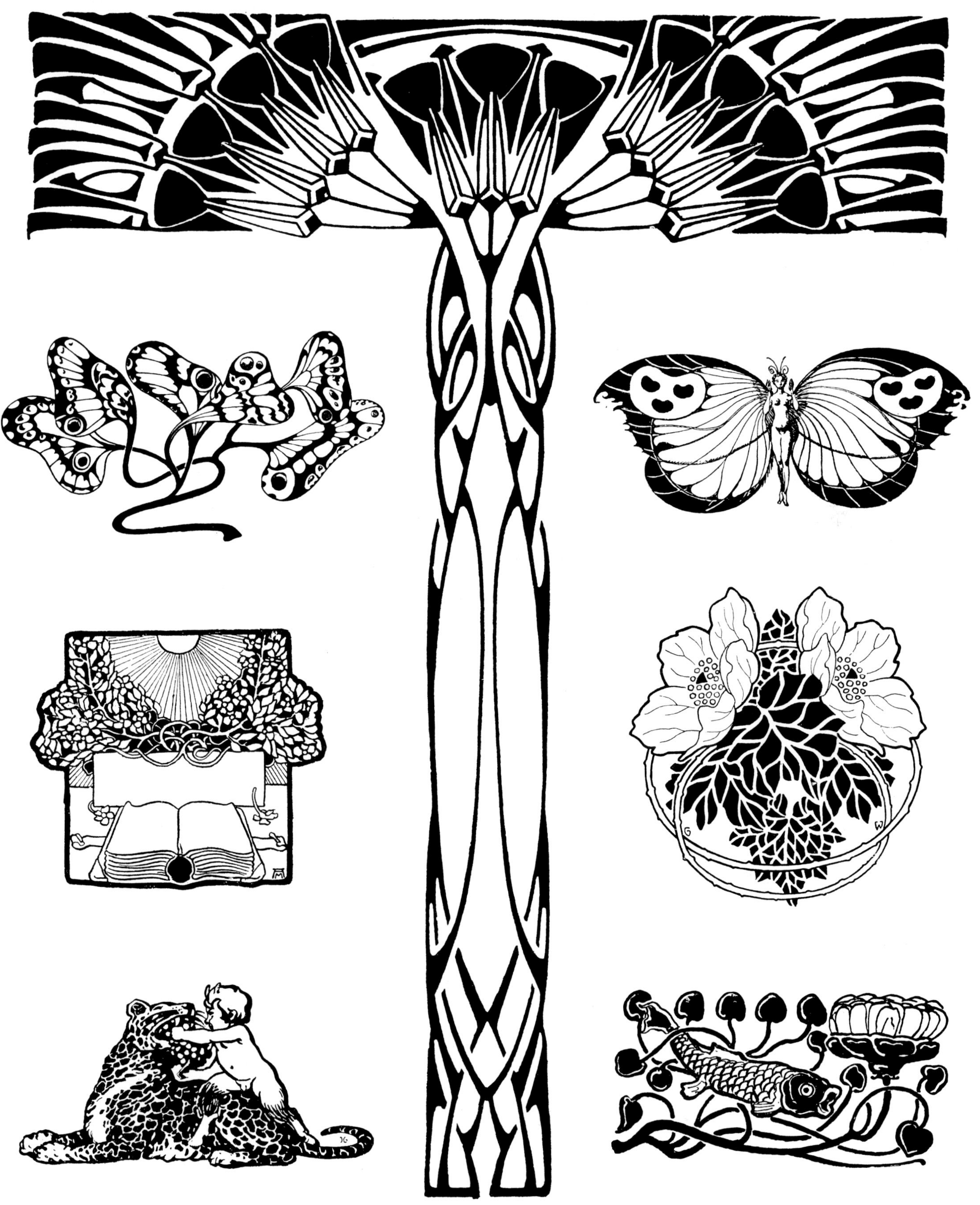

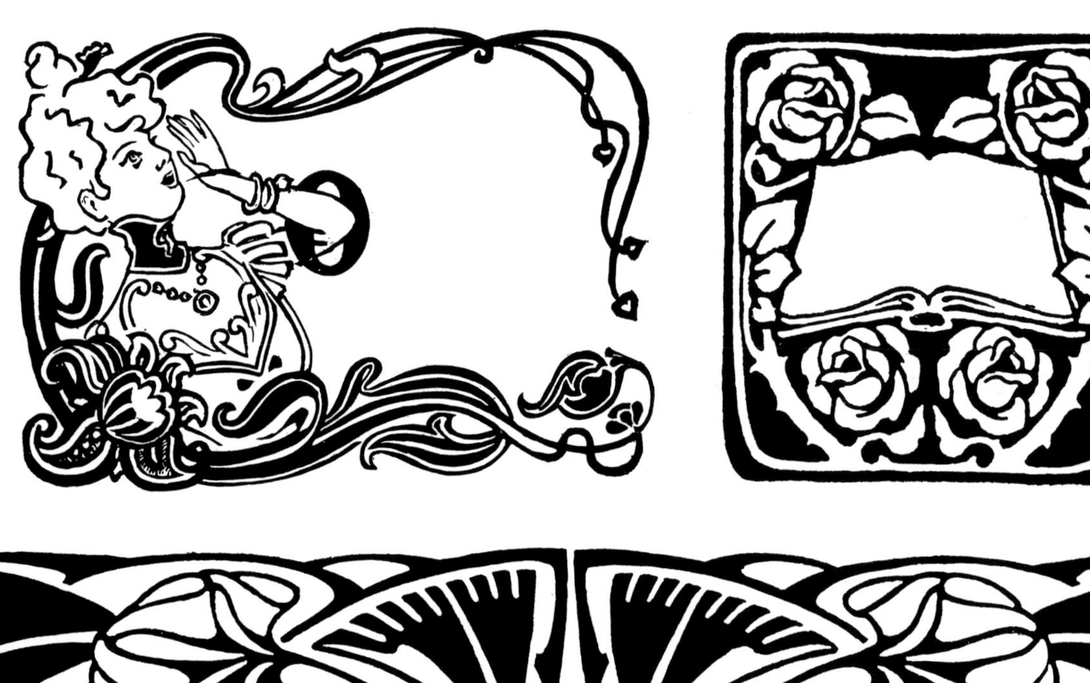

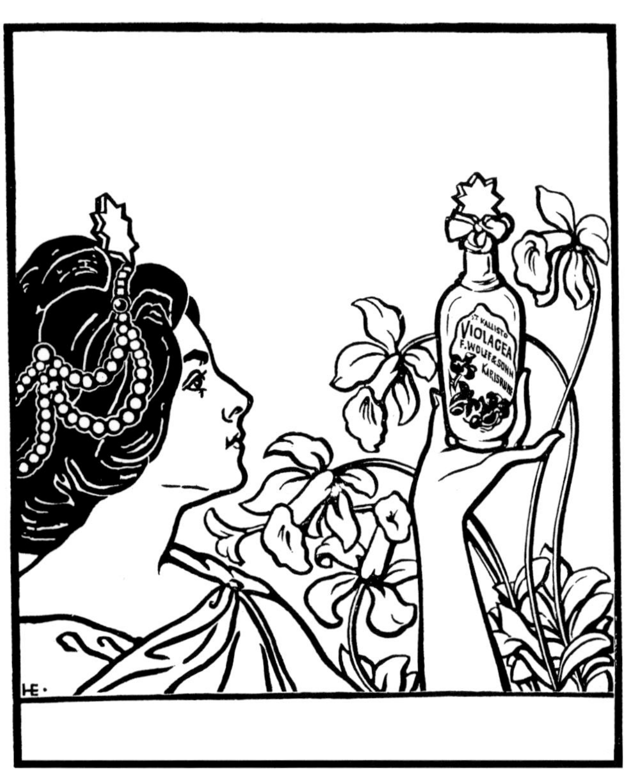

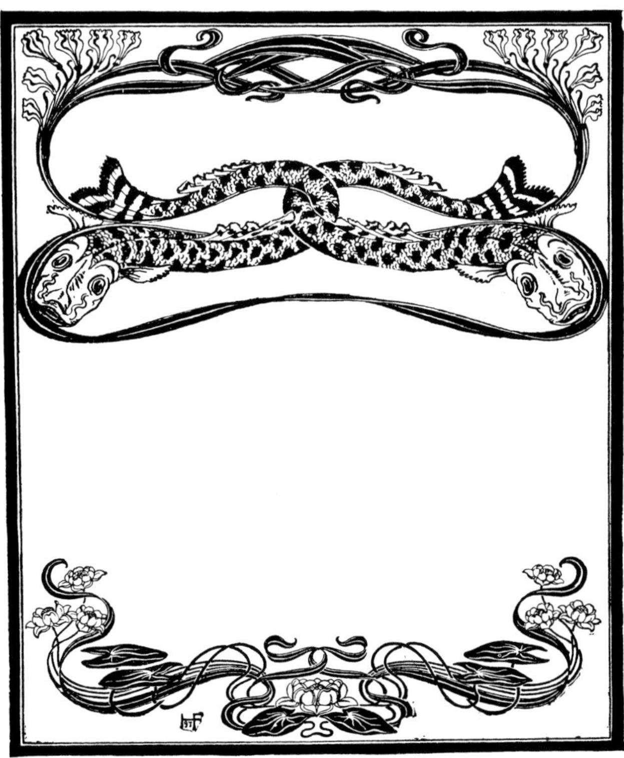

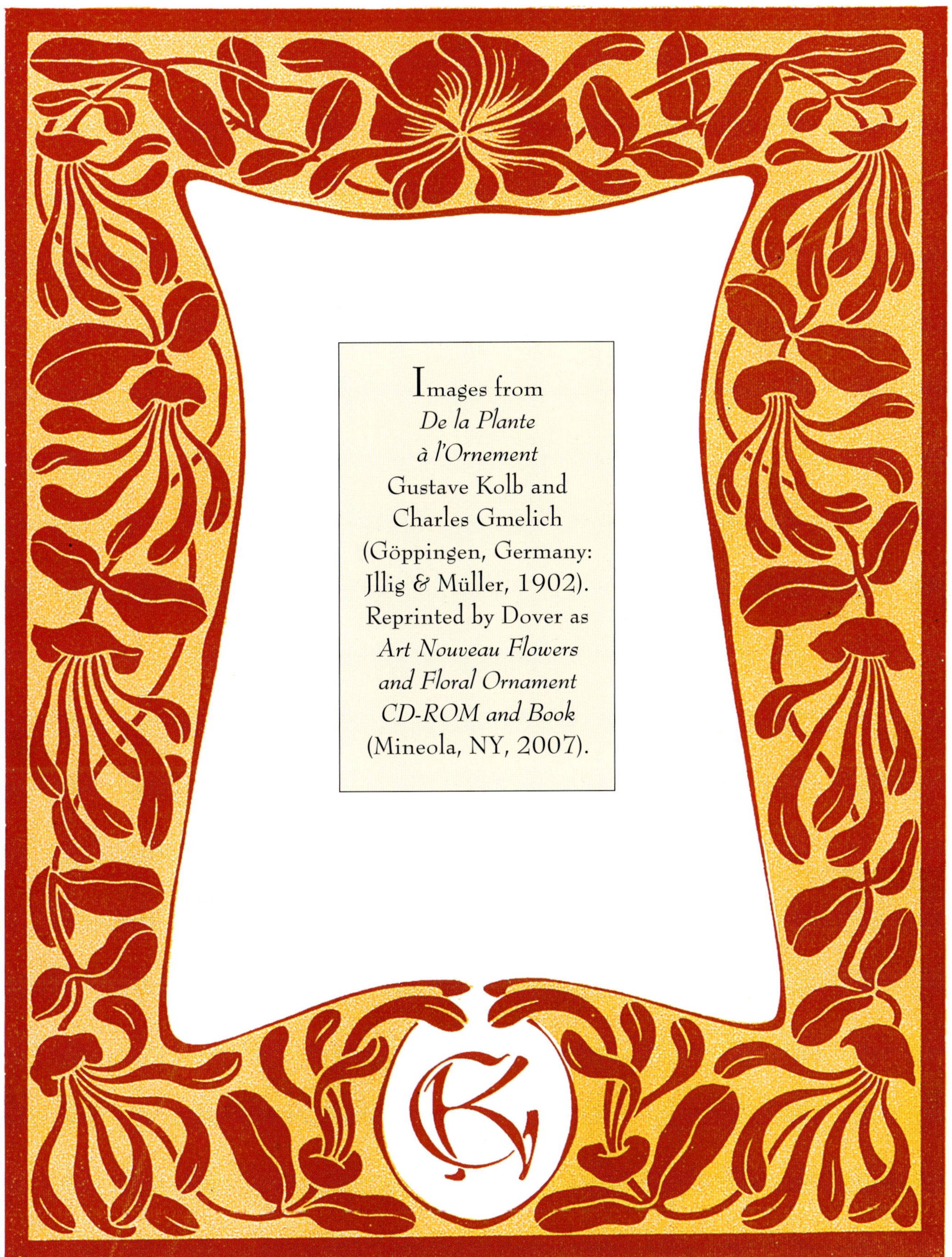

Images from
*De la Plante
à l'Ornement*
Gustave Kolb and
Charles Gmelich
(Göppingen, Germany:
Jllig & Müller, 1902).
Reprinted by Dover as
*Art Nouveau Flowers
and Floral Ornament
CD-ROM and Book*
(Mineola, NY, 2007).

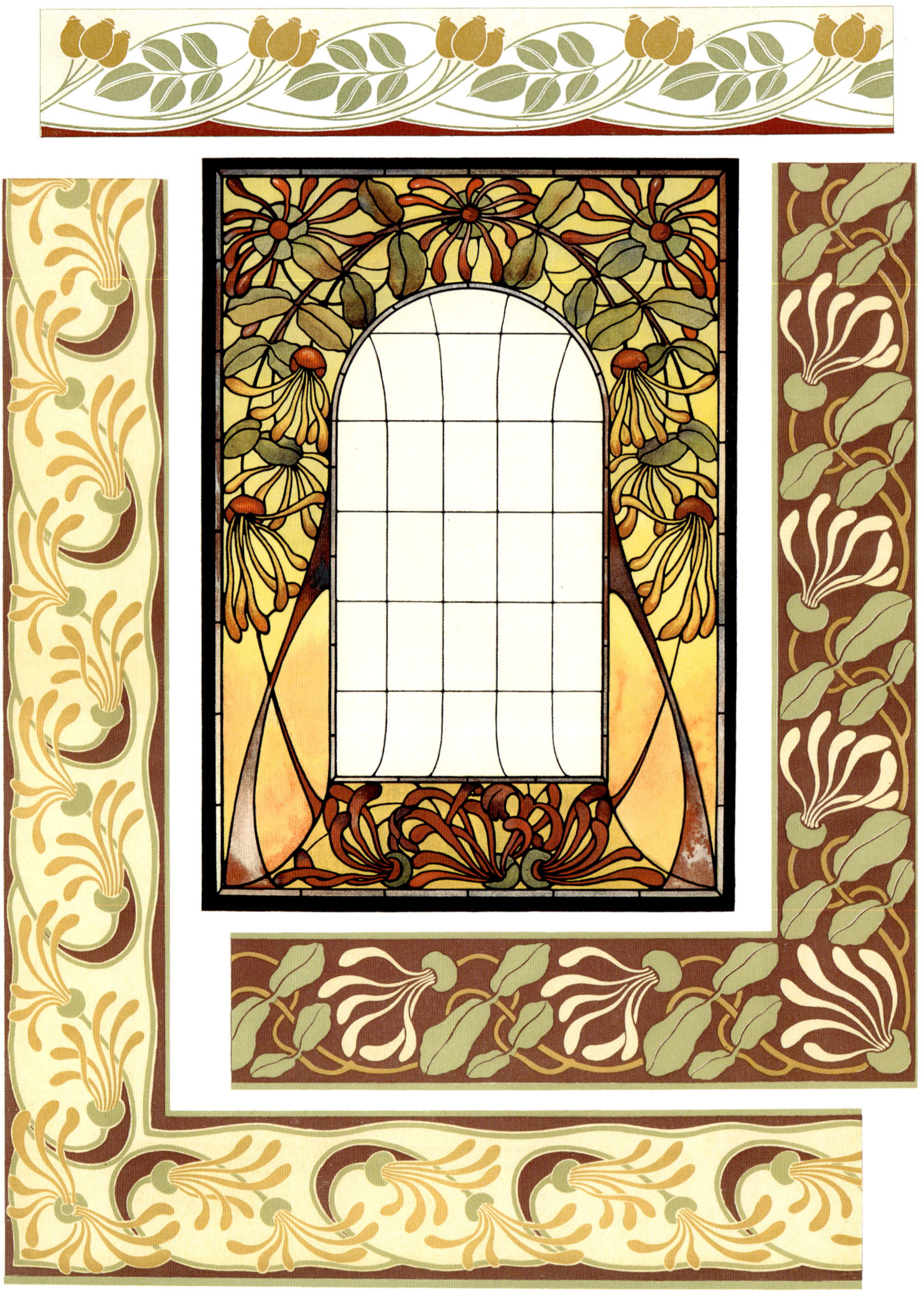

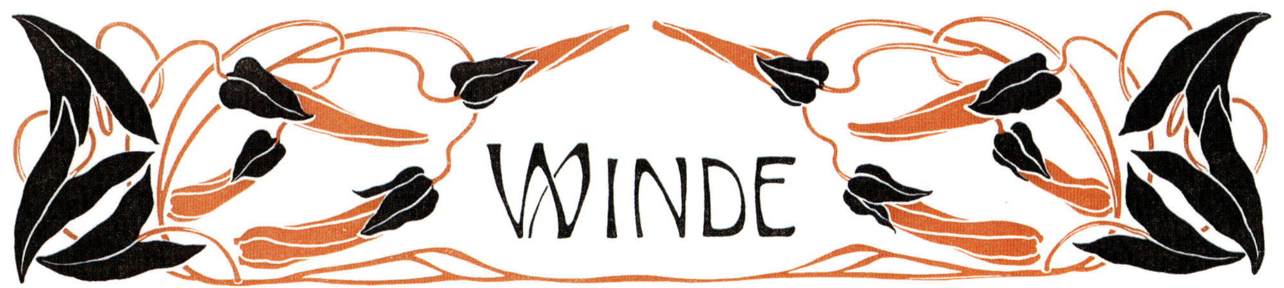

WINDE

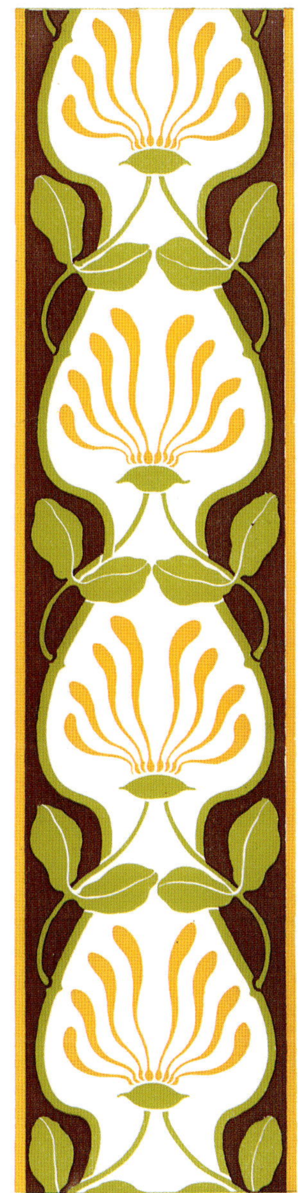

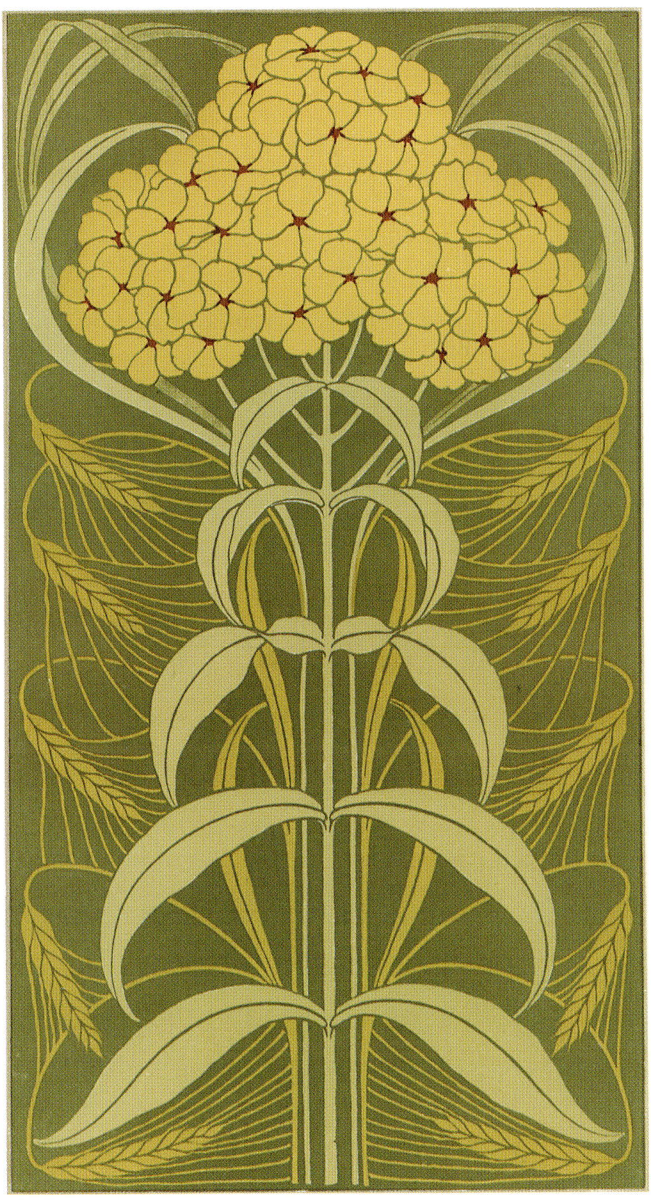

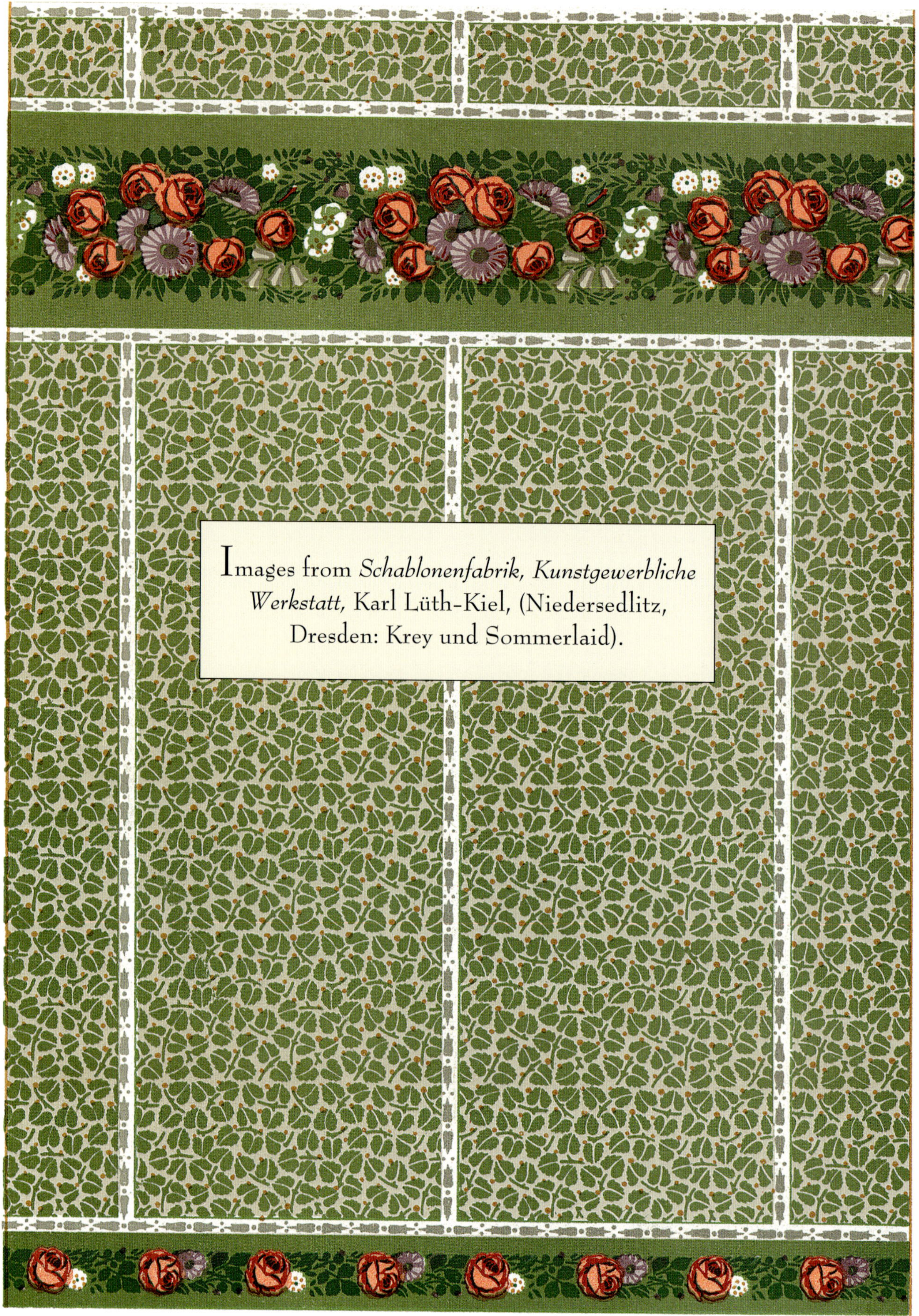
Images from Schablonenfabrik, Kunstgewerbliche Werkstatt, Karl Lüth-Kiel, (Niedersedlitz, Dresden: Krey und Sommerlaid).

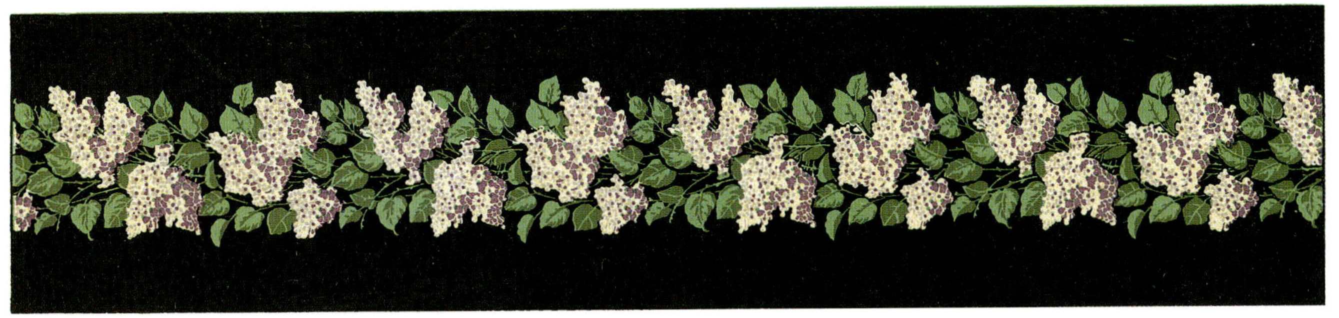

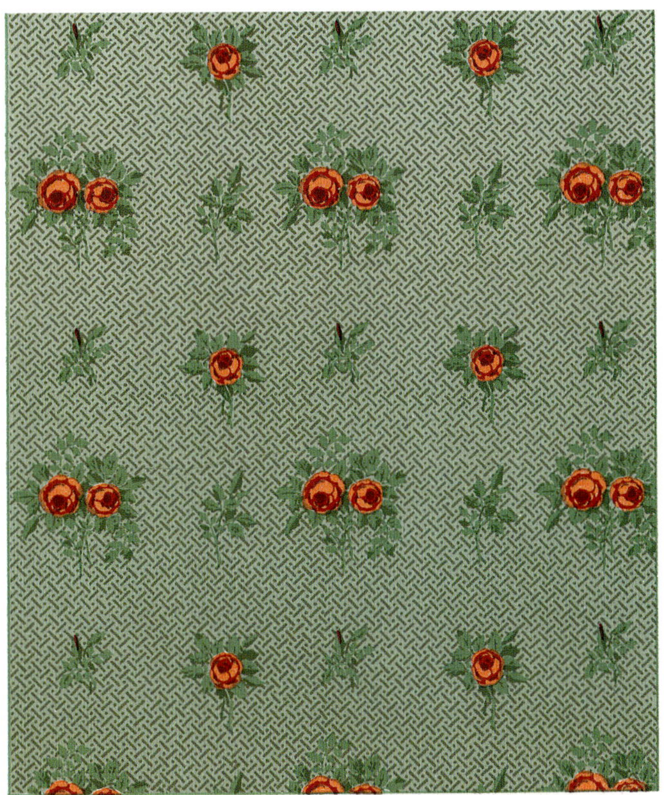

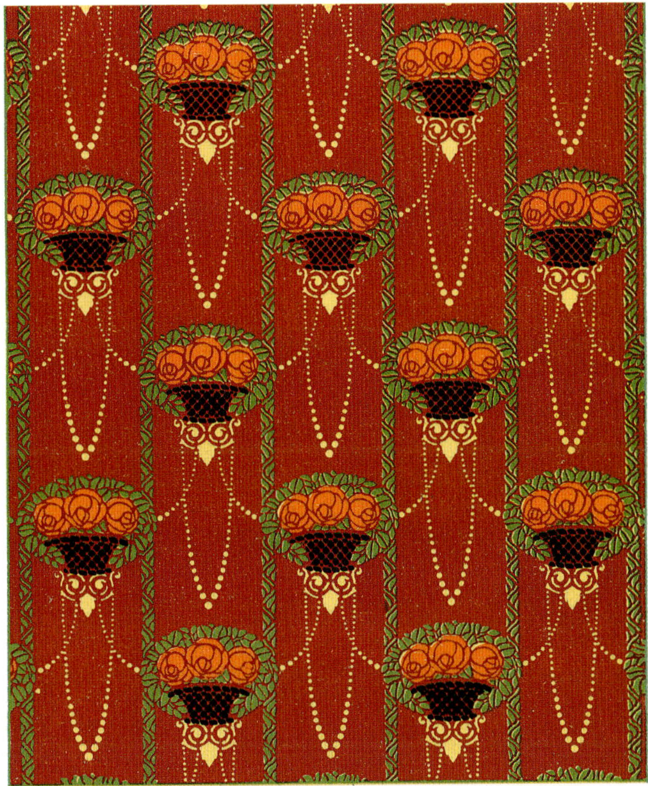

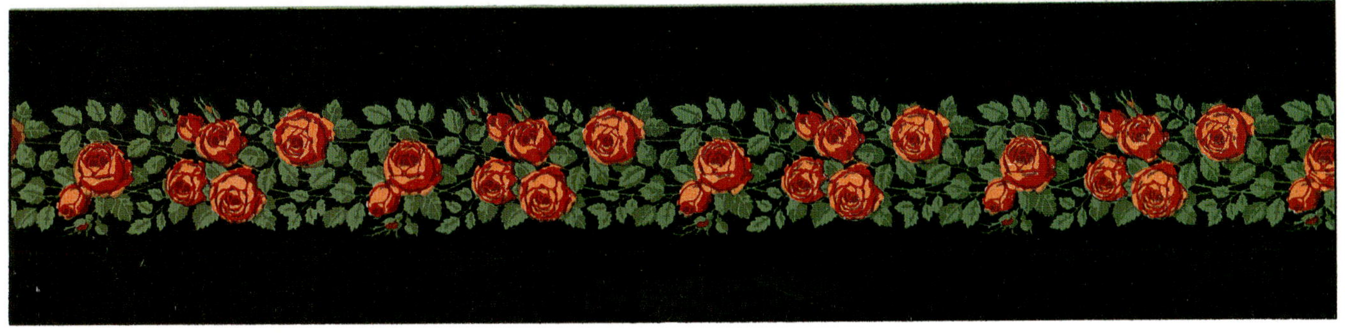

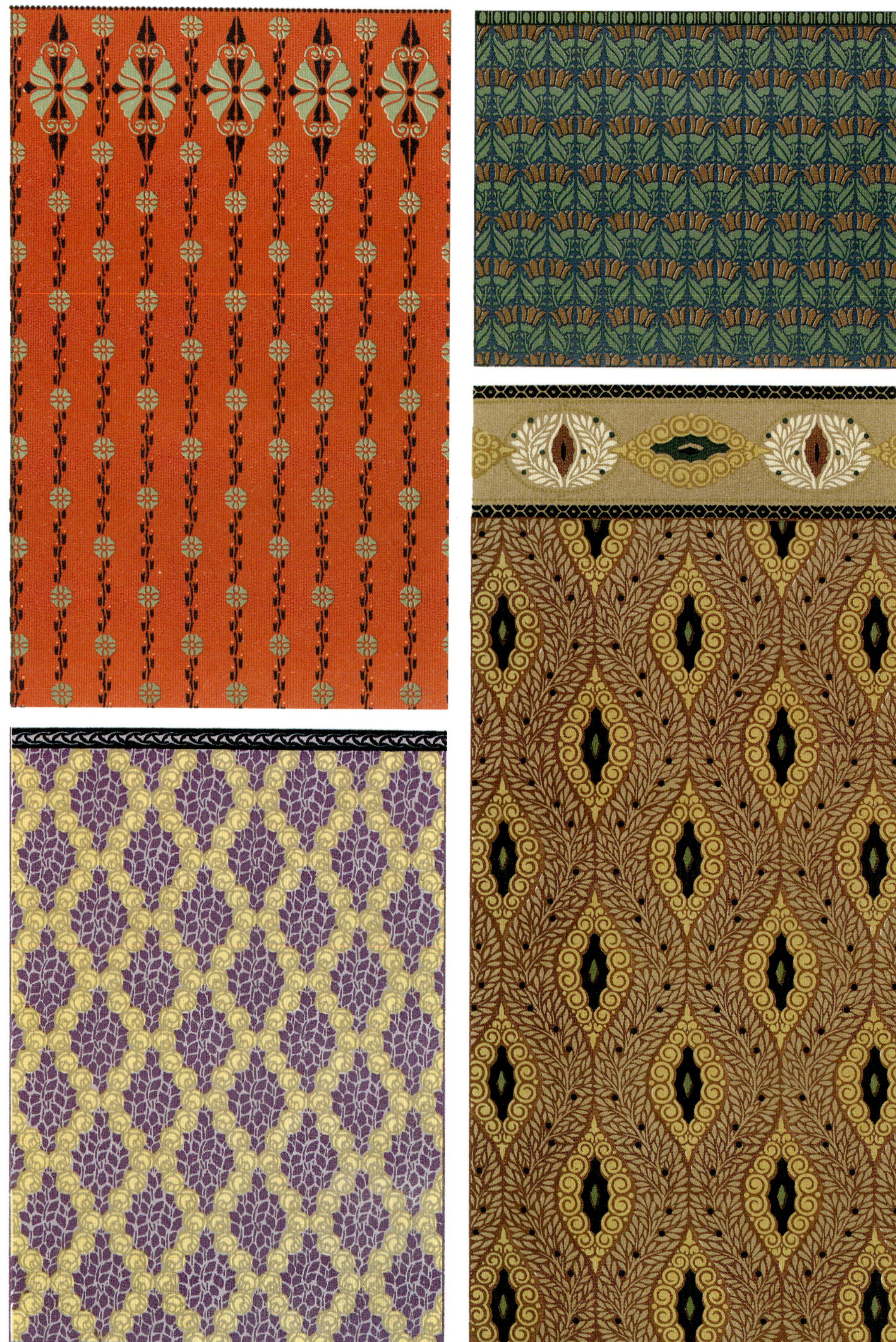

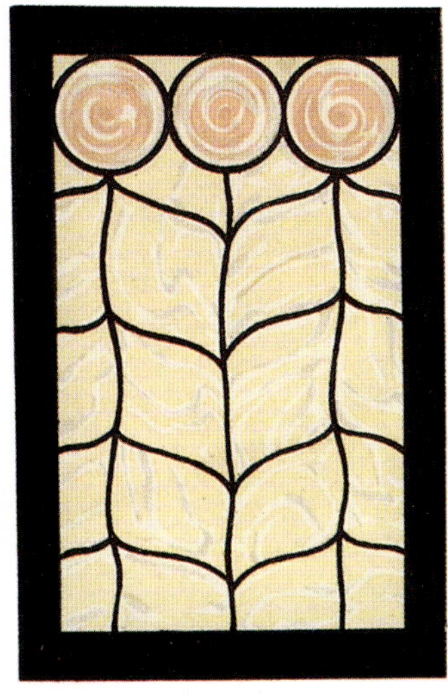
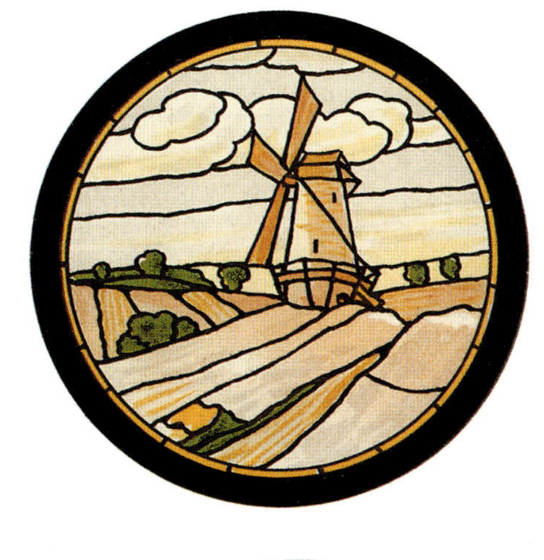
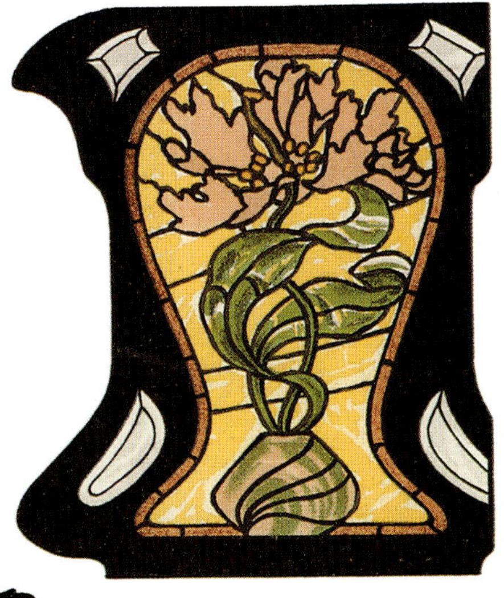
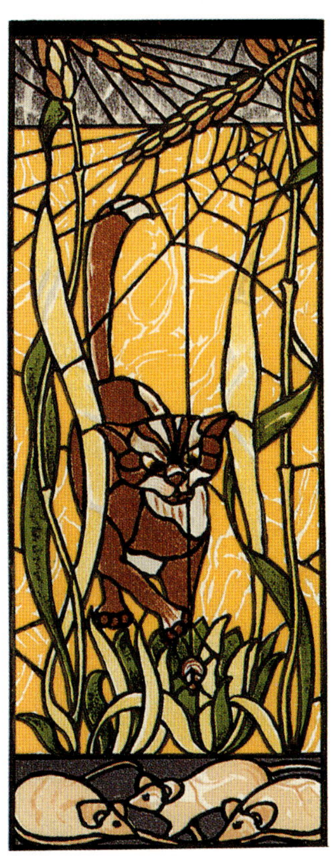
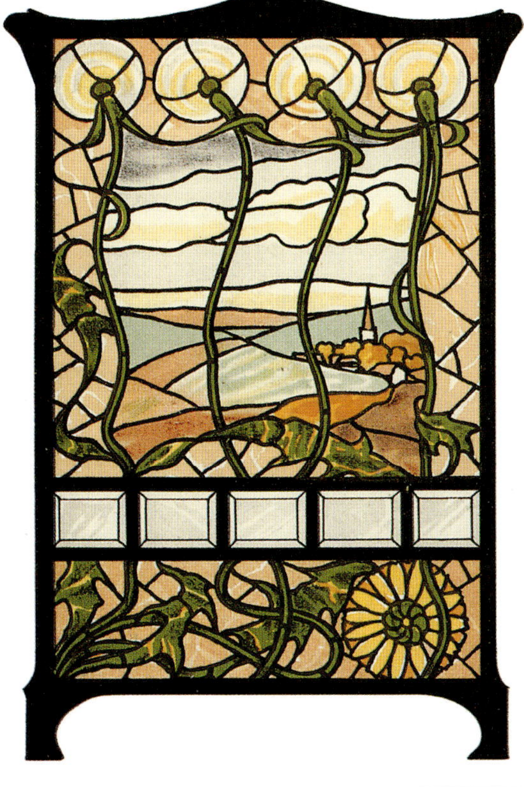
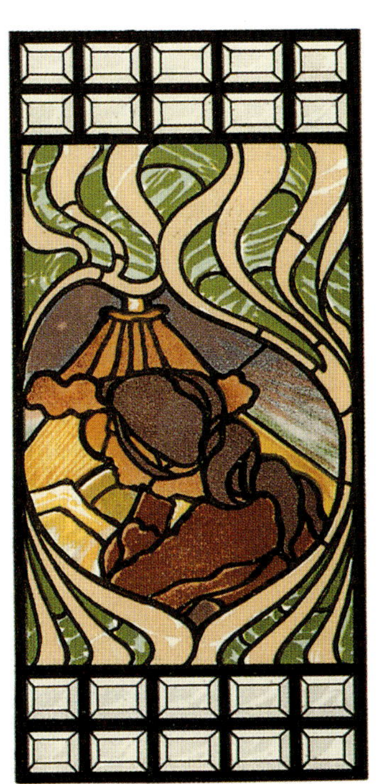

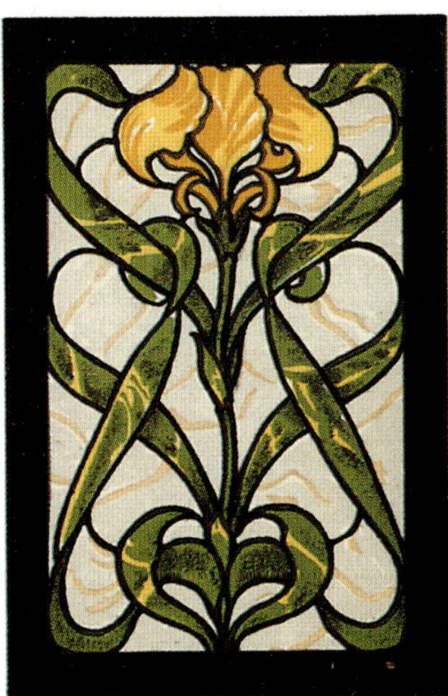

Images from *Vorbilder für Kunstverglasungen im Style der Neuzeit, Serie I* and *II* (Berlin and New York: Bruno Hessling, 1900). Reprinted by Dover as *Masterpieces of Art Nouveau Stained Glass Design: 91 Motifs in Full Color*, by Arnold Lyongrün (New York, 1989).

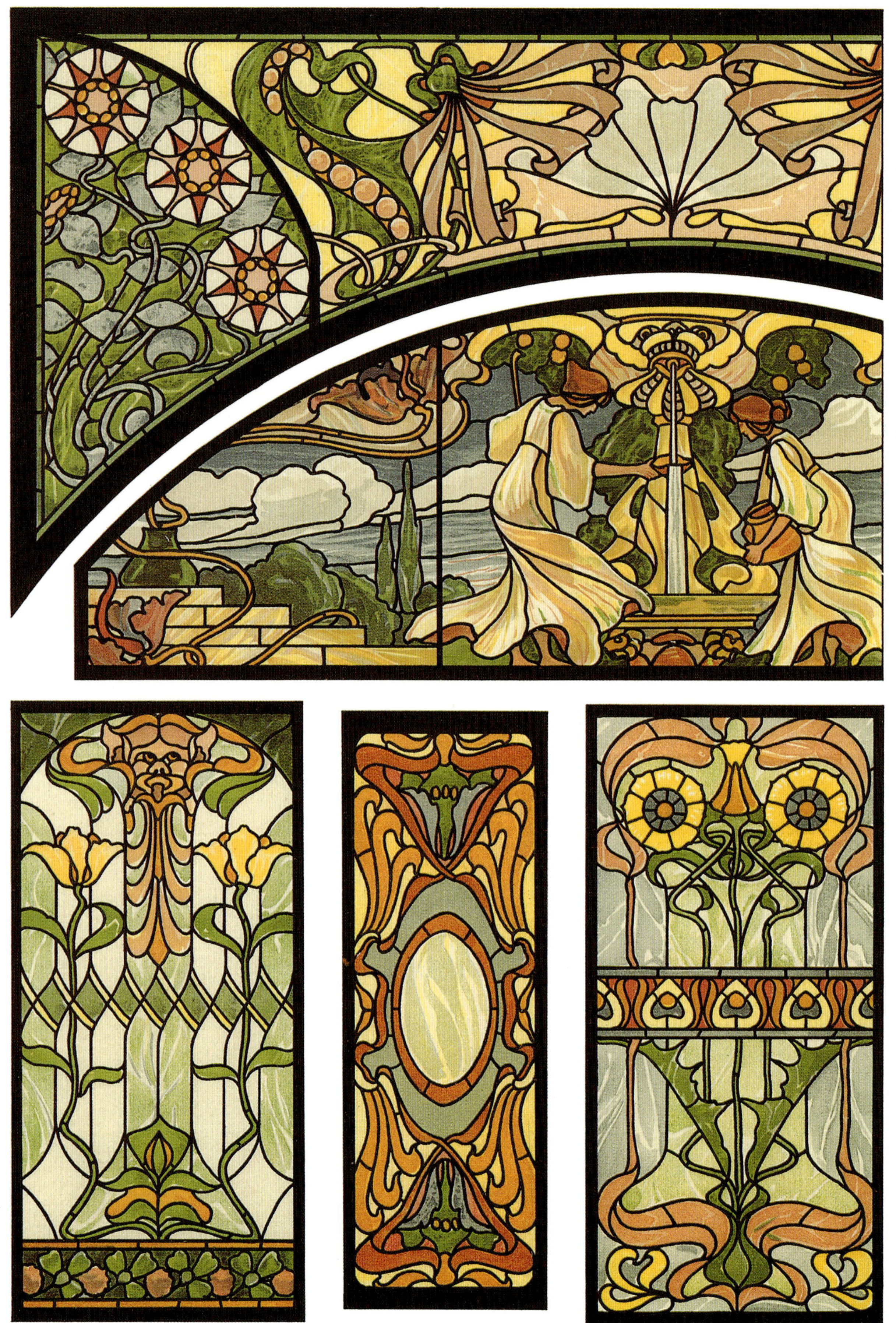

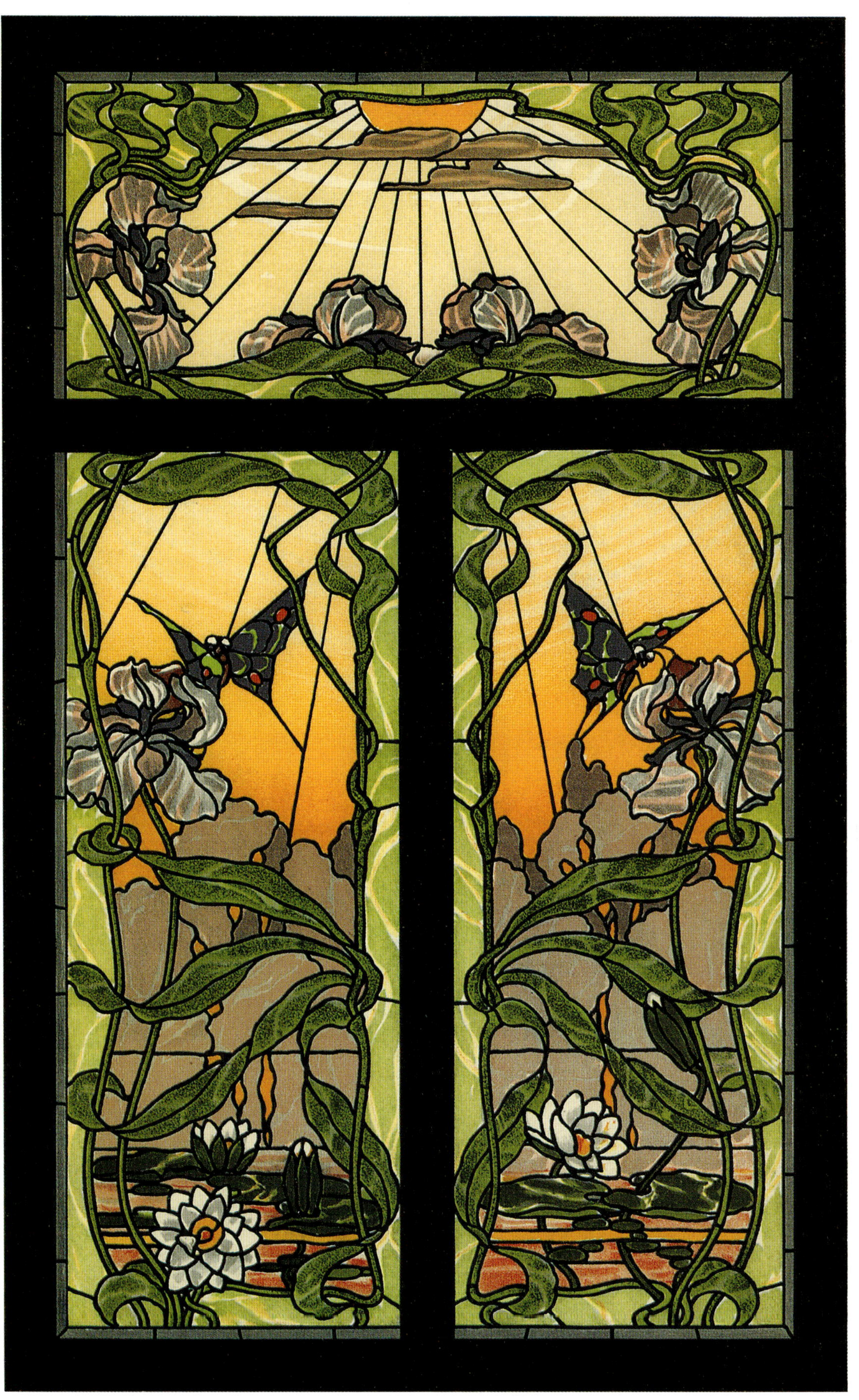

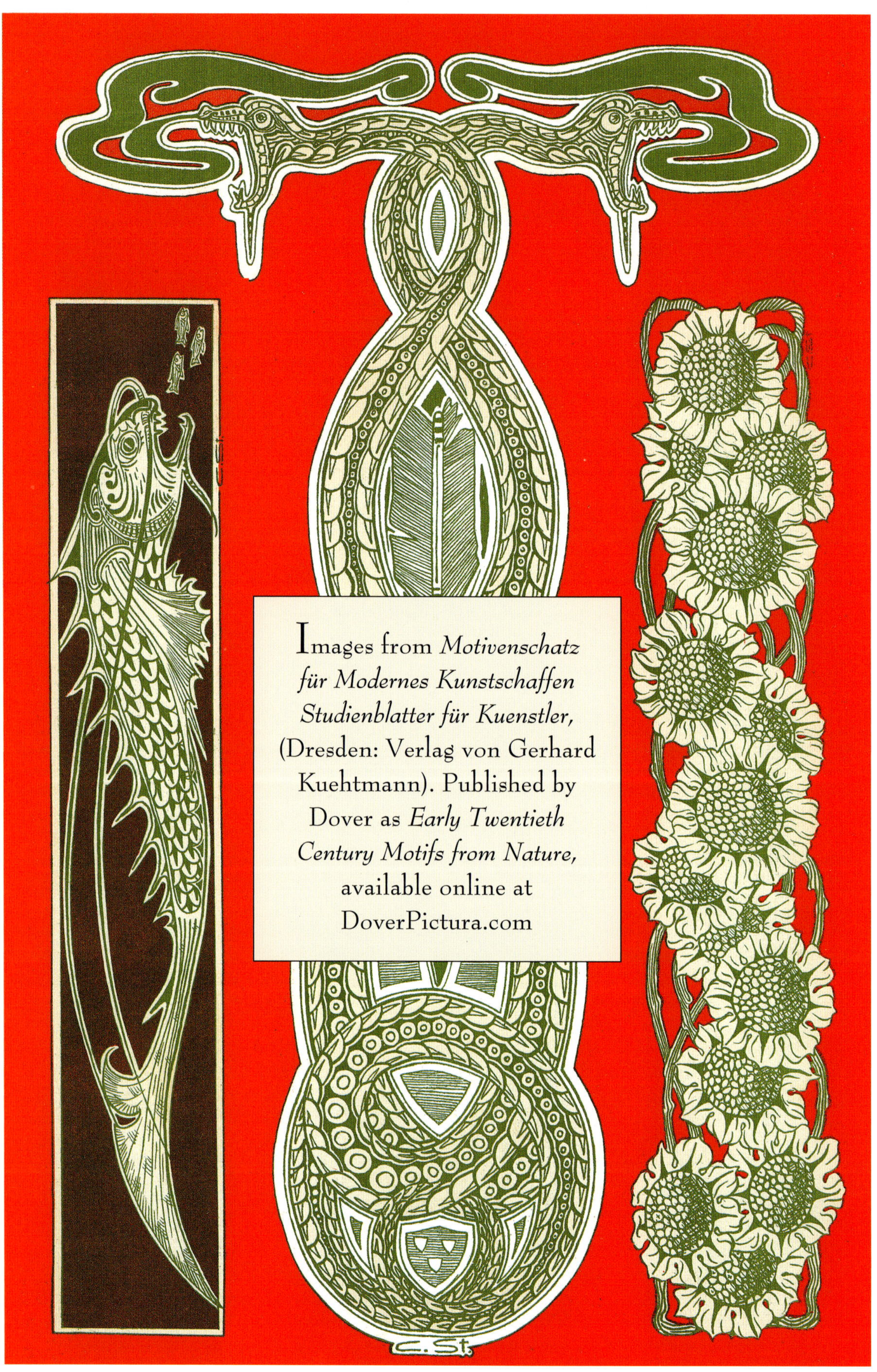

Images from *Motivenschatz für Modernes Kunstschaffen Studienblatter für Kuenstler*, (Dresden: Verlag von Gerhard Kuehtmann). Published by Dover as *Early Twentieth Century Motifs from Nature*, available online at DoverPictura.com

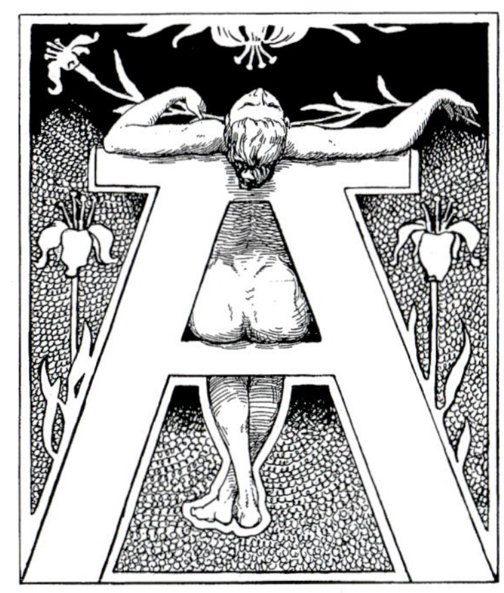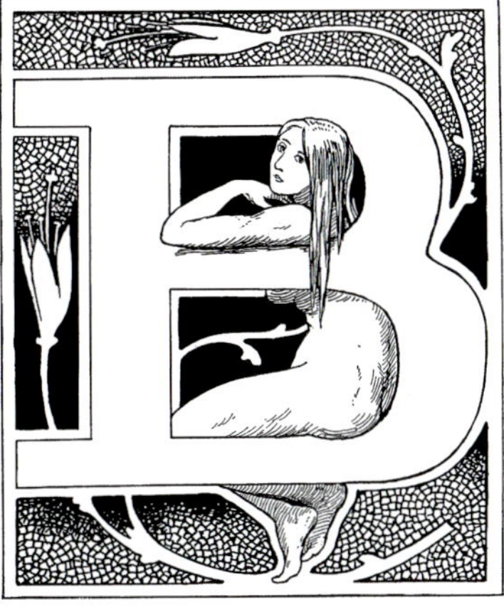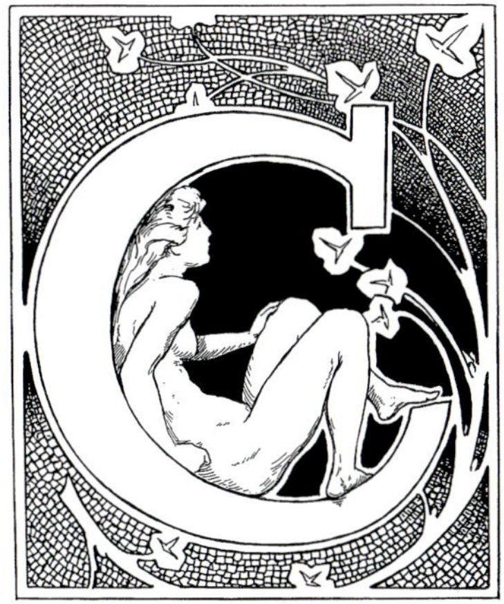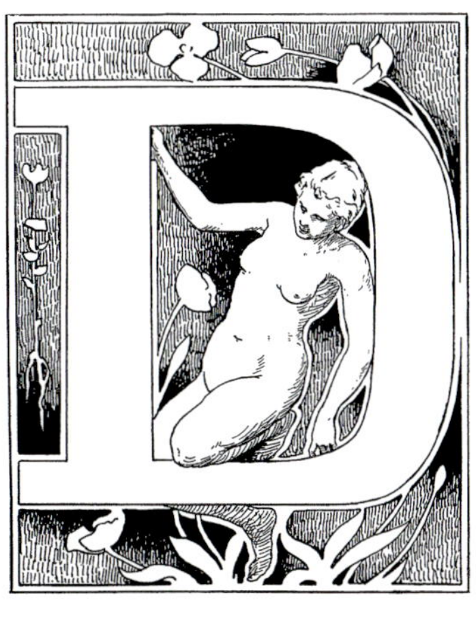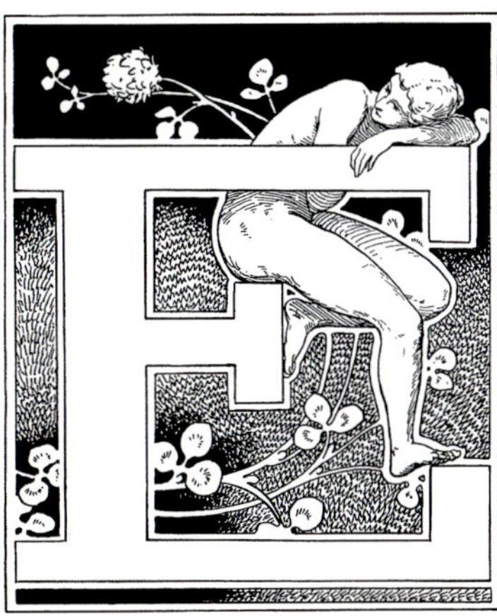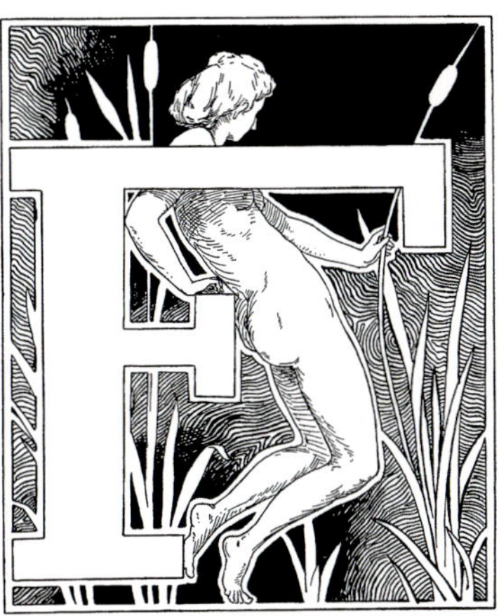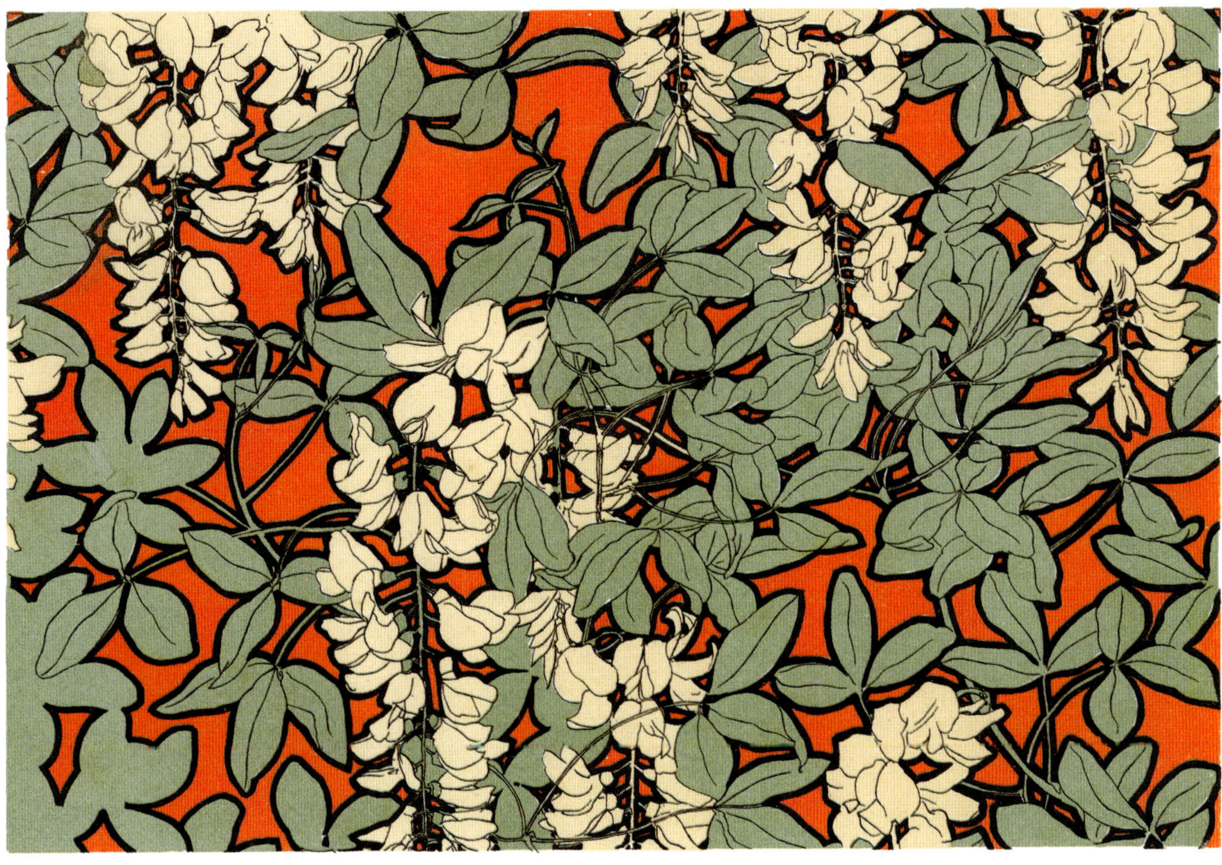

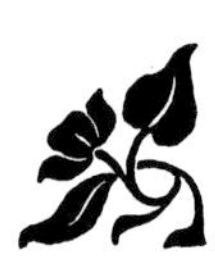
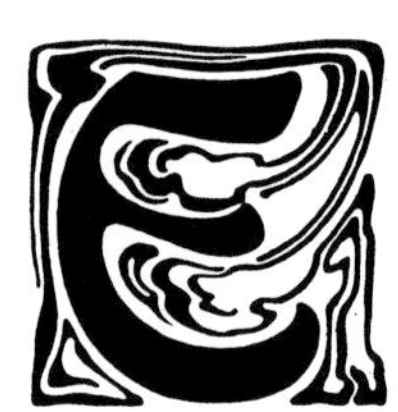
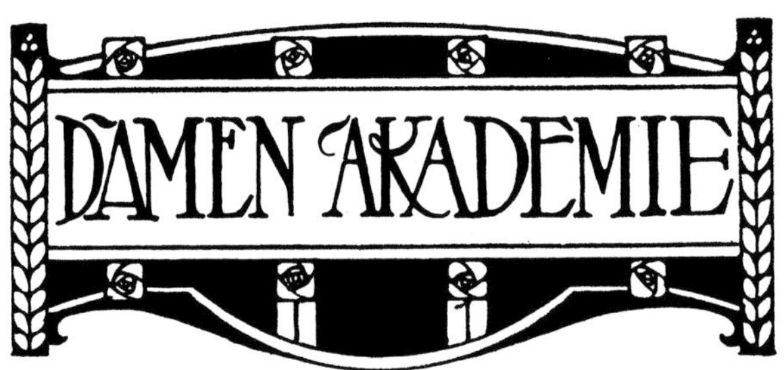

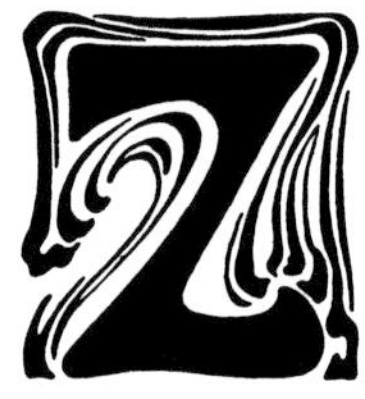
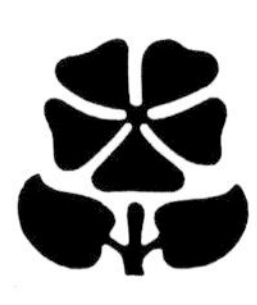

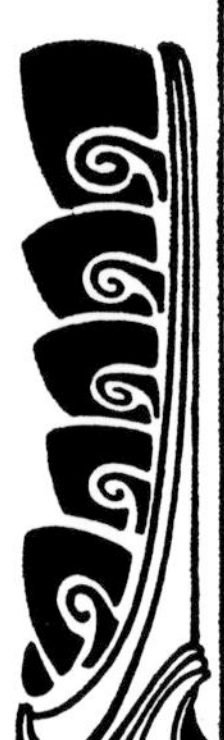

Images from *Schriftenatlas Neue Folge: Eine Sammlung von Alphabeten Initialen und Monogrammen*, edited by Ludwig Petzendorfer (Stuttgart: Julius Hoffmann, c. 1903). Reprinted by Dover as *Treasury of Authentic Art Nouveau Alphabets, Decorative Initials, Monograms, Frames and Ornaments* (New York, 1984).

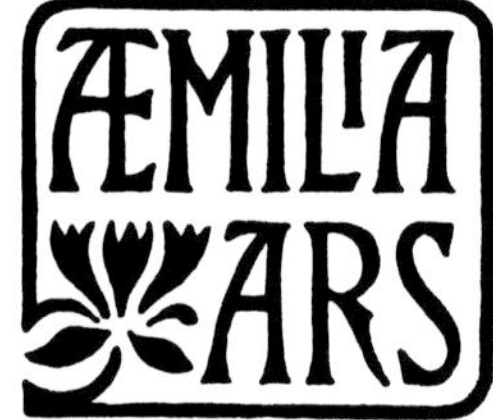

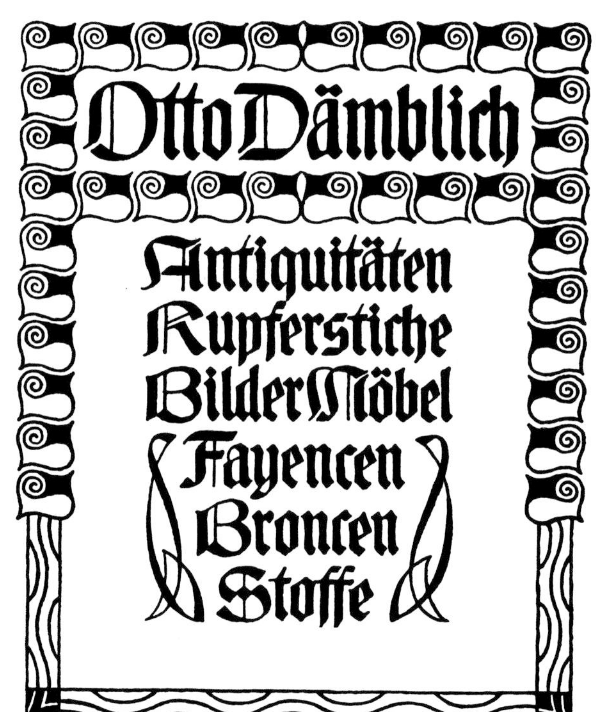

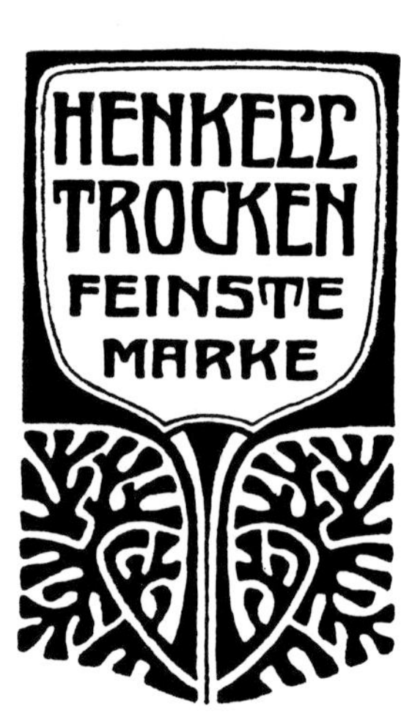

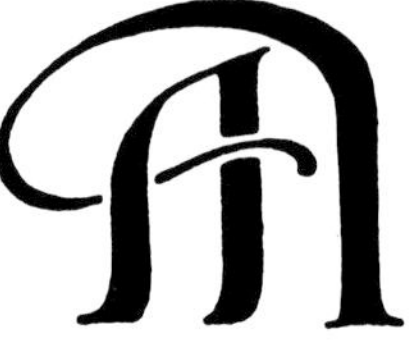

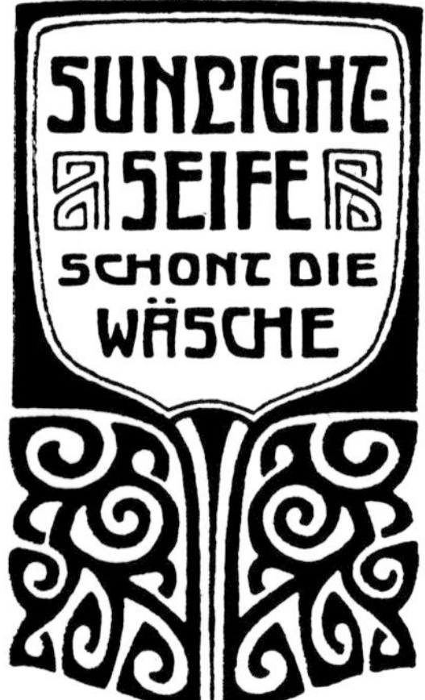

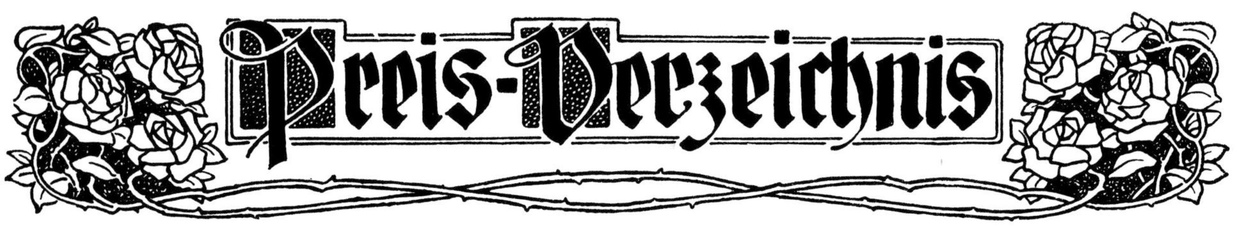

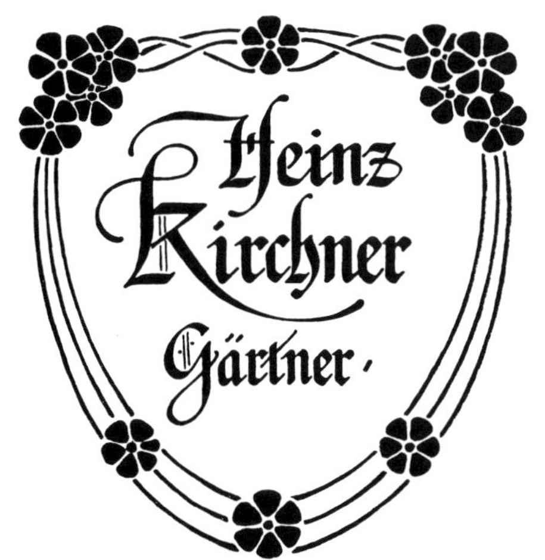

Heinz
Kirchner
Gärtner.

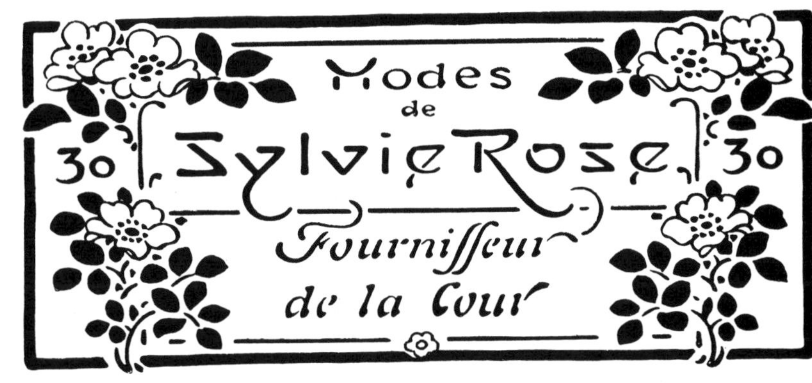

Modes
de
30 Sylvie Rose 30
Fournisseur
de la Cour

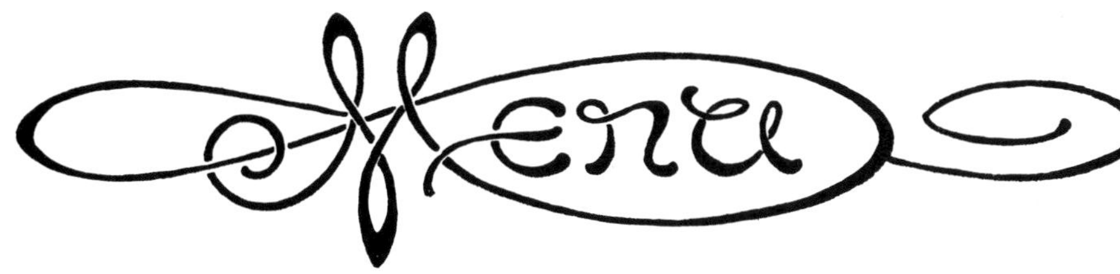

Menu

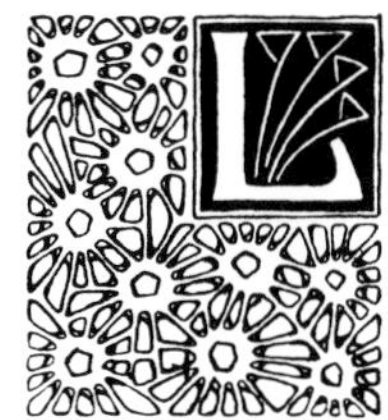

L

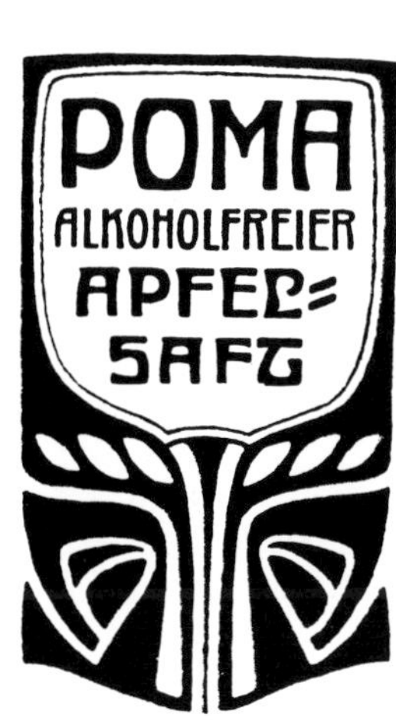

POMA
ALKOHOLFREIER
APFEL=
SAFT

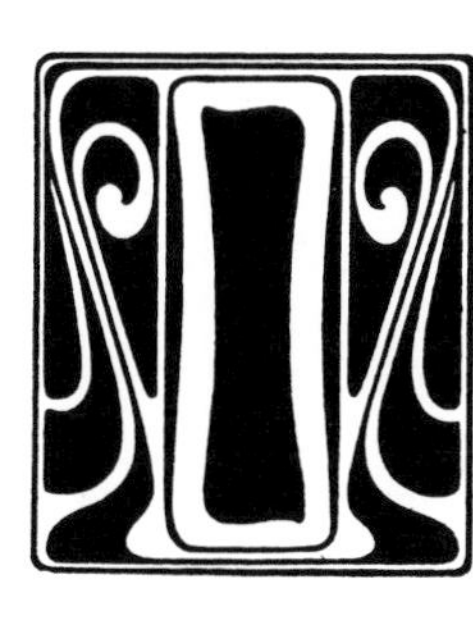

I

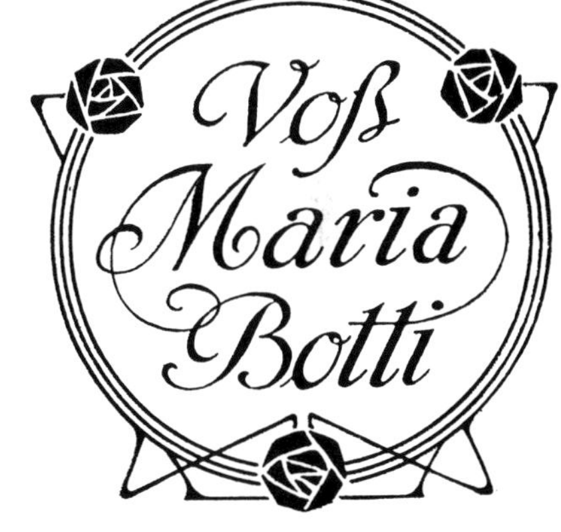

Voß
Maria
Botti

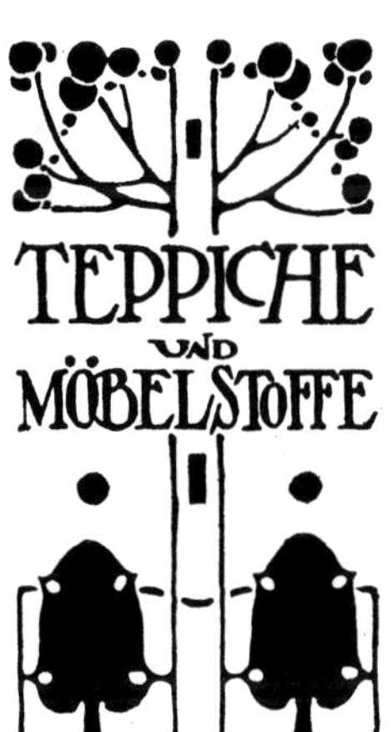

TEPPICHE
UND
MÖBELSTOFFE

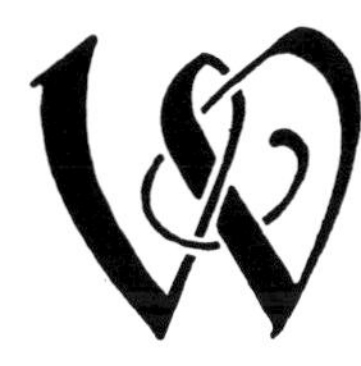

W

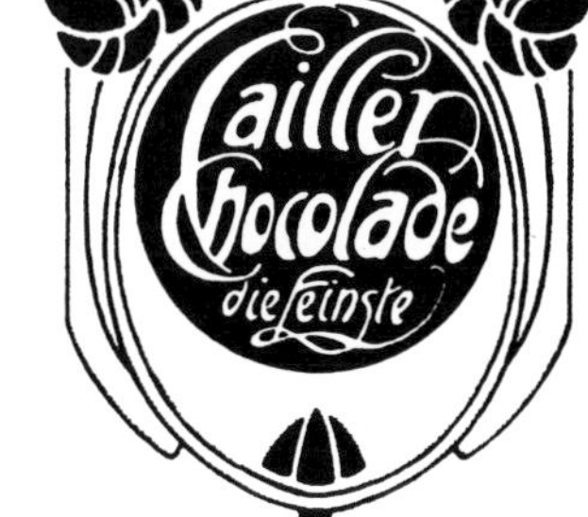

Cailler
Chocolade
die feinste

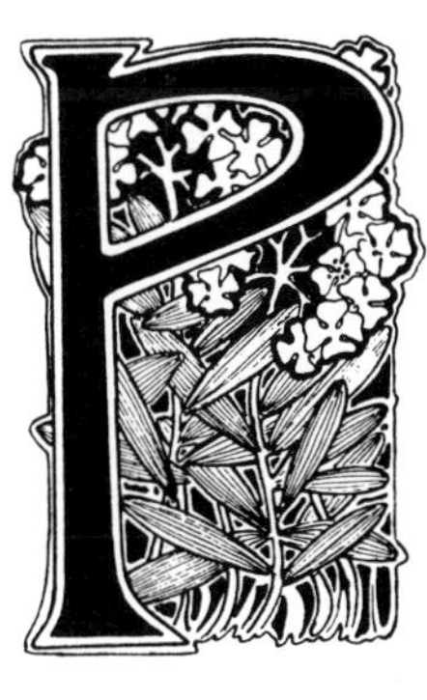

P

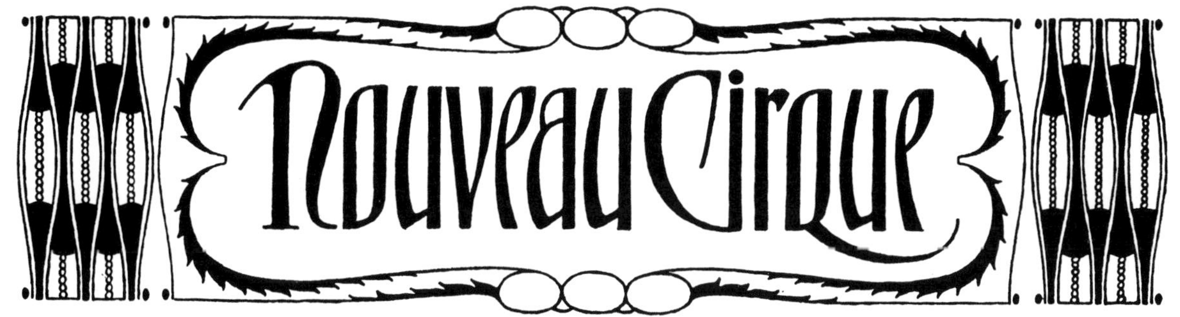

Nouveau Cirque

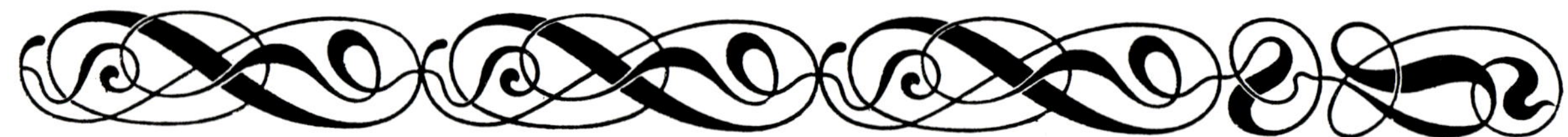

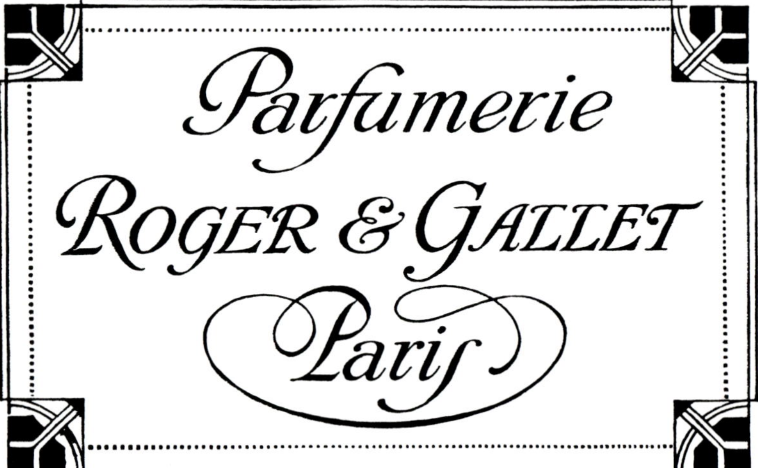
Parfumerie
Roger & Gallet
Paris

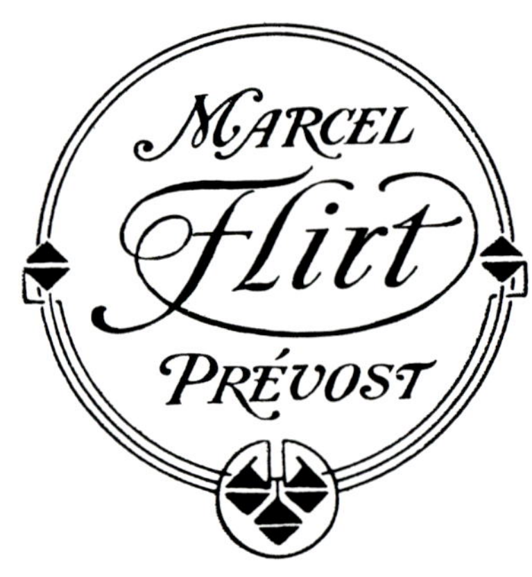
Marcel
Flirt
Prévost

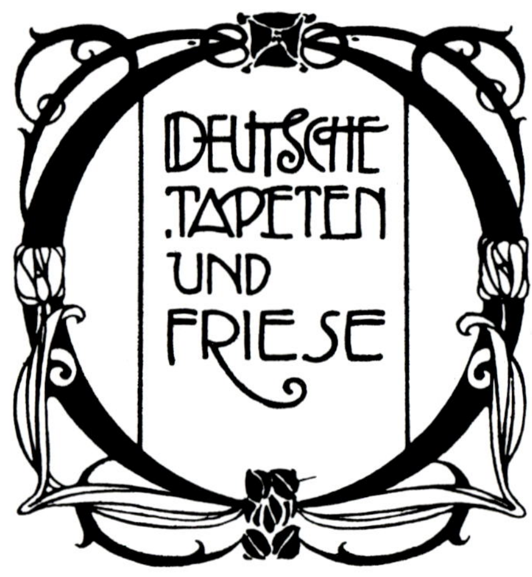
Deutsche
.Tapeten
und
Friese

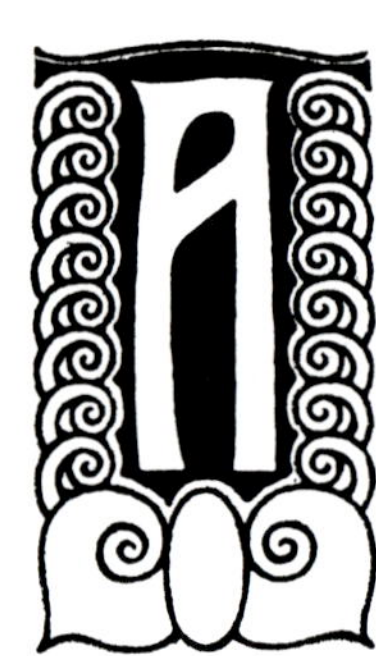
A

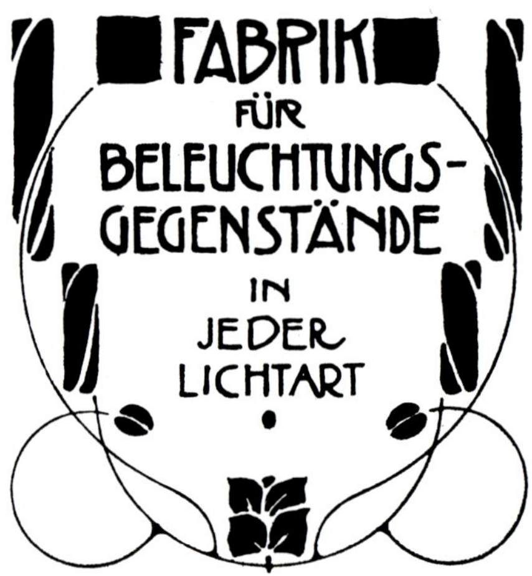
Fabrik
für
Beleuchtungs-
Gegenstände
in
jeder
Lichtart

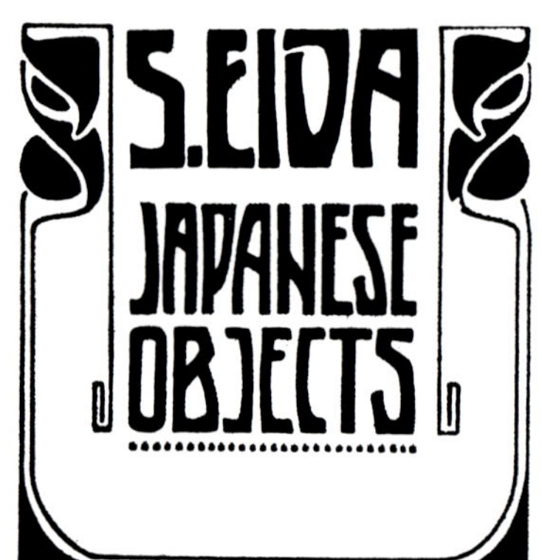
S. Eida
Japanese
Objects

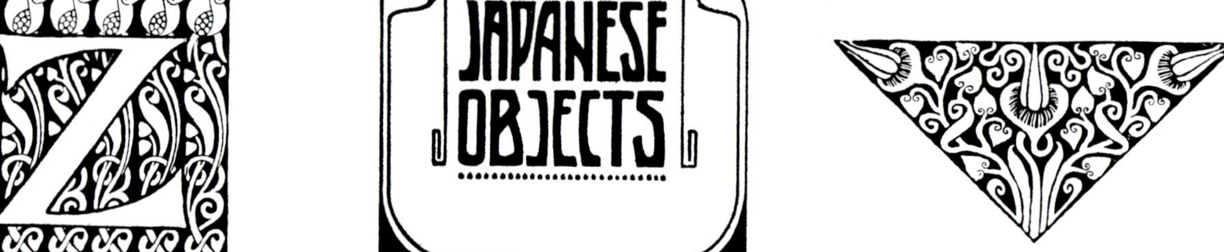
Z

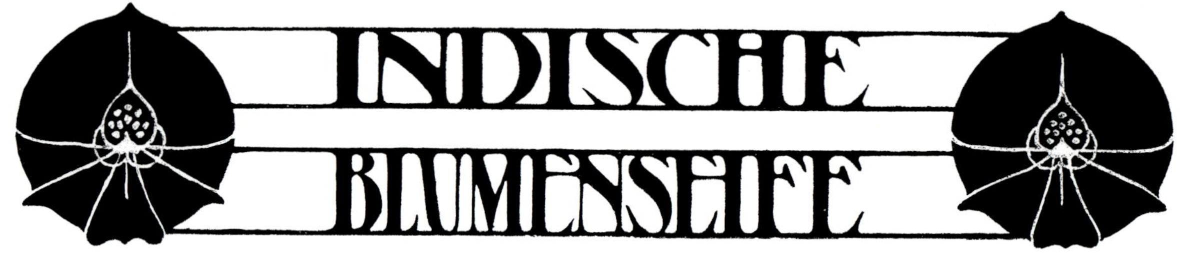
Indische
Blumenseife

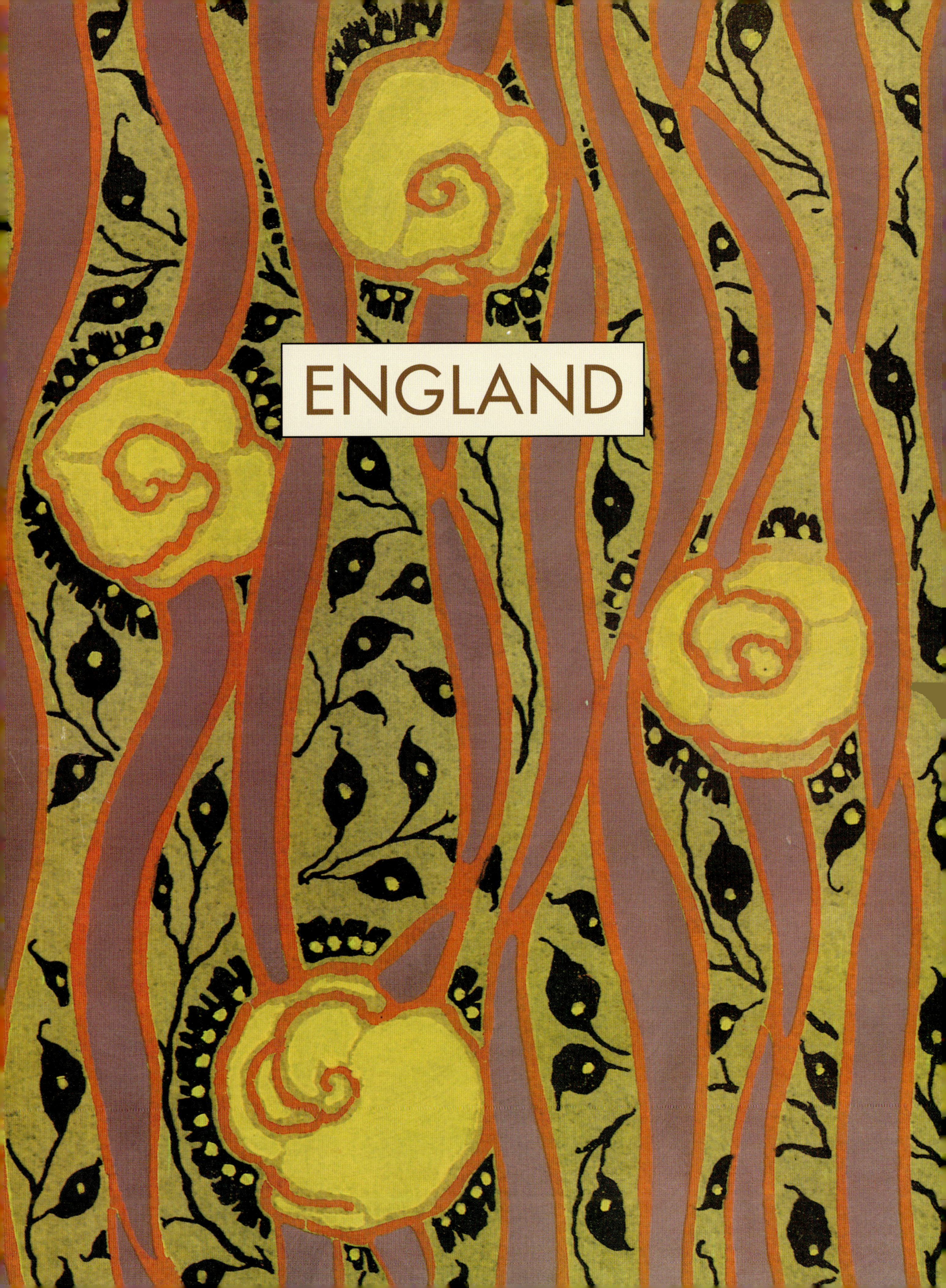

ENGLAND

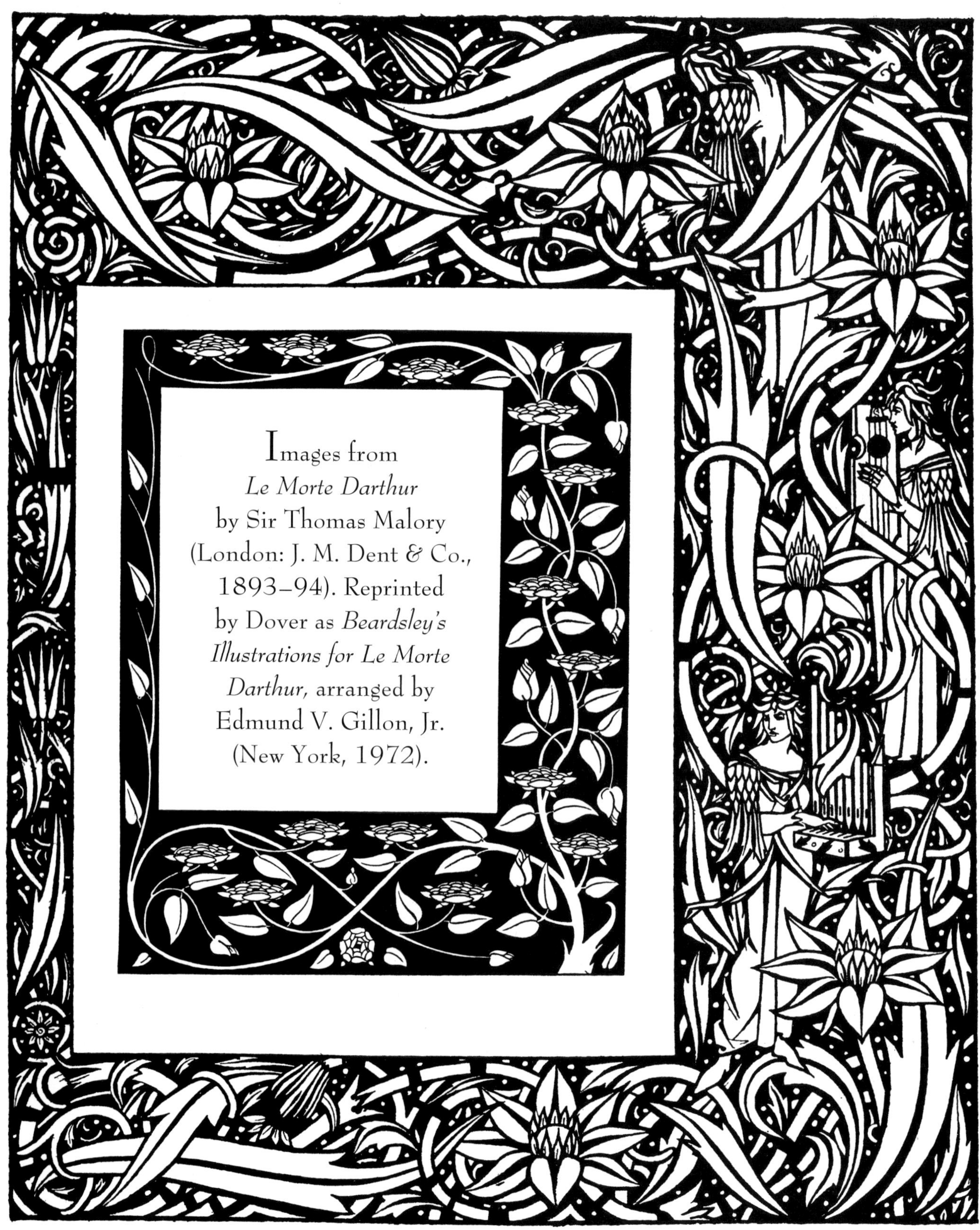

Images from
Le Morte Darthur
by Sir Thomas Malory
(London: J. M. Dent & Co.,
1893–94). Reprinted
by Dover as Beardsley's
Illustrations for Le Morte
Darthur, arranged by
Edmund V. Gillon, Jr.
(New York, 1972).

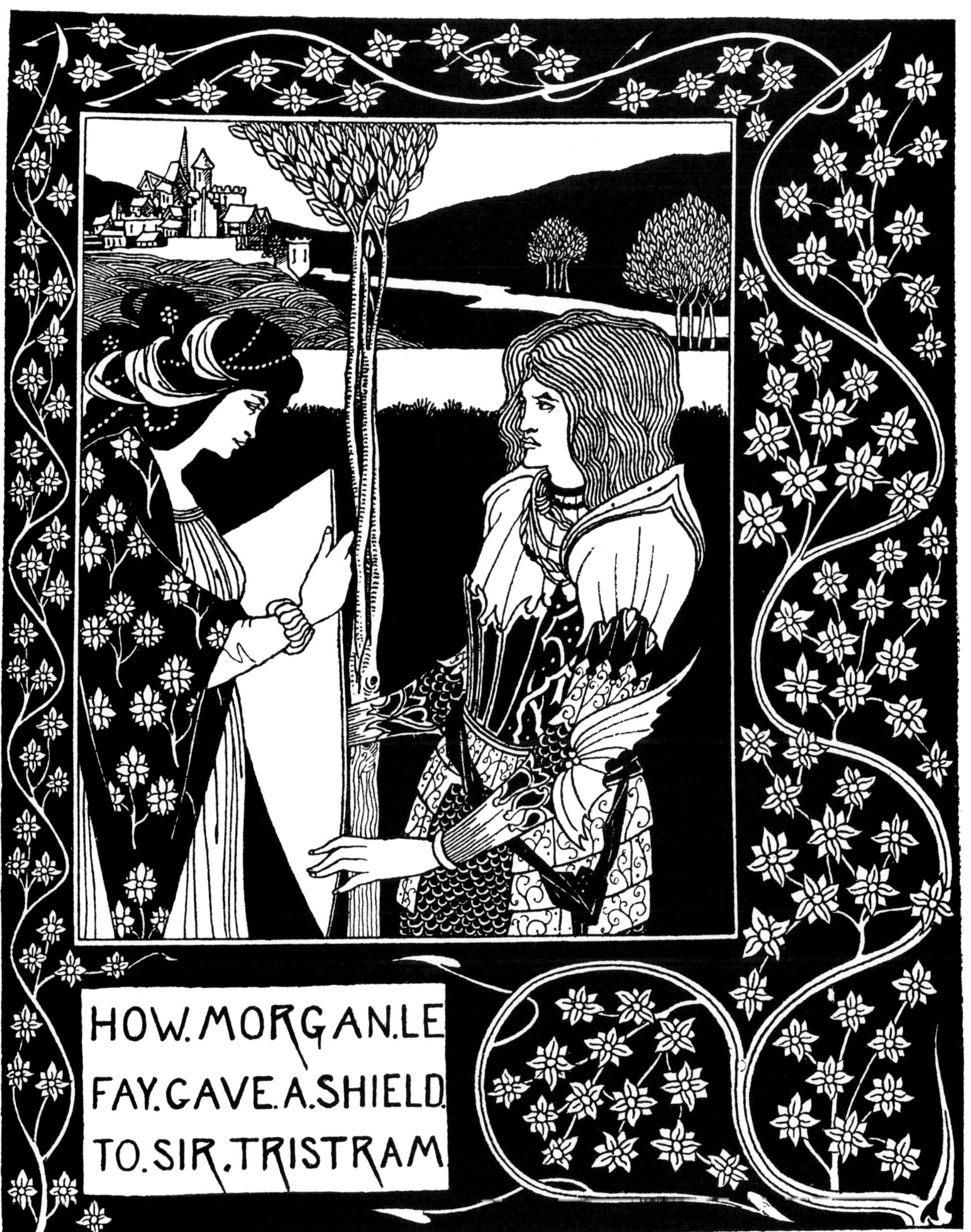

HOW. MORGAN. LE
FAY. GAVE. A. SHIELD.
TO. SIR. TRISTRAM

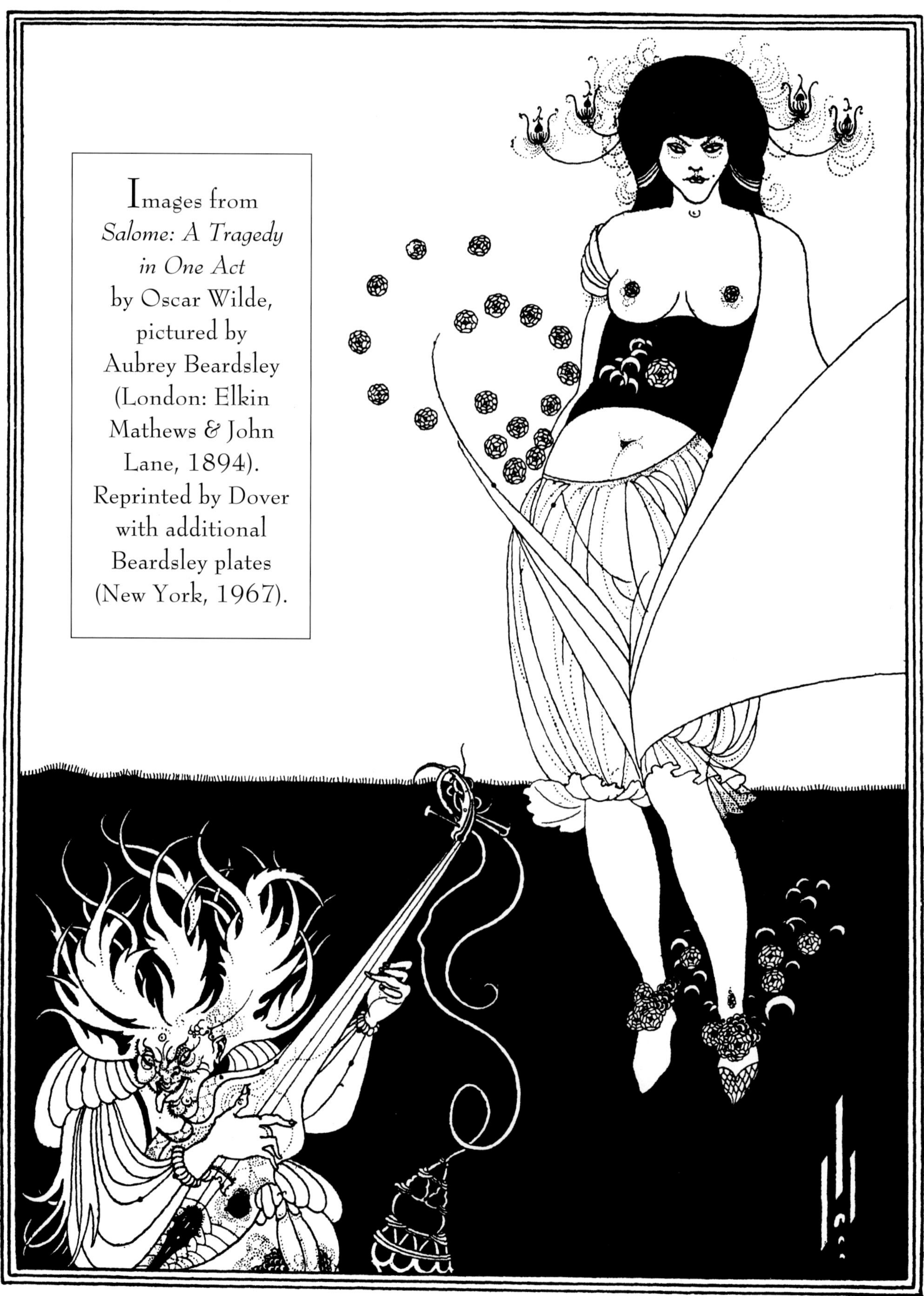

Images from
*Salome: A Tragedy
in One Act*
by Oscar Wilde,
pictured by
Aubrey Beardsley
(London: Elkin
Mathews & John
Lane, 1894).
Reprinted by Dover
with additional
Beardsley plates
(New York, 1967).

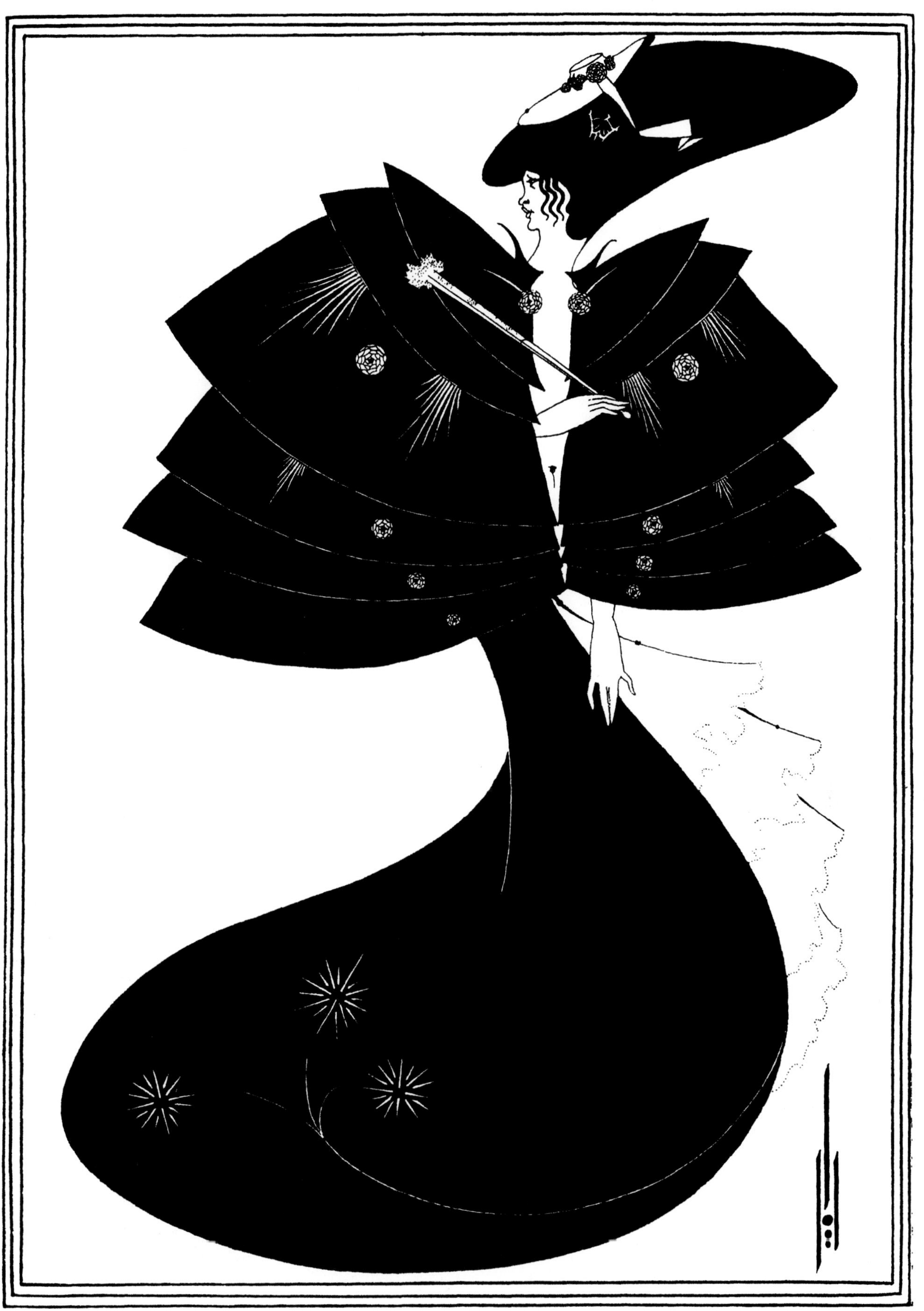

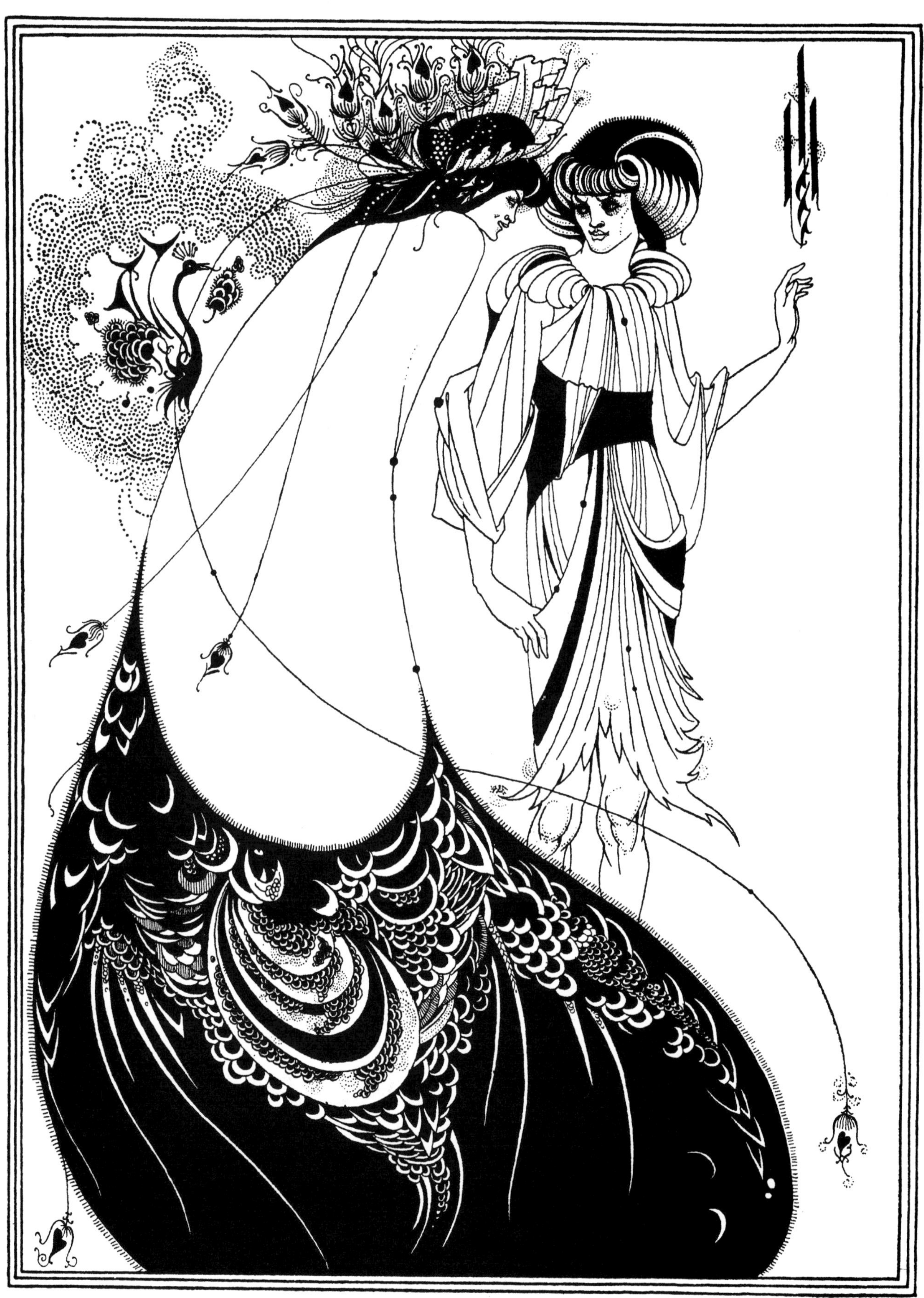

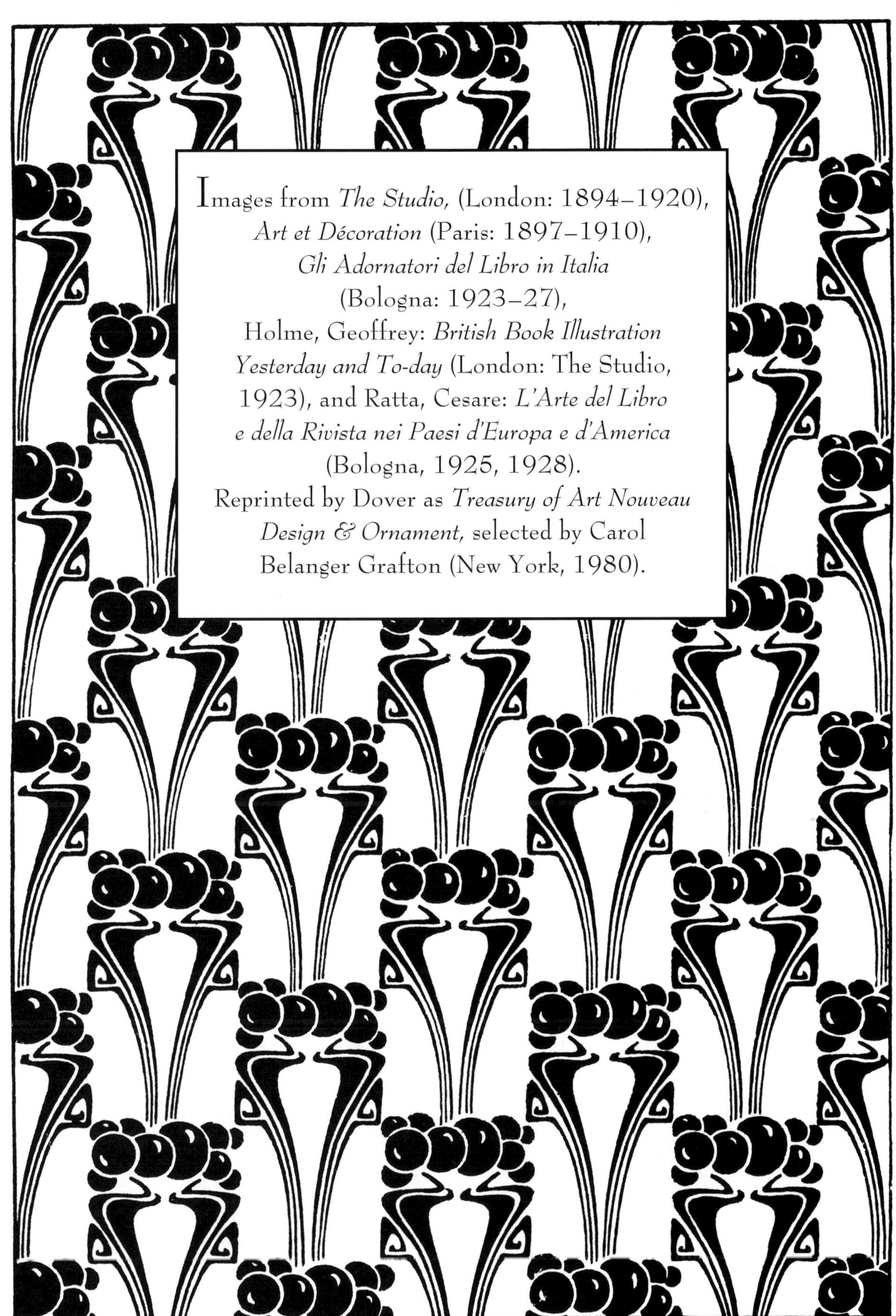

Images from *The Studio*, (London: 1894–1920),
Art et Décoration (Paris: 1897–1910),
Gli Adornatori del Libro in Italia
(Bologna: 1923–27),
Holme, Geoffrey: *British Book Illustration
Yesterday and To-day* (London: The Studio,
1923), and Ratta, Cesare: *L'Arte del Libro
e della Rivista nei Paesi d'Europa e d'America*
(Bologna, 1925, 1928).
Reprinted by Dover as *Treasury of Art Nouveau
Design & Ornament,* selected by Carol
Belanger Grafton (New York, 1980).

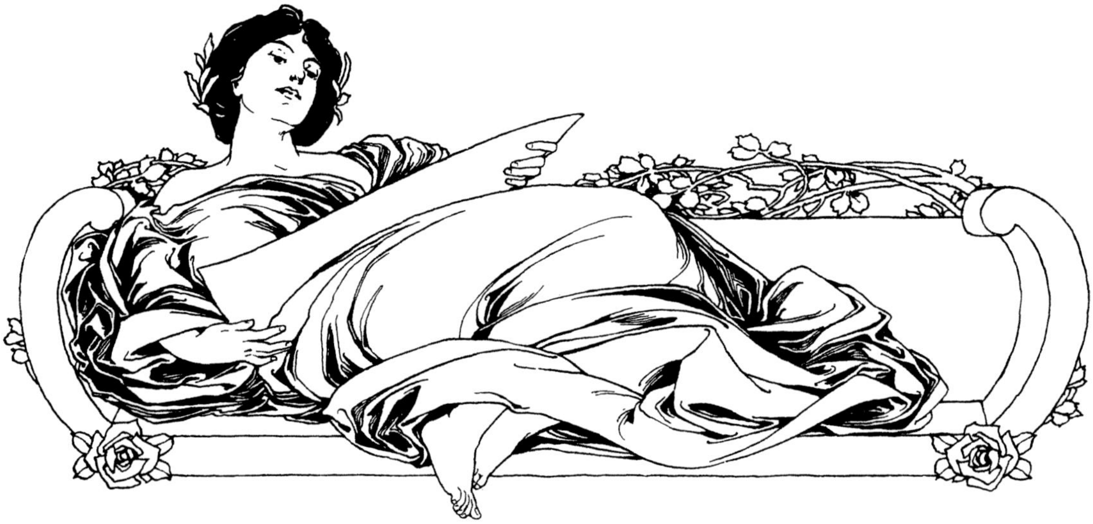

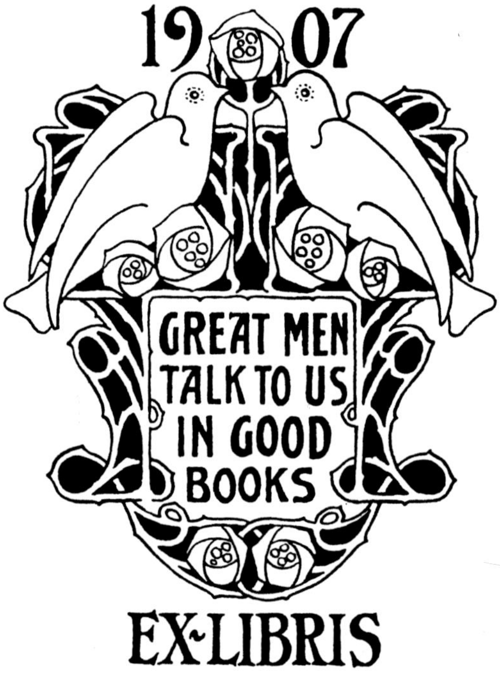

1907
GREAT MEN
TALK TO US
IN GOOD
BOOKS
EX-LIBRIS 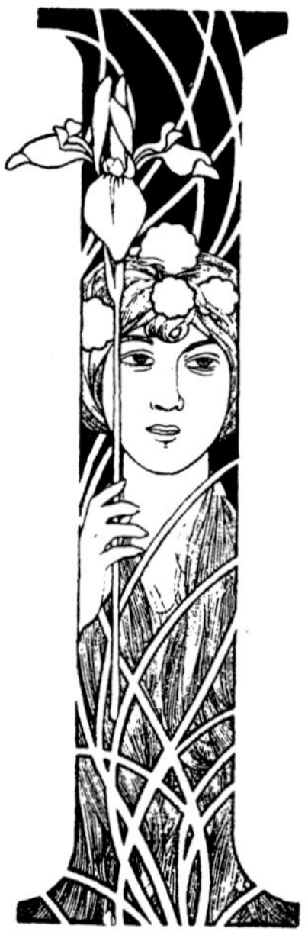
MENU 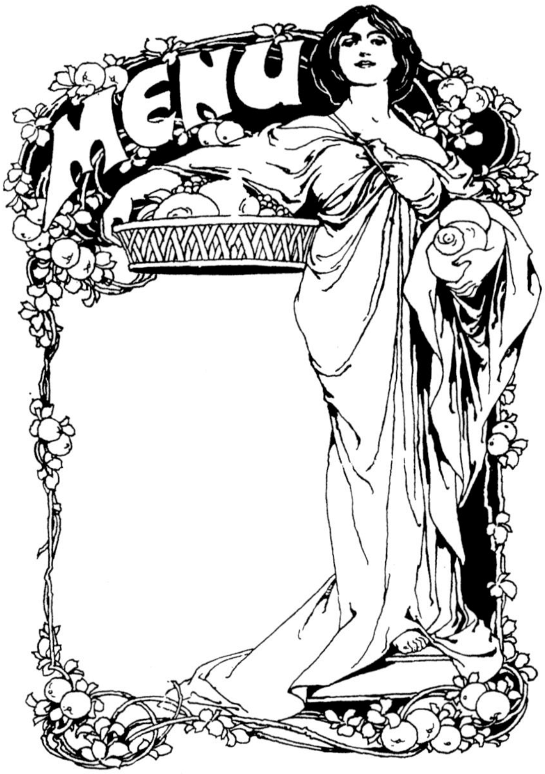

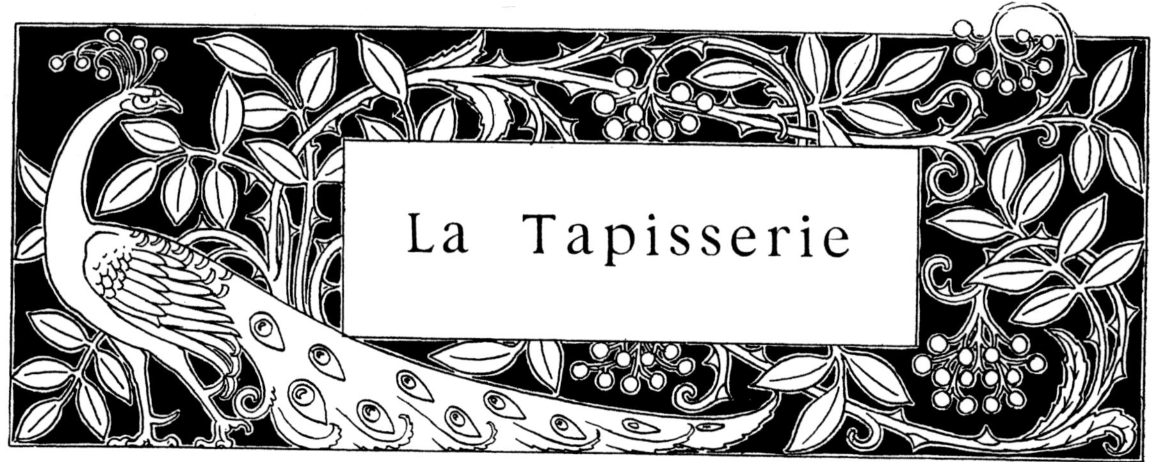

La Tapisserie

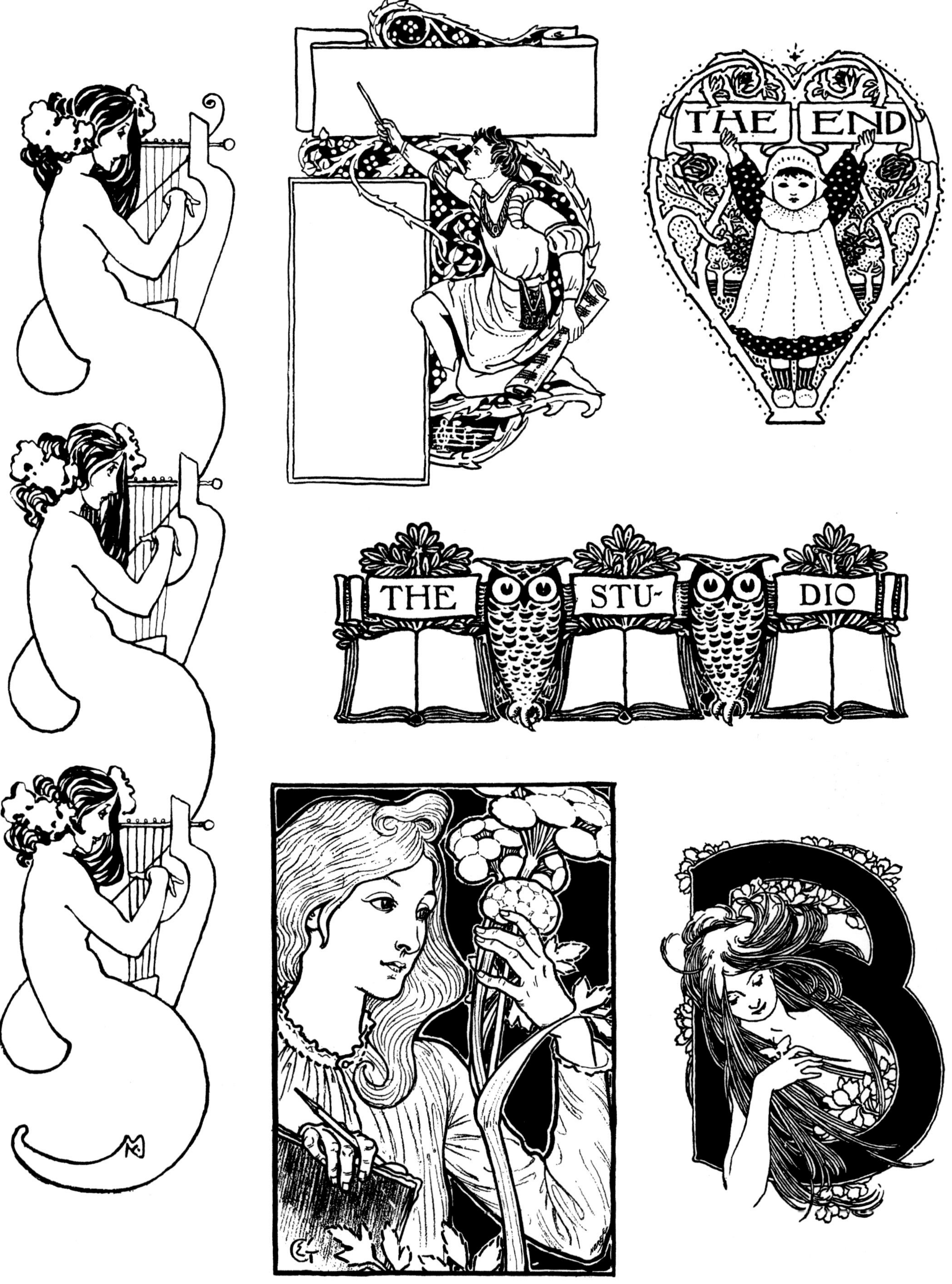
THE END
THE STU- DIO

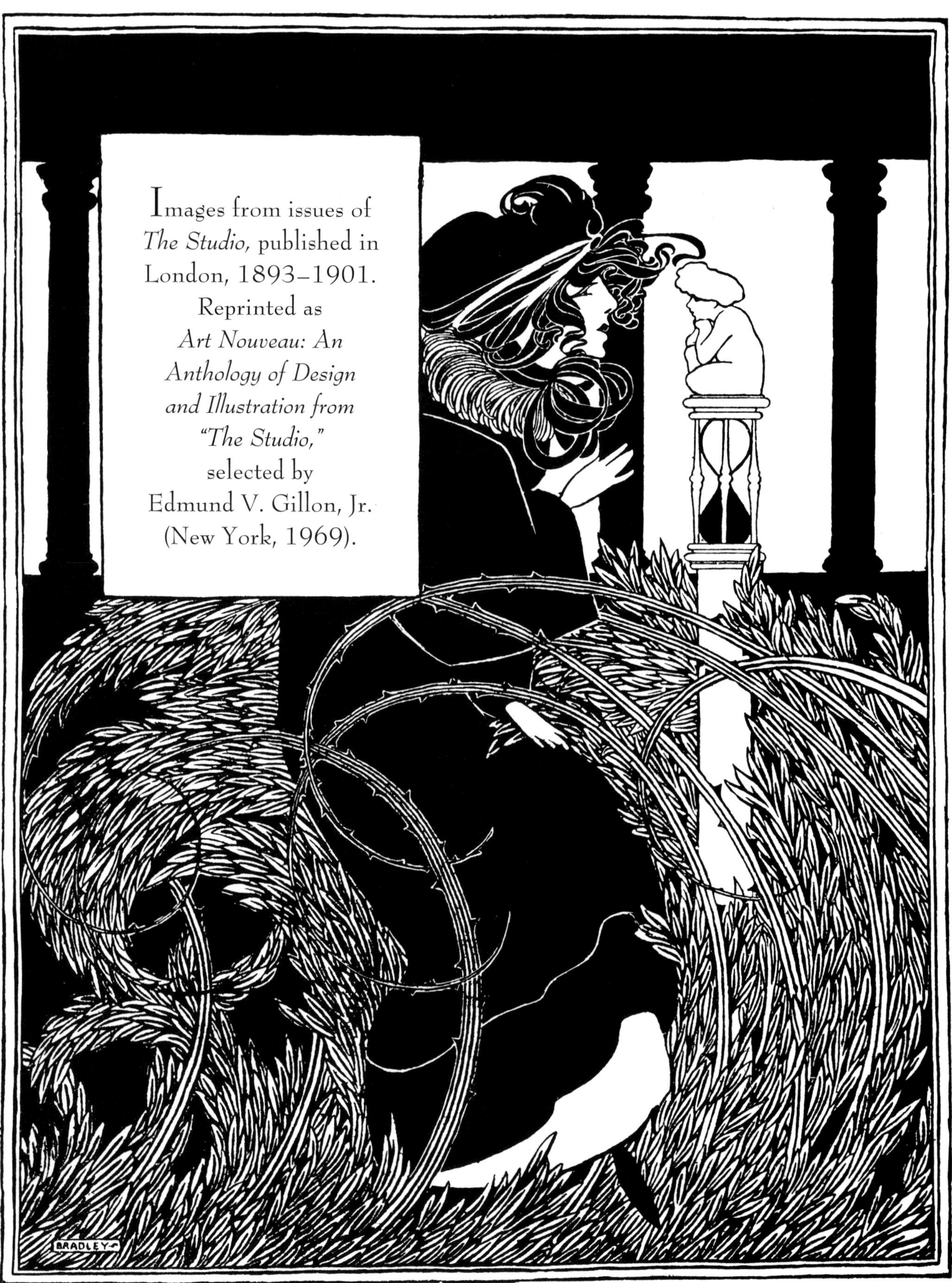

Images from issues of
The Studio, published in
London, 1893–1901.
Reprinted as
Art Nouveau: An
Anthology of Design
and Illustration from
"The Studio,"
selected by
Edmund V. Gillon, Jr.
(New York, 1969).

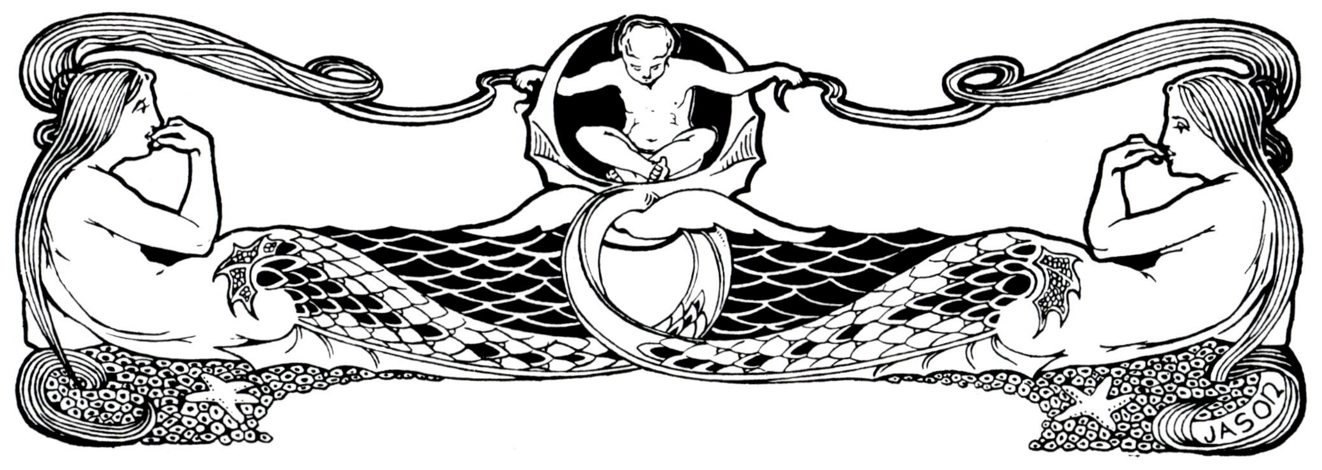

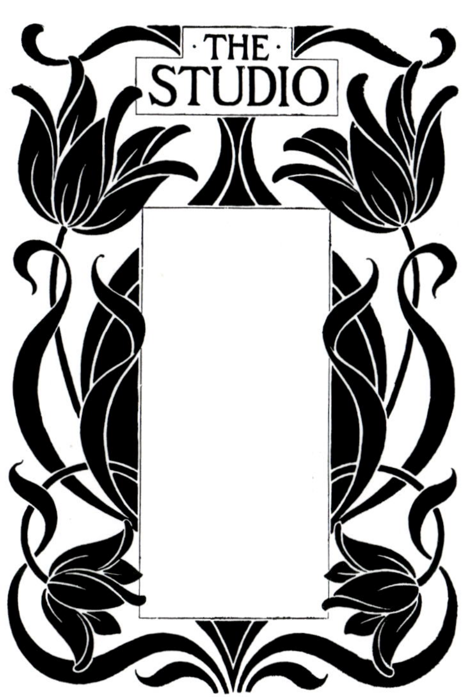

THE
STUDIO

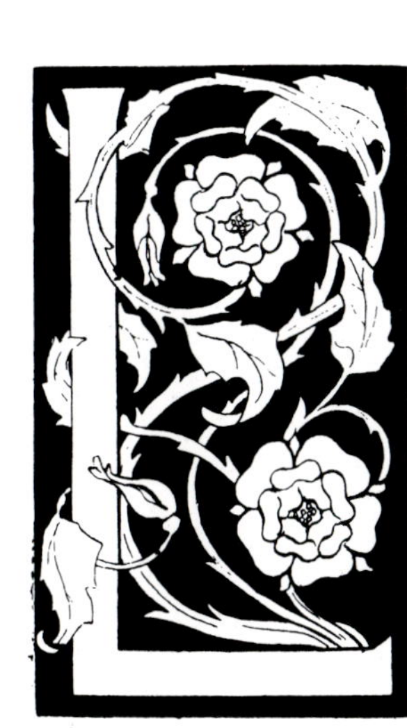

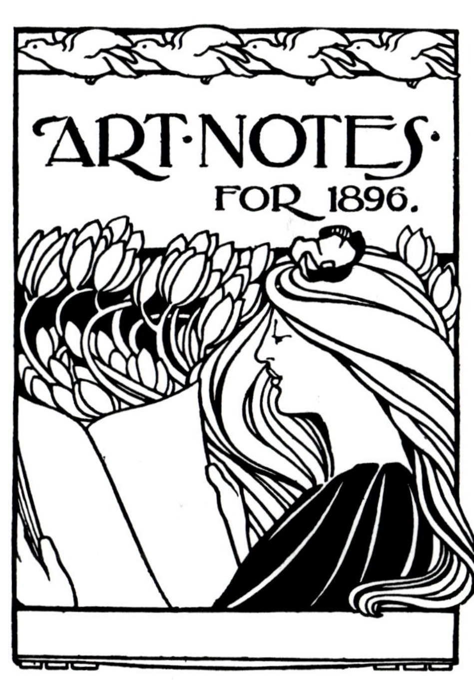

ART·NOTES·
FOR 1896.

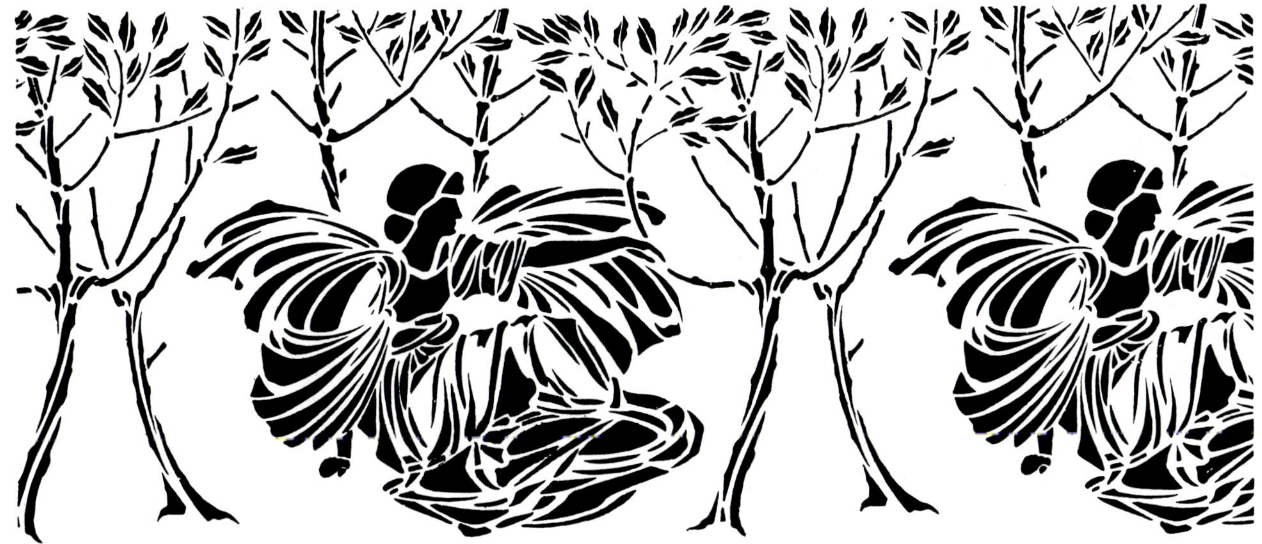

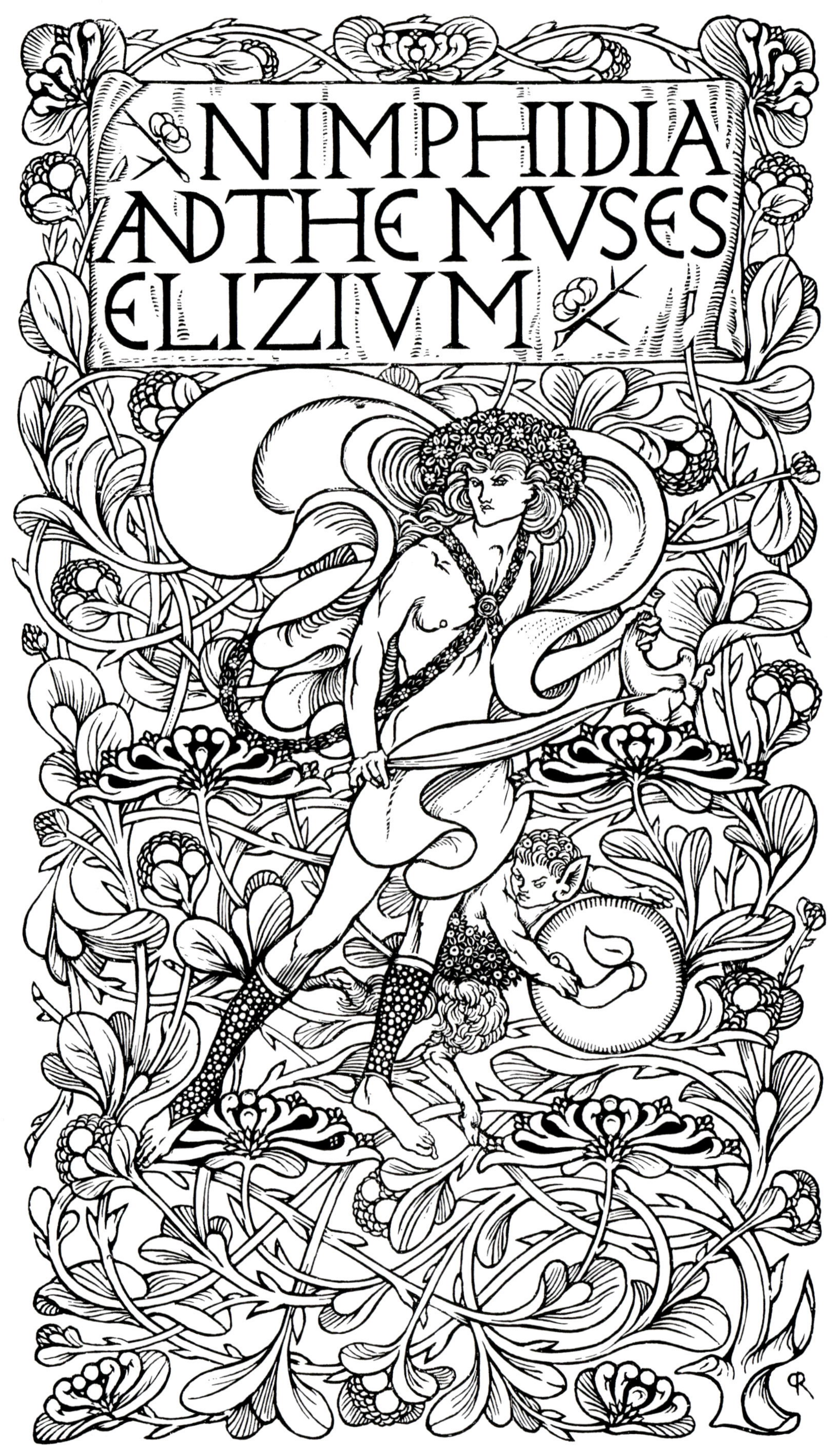

NIMPHIDIA
AND THE MVSES
ELIZIVM

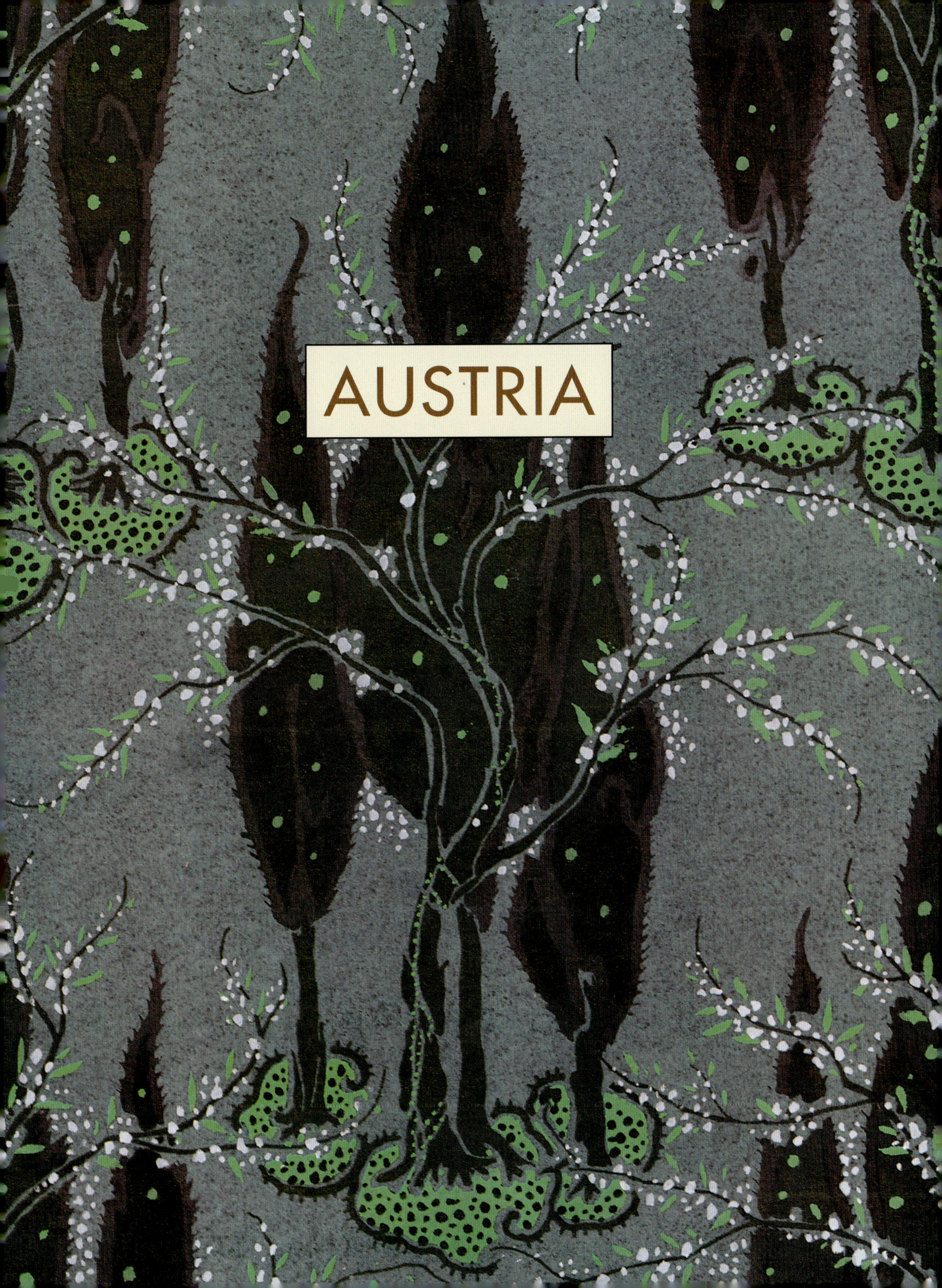
AUSTRIA

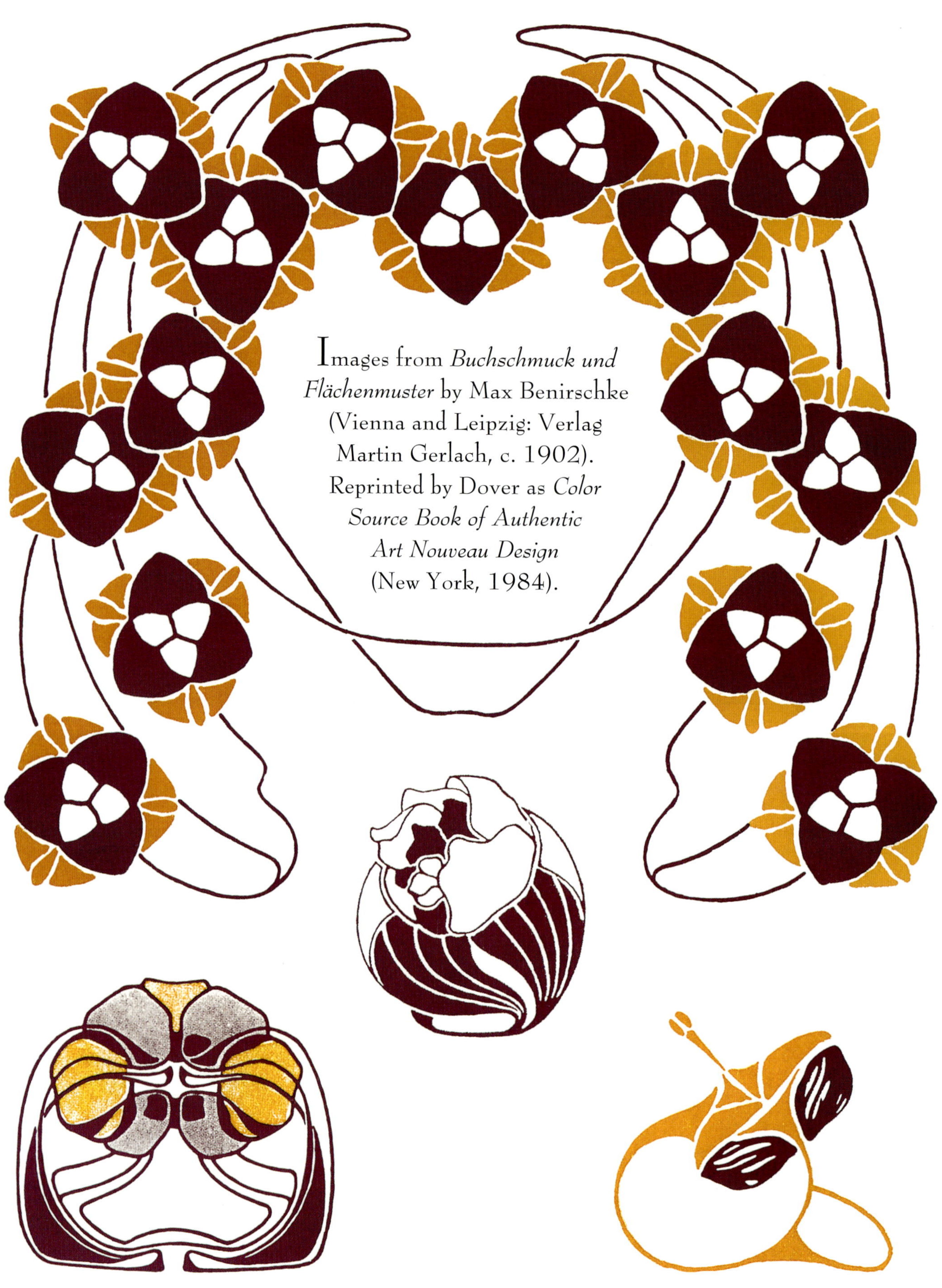

Images from *Buchschmuck und Flächenmuster* by Max Benirschke (Vienna and Leipzig: Verlag Martin Gerlach, c. 1902). Reprinted by Dover as *Color Source Book of Authentic Art Nouveau Design* (New York, 1984).

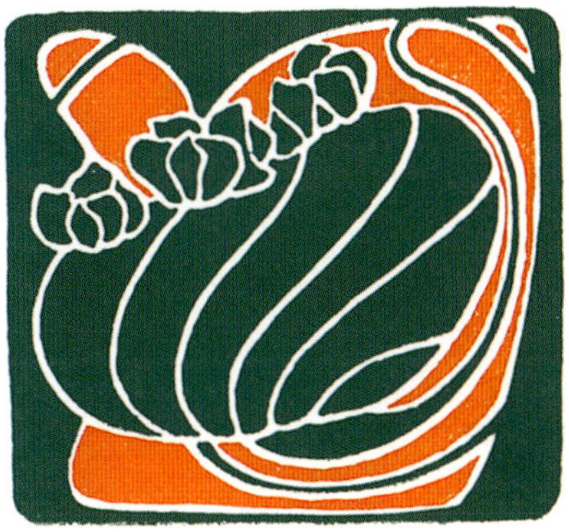

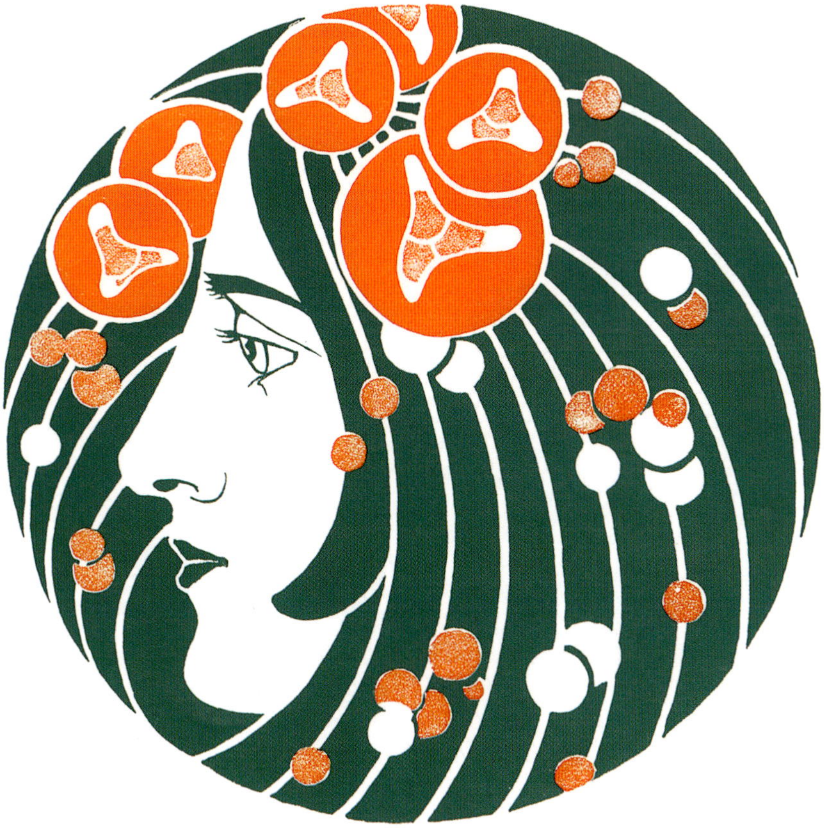

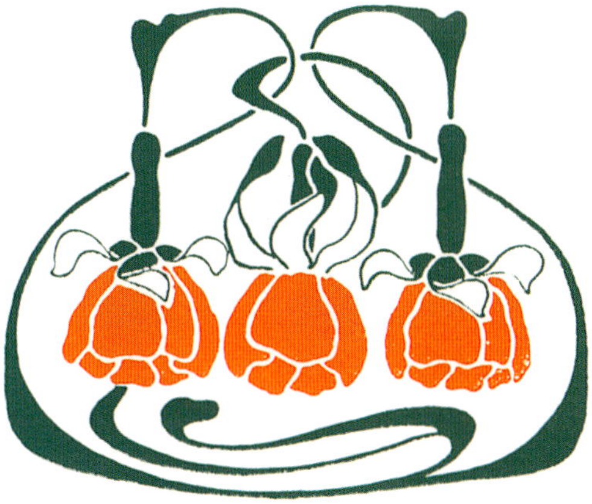

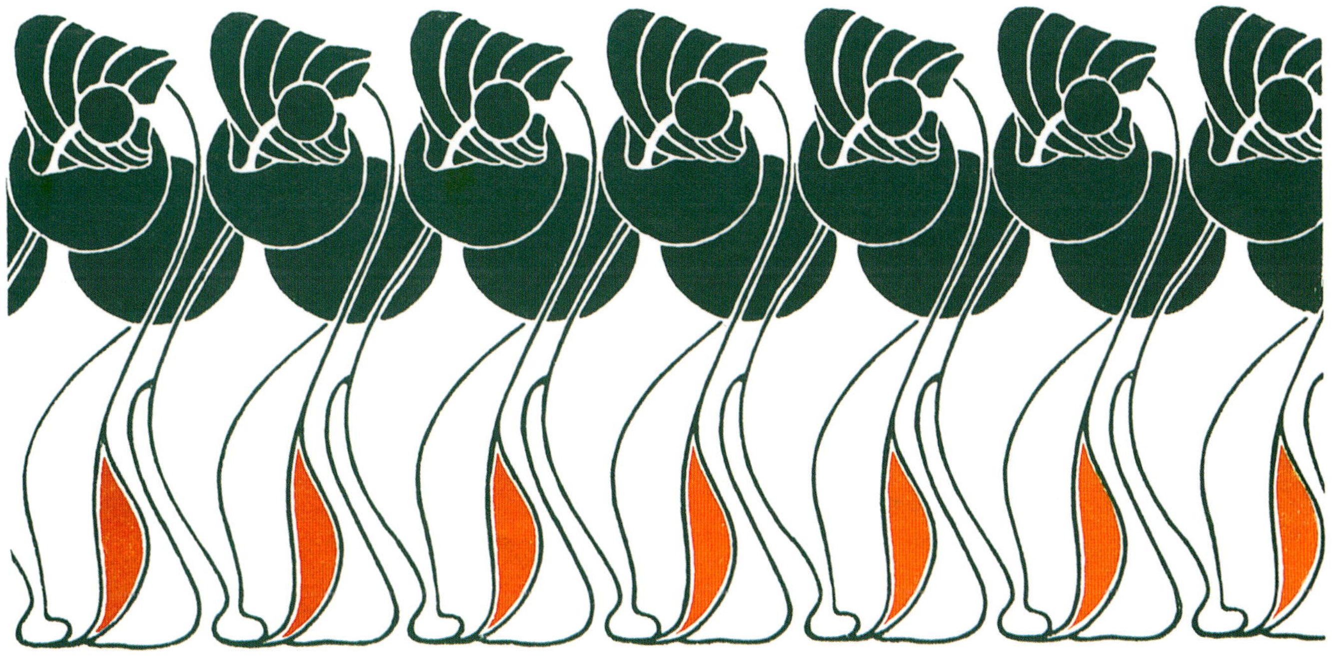

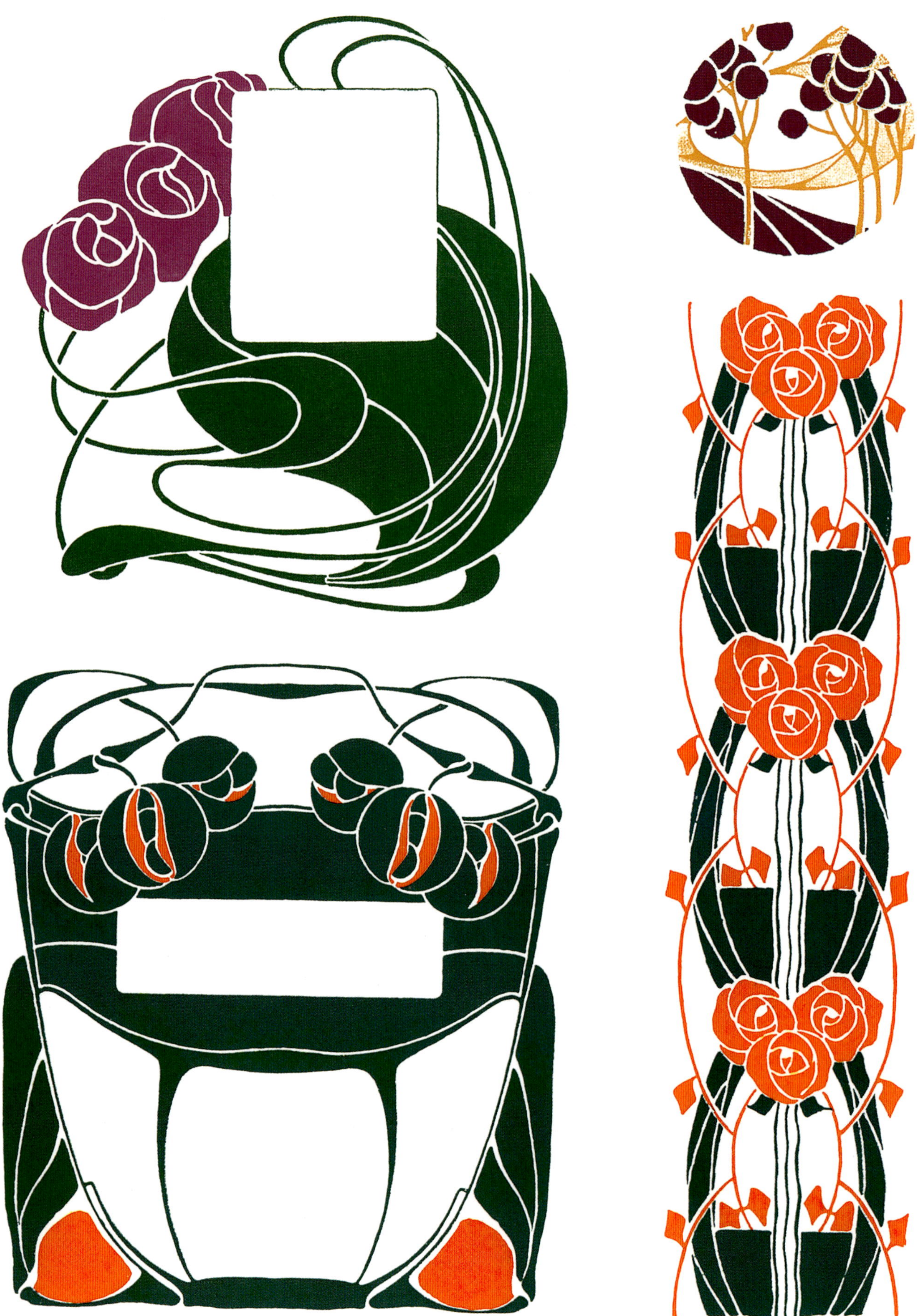

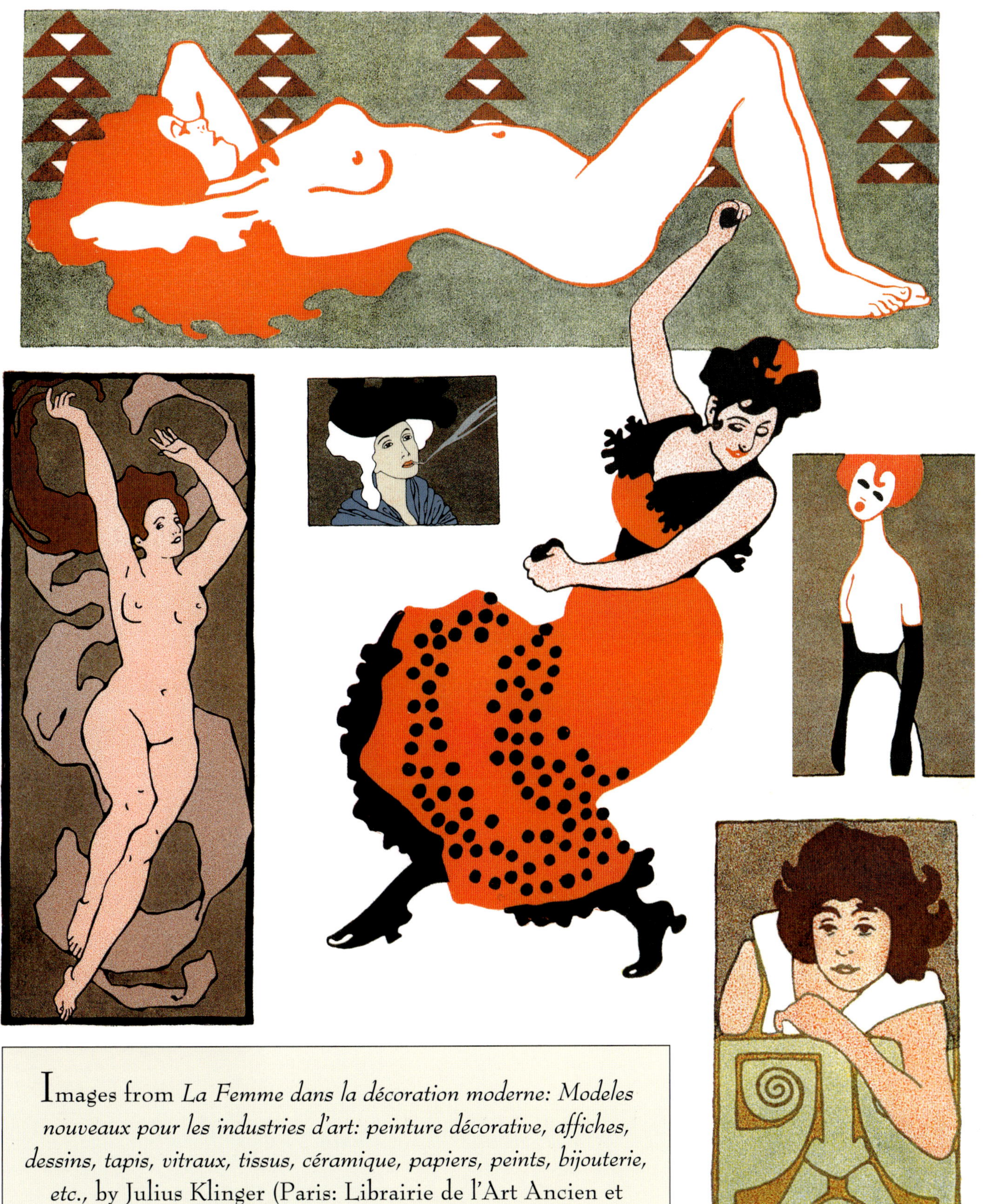

Images from *La Femme dans la décoration moderne: Modeles nouveaux pour les industries d'art: peinture décorative, affiches, dessins, tapis, vitraux, tissus, céramique, papiers, peints, bijouterie, etc.*, by Julius Klinger (Paris: Librairie de l'Art Ancien et Moderne, c. 1902). Reprinted by Dover as *The Woman in Art Nouveau Decoration* (New York, 1984).

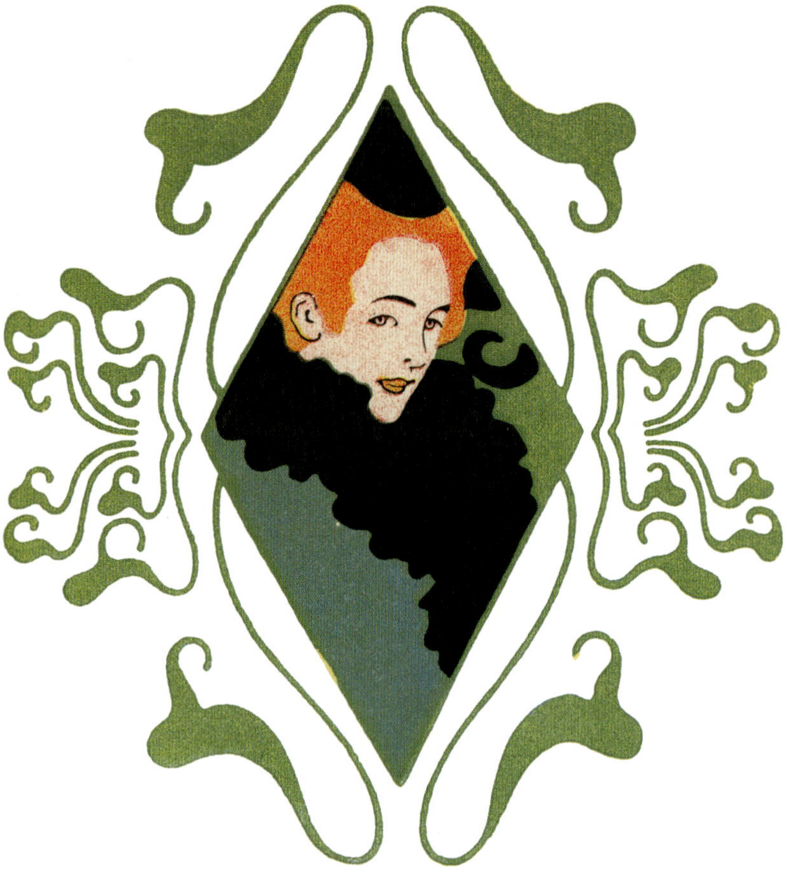

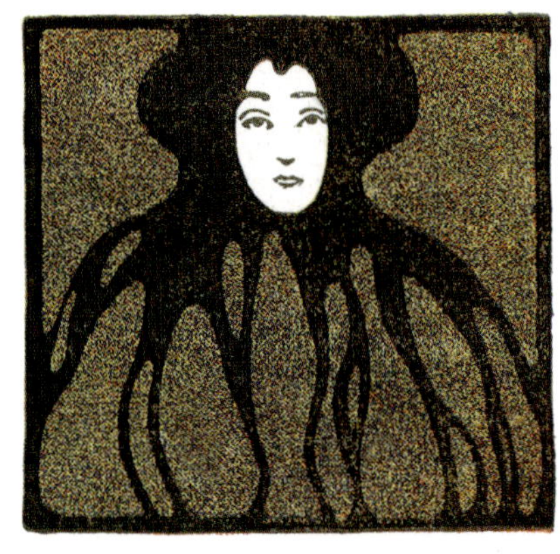

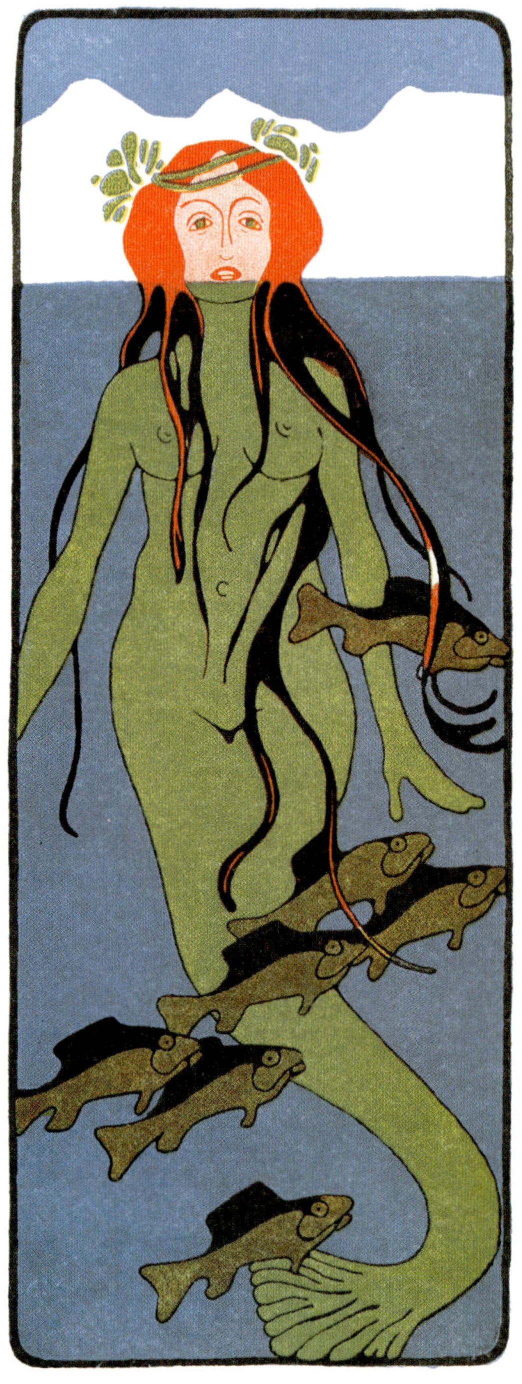

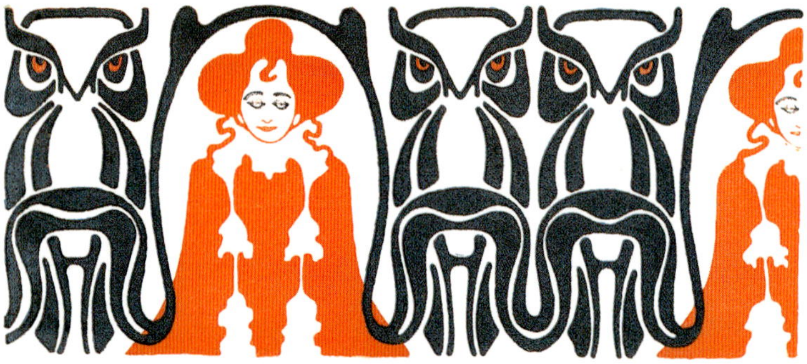

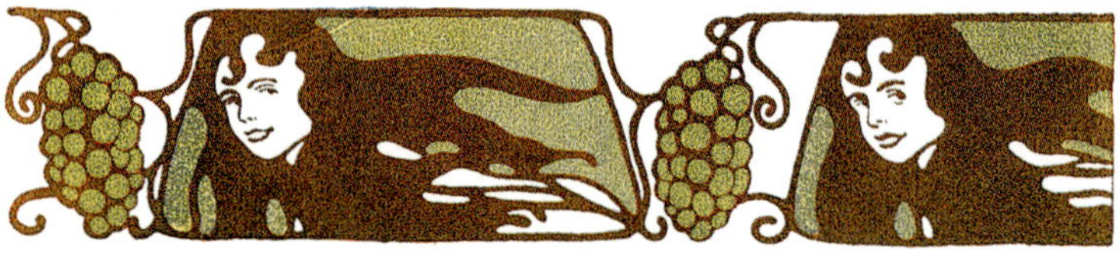

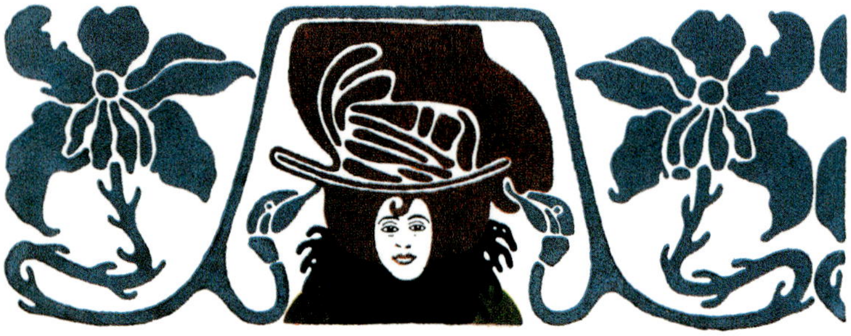

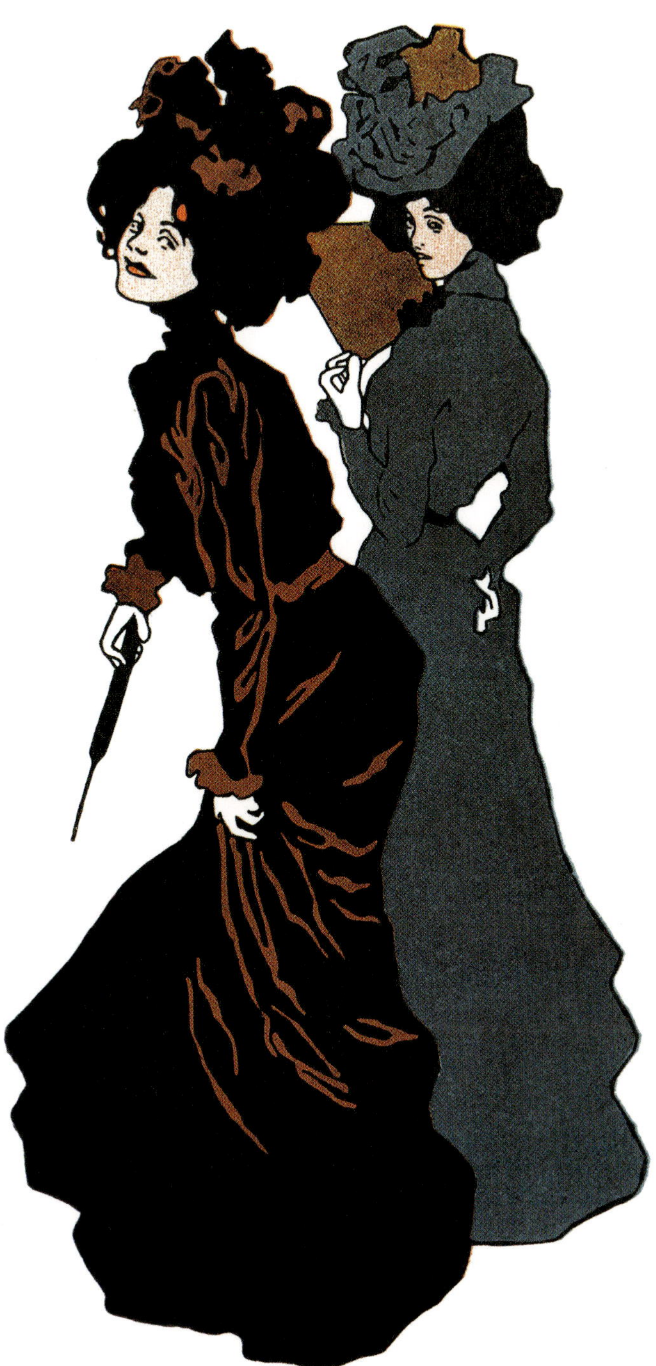

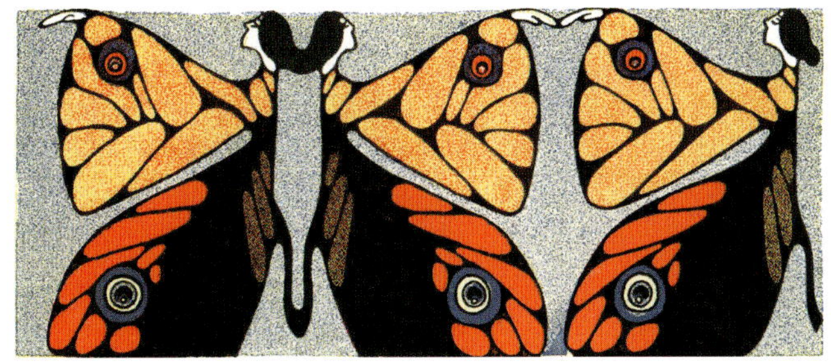

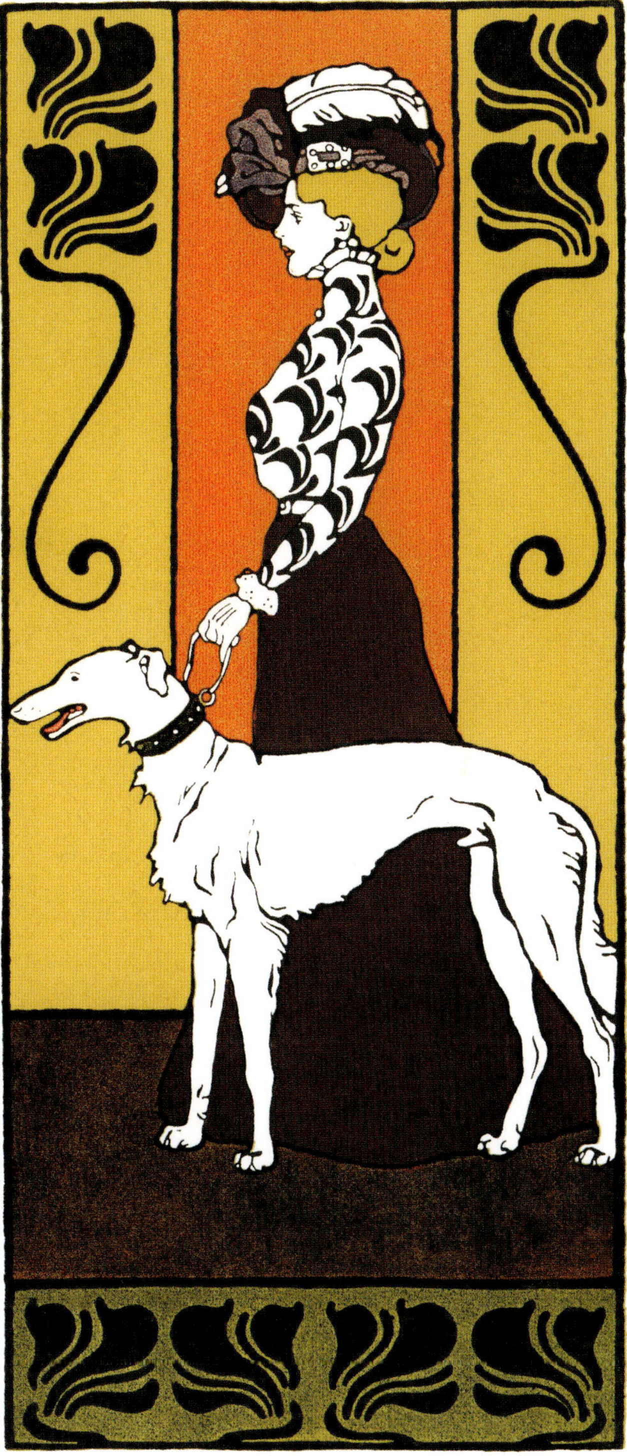

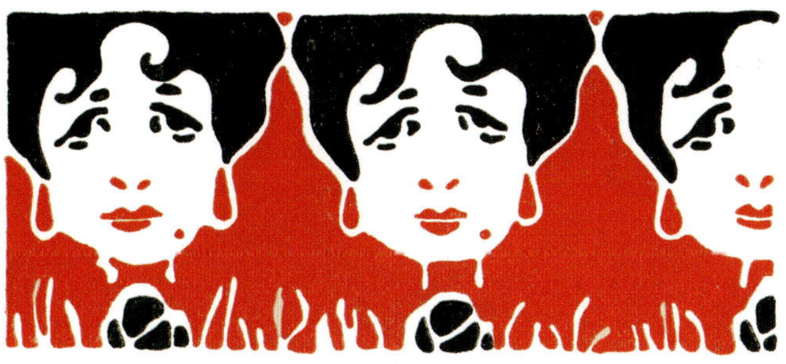

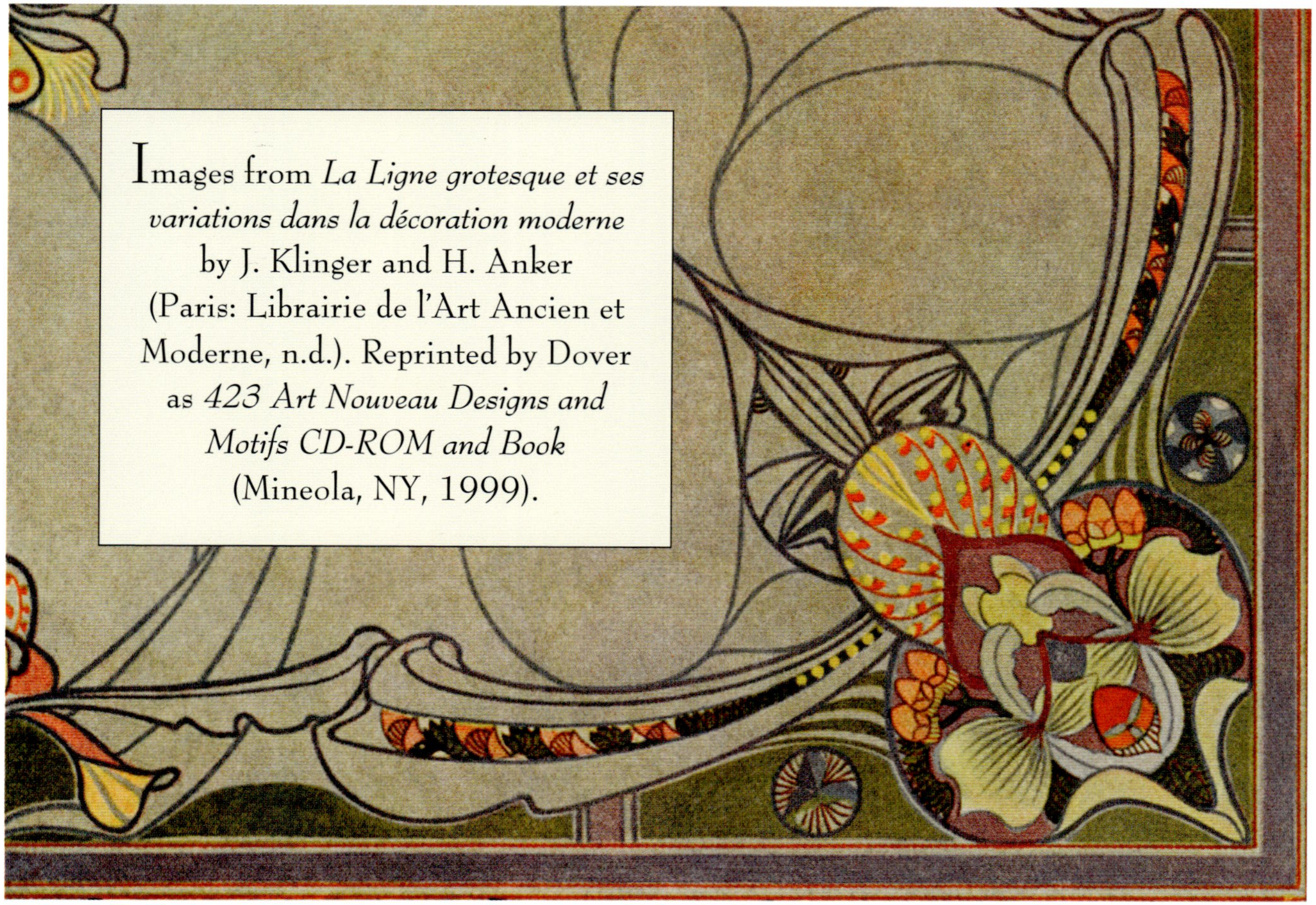

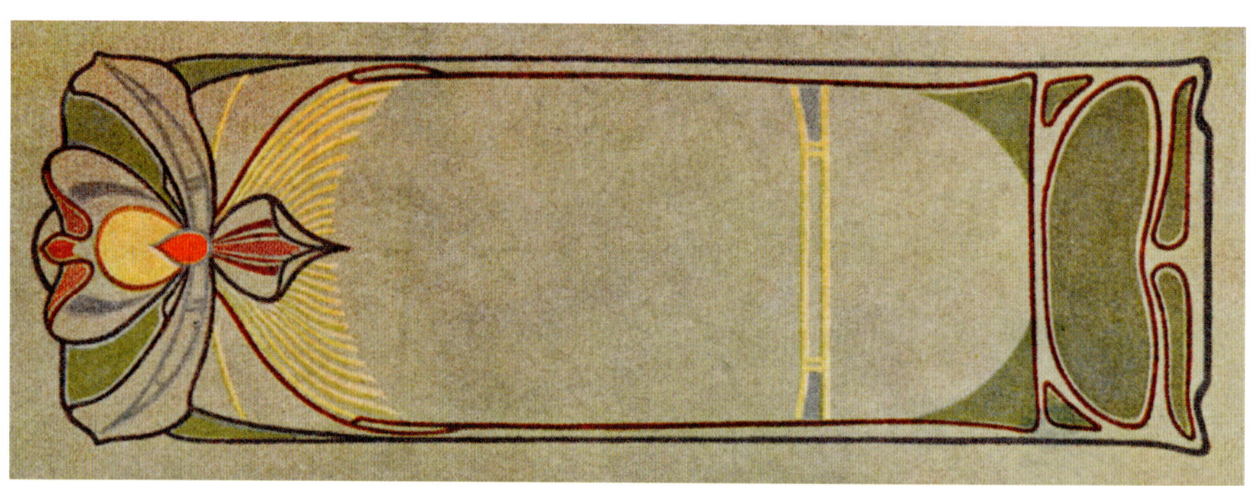

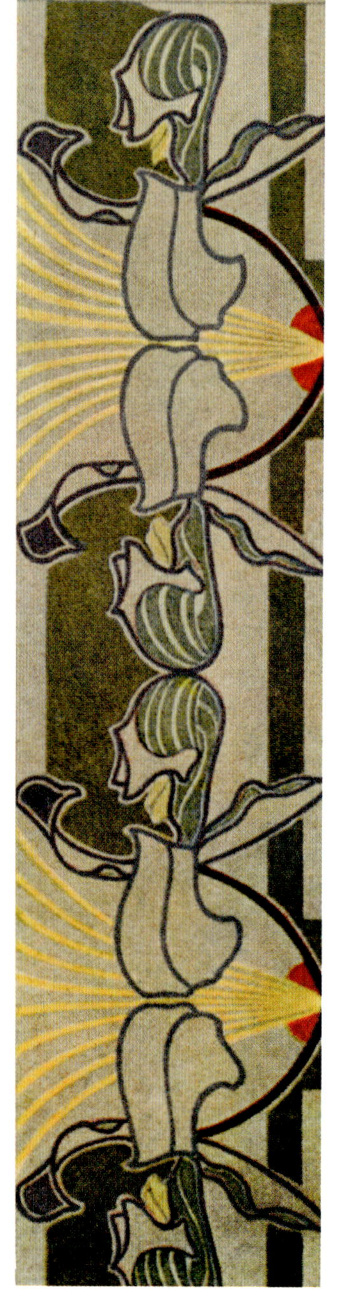

Images from *La Ligne grotesque et ses variations dans la décoration moderne* by J. Klinger and H. Anker (Paris: Librairie de l'Art Ancien et Moderne, n.d.). Reprinted by Dover as *423 Art Nouveau Designs and Motifs CD-ROM and Book* (Mineola, NY, 1999).

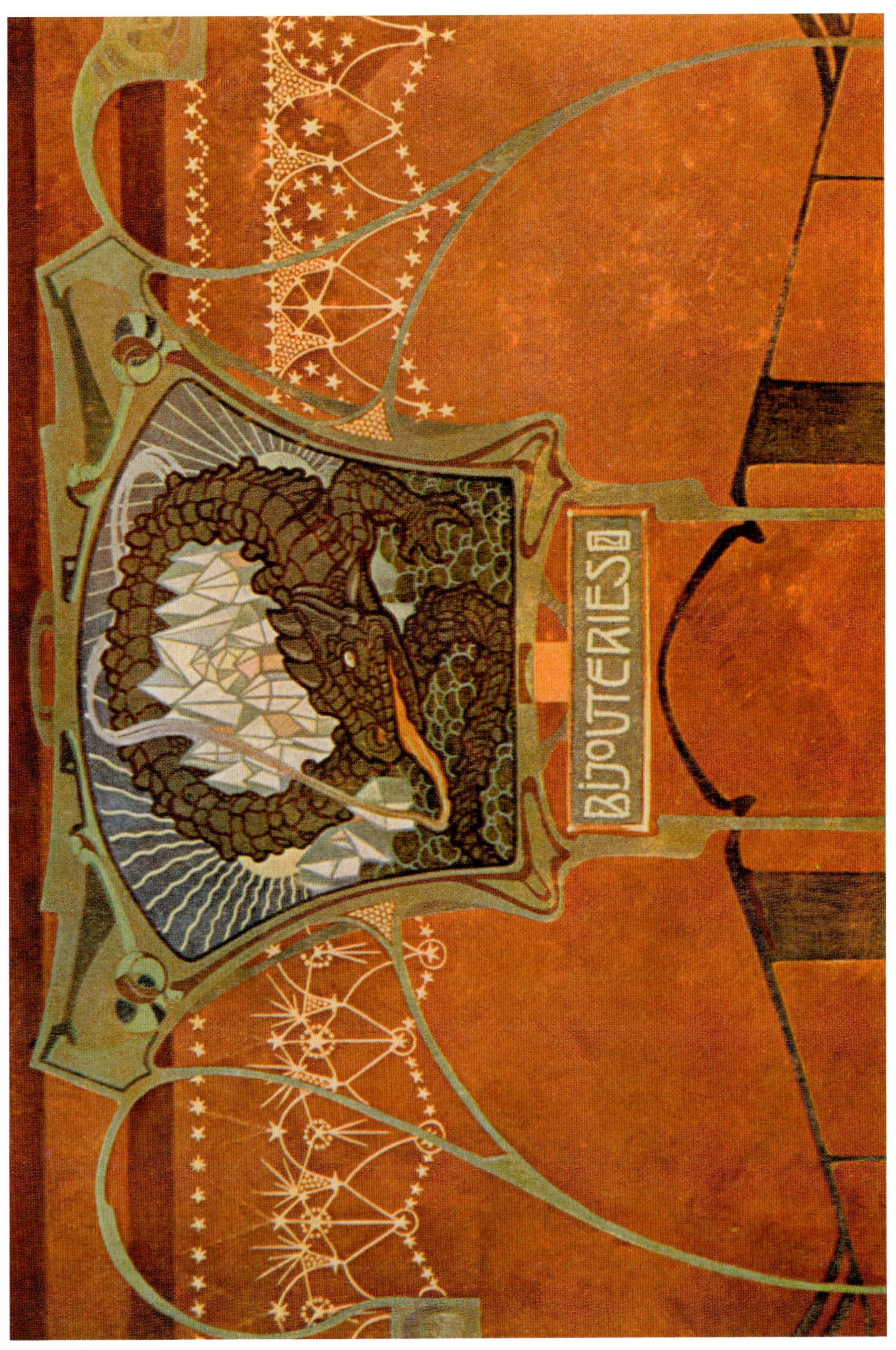
BIJOUTERIES

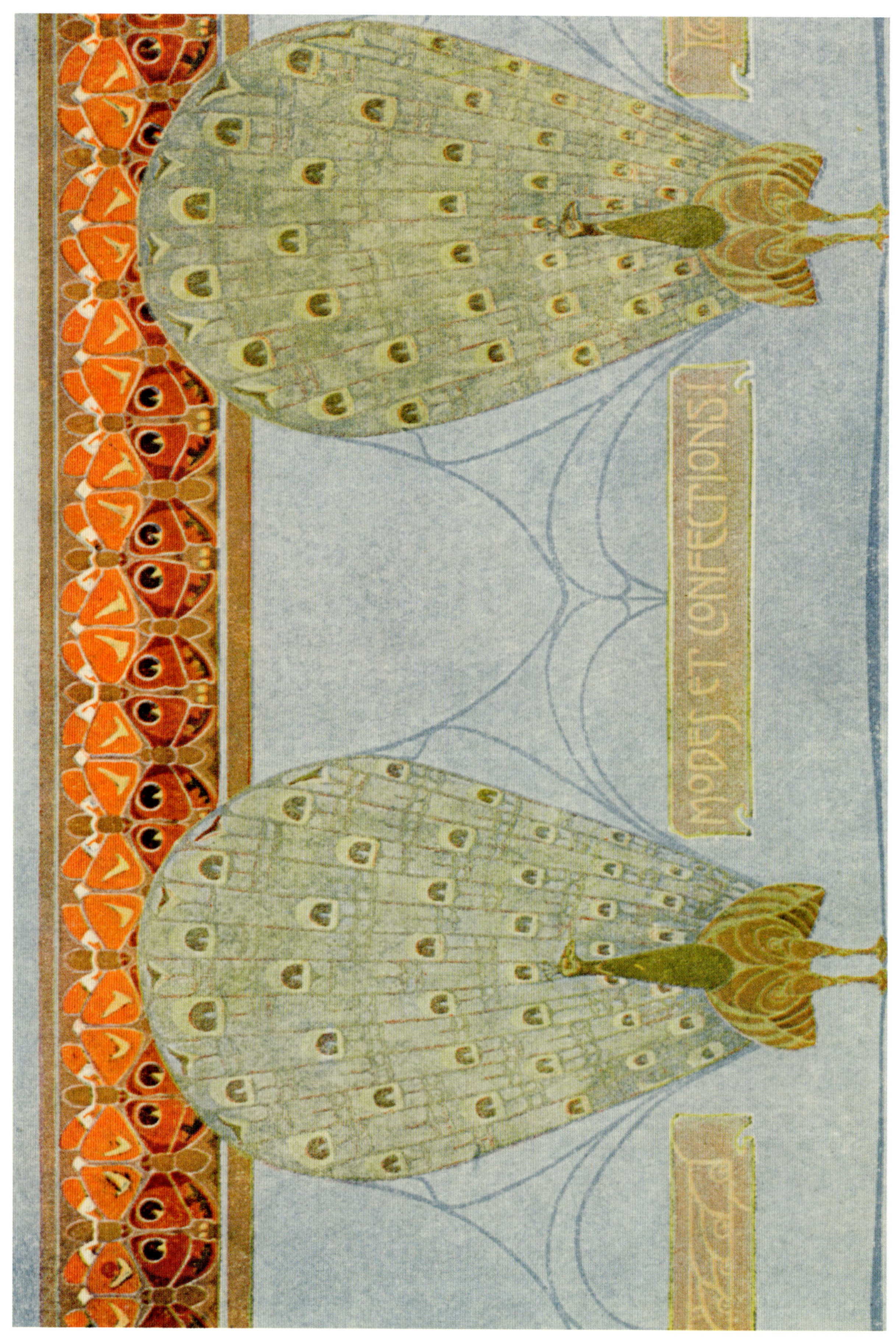

MODES ET CONFECTIONS

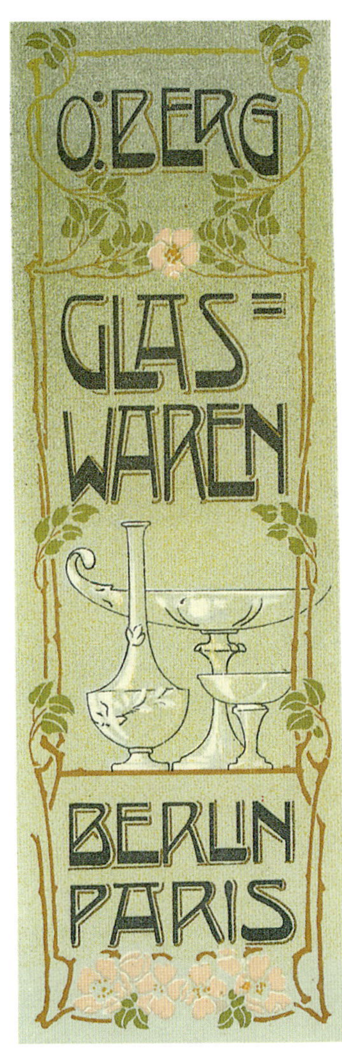

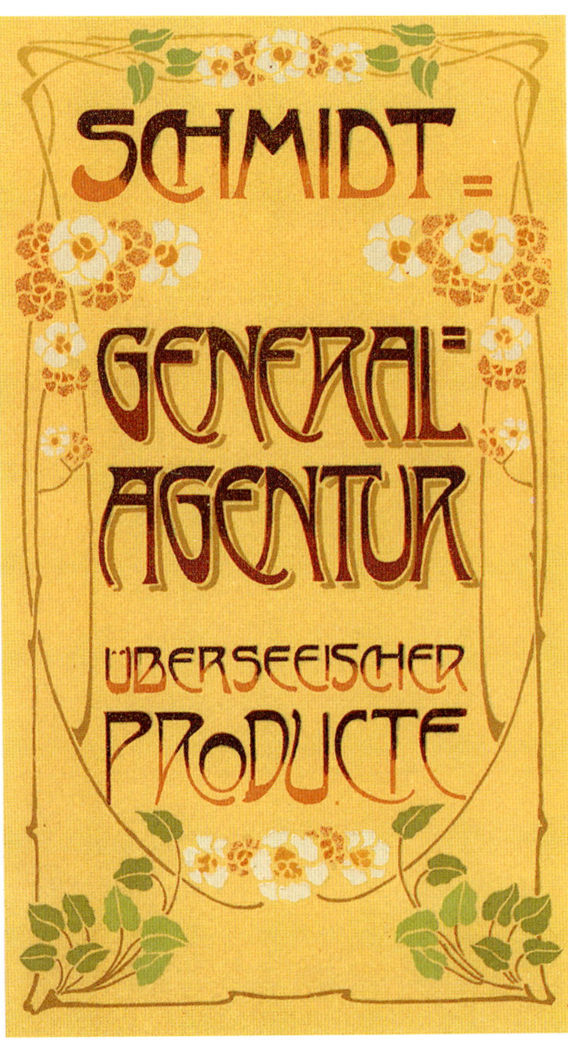

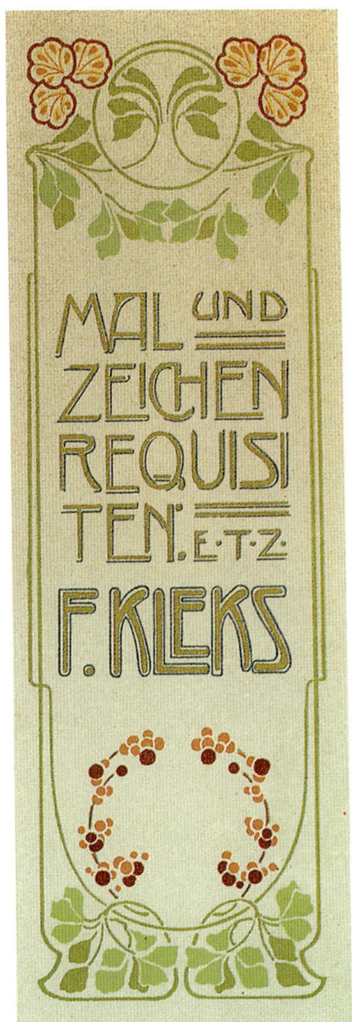

Images from *Neue Schriften und Firmenschilder im Modernen Stil: Serie I* by Josef Lehner and Eduard Mader (Vienna and Leipzig: Friedr. Wolfrum & Co., n.d.) Reprinted by Dover as *Authentic Art Nouveau Lettering and Design in Full Color* (New York, 1989).

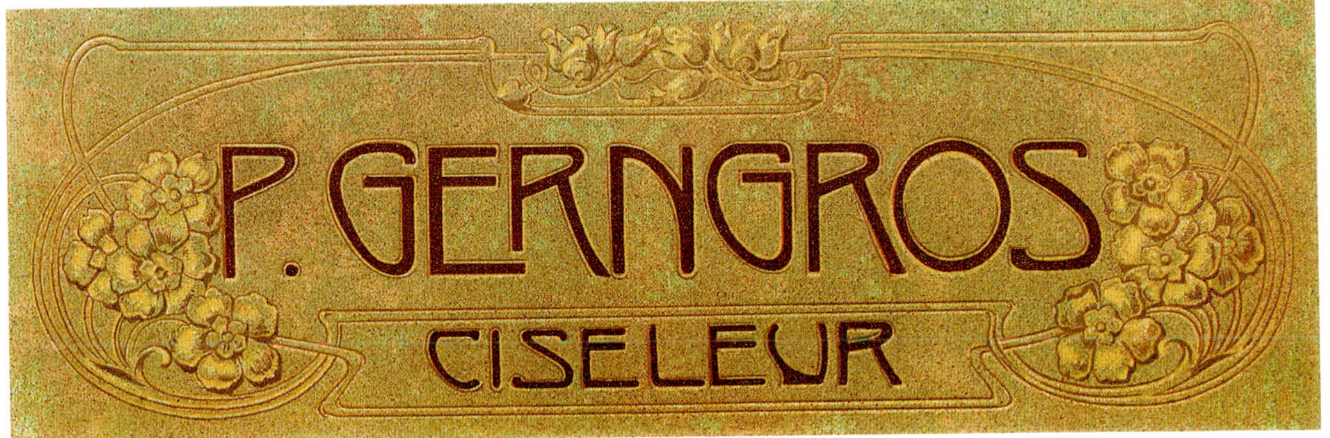

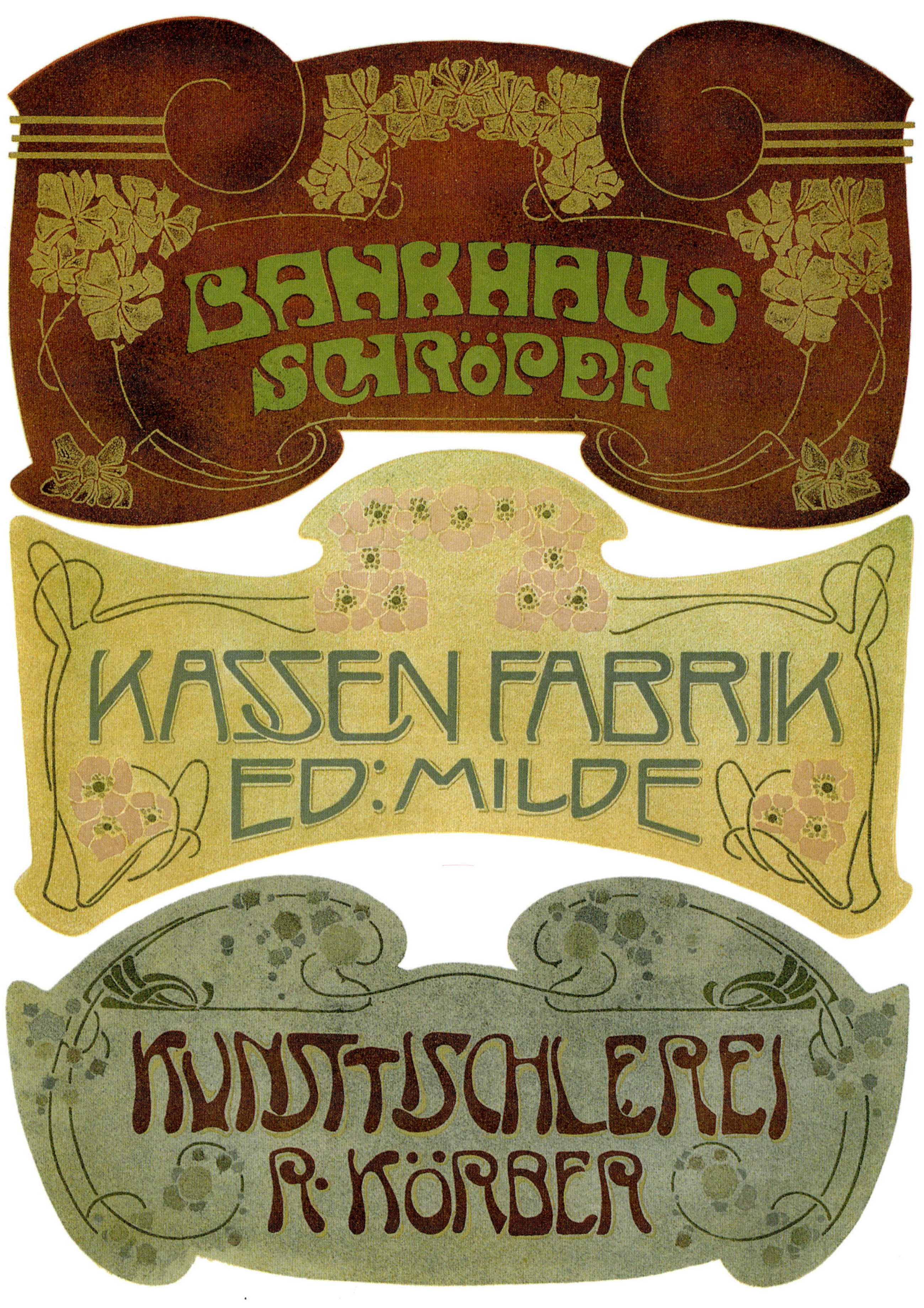

BANKHAUS SCHRÖPER
KASSEN FABRIK ED:MILDE
KUNSTTISCHLEREI R. KÖRBER

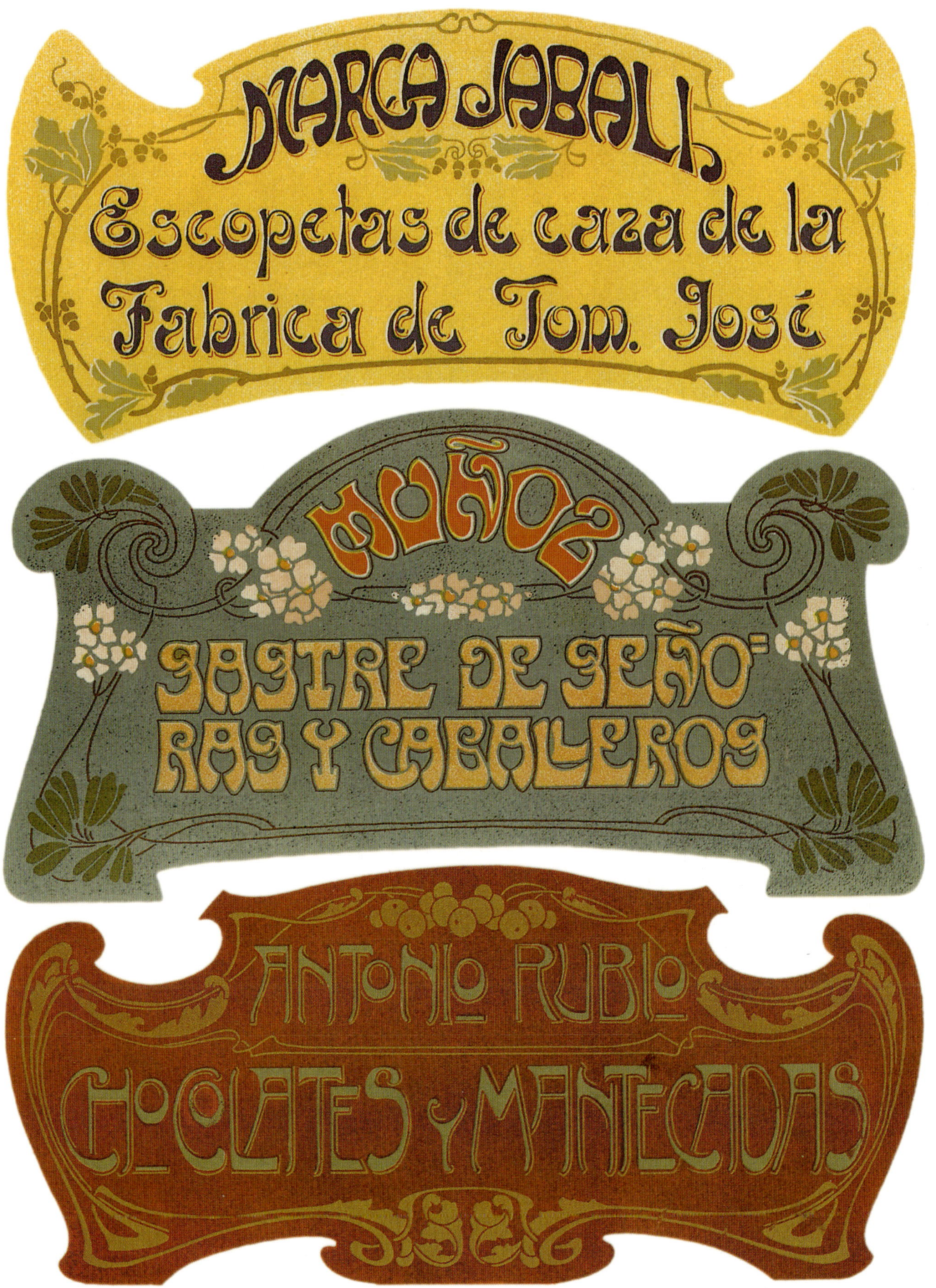

Marca Jabali
Escopetas de caza de la
Fabrica de Tom. José
Muñoz
Sastre de Seño=
ras y Caballeros
Antonio Rubio
Chocolates y Mantecadas

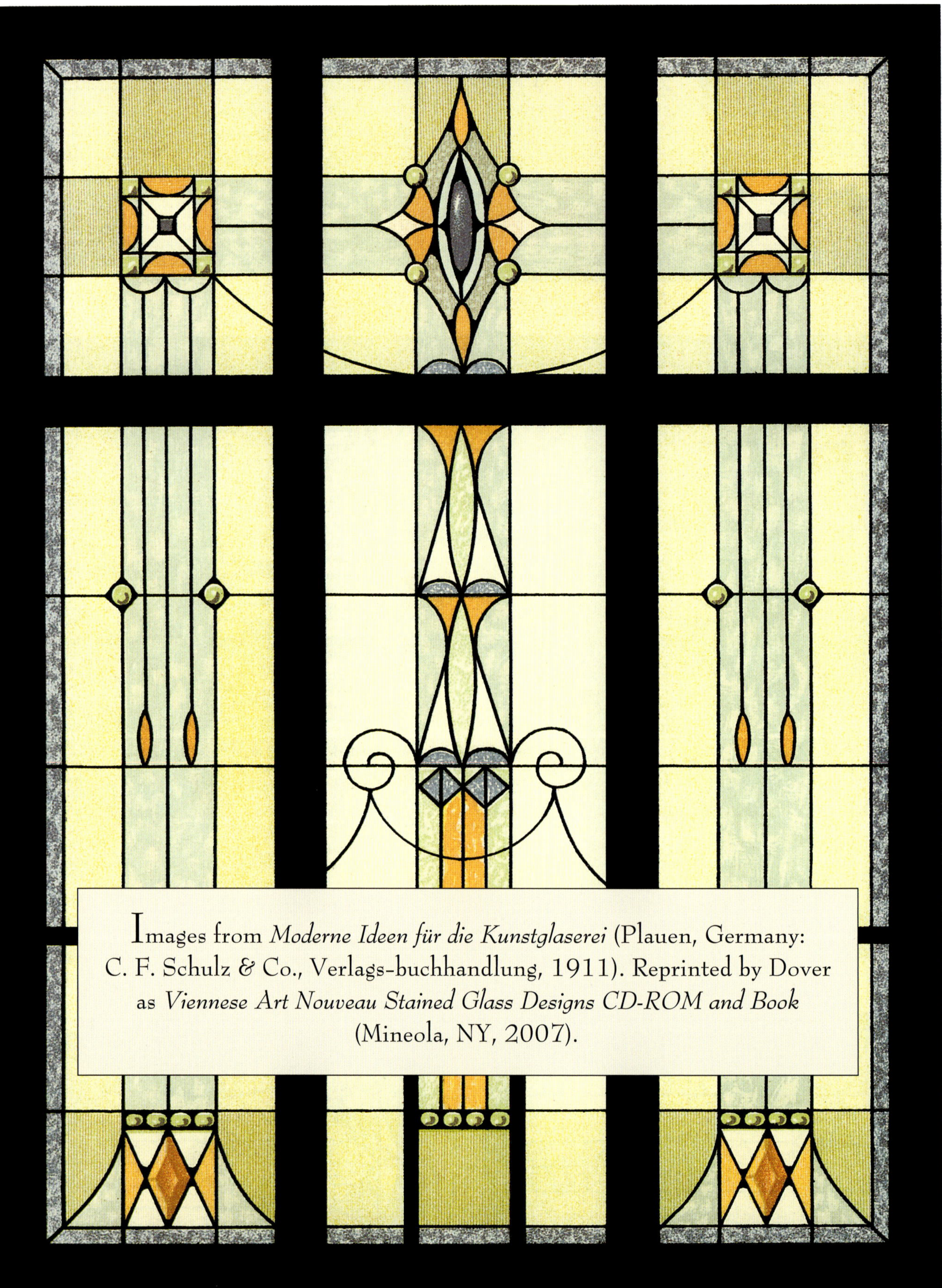

Images from *Moderne Ideen für die Kunstglaserei* (Plauen, Germany: C. F. Schulz & Co., Verlags-buchhandlung, 1911). Reprinted by Dover as *Viennese Art Nouveau Stained Glass Designs CD-ROM and Book* (Mineola, NY, 2007).

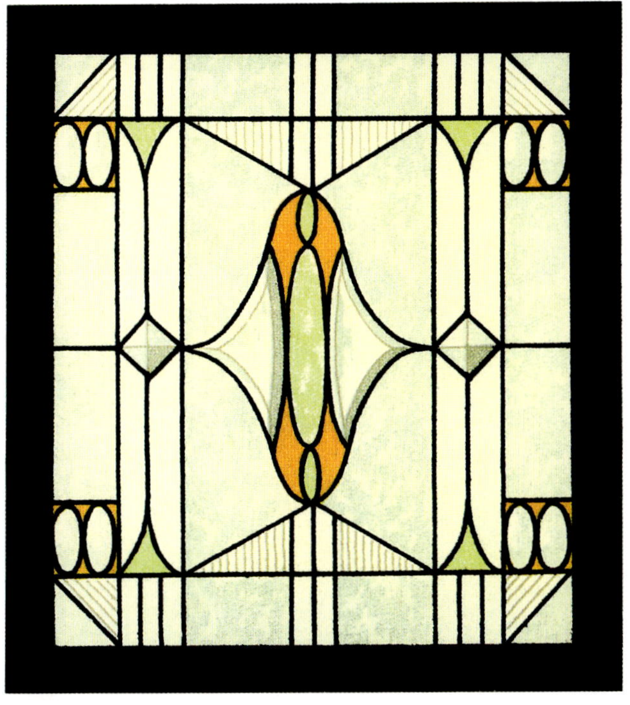

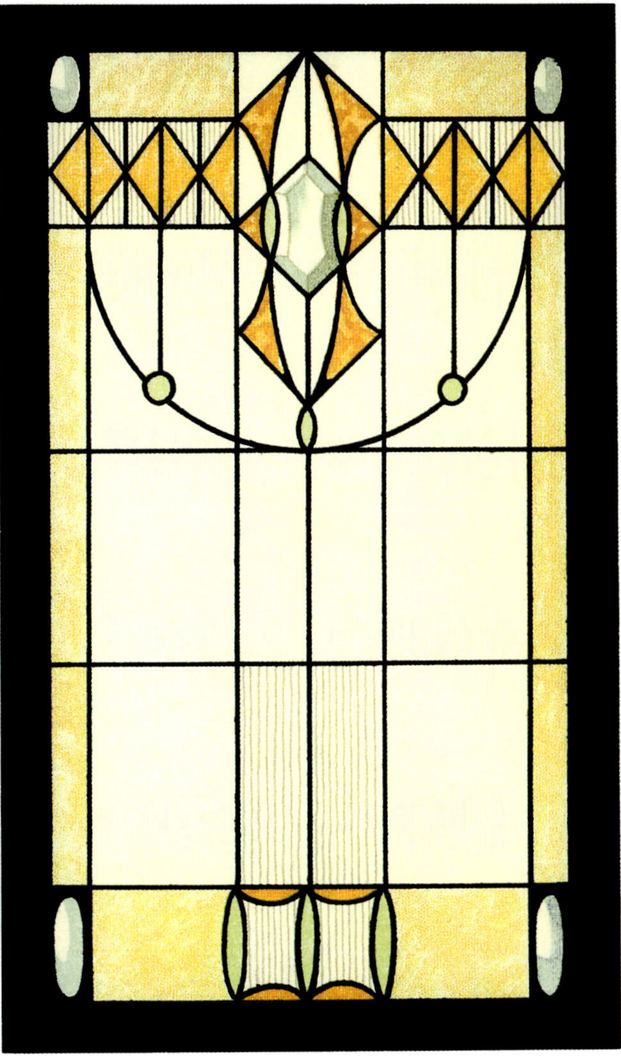

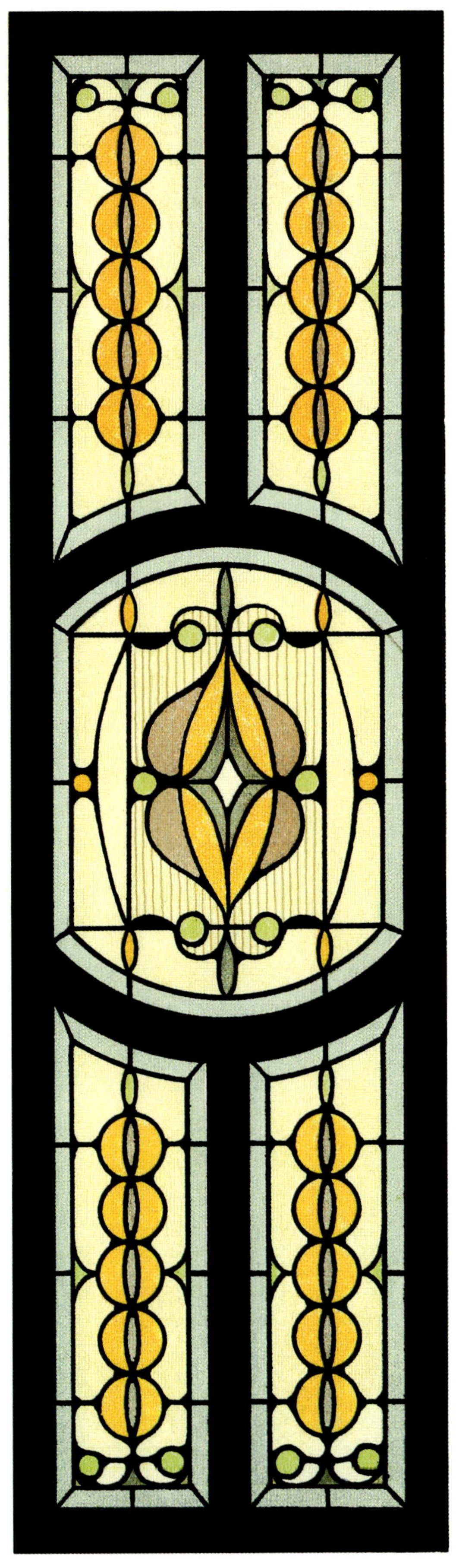

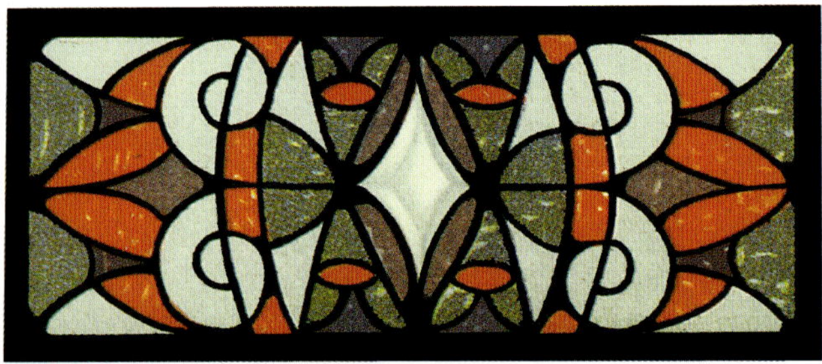

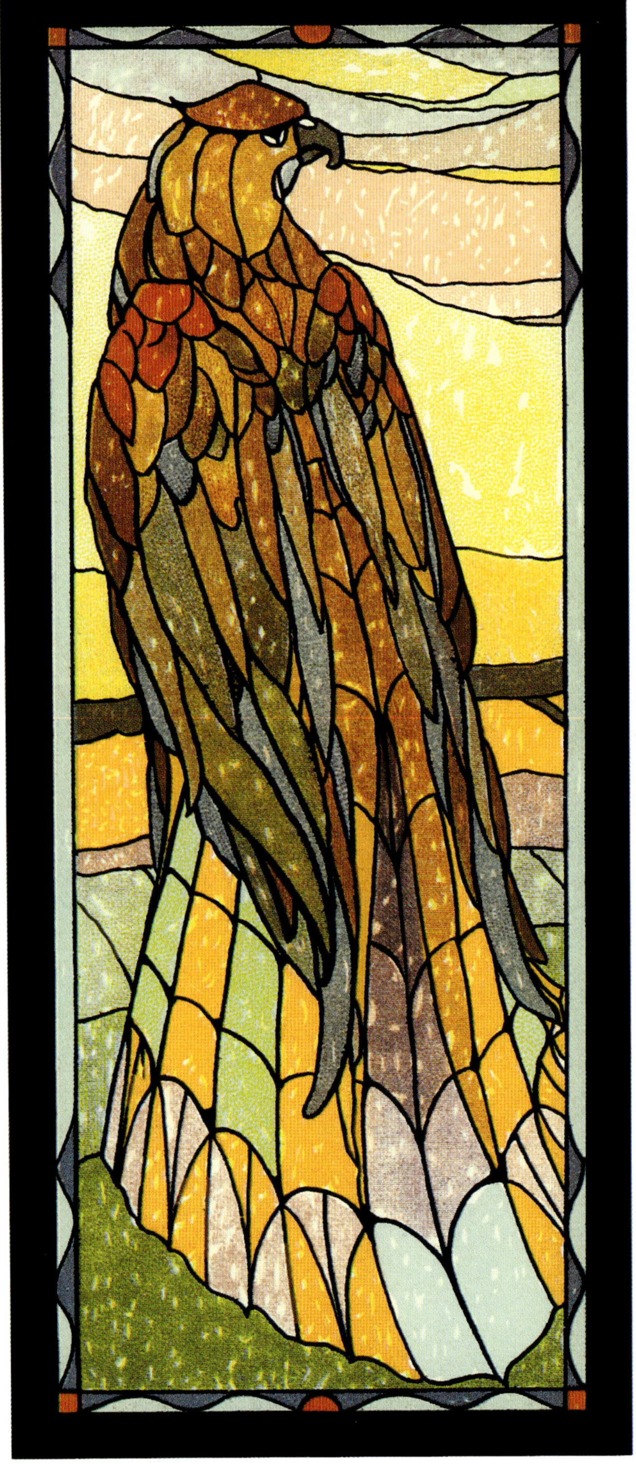

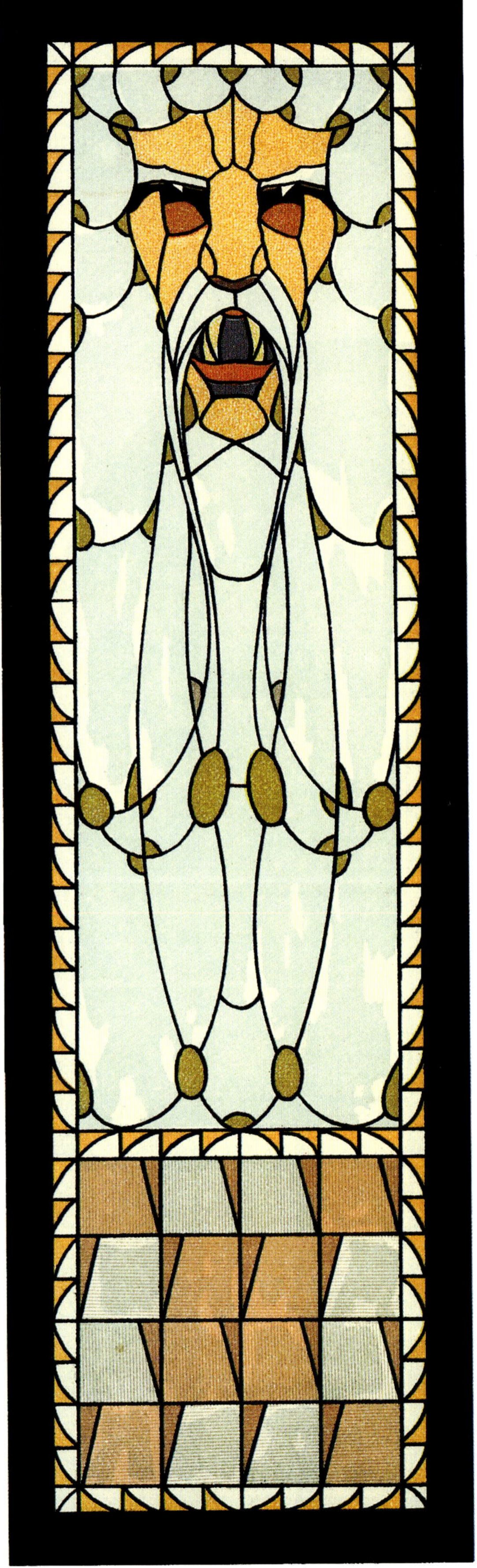

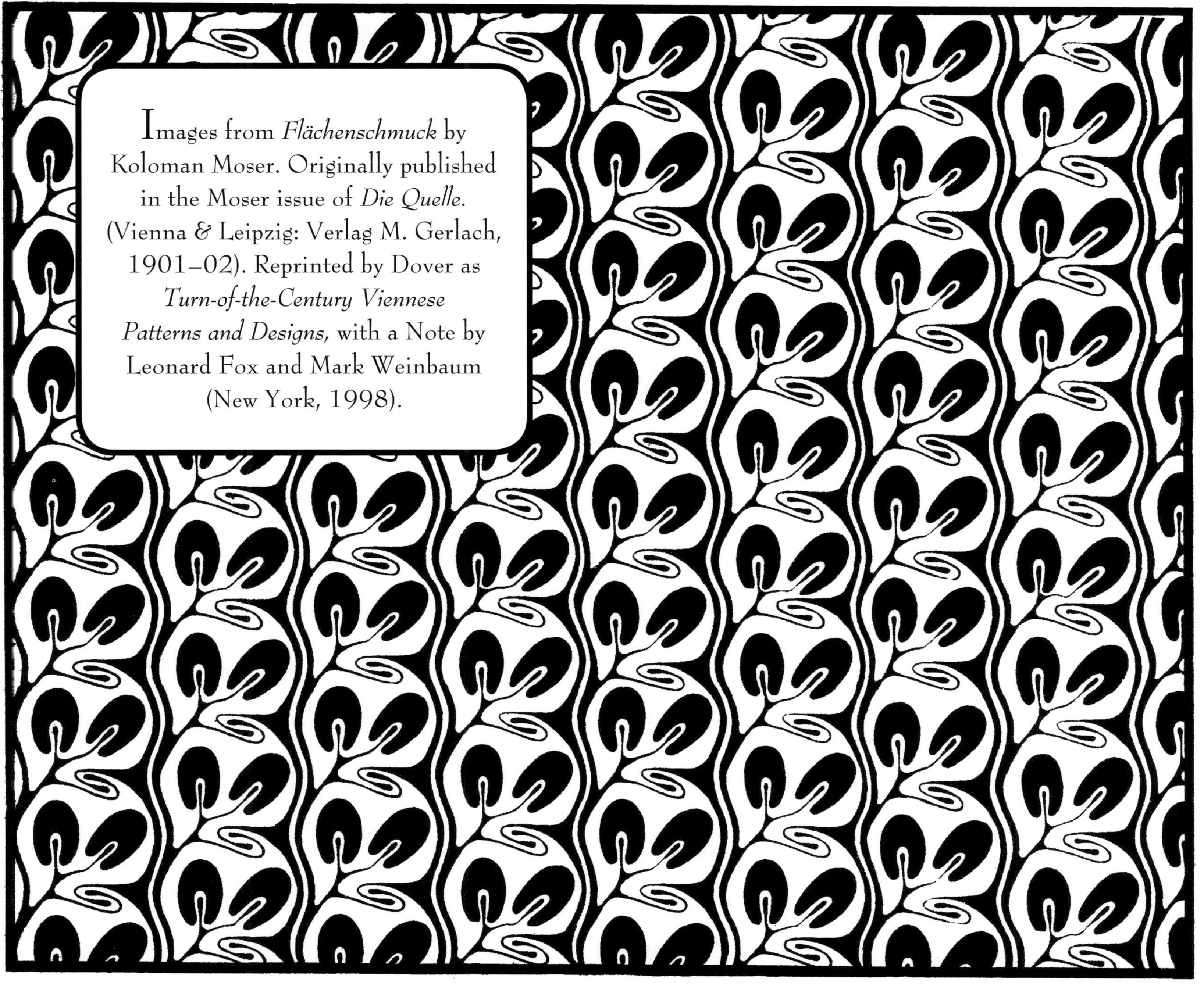

Images from *Flächenschmuck* by Koloman Moser. Originally published in the Moser issue of *Die Quelle*. (Vienna & Leipzig: Verlag M. Gerlach, 1901–02). Reprinted by Dover as *Turn-of-the-Century Viennese Patterns and Designs*, with a Note by Leonard Fox and Mark Weinbaum (New York, 1998).

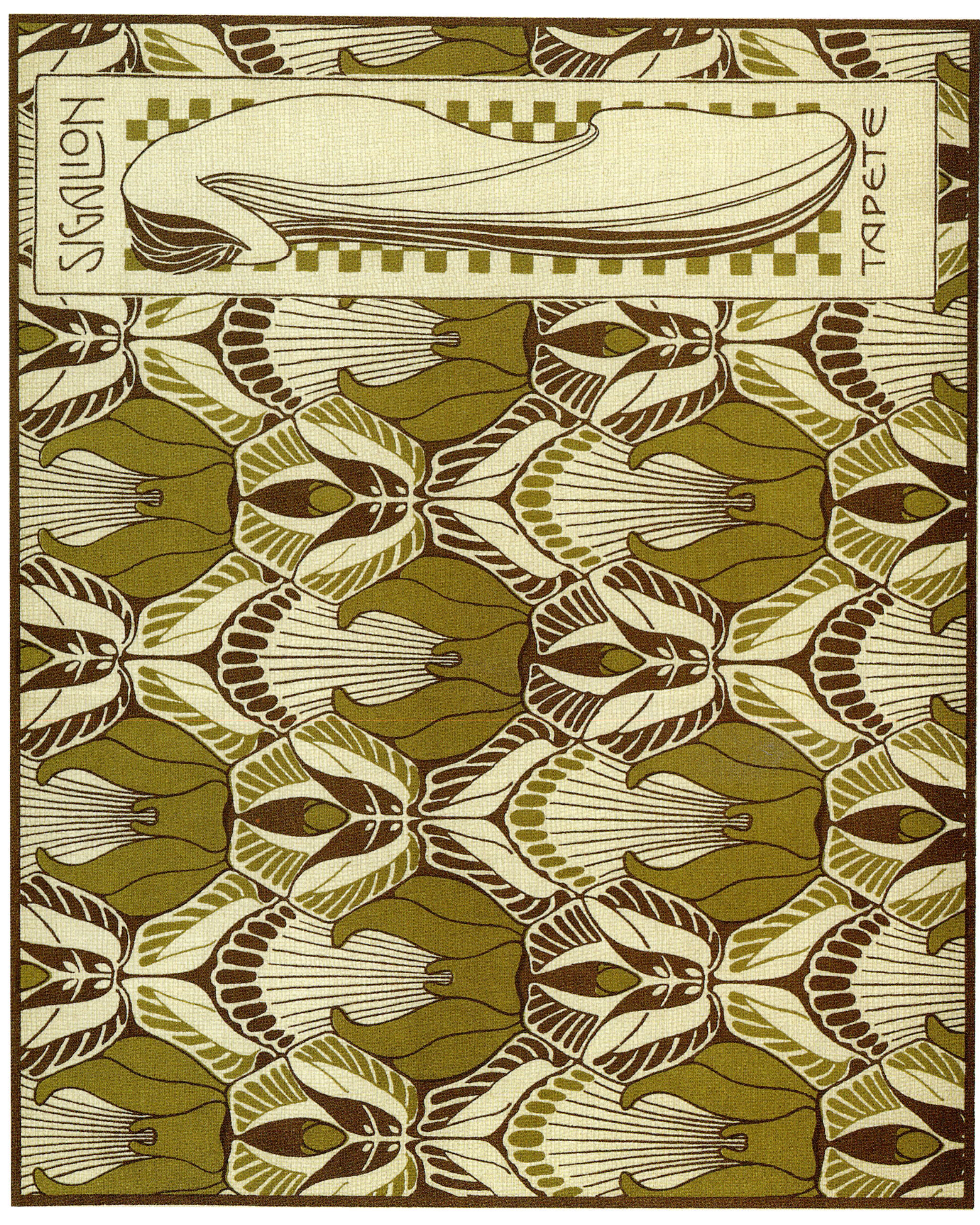

SIGNALION
TAPETE

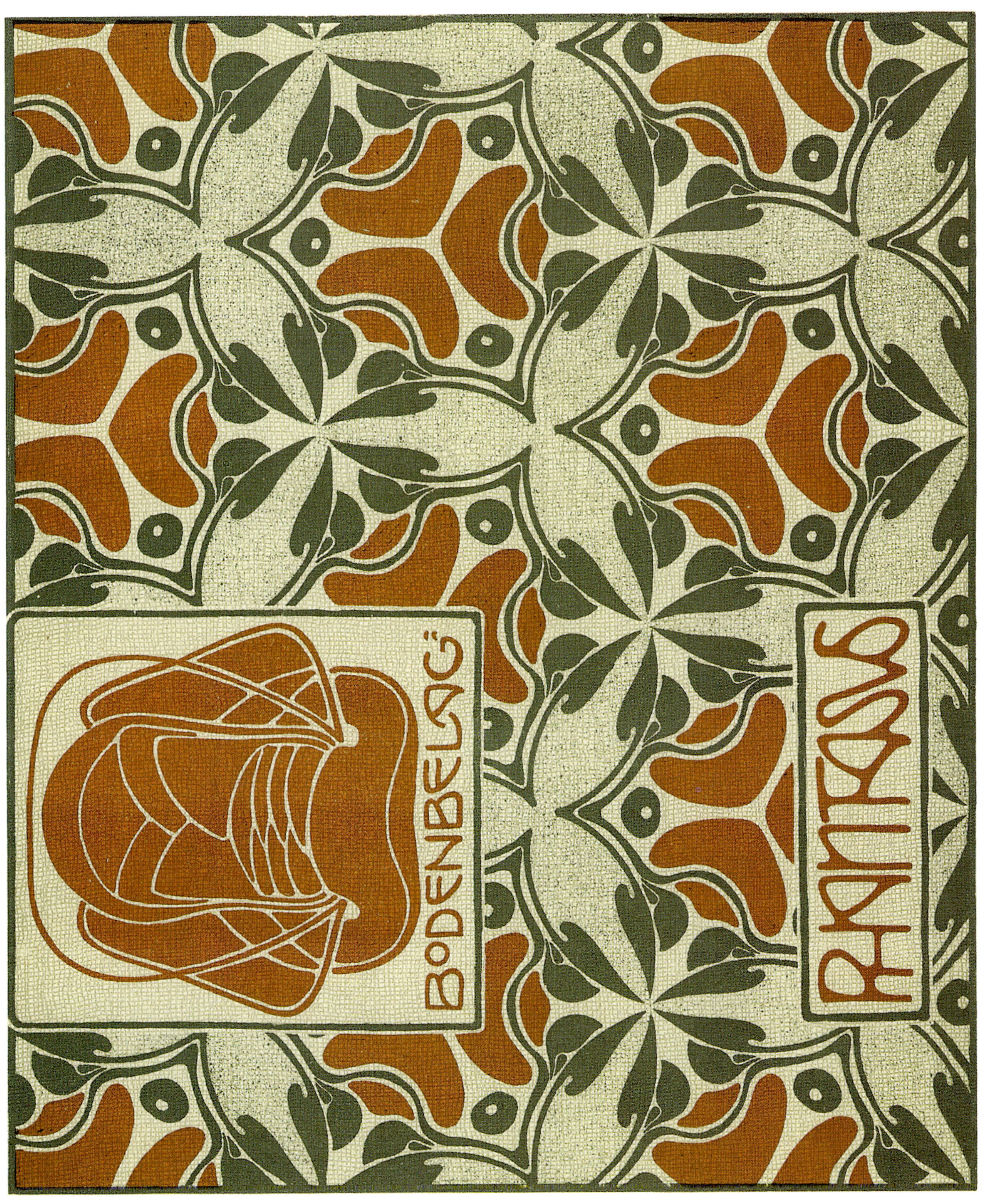

BODENBELAG

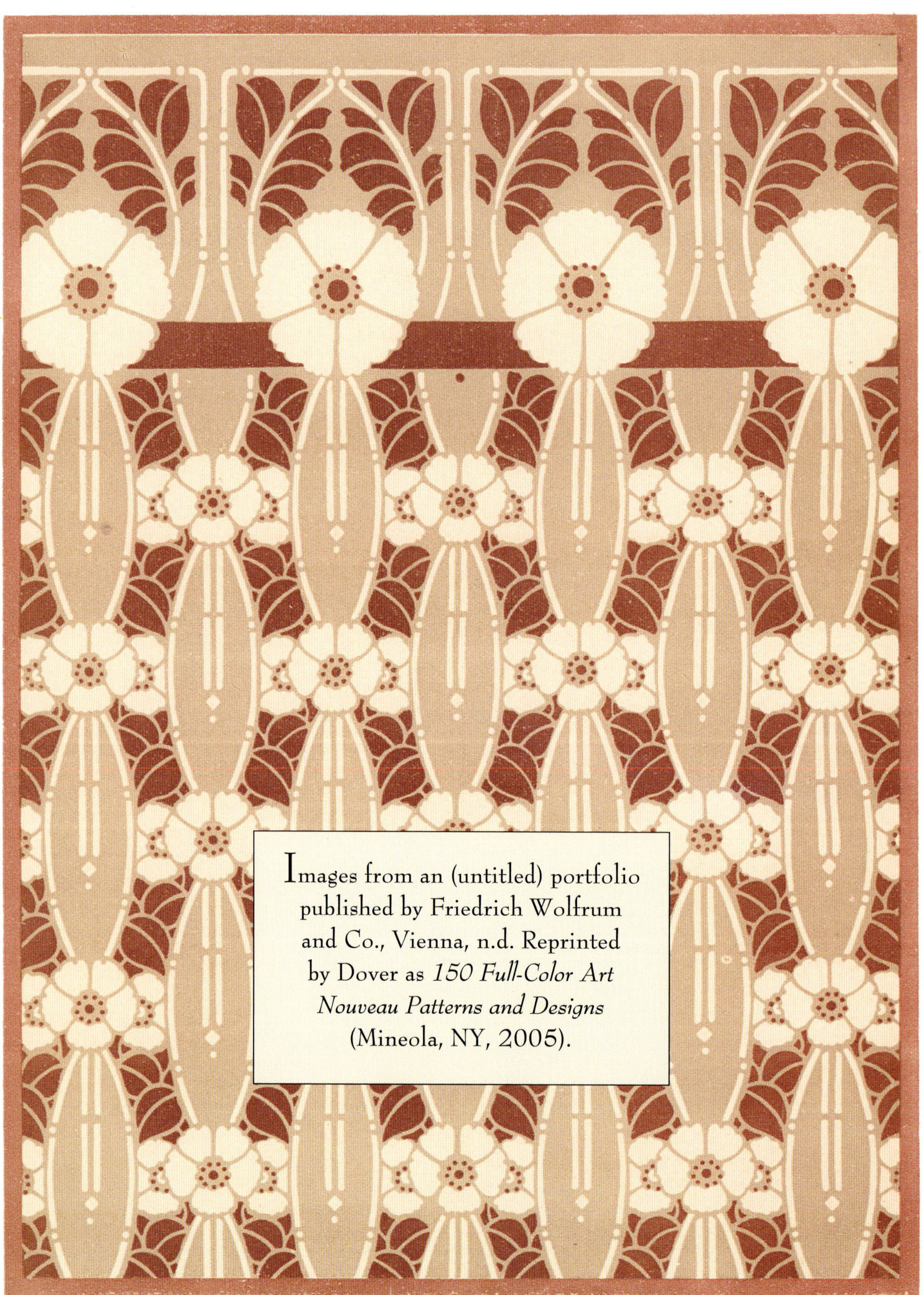
Images from an (untitled) portfolio
published by Friedrich Wolfrum
and Co., Vienna, n.d. Reprinted
by Dover as 150 Full-Color Art
Nouveau Patterns and Designs
(Mineola, NY, 2005).

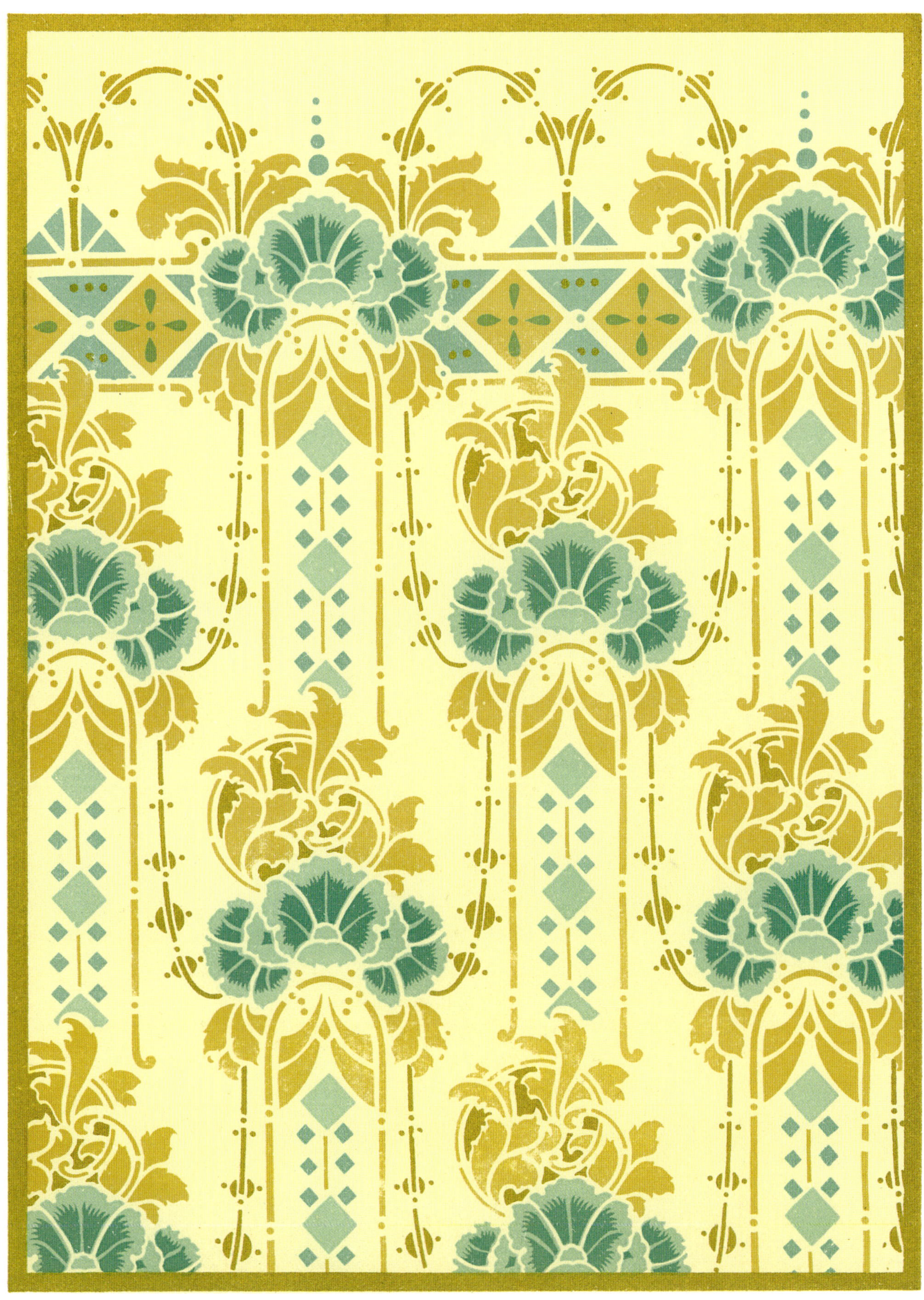

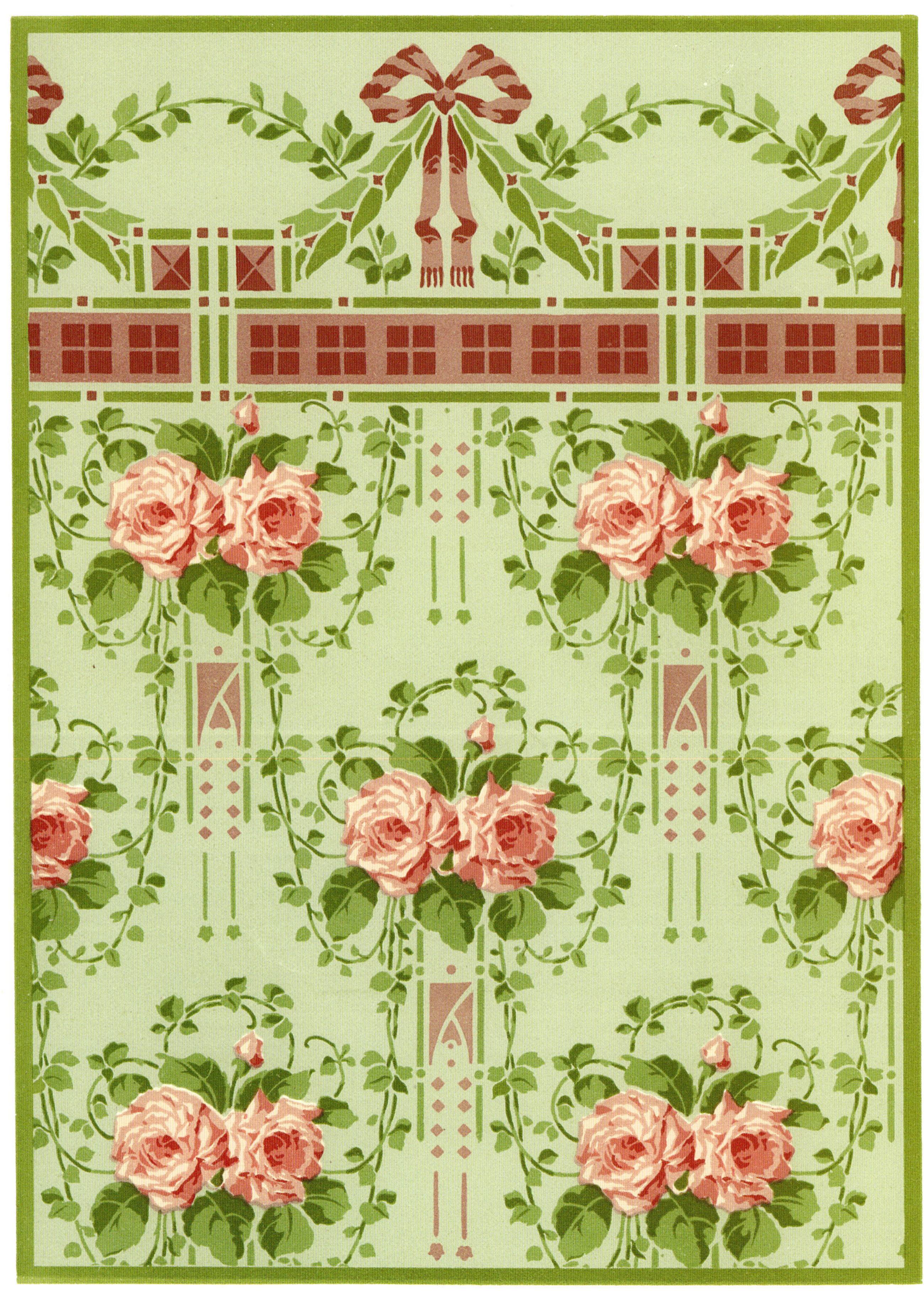

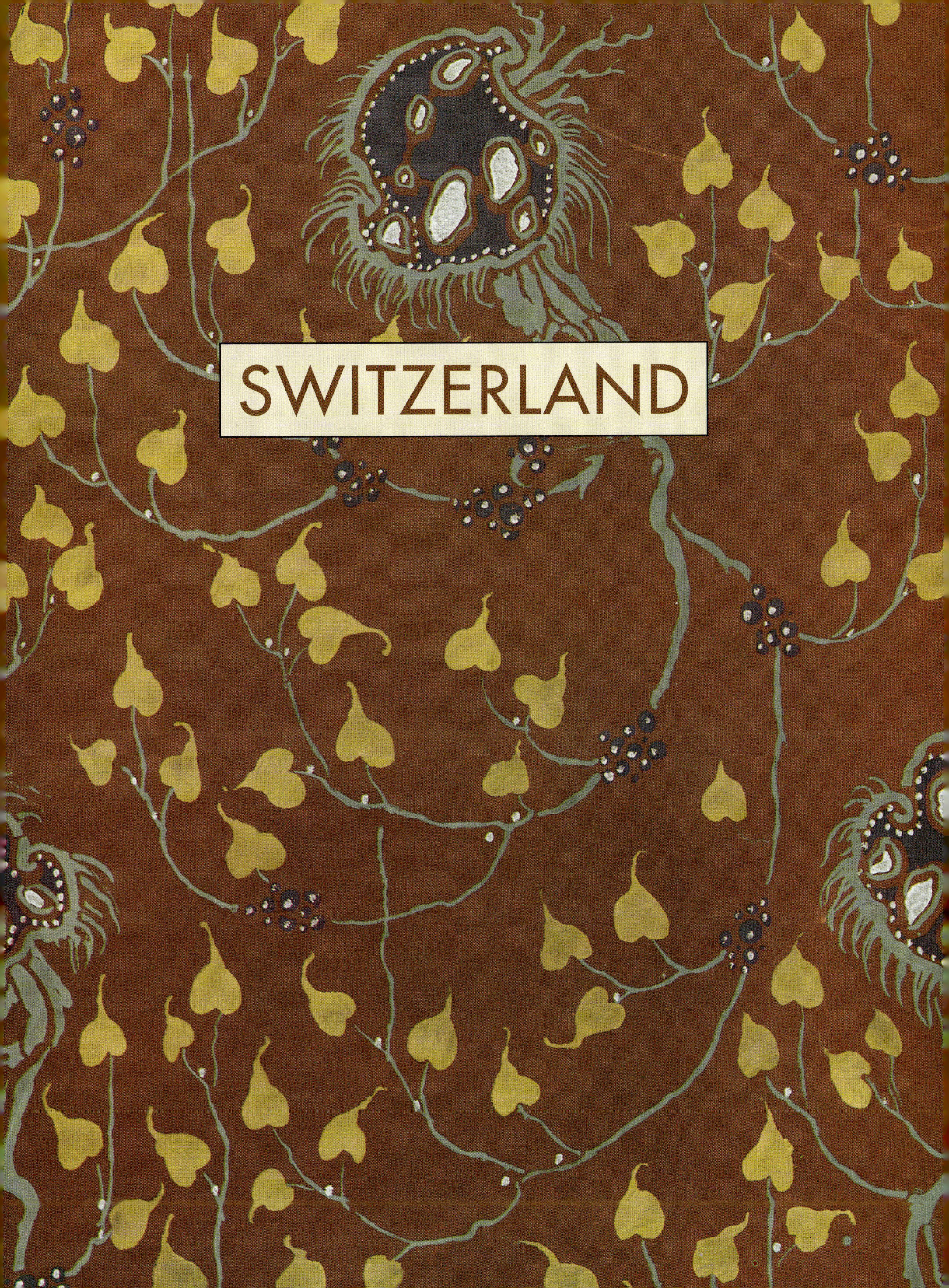

SWITZERLAND

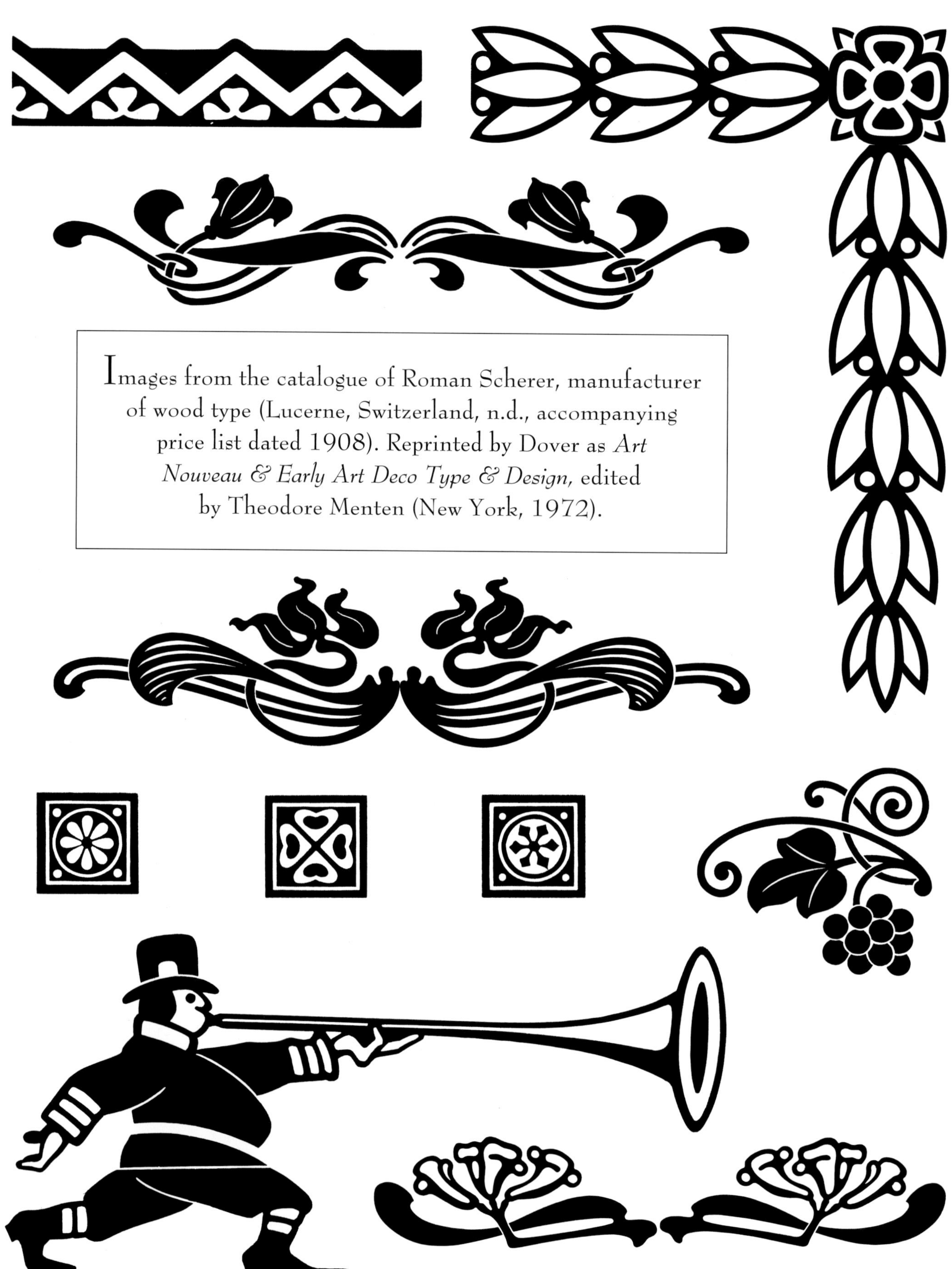

Images from the catalogue of Roman Scherer, manufacturer of wood type (Lucerne, Switzerland, n.d., accompanying price list dated 1908). Reprinted by Dover as *Art Nouveau & Early Art Deco Type & Design*, edited by Theodore Menten (New York, 1972).

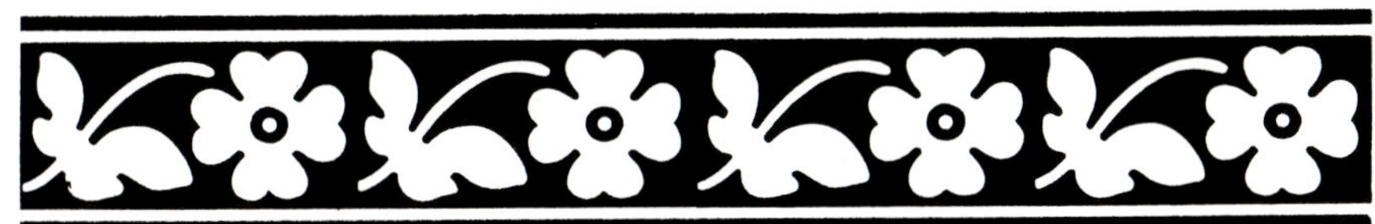
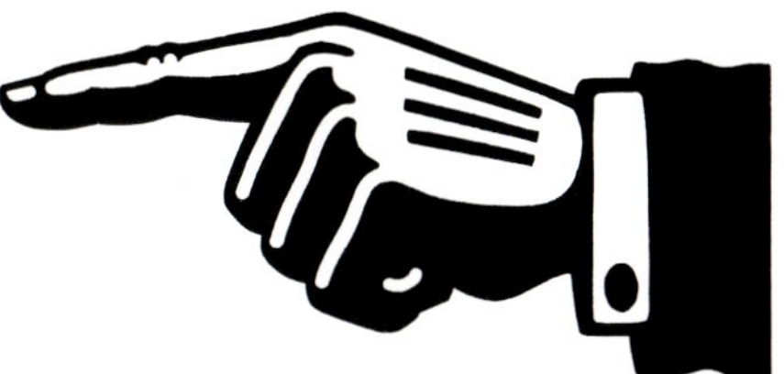
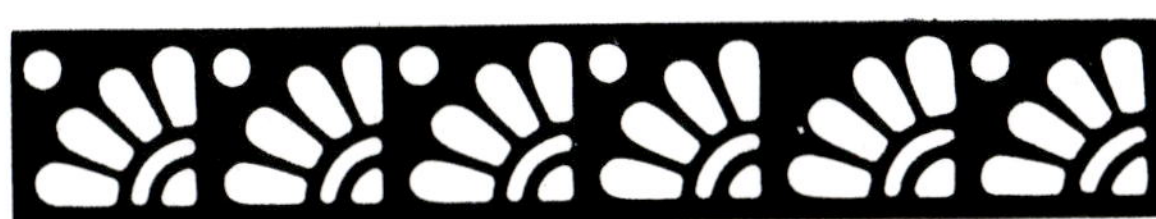
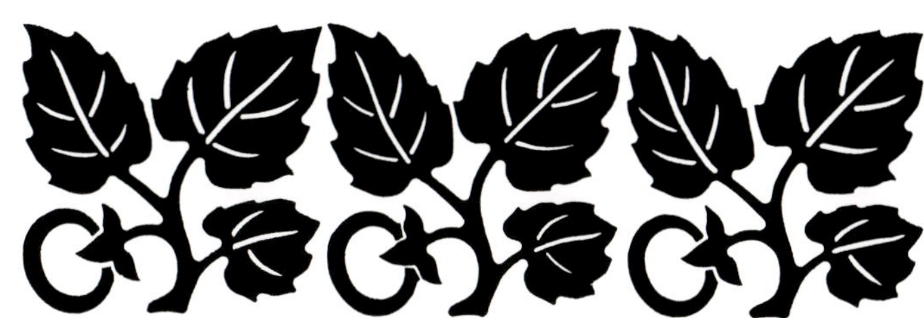

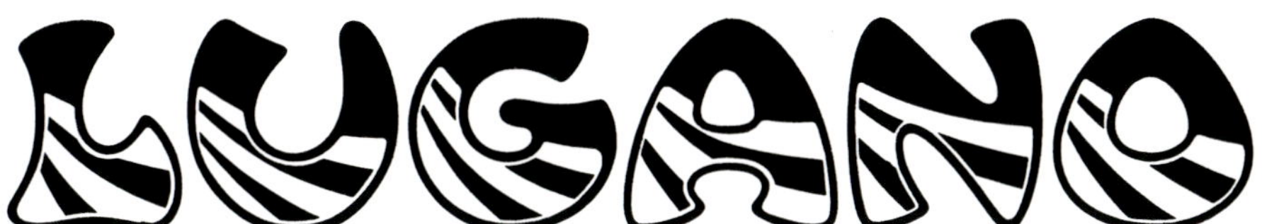
LUGANO

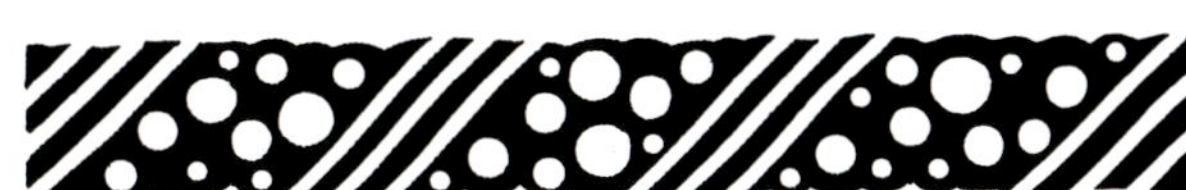
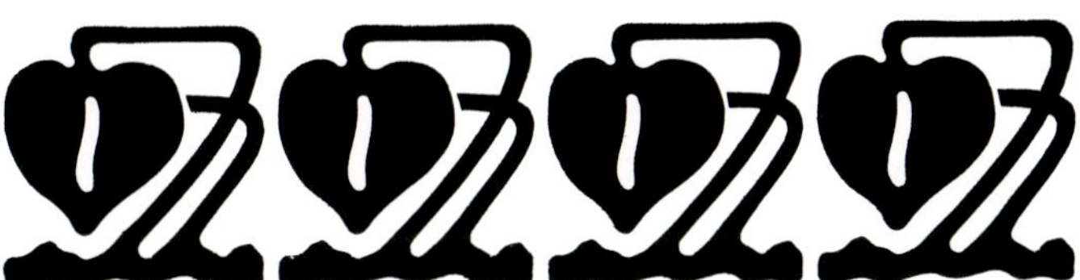
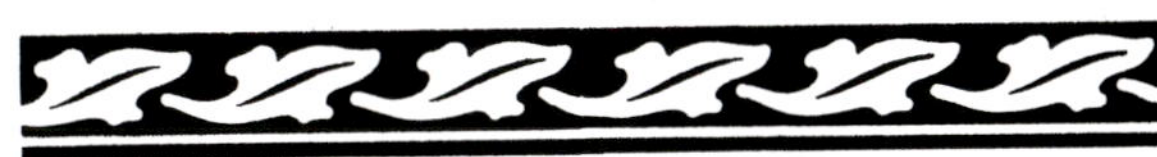
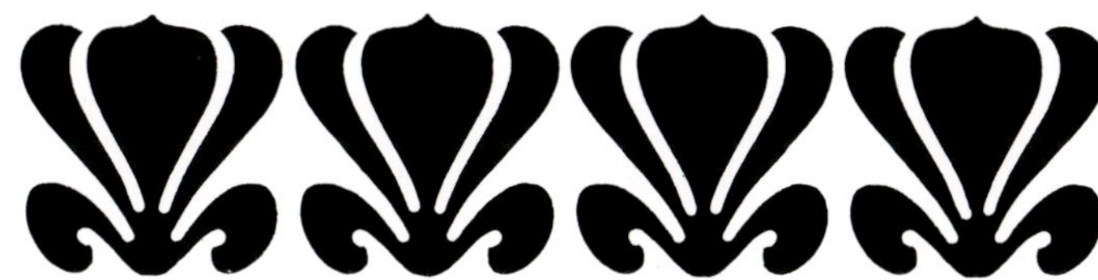
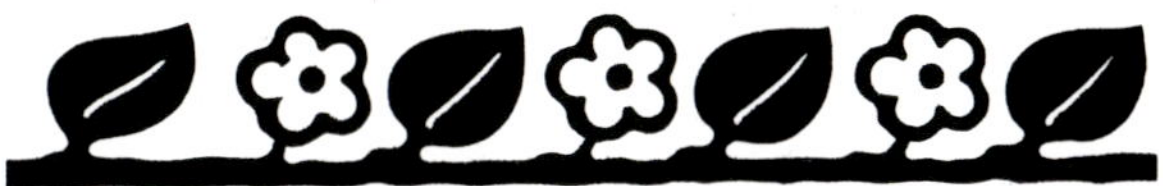
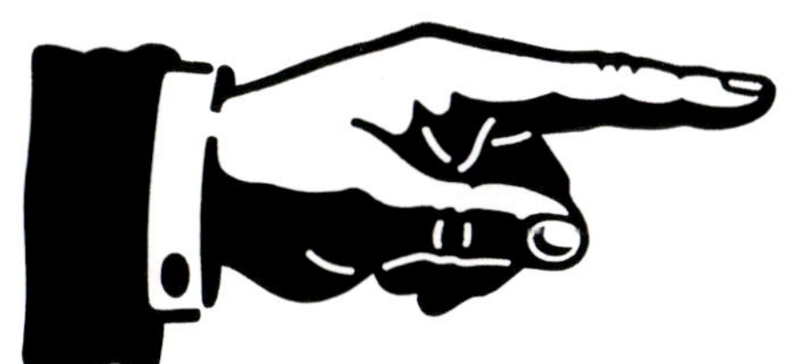
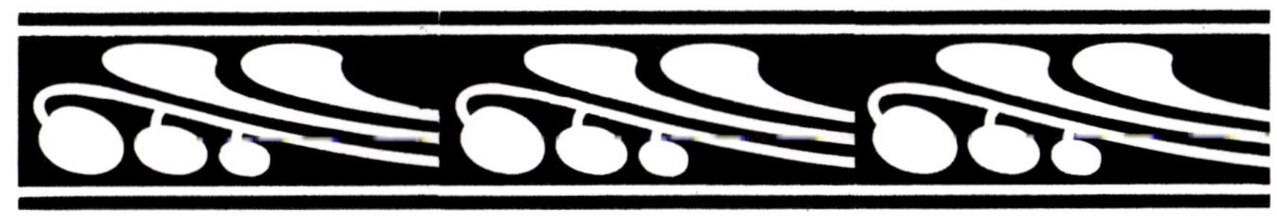

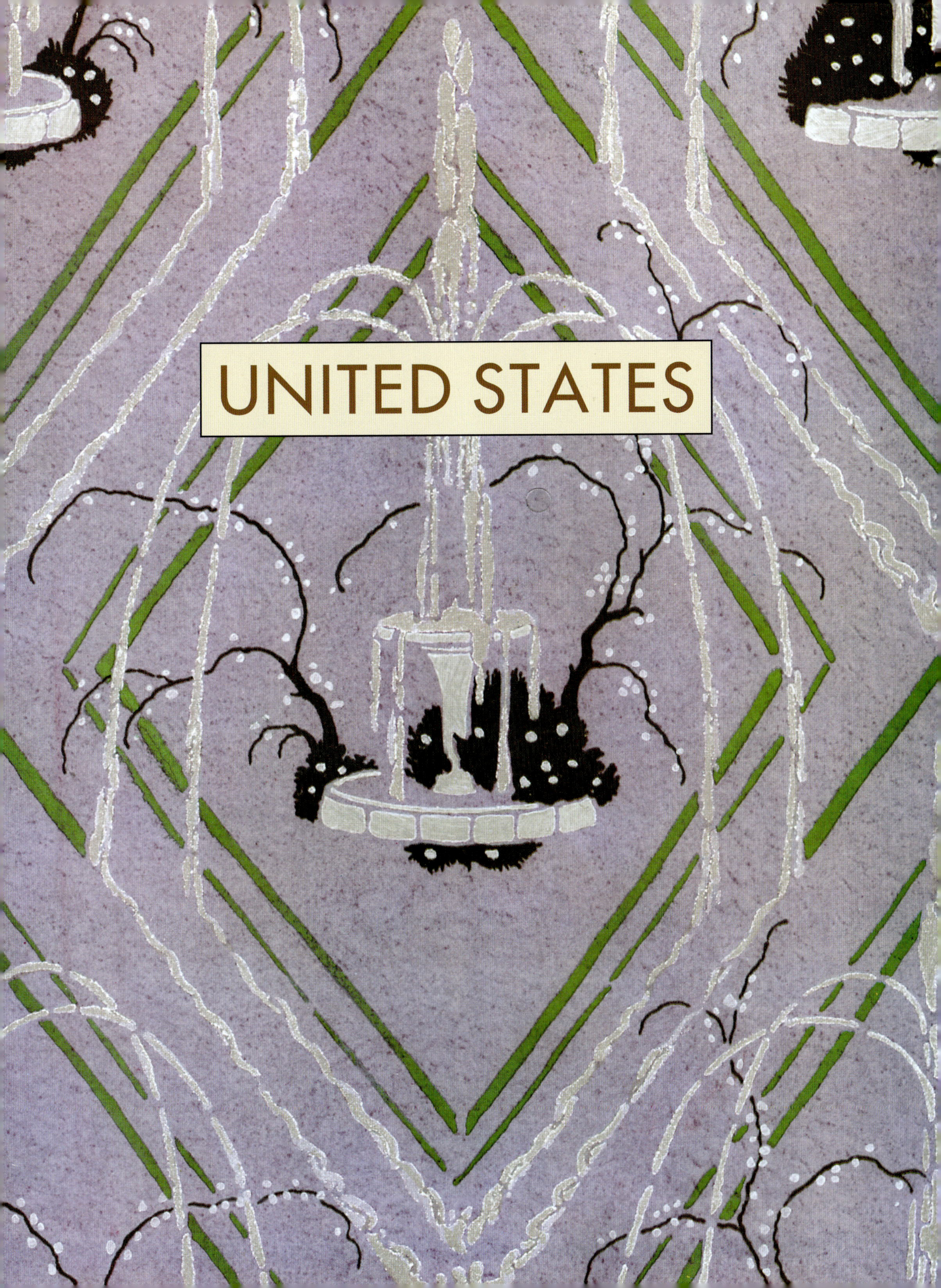
UNITED STATES

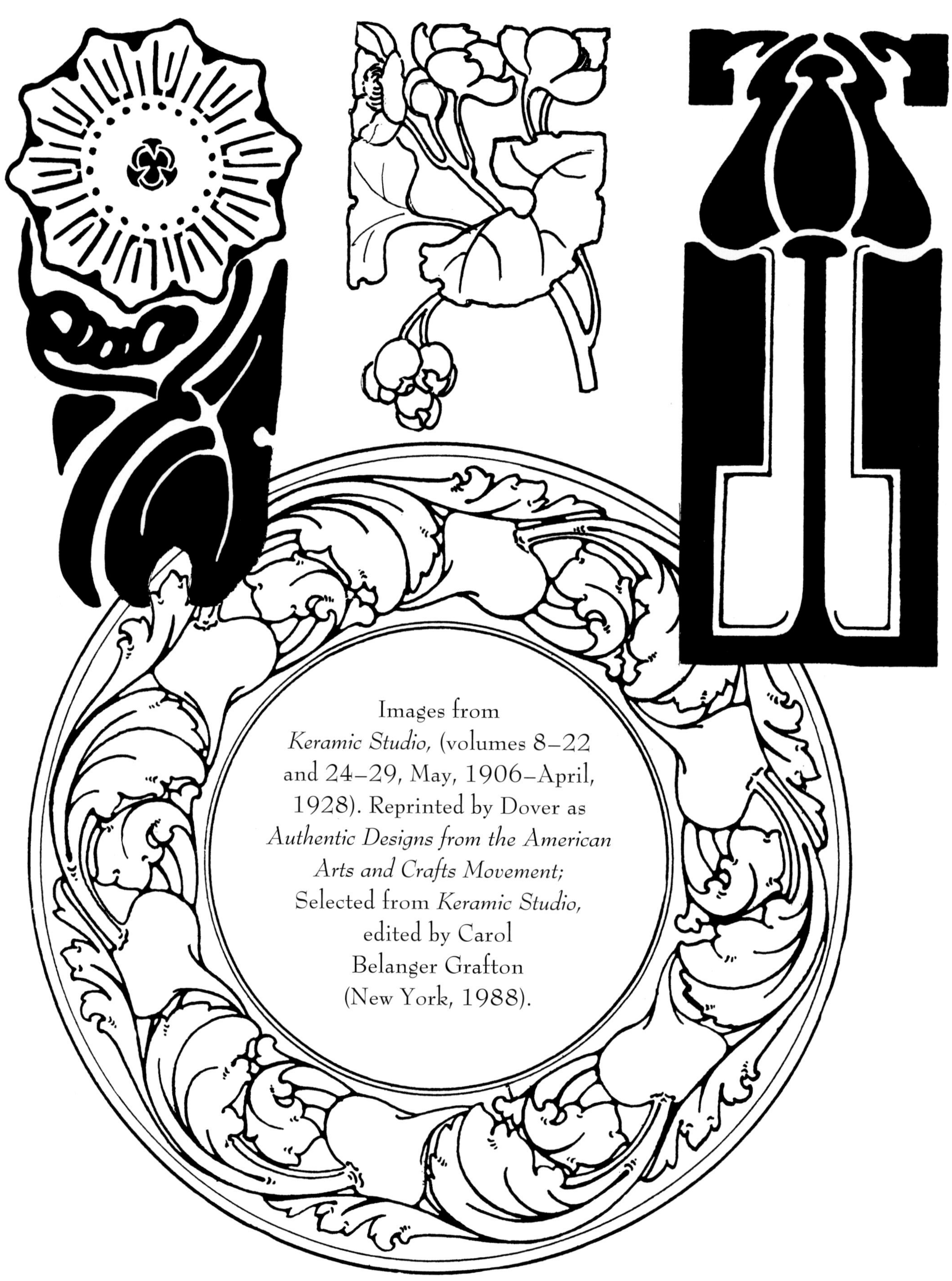

Images from
Keramic Studio, (volumes 8–22
and 24–29, May, 1906–April,
1928). Reprinted by Dover as
Authentic Designs from the American
Arts and Crafts Movement;
Selected from Keramic Studio,
edited by Carol
Belanger Grafton
(New York, 1988).

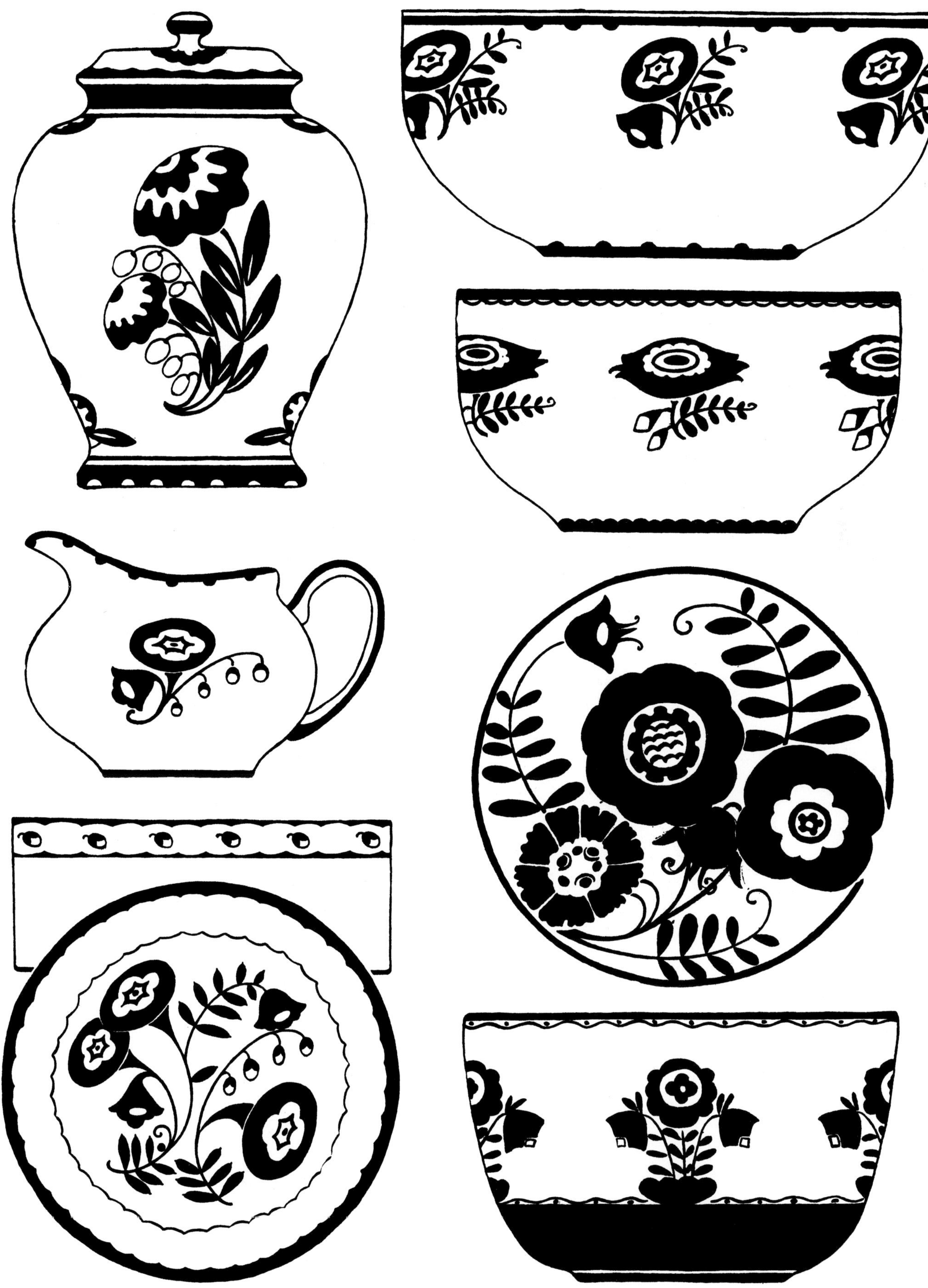

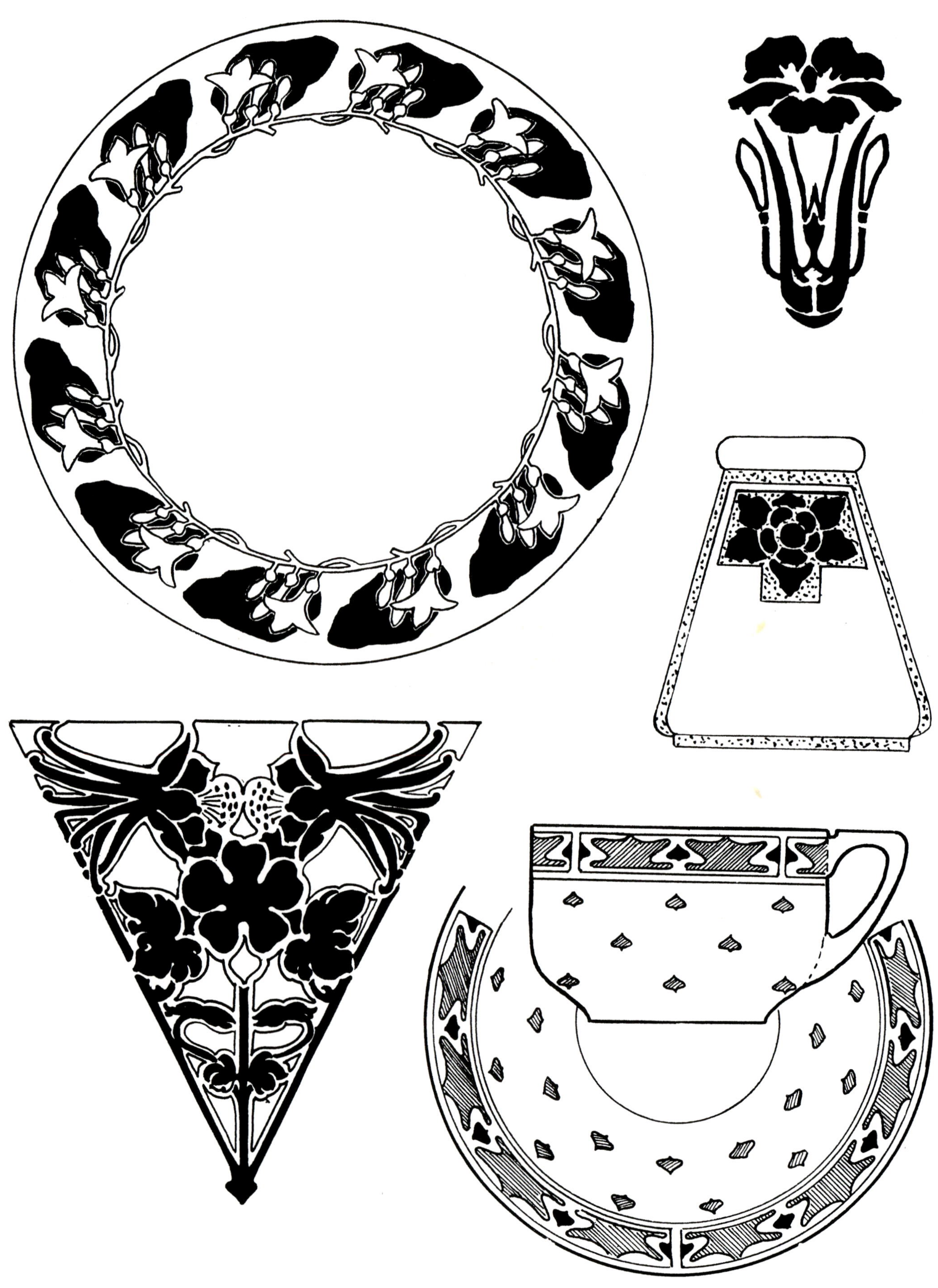

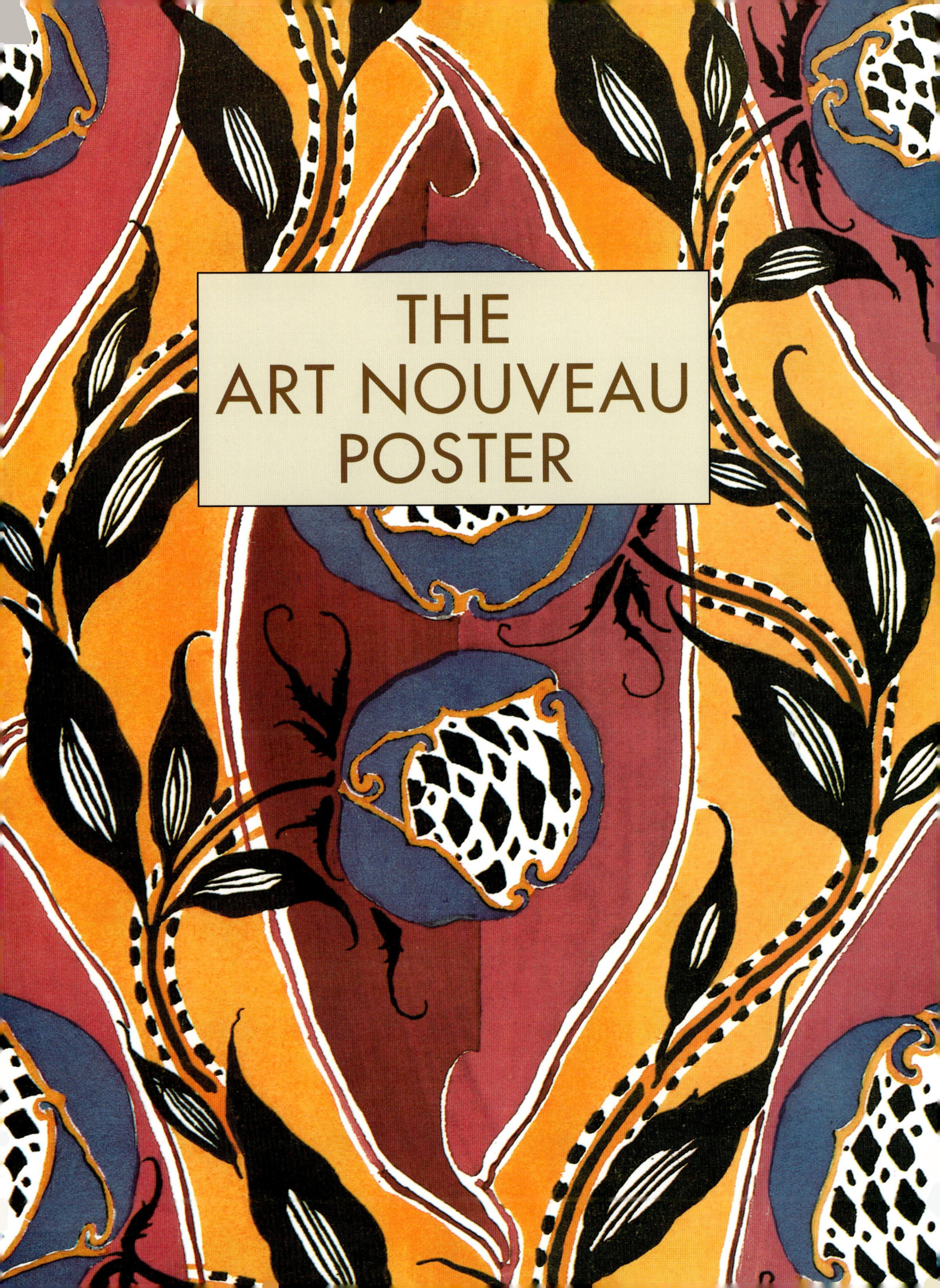
THE
ART NOUVEAU
POSTER

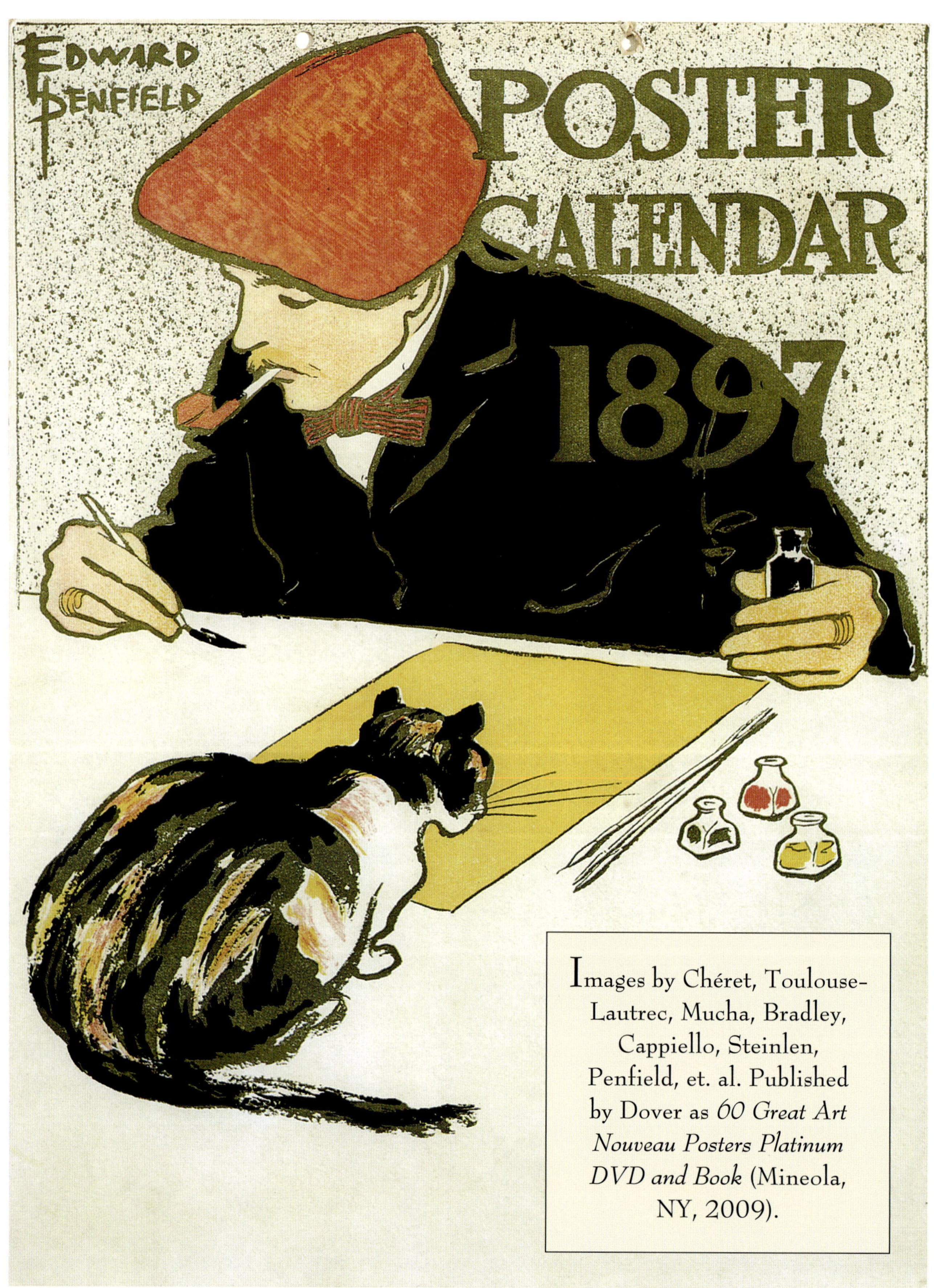

EDWARD PENFIELD (1866–1925) / *Poster Calendar,* 1897

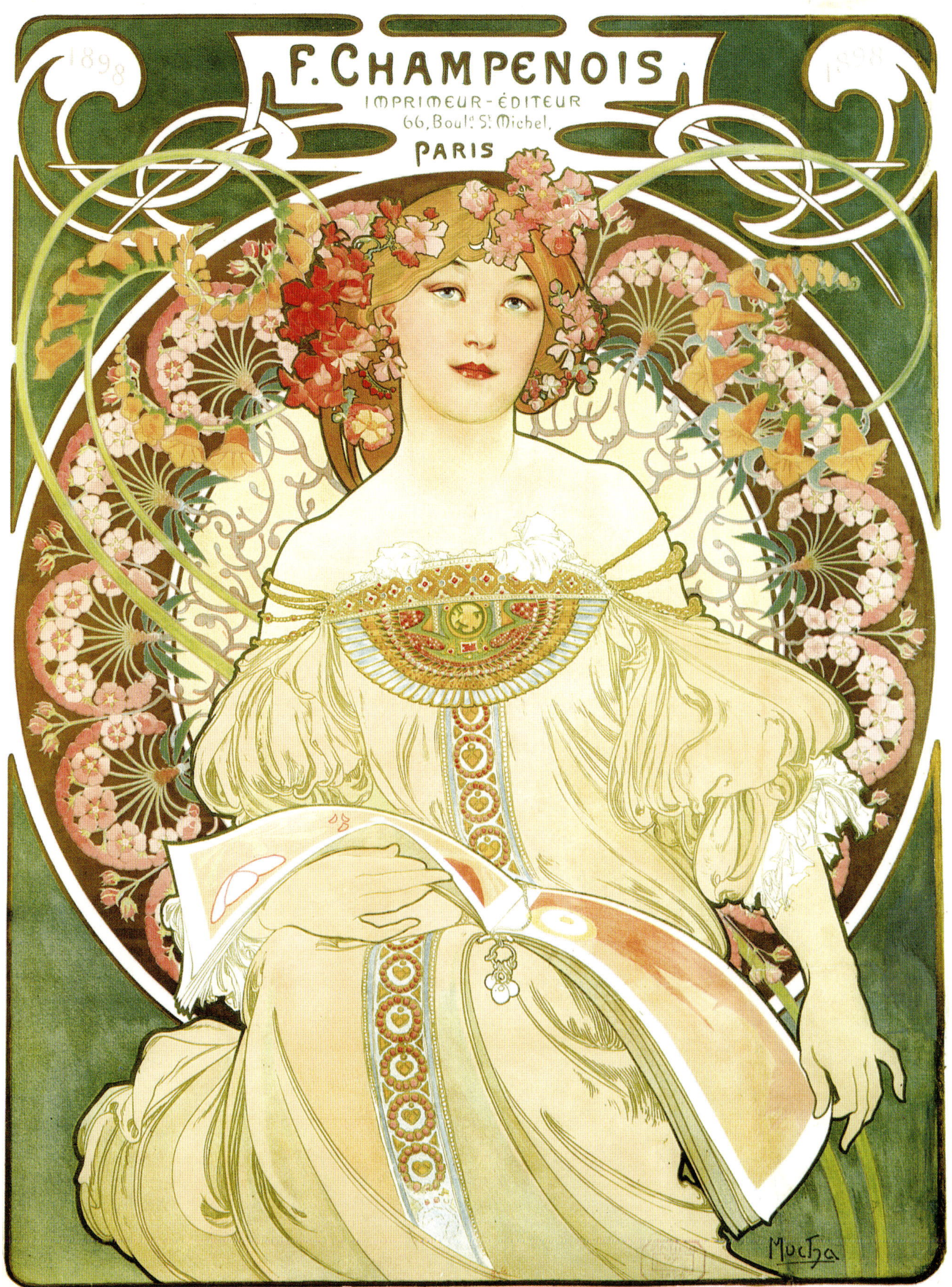

Alphonse Maria Mucha (1860–1939) / *F. Champenois Imprimeur-Éditeur*, 1897

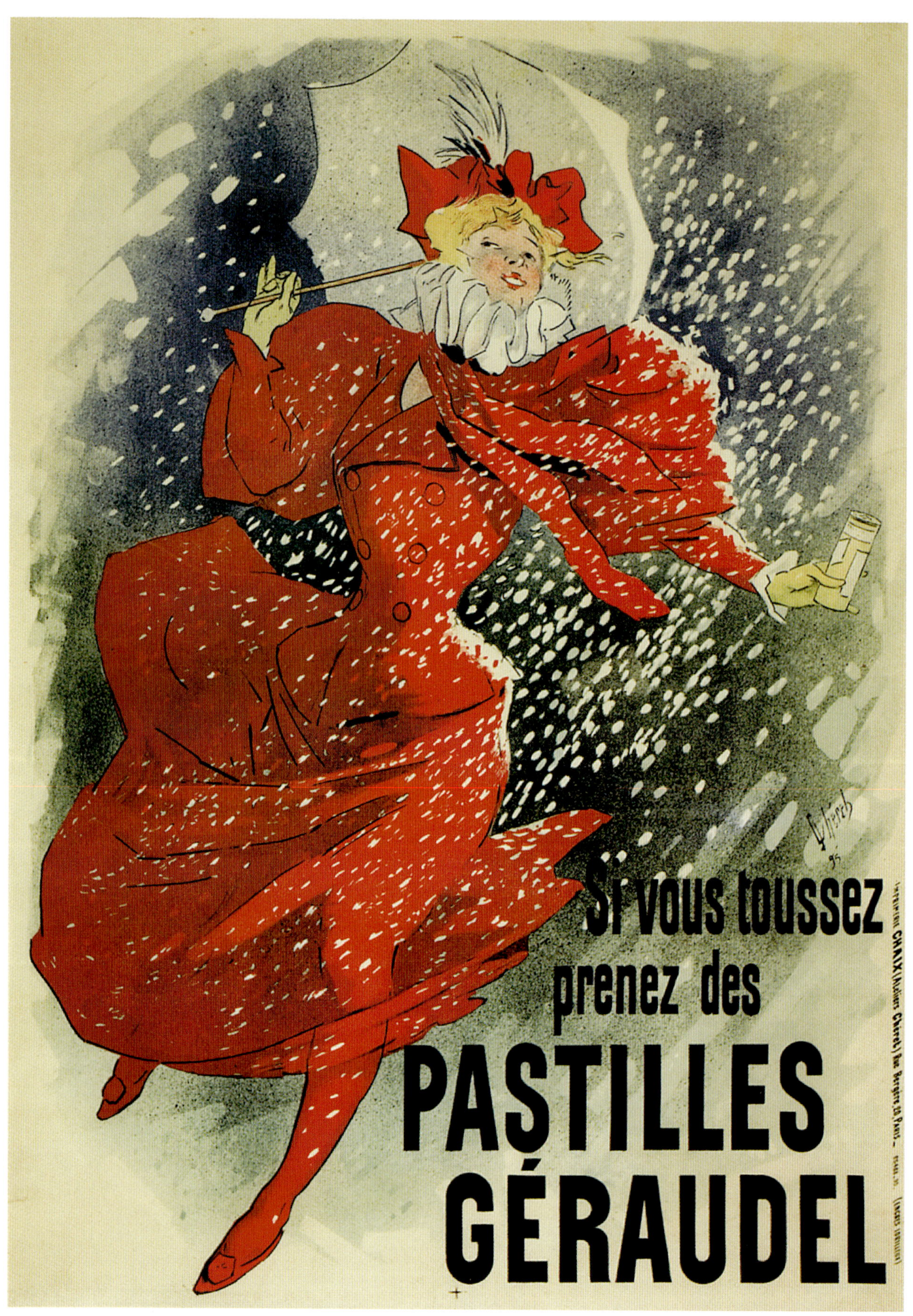

Jules Chéret (1836–1932) / *Pastilles Géraudel,* 1895

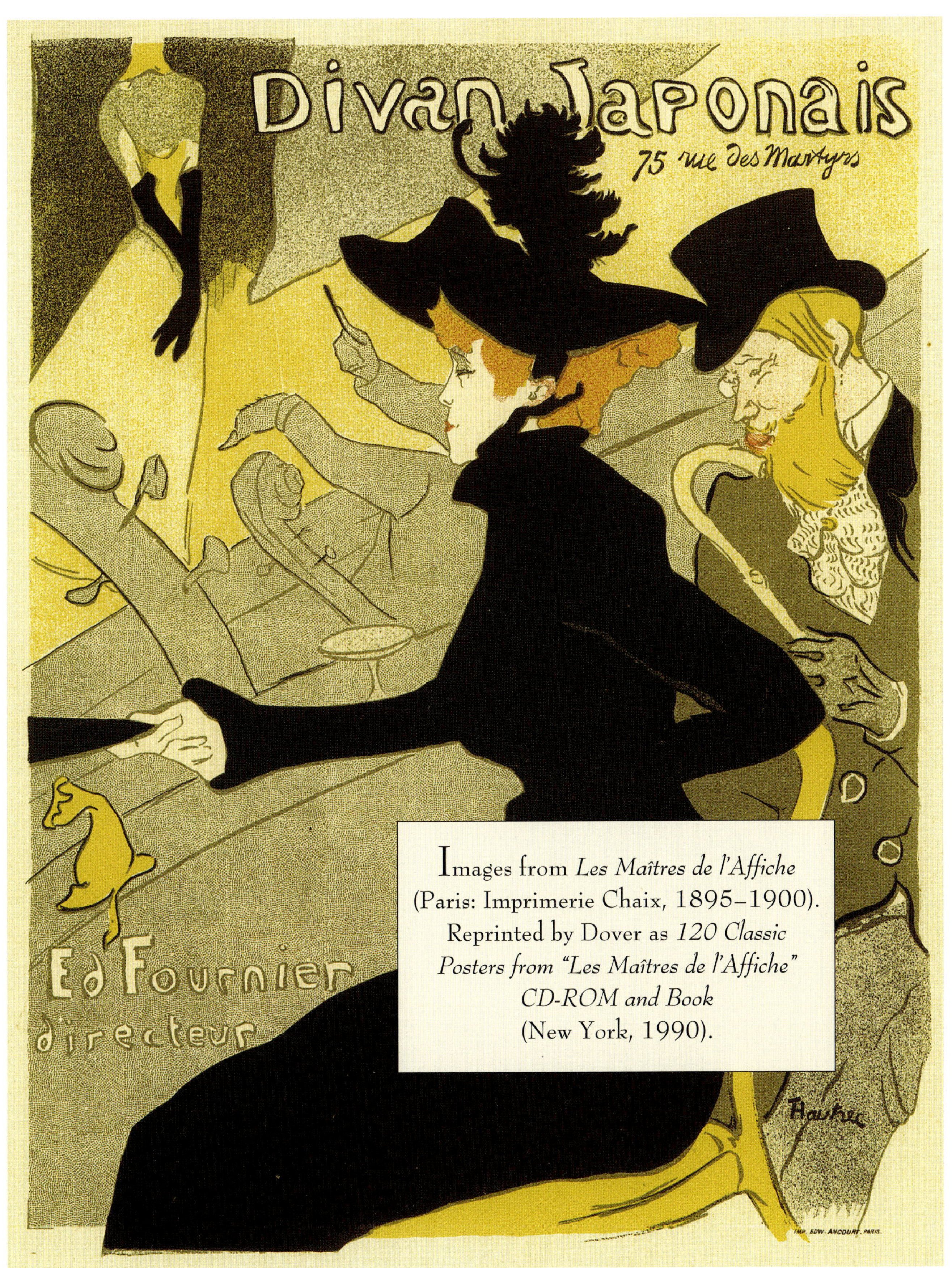

Images from *Les Maîtres de l'Affiche* (Paris: Imprimerie Chaix, 1895–1900). Reprinted by Dover as *120 Classic Posters from "Les Maîtres de l'Affiche"* CD-ROM and Book (New York, 1990).

HENRI DE TOULOUSE-LAUTREC (1864–1901) / *Divan Japonais*, 1892

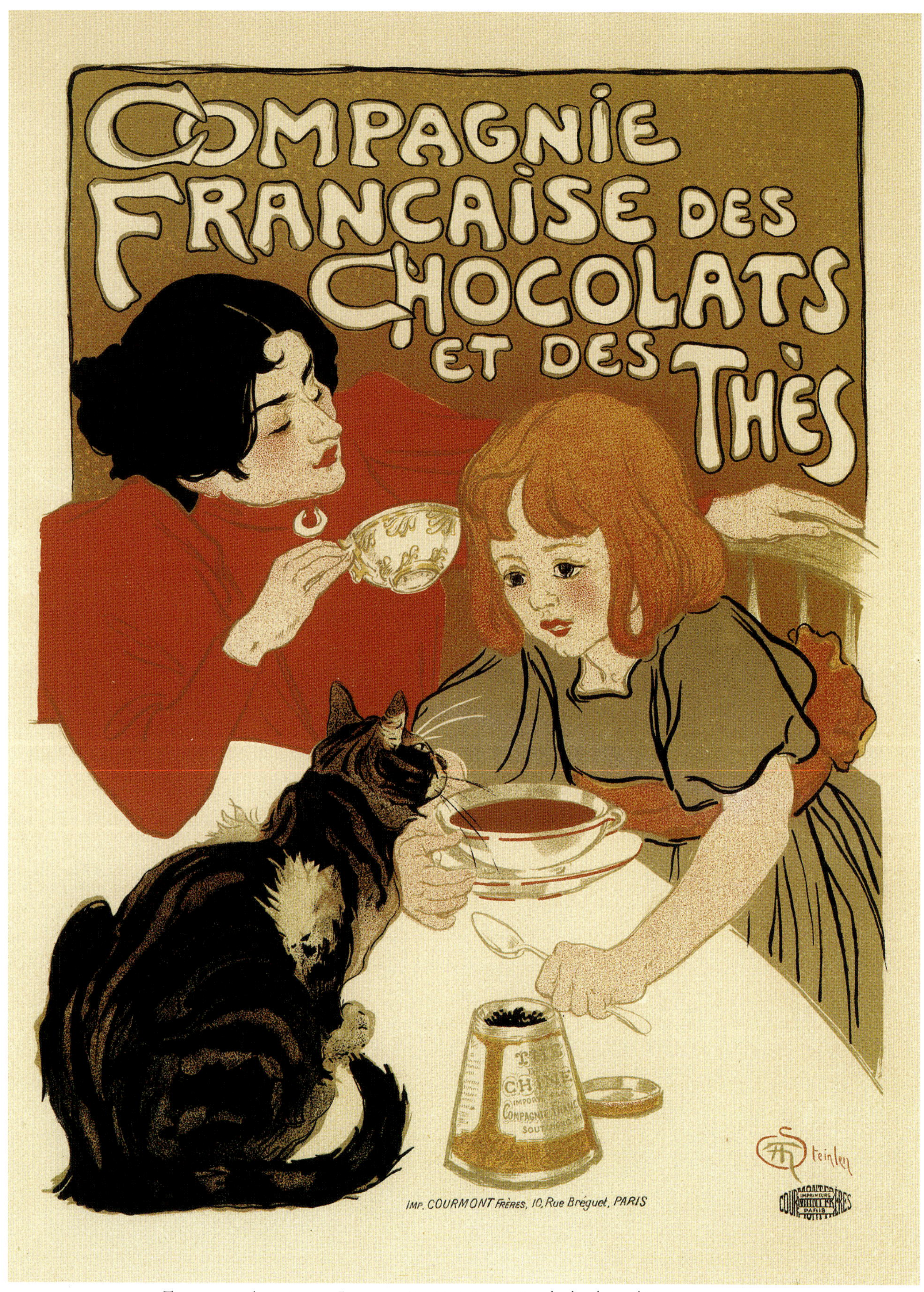

Théophile-Alexandre Steinlen (1859–1923) / *French Chocolate and Tea Company*, 1896

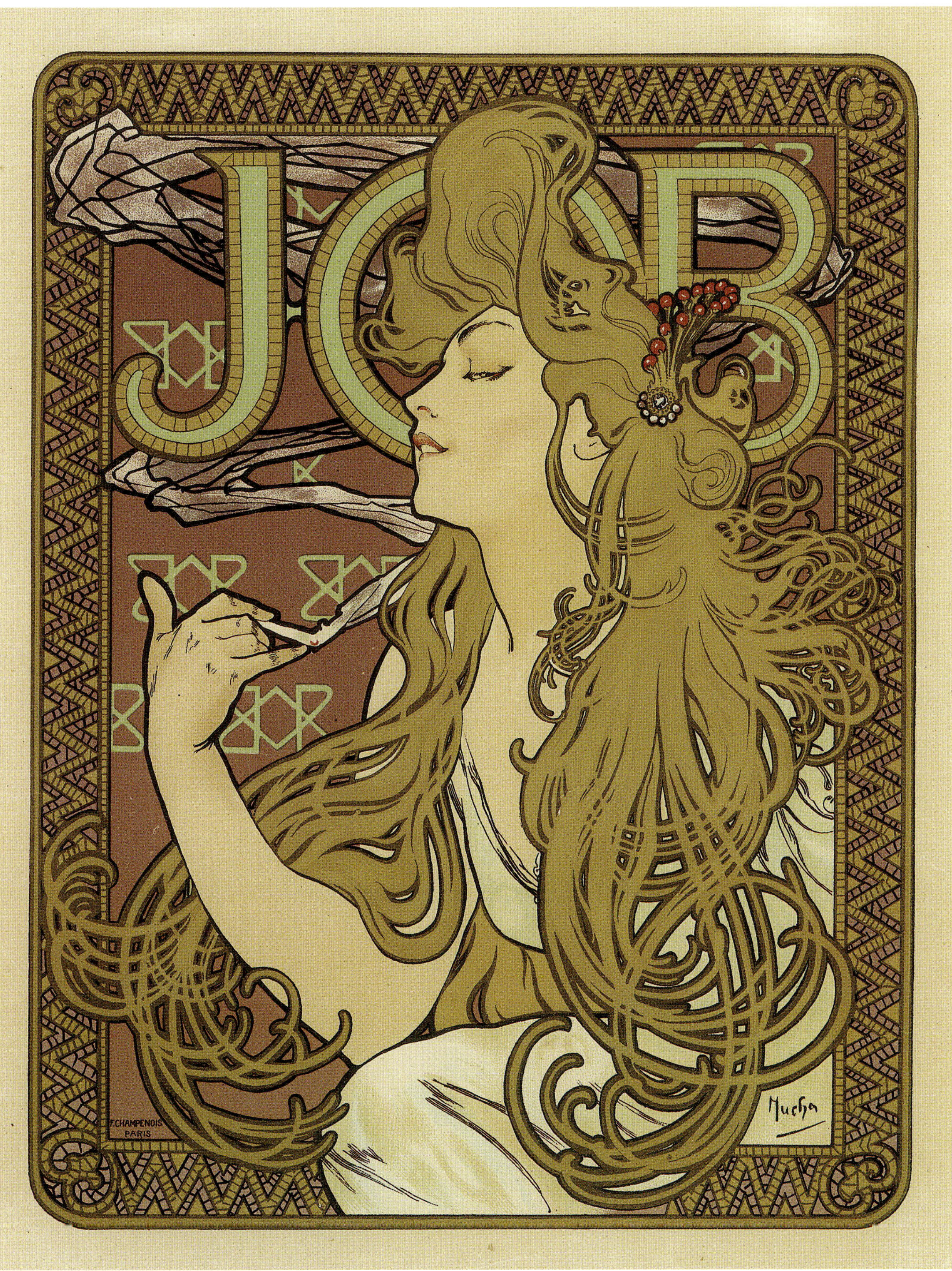

Alphonse Maria Mucha (1860–1939) / *Job*, 1898

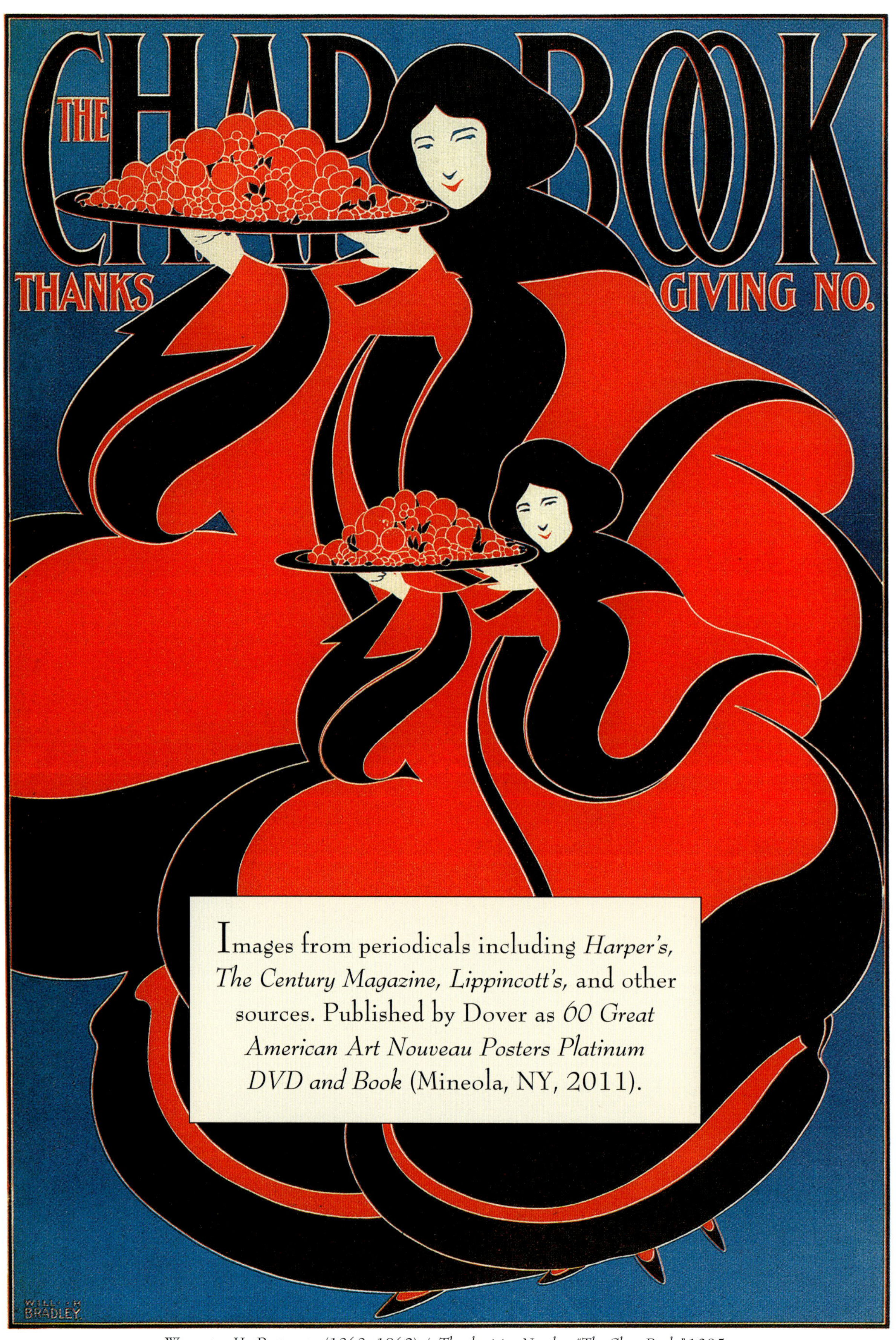

Images from periodicals including *Harper's*, *The Century Magazine*, *Lippincott's*, and other sources. Published by Dover as *60 Great American Art Nouveau Posters Platinum DVD and Book* (Mineola, NY, 2011).

WILLIAM H. BRADLEY (1868–1962) / *Thanksgiving Number, "The Chap-Book,"* 1895

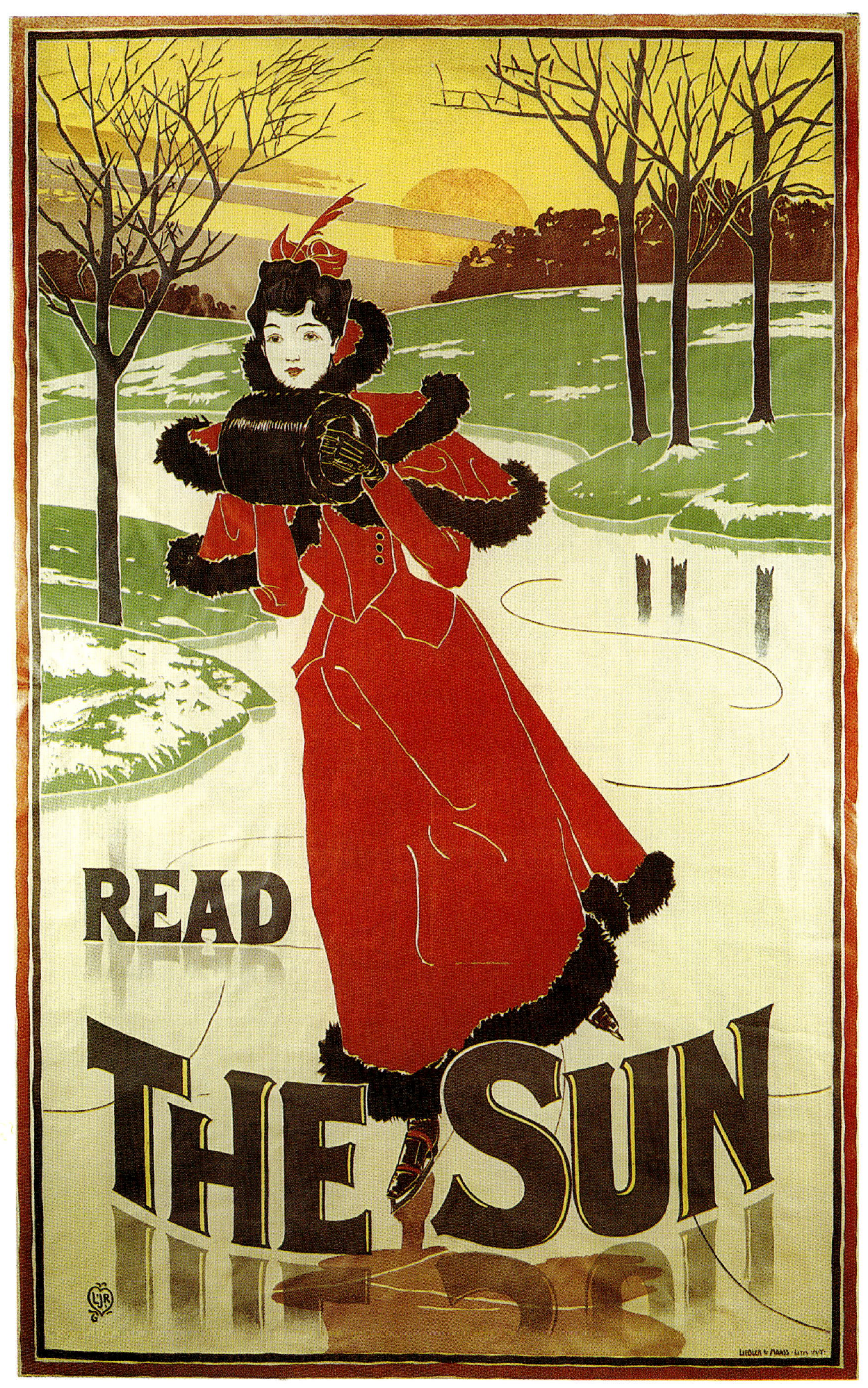

Louis John Rhead (1857–1926) / *Read the Sun*, 1895

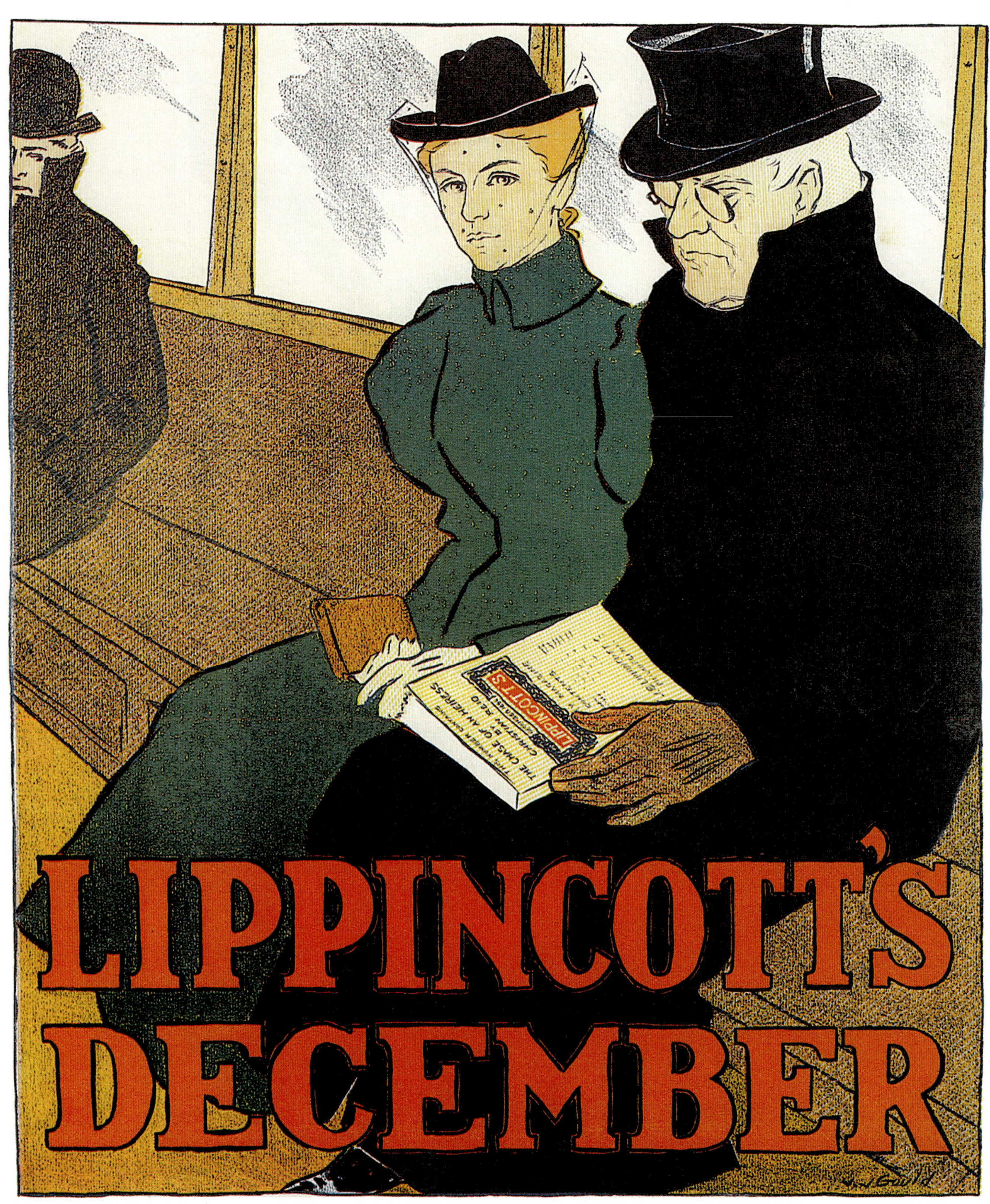

Joseph J. Gould, Jr. (1880–1935) / *Lippincott's December*, 1896

INDEX OF ARTISTS

H. Anker [dates unknown]
Plates 102–104

Austrian interior decorator and graphic artist, collaborated with J. Klinger on one of the most memorable original works on Art Nouveau decoration, *La Linge grotesque et ses variations dans la décoration moderne* (Paris, c. 1907).

René Beauclair (1877–1960)
Plates 2–4

Prolific French painter, designer, and decorative artist who worked in a variety of media including ceramics, textiles, and jewelry design.

Aubrey Beardsley (1872–1898)
Plates 84–88

English illustrator whose distinctive, erotic, and often imitated pen and (black) ink illustrations made him one of the driving forces behind the spread of the art nouveau graphic style and technique beyond the continent of Europe.

Max Benirschke (1880–1970)
Plates 96–98

Graphic artist in the Jugendstil movement.

William H. Bradley (1868–1962)
Plate 132

American illustrator and masterful poster artist whose influence on graphic style in the United States was comparable to that of Aubrey Beardsley in England. His style was also influenced by the Arts and Crafts movement and the then growing awareness in the West of Japanese woodblock printing.

A. Charayron (active 1900–10)
Plates 5–7

French graphic artist and designer. Co-author with Léon Durand of a treatise on the pochoir technique, *La Décoration Pratique au Pochoir* (Dourdan, France: Emile Thézard, n.d.).

Jules Chéret (1836–1932)
Plate 128

French painter, lithographer and masterful designer of over a thousand magnificent posters. Alphonse Mucha and other great figures of the Art Nouveau movement were his artistic descendants.

A. Desaint [dates unknown]
Plates 8–10

French interior decorator, expert colorist, and designer of decorative stencils. Published books on Art Nouveau decorative themes between 1905 and 1930.

Maurice Dufrène (1876–1955)
Plates 11–13

Prolific French designer with wide-ranging interests, worked in furniture design, ceramics, glassware and over-all interior decoration.

Léon Durand [dates unknown]
Plates 5–7

See Charayron, A.

L. François [dates unknown]
Plates 14–16

French editor of a catalogue of Art Nouveau tile designs published in Paris in 1905.

Charles Gmelich (1875–1955)
Plates 69–71

German art instructor who studied in Paris around the turn of the nineteenth century. Collaborated with his teaching colleague Gustave Kolb on a 1902 collection of Art Nouveau ornamental plates with a title which summarizes a large part of the Art Nouveau aesthetic, *Von Der Pflanze Zum Ornament* (From Plant to Ornament).

Joseph J. Gould, Jr. (1880–1935)
Plate 134

An American artistic descendent of Edward Penfield, he studied at the Pennsylvania Academy of Fine Arts, and succeeded William L. Carqueville as a poster designer for *Lippincott's*.

M. J. Gradl (1873–1934)
Plates 63–65

German designer Max Joseph Gradl, who worked in the Art Nouveau style in many areas, is best known for his jewelry designs and typography.

M. Eugène Grasset (1845–1917)
Plates 17–19

Swiss designer, based in Paris after 1871, worked in furniture, textiles, ceramics and jewelry but is best known for his graphic design, including postcards, postage stamps, and above all, posters, several of which are included in *The Maîtres de l'Affiche* collection.

J. Habert-Dys (1850–1928)
Plates 20–22

Jules-Auguste Habert-Dys published several now very rare collections of graphic designs in the 1880s and 1890s. A versatile French graphic and applied artist who started in ceramics but eventually created designs used by himself and other craftsmen and designers for fans, wallpaper, jewelry, glass, and objects d'art.

Julius Klinger (1876–1942)
Plates 99–104

An influential Austrian illustrator, painter, graphic artist, and typographer, his career flourished in Germany starting in the late 1890s when his work appeared frequently in the iconic Art Nouveau periodical *Die Jugend*. He died in the Holocaust in 1942.

Gustave Kolb (1867–1943)
Plates 69–71
See Gmelich, Charles.

Josef Lehner [dates unknown]
Plates 105–107
See Mader, Eduard.

Arnold Lyongrün (1871–1935)
Plates 75–77

German artist, studied in Paris in the 1890s and traveled throughout Europe. Worked in highly original stained glass design in the Art Nouveau style and other forms of decorative art around the turn of the century.

Eduard Mader (1858–unknown)
Plates 105–107

German Jugendstil designer. Collaborated with Josef Lehner on seminal portfolios of Art Nouveau designs and innovative typography.

Koloman Moser (1868–1918)
Plates 111–113

Austrian painter, graphic artist and designer, a founding member of both the Vienna Secession and the Wiener Werkstatte. Moser worked in many areas of applied art and design including posters, jewelry and furniture.

Alphonse Maria Mucha (1860–1939)
Plates 42–52, 127, 131

Czech artist whose poster advertising the French actress Sarah Bernhardt is one of the images which defines the Art Nouveau style. Following Jules Chéret, Mucha was the poster artist of Art Nouveau's peak years, but he also produced paintings, drawings, decorative borders, vignettes, and a great deal more.

Edward Penfield (1866–1925)
Plate 126

Art Director of *Harper's* and one of the greatest American poster artists. His many posters advertising the magazine are widely collected today.

Ludwig Petzendorfer (1851–unknown)
Plates 80–82

German editor of the greatest album of Art Nouveau typography produced during the time in which the style itself flourished, *Schriftenatlas: Neue Folge* ("Type Portfolio: New Series") a compilation of type specimens from the leading foundries of the day.

Louis John Rhead (1857–1926)
Plate 133

English born artist who emigrated to the United States and became one of the most prominent American poster artists of the 1890s, appearing regularly in *Harper's*.

E. A. Seguy [dates unknown]
Plates 23–31

French artist Eugene Alain Seguy, working first in the Art Nouveau and later in the Art Deco styles published a series of unique and magnificent design portfolios starting about 1900 and continuing into the 1930s. A master of the pochoir technique, a printing process which yields dense, striking colors through the use of stencils, it is the greatest mystery of Art Nouveau that so little is known of Seguy's life apart from his art.

Théophile-Alexandre Steinlen (1859–1923)
Plate 130

Famous for his trademark cat illustrations, Steinlen, a Swiss-born painter and printmaker also produced posters of cabaret and music-hall performers.

Henri de Toulouse-Lautrec (1864–1901)
Plate 129

With his mastery of drawing, style, color, and composition, Toulouse-Lautrec produced posters which defined Paris in the 1890s and helped usher in the great years of Art Nouveau.

M. P. Verneuil (1869–1942)
Plates 32–40

French artist and designer Maurice Pillard Verneuil studied with Eugène Grasset, and became a major poster artist in the era of Jules Chéret and Toulouse-Lautrec. A graphic artist whose popularity carried over into the Art Deco period, Verneuil worked in many areas besides graphics, including ceramic tiles, wallpaper, and textile design.

SOURCE INFORMATION

Art et Décoration. Paris: 1897–1910.

Beauclair, René. *Dessin's d'Ornementation plane en couleurs Art Nouveau*. Paris: Armand Guerinet, 1900.

Benirschke, Max. *Buchschmuck und Flächenmuster*. Vienna and Leipzig: Verlag Martin Gerlach, c. 1902.

Catalogue of Roman Scherer, manufacturer of wood type. Lucerne, Switzerland, n.d.

Charayron, A. and Durand, Léon. *La Décoration Pratique au Pochoir*. Dourdan, France: Emile Thézard, n.d.

Dekorative Vorbilder. Stuttgart: Verlag von Jul. Hoffman, Volumes 8, 10–11, 13, 15–21, 23, 1897–1912.

Dekorative Vorbilder: eine Sammlung von figürlichen Darstel-lungen, kunstgewerblichen Verzierungen, plastischen, Orna-menten, dekorativen Tier- und Pflanzen-typen, Allegorieen, heraldischen, Motiven, Traphäen, etc. Stuttgart: Verlag von Jul. Hoffman, 1889–1928.

Desaint, A. *Ideas & Studies in Stencilling & Decorating*. London: Charles Griffin & Company, Ltd., 1927.

Dufrène, Maurice. *Les Bijoux*. Paris: Librairie des Arts Décoratifs, A. Calavas, c. 1900.

François, L. (Ed.) *La Céramique Architecturale/Revetements Decoration: Album de Carreaux pour Revetements*. Paris: Faienceries de Sarreguemines, Digoin et Vitry-le-François/Utzschneider & C$^{ie.}$, 1905.

Gli Adornatori del Libro in Italia. Bologna: 1923–27.

Gradl, M. J. *Bunte Verglasungen*. Stuttgart: Julius Hoffman Verlag, c. 1905.

Grasset, M. Eugène (Ed.) *La plante et ses applications or-nementales. Second series*. Paris: Librairie Centrale des Beaux-Arts, c. 1898.

Habert-Dys, J. *Fantaisies Décoratives: Documents pour servir a la décoration des Faïences, Meubles, Tissus, Bijoux, Ap-partements, etc.* Paris: Librairie de l'Art, 1886–87.

Holme, Geoffrey. *British Book Illustration Yesterday and To-day*. London: The Studio, 1923.

Jugend: Die Münchner illustrierte Wochenschrift für Kunst und Leben, Vols. I–XVIII, 1896–1913.

Keramic Studio. Volumes 8–22 and 24–29, May 1906–April 1928.

Klinger, J. and Anker, H. *La Ligne grotesque et ses variations dans la décoration moderne*. Paris: Libraire de l'Art Ancien et Moderne, n.d.

Klinger, Julius. *La Femme dans la décoration moderne: Mod-eles nouveaux pour les industries d'art: peinture décorative, affiches, dessins, tapis, vitraux, tissus, céramique, papiers, peints, bijouterie, etc.* Paris: Libraire de l'Art Ancien et Moderne, c. 1902.

Kolb, Gustave and Gmelich, Charles. *De la Plante à l'Orna-ment*. Göppingen, Germany: Jllig & Müller, 1902.

Lehner, Josef and Mader, Eduard. *Neue Schriften und Fir-menschilder im Modernen Stil: Serie I*. Vienna and Leipzig: Friedr. Wolfrum & Co., n.d.

Les Maîtres de l'Affiche. Paris: Imprimerie Chaix, 1895–1900.

Lüth-Kiel, Karl. *Schablonenfabrik, Kunstgewerbliche Werke-statt*. Niedersedlitz, Dresden: Krey und Sommerlaid, n.d.

Moderne Ideen für die Kunstglaserei. Plauen, Germany: C. F. Schulz & Co., Verlags-buchhandlung, 1911.

Malory, Sir Thomas. *Le Morte Darthur*. London: J. M. Dent & Co., 1893–94.

Monogramme und Dekorationen. Leipzig: Verlag von Wil-helm Diebener, 1911.

Moser, Koloman. *Flächenschmuck*. Originally published in the Moser issue of *Die Quelle*. (Vienna & Leipzig: Verlag M. Gerlach 1901–02.

Motivenschatz für Modernes Kunstschaffen Studienblatter für Kuenstler. Dresden: Verlag von Gerhard Kuehtmann, n.d.

Mucha, Alphonse Maria. *Cloches de Nöel et de Paques*. Paris: Piazza et C$^{ie.}$, 1900.

Mucha, Alphonse Maria. *Documents Décoratifs*. Paris: Librairie Centrale des Beaux-Arts, Émile Lévy, Editeur, 1901.

Mucha, Alphonse Maria. *Figures décoratives*. Paris: Librairie Centrale des Beaux-Arts, Émile Lévy, Publisher, 1905.

Petzendorfer, Ludwig (Ed.), *Schriftenatlas Neue Folge: Sammlung von Alphabeten Initialen und Monogrammen*. Stuttgardt: Julis Hoffman, c. 1903.

Ratta, Cesare. *L'Arte del Libro e della Rivista nei Paesi d'Europa e d'America*. Bologna: 1925, 1928.

Seguy, E. A. *Floréal: Dessins & coloris nouveaux*. Paris: A. Calavas, c. 1914.

Seguy, E. A. *Insectes*. Paris: Editions Ducharte et Van Buggenhoudt, n.d.

Seguy, E. A. *Les fleurs et leurs applications décoratives*. Paris: Librairie des Arts Décoratifs, A. Calavas, c. 1902.

Seguy, E. A. *Papillons*. Paris: Tolmer Editeur, n.d.

Seguy, E. A. *Primavera: Dessins & coloris nouveaux*. Plauen, Germany: Christian Stoll, n.d.

Seguy, E. A. *Samarkande: 20 compositions en couleurs dans le Style oriental*. Paris: Ch. Massin, c. 1920.

Studio, The. London: 1893–1901.

Untitled portfolio. Vienna: Friedrich Wolfrum and Co., n.d.

Verneuil, M. P. *L'animal dans la decoration*. Paris: Librairie Centrale des Beaux-Arts, c. 1897.

Verneuil, M. P. *Étude de la Plante: son application aux industries d'art*. Paris: Librairie Centrale des Beaux-Arts, c. 1900.

Verneuil, M. P. *L'ornementation par le Pochoir*. Paris: Schmid and Laurens, n.d.

Verneuil, M. P., et al. *250 Bordures*. Paris: Librairie Centrale des Beaux-Arts, 1904.

Vorbilder für Kunstvergasungen im Style der Neuzeit Serie I and *Serie II*. Berlin and New York: Bruno Hessling, 1900.

Wilde, Oscar and Beardsley, Aubrey. *Salome: A Tragedy in One Act*. London: Elkin Mathews & John Lane, 1894.